The Decline
and Fall of the
Ottoman Empire

The Decline
and Fall of the
Ottoman Empire

ALAN PALMER

JOHN MURRAY

To E. R. P., with love and gratitude

© Alan Palmer 1992

First published in 1992
Reprinted 1993
by John Murray (Publishers) Ltd.,
50 Albemarle Street, London W1X 4BD

Paperback edition 1993

The moral right of the author has been asserted

A catalogue record for this book is available from the British Library

Hardback ISBN 0-7195-4934-5
Paperback ISBN 0-7195-5281-8

Typeset in 11/13 point Baskerville by Colset Private Ltd, Singapore
Printed and bound in Great Britain at the University Press, Cambridge

Contents

Illustrations

The author and publisher wish to thank the following for permission to reproduce photographs: The Hulton–Deutsch Collection, Plates 1, 2, 3, 5, 7, 8, 9, 10, 14; and The Imperial War Museum, Plates 11, 12, 13, 15, 16, 17

Preface

The greatest historian of an empire's decline and fall decided on the immense theme of his life's work when he 'sat musing on the Capitol, while the bare-footed fryars were chanting their litanies in the temple of Jupiter'. A far humbler enterprise had its origins in musings at a site no less evocative than Gibbon had chosen, but to a background of less contemplative supplications: I was seated well above the Bosphorus, while sandal-footed tourists were ordering their luncheons on the terrace of the old Seraglio.

As I looked out from this historic palace to the long white classical façade of the Dolmabahche and the green parkland of Yildiz beyond, I thought I would write almost entirely about the Sultans themselves. But when I left İstanbul I soon realized that this would be a mistake. In retrospect the most fascinating aspect of the Ottoman past is not a succession of rarely remarkable sovereigns, but the empire's geographical extent, and the way in which an astonishingly narrow ruling class imposed government on lands extending from the Danubian plains to the mountains of the Caucasus, the headwaters of the Gulf and the deserts of southern Arabia and North Africa. It has to be admitted that, although the Ottoman Empire was pre-eminent in the Balkans and the Near East for more than six centuries, when it collapsed in the wake of the First World War no one was surprised to see it disappear: long before Tsar Nicholas I's casual complaint of having 'a sick man' on our hands, foreign observers were predicting the imminent downfall of so cumbersome an institution. But how did it survive so long? The decline was certainly not rapid, nor was it in any sense constantly progressive, a steady downward graph from the autumn of 1683 when, for the second time, an Ottoman army failed to take Vienna. The reforms which arrested the decline have a particular historical interest of their own; and so, too, do the reformers who attempted to put them into practice.

Modern historical fashion favours analysis by topics at the expense of narrative. Over the two and half centuries covered by the main body of this book there are constantly recurring problems: secular and religious authority; the inadequacies of a unique form of military feudalism; movements of population; the greed of powerful neighbours; and above all, uncertainty whether to borrow from the West or to seek inspiration from Ottoman origins in north-western Anatolia. But it is easy to perceive at work in these centuries H. A. L. Fisher's famous non-pattern of 'one emergency following upon another as wave followed upon wave'; and I have therefore planned the book primarily as a work of narrative history, reflecting the form of the highly personal autocracy established in the Ottoman Empire.

I must admit that when I began research into the material for this book, the Ottoman Empire seemed as irrelevant to what was going on around us as are the Wars of the Roses. Only in the Lebanon was there a long and sad continuity of conflict. Now, however, the Ottoman past is less remote. The dynasty may have gone, but many problems that plagued the later Sultans once more make the news. For two years the cycle of history has been spinning in top gear. Half forgotten place-names are back in the headlines: towns like Basra, Mosul, Damascus or Diyarbakir; and distant outposts in Bosnia-Herzegovina or Albania in the west and along the sea coast of the Gulf or the mountain chain of the Caucasus in the east. Once again we learn of the Kurdish struggle for survival and of Armenian aspirations for independence. We are reminded of the underlying Muslim character of Sarajevo – a place-name which for three-quarters of a century has been more generally associated with the Habsburgs than with the Ottomans. We read of rival nationalities re-emerging in Macedonia and of the clash of linguistic minorities in Bulgaria. And, more gradually, we are becoming aware of the nineteen Turkic languages which, having outlived the Soviet Union, threaten to allow an Ottoman ghost – or, at least, the shade of Enver Pasha – to disturb the early years of the new central Asian republics. With a Soviet empire falling so speedily that it had no time to go into decline, the fate of Russia's former Ottoman rival in the Black Sea becomes strangely topical.

Writing about a past empire spread over three continents inevitably presents problems of nomenclature. Where any place has a name in common English usage, e.g., Salonika, Damascus, Jaffa, I have used that form. Otherwise I have generally used the place-name current in the period of which I am writing. For most of the book, İstanbul therefore appears as Constantinople, İzmir as Smyrna, Trabzon as Trebizond. In doubtful cases I have employed what I assume to be the form most familiar to the reader, e.g., Edirne rather than Adrianople. To help identify places I include a list of alternative place-names after the main narrative. The reader will also find there the dates of the Sultans who reigned in Constantinople, and a glossary explaining some of the Ottoman terms used in the text, although I hope that I have also indicated their meaning at the first point in the narrative where they appear. For proper names – some of which are of Slavonic, Greek, Arabic or Persian origin – I use the forms which seem to me to look best in English, rather than the standard Turkish spelling system (which, of course, updates Ottoman usage). Commonly Anglicized words are given the accepted form – e.g. Pasha, Vizier. To linguistic purists offended by all such inconsistencies, I apologize.

My debt to earlier historians will be clear to any reader of the bibliography. I would like to thank the staffs of the Bodleian Library at Oxford, the London Library, the Public Record Office and the British Library for their ready assistance. At John Murray Ltd I have profited from the good advice and editorial direction of Grant McIntyre and Gail Pirkis and I am grateful, too, for Elizabeth Robinson's perceptive reading of typescript and proofs. My wife, Veronica, has helped me greatly: she accompanied me on every visit to the former Ottoman lands and, as well as compiling the index, has been a stimulating critic of the book, chapter by chapter. Once again she has my deepest thanks. The book is dedicated to my aunt, Elsie Perriam, in the hospitality of whose Devonshire home the drafts of some chapters were first written.

Woodstock, Oxfordshire   Alan Palmer
May 1992

AUSTRIA-HUNGARY

Vienna

Budapest

Mohacs

TRAN-
SYLVANIA

Czernowitz

MOLDAVIA

BESSAR

O

Akkerr

Venice

CROATIA

Karlowitz

ROUMANIA

ADRIATIC SEA

ITALY

Belgrade

Sarajevo

SERBIA

R. Danube

Bucharest

Ruse

Kuch

Kain

BULGARIA

Scutari

Skoplje

Plovdiv

Monastir

Salonika

Ioannina

CORFU

GREECE

Lepanto

Athens

Navarino

MALTA

Constantin

San Ste

Chanak

M

Brusa

Esk

Smyrna

SAMOS

An

RHODES

CRETE

MEDITERRANEAN SEA

Tripoli

TRIPOLITANIA

Benghazi

CYRENAICA

Alexandr

C

EGYP

BALKAN BOUNDARIES, 1913–1914

AUSTRIA-HUNGARY

TRAN-
SYLVANIA

MOLDAVIA

BANAT

BOSNIA

SERBIA

WALLACHIA

ROUMANIA

MONTE
NEGRO

ALBANIA

BULGARIA

EASTERN
ROUMELIA

MACEDONIA

Constantinople

EPIRUS

THESSALY

GREECE

DODECANESE

PELOPONNESE

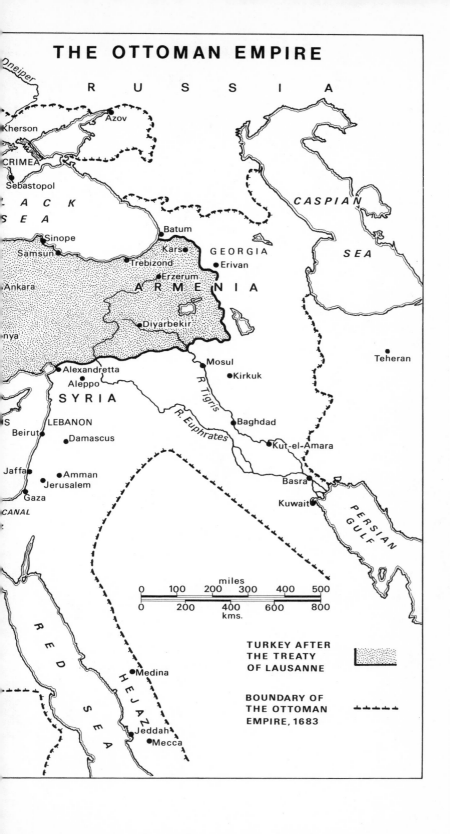

THE OTTOMAN EMPIRE

RUSSIA

Dneiper

Kherson

Azov

CRIMEA

Sebastopol

BLACK SEA

Sinope

Samsun

Ankara

Batum

Kars

Trebizond

GEORGIA

Erivan

Erzerum

ARMENIA

Diyarbekir

nya

Alexandretta

Aleppo

SYRIA

LEBANON

Beirut

Damascus

Jaffa

Amman

Jerusalem

Gaza

CANAL

CASPIAN SEA

Teheran

Mosul

Kirkuk

R. Tigris

R. Euphrates

Baghdad

Kut-el-Amara

Basra

Kuwait

PERSIAN GULF

RED SEA

HEJAZ

Medina

Jeddah

Mecca

miles

| 0 | 100 | 200 | 300 | 400 | 500 |

| 0 | 200 | 400 | 600 | 800 |

kms.

TURKEY AFTER
THE TREATY
OF LAUSANNE

BOUNDARY OF
THE OTTOMAN
EMPIRE, 1683

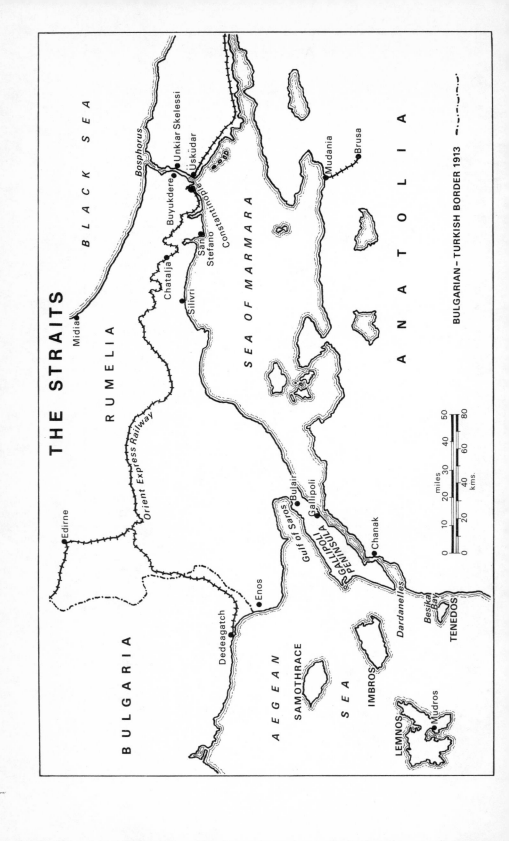

THE STRAITS

BLACK SEA

B L A C K   S E A

Bosphorus

Unkiar Skelessi

Üsküdar

Buyukdere

Chatalja

San Stefano

Constantinople

Silivri

Midia

R U M E L I A

Orient Express Railway

Edirne

Mudania

Brusa

A N A T O L I A

S E A   O F   M A R M A R A

B U L G A R I A

Gulf of Saros

Bulair

Gallipoli

GALLIPOLI PENINSULA

Chanak

Dardanelles

Besika Bay

TENEDOS

Enos

Dedeagatch

A E G E A N

SAMOTHRACE

S E A

IMBROS

LEMNOS

Mudros

BULGARIAN – TURKISH BORDER 1913 — · — · —

miles
0   10   20   30   40   50
0   20   40   60   80
kms.

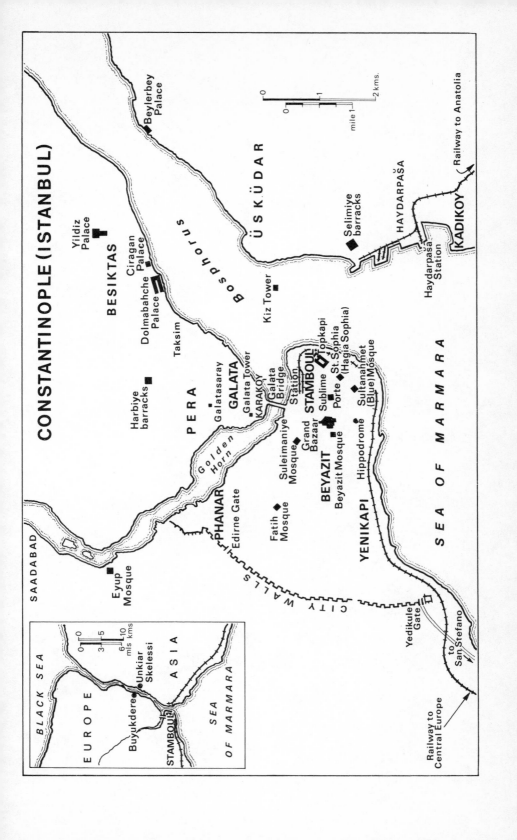

CONSTANTINOPLE (ISTANBUL)

Beylerbey Palace

Yildiz Palace

BESIKTAS

Ciragan Palace

Dolmabahche Palace

Taksim

Harbiye barracks

PERA

GALATA

Galatasaray

Galata Tower

Golden Horn

KARAKOY

Galata Bridge

Station

STAMBOUL

Topkapi

Sublime Porte

St. Sophia (Hagia Sophia)

Sultanahmet (Blue) Mosque

Suleimaniye Mosque

Grand Bazaar

BEYAZIT

Beyazit Mosque

Hippodrome

YENIKAPI

Fatih Mosque

PHANAR

Edirne Gate

Eyup Mosque

SAADABAD

CITY WALLS

Yedikule Gate

to San Stefano

Railway to Central Europe

Bosphorus

ÜSKÜDAR

Selimiye barracks

Kiz Tower

HAYDARPAŠA

Haydarpaša Station

KADIKOY

Railway to Anatolia

SEA OF MARMARA

0 __ 1 __ 2 kms.

0 __ mile 1

Inset map

BLACK SEA

EUROPE

Buyukdere

Unkiar Skelessi

STAMBOUL

ASIA

SEA OF MARMARA

0 __ 3 __ 6 mls kms
0 __ 5 __ 10

PROLOGUE

Ottomans Triumphant

'There never has been and never will be a more dreadful happening', wrote a monastic scribe in Crete when in June 1453 reports reached the island that Constantinople had fallen to the Turk. His tone of horror was echoed in papal Rome and republican Venice, in Genoa, Bologna, Florence and Naples, and in the trading cities of Aragon and Castile as the shock-wave spread across the continent. Only in England, where the imminent loss of Bordeaux to the French seemed of greater consequence, did the news arouse little concern. Elsewhere there was consternation. Constantinople may have become depopulated, impoverished and encircled by the Turks; already it had been sacked and looted in 1204 by the knights of the Fourth Crusade; but, in a medieval society increasingly conscious of its classical heritage, there lingered an idealized concept of Byzantium as the Christian legatee of Graeco-Roman civilization. Dismay was heightened by a sense of guilt. Emperor Constantine XI had called for armed support against the Muslim enemy. He received only negligible aid, together with the prospect of a coming unity between the Latin and Greek churches.

But Constantinople was doomed to fall. Only a massive relief expedition, together with diversionary assaults elsewhere around the Ottoman frontiers, might have saved it. Soon after sunrise on Tuesday 29 May 1453 the Sultan's troops found a way through a small gate in the unassailable walls at the Kerkoporta. By sunset what remained of the pillaged city lay in their hands. Constantine XI Dragases, eighty-sixth Emperor of the Greeks, perished fighting in the narrow streets beneath the western walls. After more than eleven hundred years there would be no more Christian Emperors in the East.

When Sultan Mehmed II rode his grey into Constantinople late that Tuesday afternoon he went first to St Sophia, the Church of the Holy

Wisdom, taking the basilica under his protection before ordering its conversion into a mosque. Some sixty-five hours later he returned there for the ritual Friday midday prayers. The transformation was symbolic of the Conqueror's plans. Yet so, too, was his insistence on ceremonially investing a learned Orthodox monk to fill the vacant Patriarchal throne. For Mehmed sought continuity; the 'dreadful happening' was, for him, neither a terminal end of a world empire nor a new beginning for the Sultanate.[1] He was to appropriate more than Christian altars for the service of Islam. The laws of the Byzantine Emperors served as a model for the codification he initiated. Significantly, he added to his titles *Rum Kayseri* (Roman Caesar), proclaiming himself heir to the imperial tradition which once encompassed the shores of the Mediterranean and beyond. There had been Arab empires in the Middle East but these proved transient creations. In seeking to restore Constantinople to its old greatness Mehmed the Conqueror affirmed his belief in the permanence of the Ottoman Empire by giving the Turks a capital city in European 'Rumelia' which looked out across the narrow waterway towards the Anatolian highlands, whence they had come.

Originally the Turks were nomadic horsemen from Central Asia who embraced Islam in the ninth century. Under the Seljuk leader Tuğrul they captured Baghdad, home of the earliest caliphate, eleven years before William of Normandy invaded England. The first major victory of Seljuk Turks over Christians followed in 1071, when a Byzantine army was defeated near Lake Van. Subsequently the Seljuks established a Sultanate, with its capital at Konya, on the site of the Greek city of Iconium. This Seljuk Sultanate survived until the first years of the fourteenth century, battered by pagan Mongol hordes. Local rulers then carved out principalities for themselves. Among them was Osman of Söğüt, a settlement near modern Eskişehir in western Anatolia. His dynasty became known as the 'Osmanli' in Turkish and 'Othman' in Arabic, which was corrupted into 'Ottoman' in the languages of western Europe. Osman died in 1326 when his army was besieging the Byzantine city of Brusa (Bursa today), which was captured by his son and successor, Orhan. Brusa thus became the first effective capital of an Ottoman Sultanate which survived until 1922, although the city was succeeded as capital by Adrianople (now Edirne) in about 1364 and, some ninety years later, by present-day İstanbul.

The Ottoman Turks crossed the narrow Dardanelles into Europe in 1345 at the invitation of Emperor John V Paleologus, who sought their military aid against a usurper. So formidable were the Turkish horsemen that they speedily made vassals of the Bulgars and Serbs, consolidating their Balkan gains by a decisive victory over the southern Slavs in June 1389 at Kossovo. As early as 1366 the rapid growth of Islamic power in south-eastern Europe had led Pope Urban V to proclaim a crusade, but the Ottoman advance seemed irresistible. The 'Turks' – as the multiracial subjects of the Sultan were collectively misnamed in central and western Europe – were soon feared as 'wild beasts' and 'inhuman barbarians', much as the 'Norsemen' had been in the age of the Vikings. Even before the fall of Constantinople the Ottomans had penetrated deeply into Europe, mounting devastating raids across the farmland of southern Hungary. They were checked by János Hunyadi in Transylvania in 1442 and outside Belgrade in 1456, but seventy years later the full weight of the Ottoman armies was concentrated in central Europe. At Mohács, on 29 August 1526, Sultan Suleiman I inflicted a terrible defeat on the Magyars: 24,000 *Süleyman* dead were buried on the battlefield; 2,000 prisoners were massacred; thousands more were carried back as slaves to Constantinople.

Suleiman the Magnificent, tenth Ottoman Sultan and the fourth to take up residence in the conquered city, is historically the best known of all Turkey's rulers. His reign – from 1520 to 1566, the longest of any Sultan – marks the apogee of the Ottoman Empire. He was a splendid show-pageant prince, like his near contemporaries in the West, Henry VIII of England and Francis I of France (who formed an anti-Habsburg alliance with the Sultan). The Turks remember Suleiman primarily as a lawgiver who was also a poet and scholar and a patron of the arts; fittingly, his permanent monument is the Suleimaniye mosque complex which ~~Mirman~~ Sinan, the finest of *Mimar = architect* Ottoman architects, built on the hillside looking out across the Golden Horn. Above all, Suleiman was a *ghazi* warrior, a soldier victorious *ghazi* on the Tigris as well as on the Danube, the conqueror of Belgrade, Buda and Rhodes. He ruled directly over much of southern Russia, over Transylvania, Hungary and the Balkans, Anatolia, Syria, Palestine, Jordan, and most of modern Iraq, Kuwait and the western shore of the Gulf. He was protector of Jerusalem and the Muslim holy places in modern Saudi Arabia and the overlord of Aden, the Yemen and all the North African coast from the Nile delta to the foothills of the Atlas Mountains.

Suleiman was more than a secular potentate. As *de facto* Caliph, he possessed a spiritual primacy among Muslim princes. He may also have been *de jure* Caliph; for the Caliphate, first held by the rulers of Baghdad and re-established in Egypt, had long been in eclipse. When

Suleiman's father, Sultan Selim I, captured Cairo in 1517 the last Abbasid Caliph became an Ottoman pensionary, and he is said to have transferred the shadow dignity to his new sovereign.[2] This may well have been mere legend; no Sultan claimed the caliphate *de jure* until the Ottoman Empire was in decline. But Suleiman and his heirs certainly possessed authority in the Muslim world; the Sherif of Mecca had sent Selim the keys of Medina and Mecca, placing the Holy Cities – and the pilgrim routes serving them – under his protection. On the other hand, the Sultans' religious authority was never acknowledged by zealous Shi'ites in Persia and Mesopotamia. Their divinely guided leaders claimed descent from Ali ibn Ab'Talib, the Prophet's cousin and son-in-law (whose shrine is in the modern Iraqi city of Najaf).

The Ottoman Empire was, in origin, a military institution dedicated to fulfilling the sacred obligation of extending the 'Abode of Islam' by conquering the lands of the unbelievers. Even before the fall of Constantinople the warrior Sultans had begun to bolster their personal despotism by developing a system under which selected Christian-born slaves, converted to Islam, became an imperial bodyguard. From within this priviliged caste the Sultans came to find most of their ministers (viziers) and military commanders (*ağas*). Suleiman I completed the work of Mehmed II in modifying this machine, geared for continous frontier war, into an imperial administration run by personal slaves through what were, in effect, armies of occupation.

'Whoever assaults the Turk must be prepared to meet his united forces . . . because those near the ruler's person, being all slaves and dependent, it will be more difficult to corrupt them.' This grudging admiration for Ottoman rule in Machiavelli's *The Prince*, written shortly before Suleiman's accession, points shrewdly to the basic source of strength in the imperial autocracy.[3] It could not function without total reliance on 'those near the ruler's person'. For the efficient adminis-tration of his empire a strong Sultan could turn confidently to the *divan-i hümayun* (a council of ministers, and a court of law) and especially to his chief minister, the Grand Vizier, who was generally the most privileged of imperial slaves. But within this centralized state, the Sultan also had to depend on the loyalty of each governor (*beylerbey* or, later, *vali*) whom he appointed to a province (*beylerbik* or vilayet). Beneath the governor would be several beys, heads of each county (*sanjak*) in the province. Rank was shown by the title of Pasha accorded to gover-nors and symbolized by the bestowal of ceremonial horsetails: one to a bey; two to a governor; three to the Grand Vizier; four to the Sultan himself.

beylik

A Sultan was more than an all-powerful sovereign. He was the greatest of land-owners; all newly conquered territory passed into his possession. In the cities, especially in the capital, most landed property constituted *vakif*, a pious foundation (plural *evkaf*) under the control of a religious institution, but when Suleiman came to the throne, almost ninety per cent of land outside the towns was, technically, crown property and therefore under state ownership. By using this crown land as a basic source of revenue for his government, Suleiman built up an Islamic counterpart to Western feudalism, exploiting the slave basis of the empire, even at the lowest level in the social scale. In the Balkans and Anatolia a fief (*timar*) of land would be allocated to a mounted soldier (*sipahi*) who, while having no rights of ownership, became the Sultan's representative on the 'estates' assigned to him. The *sipahi* was charged with the maintenance of order, and with encouraging agriculture so as to raise the yield from the fields; but, above all, he was responsible for collecting agreed taxes from the peasants which, after deducting a sum for the upkeep of himself, his horse and his family, he would forward to the central government. It was a cumbrous system, needing the maintenance of a co-ordinated discipline across the empire in order to intimidate the feudatories into collaboration. Under Suleiman this *timar* system worked; he died with a full treasury.[4] Less skilful Sultans did not.

The Caliphate ensured that Suleiman could bring an aura of Koranic respectability to vexatious exigencies of government. If he sought an interpretation of Islamic Holy Law (*şeriat*), he might turn to the collective wisdom of Muslim divines, as voiced by the religious establishment (*ulema*). More specifically, he would seek and receive authoritative advice from its hierarchical leaders, an inner circle known as the *ilmiye*, whose chief spokesman was the *şeyhülislâm* (Chief Mufti). The *ulema* were a favoured section of the community, exempt from taxation; they decided, not only strictly religious matters, but questions concerning the form of justice practised in the state, and the character and conduct of education as well. Important rulings would be issued in the form of a carefully considered legal opinion (*fetva*), generally in the name of the Chief Mufti. For Suleiman the *şeriat* was a sound support for government, a source of reference from which there could be no appeal.[5]

Almost imperceptibly, these religious institutions began to provide Ottoman government with a constitutional check, limiting a Sultan's autocracy. So respected were the religious leaders that they could even deliberate on the worthiness of a Sultan to retain his throne. They never questioned Suleiman's regnal rights nor, more surprisingly, those of his successor, the aptly named 'Selim the Sot'. But by 1610 the influence of *ulema* and *ilmiye* in making or breaking sultans was considerable; and it remained so throughout the Empire. Of twenty-one Sultans whose reigns ended between 1612 and 1922, thirteen were deposed under the authority of a *fetva* given by the Chief Mufti in response to questions framed by political enemies on a sultan's observance of Holy Law.[6]

After Suleiman's death the qualities of kingship shown by the Sultans deteriorated rapidly. Although Selim was something of a scholar and his grandson Mehmed III led a successful campaign in Hungary, none were both fine warriors and wise rulers in the old tradition. No Sultan acceding later than 1595 had any experience of active military service before coming to the throne. Murad IV, the strong-willed sovereign on the throne between 1623 and 1640, showed ability as a military commander in the Caucasus and Mesopotamia, but he was forced to spend much of his reign reasserting his authority over rebellious soldiery in the provinces. And though Murad was an able Sultan even he died from heavy drinking at the early age of thirty-one. Most rulers contentedly left the shaping of policy to others at court – to a Grand Vizier or an *aga*. Of particular influence in several reigns during the late sixteenth and early seventeenth centuries were the intrigues of a *Valide Sultana* (Princess Mother); palace power games were played with such intensity in these years that they have been called 'the Age of the Favoured Women'.

Modern academics frown austerely at so romantic and evocative a label. But even if they minimize the significance of harem politics, historians concede that by the mid-seventeenth century there is ample evidence of an empire slipping into decline.[7] They can point to at least six signs of chronic weakness: inflation, exacerbated by cheap silver from Peru circulated by traders from Genoa and Ragusa (Dubrovnik) and causing a threefold increase in the cost of basic food; failings in the pyramidical structure of *timar* tax collection; the growth of banditry, following a population explosion in Anatolia; ruinous fires in several overcrowded cities; an inflexible adherence to old ways of waging war and governing conquered lands; and (from 1536 onwards) the grant of 'Capitulations' – the treaties which, by giving special legal rights and tariff concessions to Europeans who resided within the Ottoman Empire, ensured that profitable trades should fall increasingly into foreign hands. Yet although modern historians may acknowledge that the Ottoman Empire had passed its zenith, these signs of crumbling power went unperceived by contemporaries, whether they were the

Sultan's subjects, or foreign observers. Even in decline the Ottomans clung to their cherished mission of thrusting the frontiers of Islam deeper into the marchlands of Christendom. Only when the seventeenth century was well into its final quarter did the truth begin to dawn on Western monarchs. It was then, in 1683, that, from news of a battle in the hills above Vienna, they recognized that the Sultan's armies were as fallible as their own. The legendary 'Grand Turk' need no longer be feared.

That he possessed astonishing powers of resilience, they were equally slow to perceive.

CHAPTER 1

Floodtide of Islam

It was 7 July 1683, and the people of Vienna sweltered restlessly under the sultry heat of a midsummer evening. Since early that Wednesday morning, when Emperor Leopold I returned hurriedly from hunting stags in the Wienerwald, fearful rumours had swept through the city. A vast Turkish army was said to be advancing westwards from the Alföld, the cultivated Hungarian plain around Lake Balaton. For several days thousands of refugees had poured into the Habsburg capital, bringing tales of burning villages and of savage atrocities on men, women and children. Now, from high ground east of the city, onlookers could see a great dust storm; it was raised, they said, by the approach of warrior horsemen following the green banners of Islam in a frenzied assault on Catholic Christendom.

Ottoman Turks had fought Christians, Orthodox or Catholic, for many generations, and there is no doubt that by now the Sultan's armies were less formidable than when the Janissaries stormed the walls of Constantinople. But even if the people of Vienna had been aware of signs of weakness in the approaching enemy, the knowledge would have brought them little comfort. In 1683, as in Shakespeare's day, 'the Turk' was still regarded as 'the terror of the world'. For a century and a half, the heartland of Hungary had been subject to the Sultan's rule. As far west as Esztergom, where Hungary's sainted king Stephen was born long before Habsburg or Ottoman entered history, a cluster of minarets crowned the fortress hill above the Danube. And, for the Viennese, it remained an unpleasant thought that Esztergom was within a hundred miles of the Wienerwald.

Yet, as an episode in folk legend, the peril was not unfamiliar to them. Three years after Hungary's disastrous defeat at Mohács it had looked as if the Habsburg capital, too, might soon pass under Turkish rule. In September and October 1529 Sultan Suleiman I had encircled Vienna with a quarter of a million men and three hundred siege guns, only to pull back into Hungary when endless rain threatened to bog down his army in the mire. The danger had receded, but the nightmare fear of Turkish invasion remained throughout the years of the Counter-Reformation. After 1529 Austrian prelates, alarmed by Suleiman's deep incursion into Catholic Christendom, insisted that the parochial clergy of central Europe should establish a warning system, the *Türkenglocken*, a peal of bells which would alert the soldiery to the coming of the Turks and summon the Catholic faithful to pray for deliverance from Islam.

A century passed with no need for the *Türkenglocken* to ring out across Austria. Once Suleiman's long reign ended in 1566 the Sultanate, weakened by palace rivalry and intrigue, became militarily a less formidable institution. But the latent menace of Ottoman invasion was ever-present; and the church bells tolled their warning in July 1664, when a powerful army was thrown back at Szentgotthárd on Hungary's historic western frontier. Now, in this stifling summer of 1683, Vienna was threatened yet again with Turkish occupation. After a winter and spring of negotiations between Austrian and Ottoman diplomats, the vanguard of a massive army had crossed the western edge of the Hungarian plain in late June. Fighting alongside the invaders were Hungarian insurgents led by an ambitious Magyar nobleman, Imre Tököly. But what most alarmed the Austrians were the irregular *akinji* outriders, undisciplined skirmishers plundering far ahead of the main, well-disciplined Ottoman army. When, on this first Wednesday in July, news reached Emperor Leopold that the crescent flag was flying over the citadel of Györ, he thought the threat imminent. Györ was only eighty-five miles away: the imperial family would leave Vienna at once before the dreaded *akinji* closed in upon the capital.

At eight o'clock that evening a cavalcade of heavy carriages set out from the Hofburg, lumbering across the moat bridge of the Schweizerhof Court to head for the road westward, towards Melk and Linz. The departure of the imperial family confirmed the people of Vienna's worst fears. Hundreds of refugees sought to accompany the Emperor and his escort, so impeding their progress that the nine-mile journey to Korneuburg took four hours. As Leopold stepped down from his carriage soon after midnight, he could look back over Vienna and see the spire of the Stephans-Dom silhouetted against a glowing eastern rim of hills fringed with fire.[1]

But as the invaders approached Vienna they checked their pace of advance. The best troops had already travelled more than halfway across Europe, covering almost a thousand miles since leaving their barracks beside the Bosphorus at the end of March. Now, with the wooded hills of the Wienerwald in sight, their commander anticipated a stiffening resistance. He was not to know there were serious gaps in the defences of the *Antemurale Christianitatis*, 'the Front Line of Christendom' (as a Dutch contemporary called Vienna); and he was sceptical of reports from deserters that the city was garrisoned by no more than 12,000 regular troops. Not until Tuesday, 16 July – six days after Emperor Leopold's flight – did the Turkish vanguard reach the outer line of Vienna's fortifications.

In 1529 Sultan Suleiman I had conducted the siege of Vienna in person, receiving on the plains beside the Danube the first check to Ottoman arms in seventeen years of war on three continents. Not that Suleiman had been defeated; he had merely failed to capture a city which seemed less naturally defensible than so many fortresses already taken along the middle Danube. But by 1683 the character of the Sultanate was different. Mehmed IV, who had been on the throne for the preceding thirty-five years, was a spendthrift hedonist, a vigorous horseman but no soldier; in Ottoman history he is labelled '*Mehmed Avçi*' (Mehmed the Hunter) and he is remembered, in epic verse as well as in prose, for mobilizing thousands of peasants as beaters in the woods around Edirne. Eight years after his accession he had the good fortune to find a gifted family who provided him with two first-rate Grand Viziers, Mehmed Köprülü and his son, Fezil Ahmed. Their reforms and administrative efficiency brought him the full treasury into which he dipped for his hunting campaigns, but they also enabled him to raise the powerful force which set out on this second march on Vienna. Sultan Mehmed was prepared to ride as far as Belgrade with his troops. He would not, however, risk a personal rebuff. Far better to entrust so ambitious an enterprise to his close companion Kara Mustafa, who on Fazil Ahmed's death in November 1676 had become Grand Vizier.[2]

No Ottoman commander possessed greater military experience. In 1672 on the river Dniester Kara Mustafa had outwitted the great Polish soldier, John Sobieski, to secure the fortress of Kamenets Podolsky for the Turks and their Tatar vassals. Two years later he had taken the town of Uman, having his Christian captives flayed and sending their stuffed hides as a gift to the Sultan. His origins remain decently obscure; he was not a Köprülü by birth, but had been educated and personally advanced as if he were Fazil Ahmed's foster-brother; and

in June 1675 he strengthened his power at court by marrying Princess
Küçük, daughter of the recipient of those grisly trophies from Uman.
It was rumoured that the Grand Vizier brought with him a full complement of camp followers, including 1,500 concubines and 700 black
eunuchs to guard them. Many grotesque tales of his way of life rest
on a basis of fact, but this legend is almost certainly apocryphal. Nevertheless, he seems to have possessed a sexual appetite difficult to satisfy
and matched only by the scale of his ambition. To succeed where
Suleiman failed would make him as famous a commander on land as
Hayruddin 'Barbarossa' at sea, more than a century before.

He began by showing great efficiency. Within two days of inspecting
Vienna's outer defences he completed the investment of the city. On
14 July a bad fire wrecked many town palaces of the magnates, the
smoke drifting over the Ottoman lines causing Kara Mustafa to fear
that Vienna might be in ruins by the time the prize fell into his hands.
Accordingly he gave orders for the construction of a huge camp beyond
the fortifications and siege works, a military headquarters which would
make a worthy home for the Sultan's paladin. Within little more than
a week a tented city sprang up between Vienna itself and the north-
western hills of the Wienerwald. His adversaries were much impressed
by this curious display of Ottoman splendour. An Italian count serving
in the Habsburg army has left a description written that summer:
'It is impossible for anyone to conceive how broad a stretch of land
they covered. Centred in the middle of the camp arose the Grand
Vizier's pavilion, looking like some splendid palace surrounded by
several villas, the tents being of different colours, all of which made
for a richly pictorial diversity.'[3] More than three centuries after the
siege, Vienna still possesses a Türkenschanz Park. But it is no longer
an open space. A wealth of fine trees surrounds the hillock at the centre
of the old Turkish encampment. Felicitously, there is also an 'adventure
playground' for the young.

For sixty days Kara Mustafa remained in his palatial camp, concentrating 200,000 men around the twelve bastions and defensive palisades
of the city walls. The Austrian campaign confirmed not only his personal reputation for cruelty, but the widespread belief in Western
Europe that the Sultan's troops were a barbarian horde. In reality,
the Ottoman regular army was no better and no worse than other
campaigners. It was otherwise with their commander; Kara Mustafa,
though casual in his religious observance, exhibited a fanatical hatred
of Christians; he was 'the scourge of mankind', a Venetian envoy wrote
to the Doge.[4] He retained a row of severed heads to commemorate his

11

seizure of Hainburg, a fortified village some twenty miles down the Danube; and on 16 July his troops slaughtered four thousand villagers in outlying Perchtoldsdorf. During the first week of the siege he ordered the systematic killing of prisoners, exhibiting their heads to demoralize the Austrian troops manning the defences. By late July marauding *akinji* horsemen, over whom Kara Mustafa had little control, were sweeping up the Danube, carrying rapine and devastation as far west as Enns. Only a few fortified abbeys, like Melk, high on a cliff face above the river, survived as Christian islands cut off by this raging floodtide of Islam.

Emperor Leopold I – by now in Passau – urgently sought aid. Subsidies from the Pope, a rush of volunteers from the young nobility in northern Italy and Franconian Germany, and the mustering of armies by the Electors of Bavaria and Saxony, held hope of relief for Vienna. There remained, too, the prospect of substantial backing from the crack Polish troops of King John Sobieski, once they could complete a long march southwards from beyond the Carpathians; Sobieski had old scores to settle with Kara Mustafa. Yet it could be argued that the chief hope for Vienna lay in the weaknesses of the Grand Vizier's character, in the greed which made him at heart no better than a bandit chieftain. A frontal assault on the city, with walls breached and the attackers granted the traditional three days of looting, street by street, would prove less profitable for him personally than a capitulation on agreed terms; a formal surrender would allow him to secure for his own coffers the rich booty of Vienna's remaining palaces and churches. Only in the last days of August, as John Sobieski's advance columns reached the northern bank of the Danube, did Kara Mustafa finally give up hope of starving the city into surrender and order an all-out attack on its southern defences.

By 7 September Sobieski had made contact with the Germans under Charles, Duke of Lorraine, and a relief army of 80,000 troops was concentrated along the northern crest of the Wienerwald. On that Tuesday evening, camp fires on the Kahlenberg heights let Count Starhemberg, the commander of the Vienna garrison, know help was at hand. Kara Mustafa, too, saw the fires and, from interrogated prisoners, was well aware of the strength of the armies marching against him. Urgently he pressed the skilled Turkish *laguñçi* (sappers) into digging parallel trenches and tunnels to undermine Vienna's outer defences. An exploding mine at last breached the walls on the morning of 12 September. But it was too late. The Ottoman troops could not exploit their success; from five o'clock on that Sunday morning,

lağımcı

a fierce battle had been taking place along the wooded spur of the Kahlenberg and through the terraced vineyards of the lower slopes. As the light began to fail, German infantry reached the outskirts of the great Turkish camp. With the setting sun behind them, Polish cavalry bore down upon the tented city to consolidate the victory and ensure the relief of Vienna. The Grand Vizier abandoned many of his trophies, including a prize steed, richly caparisoned. As dusk fell he was seen speeding eastwards towards Györ on a lighter horse and almost unrecognizable, with his right eye bandaged.[5]

In 1529 Suleiman the Magnificent retired from Vienna of his own volition and in good order; in 1683 Kara Mustafa's troops were forced to retreat, their commander fleeing defeated from the field. No one can choose a precise date and say 'On this day the Ottoman Empire passed into decline', but there is no doubt that the scattering of the Turkish camp outside Vienna on that September evening forms one of history's greatest turning-points. No Ottoman army had been routed so dramatically in any earlier encounter. Yet, rather strangely, the fierce combat along the slopes of the Kahlenberg never figures in any list of 'decisive battles of history'. No doubt the events of that Sunday seemed of little importance at first, except to Emperor Leopold; militarily they possessed no particular interest; and they did not lead to the immediate conclusion of a peace settlement. Only with the passage of time has the true significance of the battle become clear. For although there were to be many more encounters in the Danubian plain, never again did an Islamic host pit its might against the walls of Catholic Christendom.

No attempt was made by Sobieski or Duke Charles to pursue the demoralized enemy immediately after the relief of Vienna. They lingered on the outskirts of the city until Emperor Leopold returned, on the following Tuesday. By then, Kara Mustafa had put the rivers Leitha and Raab between his army and the victorious Christians. Once he reached the Alföld, he was able to regroup his shattered cavalry and fall back upon the citadel of Buda. At the same time he looked for scapegoats in order to convince the Sultan that he was not himself at fault. He could not take vengeance on the insurgent Hungarians, for their canny leader slipped away to the north-east and was using Sobieski as an intermediary to save him from the Emperor's wrath, with some success. But the Ottoman regimental commanders remained in the Grand Vizier's power. They suffered for the failure in front of Vienna. More than fifty pashas were strangled by Kara Mustafa's personal bodyguard in the week which followed the battle on the Kahlenberg.

These deaths of course made no difference to the outcome of the campaign. Momentarily, at the end of the first week in October, the Grand Vizier's deputy inflicted a severe check on the Poles at Parkan, a river crossing beneath Esztergom. But two days later a combined Christian army, commanded by Charles of Lorraine, reversed the decision at Parkan and finally broke Turkish resistance along the middle Danube. On 24 October Esztergom surrendered after a brief bombardment. Although earlier in the century Austrian troops had captured towns and villages in which the Turks had set up mosques, Esztergom became the first Islamicized city in Catholic Europe to be recovered by a Christian army.

Even before the fall of Esztergom, Kara Mustafa had left Buda and set out for Belgrade. As the army retreated across the Pannonian Plain he ordered more executions, for he was determined to keep news of the disasters in Austria and Hungary from reaching the Sultan's court for as long as possible. Geographically, the middle Danube might constitute a remote north-west frontier for the empire. But the Grand Vizier was under no illusions about the Sultan's reaction to military failure. Mehmed IV was not a charismatic leader; like so many members of the Ottoman family, on the most solemn occasions he looked 'a wretched contrast to his splendid trappings', as a Venetian diplomat had commented earlier in the year; but, however unimpressive his parade horsemanship might be, Mehmed remained 'the Grand Turk'.[6] A single military defeat, even as distant from his capital as the middle Danube, signified an ominous diminution of imperial power. His Grand Vizier had failed Mehmed in the very lands where, for ten generations, the Sultans had been accustomed to expect victories from their army.

When on 17 November Kara Mustafa reached Belgrade's citadel, on its limestone cliff above the confluence of Danube and Sava, his expectancy of life was low. He could not execute every witness of his lack-lustre generalship without confirming suspicions already circulating at the Sultan's court; and, though he sought to bribe many survivors of the campaign, there was no certainty that money would ensure a lasting silence. His fate – and, a few years later, the fate of his sovereign – illustrates the inherent self-discipline which still shaped Ottoman ruling institutions as the Empire embarked on a long delaying action against the resilient West.

At Belgrade Kara Mustafa was still, for the moment, Grand Vizier. In the Kalemegdan Fortress he retained the symbols of office with which Mehmed IV had invested him seven years before – the Imperial

Seal and the Key to the Kaaba – and also the Holy Banner (*sancaği şerif*) which the Sultan had handed to him in May, here in Belgrade, on his appointment as Commander-in-Chief. But although his office ensured that Kara Mustafa still possessed a terrifying authority over his battered army and the towns and villages of Serbia, he knew that generals who suffered defeat while carrying the *sancaği şerif* into battle had no right to expect pardon. Old personal enemies surrounded Mehmed IV, who was holding court at Edirne, a favourite residence where Kara Mustafa had often ridden beside him on hunting expeditions. When a Grand Vizier set out to lead a campaign for his sovereign the day-to-day business he would have undertaken as chief minister was entrusted to a deputy, and as reports from the Danube seeped through to Edirne it was easy for the deputy and other members of the Divan to convince the Sultan that Kara Mustafa had shown himself unworthy of the responsibilities assigned to him. Mehmed realized that if the Grand Vizier were allowed to live, the humiliating burden of a defeat by infidel armies would pass to the Sultan-Caliph himself.

Such reasoning sealed Kara Mustafa's fate. On the last Saturday in December he was at his midday prayers when two senior Court dignitaries reached the Kalemegdan citadel from Edirne. They brought with them a double command from the Sultan to his son-in-law: he must surrender to the imperial emissaries his symbols of civil and military authority; and he should then 'entrust his soul to Allah, the ever Merciful'. Kara Mustafa completed his prayers, took off his turban and mantle of state, and allowed the executioner to throttle him speedily. There was about the timing of his death a strange irony. As the bowstring tightened around Kara Mustafa's neck in Belgrade, far away in Vienna and Esztergom and in towns and villages which had so long feared the coming of 'the Turk', the church bells were ringing out to celebrate Christmas. It was on 25 December that his co-religionists executed the arch-persecutor of Christians.[7]

The body was decapitated, the head skinned, stuffed, and sent to Mehmed IV as proof that the sovereign's orders had been carried out. But Nemesis had not finished mocking the unfortunate Kara Mustafa. In later campaigns the head fell into Austrian hands. Three hundred years after the siege the curious tourist could see it mounted in a glass case on the first floor of Vienna's *Historisches Museum*, a grisly relic of a turbulent age. But the skull is no longer on display. A spirit of reconciliation now prevails in the Austrian capital. Old enmities dissolve in the mystery of time past.

CHAPTER 2

Challenge from the West

Sultan Mehmed IV was sovereign of more than thirty million subjects, twice as many as King Louis XIV and six times as many as Emperor Leopold I. Even after the disaster on the Danube, his empire remained formidable. He ruled over almost the whole of the Balkans, up to the eastern approaches to Zagreb, and his troops held outposts along the Polish river Bug and the Russian rivers Don and Dnieper. In Europe alone his lands were greater in area than France and Spain taken together, while in Asia Minor he was direct ruler over a vast region which stretched as far south as the head-waters of the Red Sea and the Persian Gulf, and he held as tributary states the Caucasian lands eastwards to the Caspian Sea. Rhodes, Crete and Cyprus acknowledged his sovereignty; so, too, did Egypt and the lower Nile valley, and he could claim vassal authority over Tripoli, Tunis and Algiers.

Along most of these frontiers there was, however, a clear limit to imperial expansion, well defined on the map. In the East the Ottoman advance was checked by a combination of geography and military science, to which might be added the religious hostility of convinced Shi'ites: the Safavid dynasty of Persia possessed the skill to exploit natural defences high in their mountainous central plateau; and it was never likely that the Ottomans would emulate the early Arab invaders and reach the Punjab. In the South the barrier to expansion was purely geographical: sand imposed a natural frontier, and apart from protecting the pilgrim trail to Medina and Mecca, there seemed no reason for the Ottomans to penetrate deeply along caravan routes into the Sahara or the Arabian deserts. The south-western limits were also settled long before the closing decades of the seventeenth century, for new conquests in that direction depended on sea power, and Turkish shipyards did not build vessels stout enough to face the challenge of the Atlantic. Although the Sultan's calm-water fleet was still effective to the east of the Sicilian narrows, Ottoman maritime pretensions never fully recovered from their defeat in 1571, when Don John of Austria's Spanish, Genoese and Venetian armada gained a decisive victory at Lepanto in the Gulf of Patras. Thereafter successive Grand Viziers left naval harassment of the Sultan's Christian enemies in the western Mediterranean to 'Barbary pirates', untrustworthy allies though these notorious corsairs often proved to be.

Yet, while mountains, sands and ocean confined Ottoman power in three directions, there was no natural obstacle to the north of the Balkans, short of the Carpathians and the Alps. An artificial barrier, a string of fortresses built by the Habsburgs in the late sixteenth century, formed the so-called 'Military Frontier' across western Croatia, but the Danubian plain formed a vast arena in which generals who could master the changing techniques of military science might engage the enemy in battle. In the fifteenth century the Turks had soon perceived the value of cannon; even as early as 1453 a 'super-gun' twenty-six feet long lobbed stone balls against the walls of Constantinople. But they did not maintain their lead in exploiting new weaponry. The relief of Vienna and the fall of Esztergom showed the world what several foreign travellers had suspected over the past half-century: the Ottoman war machine was beginning to seize up. It may have enabled the Sultans to raise a standing army earlier than other sovereigns in Europe, but the Danubian campaign had shown that Kara Mustafa's combination of specialist troops, feudatories, daredevil light horsemen and untrained auxiliary plodders could not match the new professional soldiery of the West. Turkish flintlock muskets remained deadly, but heavy artillery trains drawn by oxen, buffalo or camels made slow and lumbering progress across the Danubian plain.

Catholic Christendom sought speedily to exploit the advantage won by Sobieski and Charles of Lorraine by weaving, for the first time, a grand strategic design against 'the Turk'.[1] In March 1684 emissaries from Venice, Poland and Austria came together, with the backing of Pope Innocent XI, to create a new 'Holy League', an offensive coalition which would threaten other frontiers as well as the Danube basin. During these discussions in Venice the earliest provisional plans were outlined for partitioning the Ottoman Empire in Europe and – more vaguely – in the Middle East, too. Louis XIV, whose ministers maintained profitable relations with successive Grand Viziers, was disinclined to associate France with any crusading Holy League, but it was hoped Orthodox Russia, Protestant Germany and even Muslim

Persia would act in concert with the three Catholic Powers.

These plans were over-ambitious: Persia failed to respond to the Capuchin missionaries who served as envoys from Venice; German Lutheran participation was minimal; and another two years passed before the Russians went to war, then only to mount an expedition against Mehmed's tributary ruler, the Tatar Khan of the Crimea. But, although the coalition remained incomplete, the Holy League was able to attack Mehmed IV in rapid succession on several fronts. These operations marked the start of thirty-five years of almost continuous warfare, in which the Sultan's enemies sought to roll back the frontiers of Islam and prove that the great empire built up by Suleiman was set in fatal decline.

The fighting began where it had ended in the previous autumn. Duke Charles of Lorraine continued the war in the Alföld, securing Pest and most of northern Hungary in two summer campaigns, taking Buda after a month's siege on 2 September 1686, and defeating the Turks heavily eleven months later near the historic battlefield of Mohács. Charles's victory allowed Habsburg armies to clear the Ottomans from most of Croatia and Transylvania. In the first week of September 1688 the Austrians carried the war into the Balkans by storming Belgrade, the capital of a provincial pashalik for more than a century and a half. In the following summer they advanced to Niš and Skopje, penetrating to within four hundred miles of Constantinople by the autumn.

Meanwhile Venice, too, opened up a battle front in the Balkans. Raids on Ottoman outposts along the southern Dalmatian coast and in Bosnia were followed in 1685 by a new campaign in Greece. Francesco Morosini, a former Doge in his late sixties, landed at Tolon in the Peloponnese – the 'Sanjak of the Morea' – and encouraged revolts in Epirus and the Mani. By August 1687 this 'Venetian' force, which included Lutheran mercenaries under the Swedish adventurer Count John Königsmarck, had ejected the Turks from all the Peloponnese except the defiant rocky promontory of Monemvasia. A month later Morosoni's men swept across the isthmus of Corinth and thrust forwards, by land and by sea, to the Piraeus. They then attacked the tumbledown cluster of homes and shops around the Acropolis which was all that remained of the greatest of classical cities. After ten days of intermittent bombardment the Ottoman troops surrendered. Not, however, before irreparable disaster had hit Athens.[2] On the evening of 26 September 1687 a German mercenary fired a mortar from the Mouseion Hill which blew up a Turkish powder magazine in the

Parthenon; the frieze and fourteen columns crashed to the ground. A few days later Morosini ordered the carved horses and chariot of Athena to be removed from the west pediment and shipped to Venice as a trophy of war, following the marble Lion of the Piraeus which was already on its way to embellish the gates of the Doge's arsenal. The task of lowering the group proved too hard for Morosini's unskilled labourers. Horses and chariot fell to the ground, in ruins. The classical heritage of Athens suffered more from Morosini's expedition than from any depredations inflicted during the past two centuries of Ottoman rule – although it was, of course, the Turks who used the Parthenon as a gunpowder store.

Alarming rumours of the Holy League's strategic counter-offensive filtered through to Constantinople. So, too, month after month, did thousands of hungry and desperate refugees. There was no escaping the effects of the war in the capital or on either shore of the Bosphorus. Bread prices doubled in 1686 and again in 1687; banditry flourished in Rumelia; fields went untilled in the fertile regions because labourers had been conscripted into Kara Mustafa's army. Sultan 'Mehmed the Hunter' chose to remain as long as possible at Edirne, fearing for his life in the capital. Early in his reign Mehmed had been well served by two members of the Köprülü family. Now a third, Ahmed's younger brother Mustafa, became the natural leader of an opposition group, intent on checking the decline of the Sultan's authority in the Empire's outlying provinces.

Mehmed was hopelessly discredited and it was too late for Mustafa Köprülü to save him. Defeat at Mohács, followed closely by news of Morosini's advance into Attica, cost him the Sultanate. Four predecessors had already been cast from the throne in the first half of the century. Last of them was Mehmed's father Ibrahim 'the Mad', deposed on 8 August 1648 after an eight-year reign made memorable by a frittering-away of harshly extorted funds, and by tales of one terrible night on which he was said to have ordered the drowning of two hundred and eighty concubines. No one grieved for Ibrahim when, ten days after losing his throne, he was strangled by his own *cellad* (Chief Executioner). Now, in 1687, with angry and underpaid soldiers flocking into the capital, it seemed probable that Mehmed would suffer his father's fate. But neither the Divan nor the *ulema* wished to weaken further the twin institutions of Sultanate and Caliphate by a second murder. Mustafa Köprülü favoured bloodless deposition, with Mehmed IV surrendering sovereignty to his 45-year-old half-brother Prince Suleiman.

Abdications seldom go smoothly, even among the dynasties of mono-gamous societies, and in the Ottoman Empire the structure of the harem system constantly raised succession problems.[3] Before the nine-teenth century it was rare for there to be an heir-apparent, a well-groomed prince ready to come forward immediately after a Sultan's death or deposition. Most Ottoman rulers favoured several Sultanas, as well as concubines lower down the harem hierarchy who might have borne them sons. So intricate was the problem that in the fifteenth and sixteenth centuries the brothers and half-brothers of a new Sultan were generally strangled on his accession day, thus eliminating rival claimants who might become the centre of palace intrigue: five brothers of Murad *IV* had perished by the bowstring on 21 December 1574; and on 28 January 1595 the killing of a record eighteen brothers of Mehmed III left the dynasty so short of males that religious leaders began to question the morality and wisdom of mass fratricide. It was accordingly decided that close male relatives should henceforth be confined to a *kafe* (cage), one of several small apartments in the Fourth Courtyard of the Sultan's principal palace, the Topkapi Sarayi. Apart from Mehmed himself, who acceded at the age of six, all fifteen Sultans between 1617 and 1839 awaited the call to the throne in this small world, with its marble terrace looking out across a garden to the Golden Horn and the Bosphorus.[4]

Some princes suffered no more than nominal confinement. But Suleiman, only three months younger than Mehmed, entered the *kafe* at the age of six and reached middle age knowing nothing of the world beyond what he could see from the Fourth Courtyard. Thirty-nine years in the *kafe,* out of touch with public affairs, was no preparation for a reign. Nevertheless, on 9 November 1687 the Viziers duly pro-duced the dazed, puzzled and half-forgotten Prince from the inner apartments of the Topkapi; he was, a Frenchman noted, of 'long, lean and pale appearance'.[5] The Viziers waited on Mehmed IV with a *fetva* requiring his abdication. He accepted his deposition fatalistically and was duly transferred to the *kafe*, while Suleiman II was ceremonially girded with the sword in the sacred mosque at Eyüp, an occasion corresponding to a coronation. At least Mehmed's life was spared. But a final irony was reserved for him. Eventually he left the Topkapi and, under close escort, journeyed northwards, back to Edirne and the favourite palace from which he had so often ridden out hunting. But there were to be no more 'sporting campaigns' for Mehmed. His life ended in a virtual imprisonment which denied him all plea-sure. When he died in January 1693 some said it was of gout, some of poison, but many maintained that it was from melancholia.

By then Suleiman II was dead, too. In June 1691, barely three and a half years after being girded with the sword, he succumbed to dropsy as he was about to set out from Edirne on a campaign against the Austrians. In death he was honoured as never in life, for his embalmed body was brought to the *turbe* (tomb) of his great namesake in the Suleimaniye complex, beside the finest imperial mosque in the capital. He had achieved more than seemed likely when he emerged from the *kafe*. In the first days of March 1688 he personally led troops who hunted down rebels, outlaws and the most blatant racketeers in the Stamboul and Galata districts of Constantinople; he promised to lift the burden of extra war taxes; and at last, in October 1689, appointed Mustafa Köprülü as Grand Vizier – a courageous decision, for the Köprülüs were a formidable family with the confidence to make or unmake Sultans. The Grand Vizier showed himself a sound general; Niš and Belgrade were recaptured in the autumn of 1690 and a defence line re-established along the Danube. Suleiman II was ready to ride northwards with him for an advance into Hungary when death struck the Sultan down.

Mustafa Köprülü did not return to Stamboul for Suleiman II's funeral. The Viziers fetched from the back apartments of the palace yet another half-brother, Prince Ahmed, ten months junior to Suleiman and with a full forty-three years of the *kafe* behind him. There was no time for the sword-girding 'coronation' at Eyüp, only for an improvised ceremony in Edirne's Eşki mosque. Then Mustafa Köprülü set out at *Eşki* once for the Danube battle front, leaving Ahmed II to receive instruction in government from the Divan. Less than a month later, the Grand Vizier's army was ambushed at Szlankamen, thirty miles north-west of Belgrade, on the edge of the wooded Fruska Gora. Mustafa Köprülü was fatally wounded and his army scattered.

Was there perhaps at this moment a chance for the Holy League to recover the Balkans? If so, the opportunity was missed. After the death in 1689 of the neo-crusading pope Innocent XI, political objectives – and papal funds – contracted. Lack of allied cohesion led to isolated campaigns rather than fulfilment of the grand strategic master plan conceived in Venice on the eve of the war. Even before Morosini's return to his native city in 1688 the Venetian expedition to Greece was losing momentum; the Turks soon recovered Athens, although Venice held on to the Peloponnese. Polish and Russian internal affairs weakened pressure on the Ottomans from the north, while along the Danube the Germano-Austrian contribution to the League was necessarily restrained by the need to keep armies in the field against Louis XIV. A popular uprising forced the Venetians to abandon the strategically important island of Chios, and stubborn Turkish resistance thwarted the young Peter the Great's first attempt to take Azov, the Black Sea fort commanding the mouth of the river Don. But these isolated outposts of the Ottoman Empire could not be supplied regularly with arms or reinforcements; and in June 1696 a newly constructed Russian fleet enabled Peter to take Azov and begin the long contest of the Tsars for mastery over the Black Sea. A westernized Russia, bearing down on the Ottoman Empire from the north, soon posed a far more serious threat than had old Muscovy.

Tsar and Sultan were faced by a similar menace to their authority: the over-mighty power of a privileged military corps. To impose westernization Tsar Peter had first to destroy the Moscow garrison, the *streltsy*. It was a misfortune for the Ottomans that no eighteenth-century Sultan was prepared to destroy the comparable institution within his empire, the Janissary Corps.[6] Historically the corps dated back to the late fourteenth century when Ottoman power was shifting from Asia Minor to the Balkans. Sultan Murad I created the Janissaries (*Yeni Çeri*, new soldiery) as a slave bodyguard; they became a nucleus of the first standing army in modern Europe. Some fifty years later a regular pattern of enforced tribute, the *devşirme*, was introduced and served as the chief source from which the Janissary Corps was raised: Christian peasant fathers were required once in five years to report to the local administrators the number of sons in their family; one in five boys, usually a child aged about six or seven, were then taken by the Sultan's officers and obliged to become Muslims. Theoretically the tribute was levied throughout all the Christian regions of the Empire, but it fell heaviest on modern Bosnia, Albania and Bulgaria. A few bright and intelligent slaves were sent for special training at the palace school in Constantinople; there was nothing to prevent them becoming high officials, and several rose to be Grand Vizier. But most of the *devşirme* tribute became soldiers. They were brainwashed into absolute loyalty to the Corps, their military family.

In 1453 the Janissaries forced their way into Constantinople at the crucial hour of the final assault on Byzantium; a century later they were the spearhead of Suleiman the Magnificent's army. In these years the corps was bound by a strict and well-defined code of life: absolute obedience to their officers; perfect accord between each unit; abstinence from alcohol; observance of Muslim piety; enlistment only from the *devşirme* or from prisoners-of-war; no beards; no marriage;

no pursuit of a trade or profession other than soldiery; and acceptance of seniority as a basis for promotion, of residence in barracks (with safeguards for retirement), of capital punishment in a reputedly merciful form, of corporal punishment on the orders of Janissary officers, and of demands for training or exercise at any time. They could count on good pay and rations and, from 1451 onwards, they received a special distribution of Accession Money each time a new Sultan was girded with the ceremonial sword. Since only seven Sultans acceded during a span of a hundred and fifty years, Accession Money formed a not unreasonable occasional bonus payment.

But by 1620 the Janissaries were not so much a standing army as a standing menace.[7] Their code was neglected. Legal marriage was first permitted in 1566, the year of the great Suleiman's death. Soon afterwards sons of Janissaries were allowed to join the Corps, even though as Muslims they could not themselves be bound in the slave obedience that ensured strict discipline. The last comprehensive levy in south-eastern Europe was raised in 1676; already by then there were instances of Muslim fathers lending sons to Christian families so that they could find their way into such a powerful and prestigious body of men. By the start of the seventeenth century the communal life of the Corps was less binding; Janissaries acquired their own homes in garrison towns; if not campaigning, they practised trades; many behaved like a civilian reserve militia rather than as the core of the Sultan's army. Yet while greedy to acquire new rights, they remained jealously possessive of old privileges. Accession Money became, not a reward, but a form of extortion. When in 1623 Murad IV became the fourth Sultan to accede in six years, the Grand Vizier informed the senior generals of the Janissaries that the treasury was empty, and they agreed that their troops would forgo the bonus; but, in a mutinous mood, the Corps insisted on its rights: gold and silver plate from the Topkapi Sarayi was melted down and minted into coin for their benefit.

A strong and fearless ruler would have suppressed the Janissaries. But how? Unlike the Russian *streltsy*, the corps was not based on any single centre in the empire. There had long been Janissary barracks in Constantinople, in the larger provincial cities, and in conquered capitals such as Cairo and Damascus. Suleiman, aware of the potential danger constituted by the Corps, encouraged the growth of an Imperial Bodyguard of dragoons (*silahtar*). Under his successors this regiment was recruited from the richer Turkish nobility and in any campaign remained close to the Sultan's person. Yet while the *silahtar* was a small élite force, the Janissaries could number 90,000 men organized in more than a hundred battalions (*orta*), if fully mobilized. They included what might be regarded as a proto-commando brigade, the *serdengeçti* ('those willing to give up their heads'), an initial infantry assault force. If the Ottoman Empire was to meet the military challenge from the West, the Sultans needed the Janissaries, provided the Corps would fight as loyally and ferociously as in the days of Mehmed the Conqueror and Suleiman the Magnificent.

Briefly it seemed as if they might. Under Mustafa II, who came to the throne in February 1695, a vigorous attempt was made to halt the Austrian advance.[9] Within eleven weeks of his accession Sultan Mustafa appointed as *şeyhülislâm* Feyzullah Effendi, his former tutor. As principal interpreter of Holy Law it was Feyzullah Effendi's task to win support from the conservative *ulema* for renewed war on the Danube. Resistance to the Habsburgs required more taxation and greater personal suffering in the villages of both Rumelia and Anatolia, for a new campaign would once again denude the fields of labourers. Feyzullah Effendi became more than a spiritual leader; in the absence of a strong Vizier he was the Sultan's chief executive, capable of scaring reluctant provincial pashas into raising troops for the Sultan and of checking the mutinous tendencies of the Janissaries. Theoretically the Janissary Corps was at full strength, although in practice no more than 10,000 men were ready for service in Europe and the *orta* stationed in Egypt remained wildly undisciplined. But by the early months of 1696 a formidable army had gathered around the holy banner. Feyzullah Effendi and the *ulema* would, under the protection of Allah, control the Ottoman Empire from the capital while, once again, a Sultan led his army into battle.

At first Sultan Mustafa's generalship met with some success. He defended Temesvar (Timişoara) against Emperor Leopold's troops, enabling the Turks to keep a firm foothold north of the Danube. But in the late summer of 1697 he became over-ambitious, advancing northwards from Belgrade, into the rich Hungarian granary of the Backsa (now the Serbian Vojvodina). Near the small town of Zenta the Sultan's engineers improvised a bridge of pontoons across the lower Tisza, broad and fast-flowing at this point, not far from the river's confluence with the Danube. It was while the army was crossing the Tisza, late in the evening of 11 September, that the Austrians struck. Under the inspired leadership of Prince Eugene of Savoy they cut the Turkish force in two. Possibly as many as 30,000 men in the Ottoman army perished, killed on the battlefield of Zenta or drowned in the waters of the Tisza. Clusters of corpses formed 'islands' in the river, Prince Eugene reported back to Vienna soon after the battle. His 'decisive victory' marked the start of the Prince's brilliant career; it made him 'the most renowned commander in Europe', comments Lord Acton, anticipating the victorious partnership of Eugene and Marlborough in the War of the Spanish Succession.⁹ For the Turks, however, Zenta was decisive as an end of an era rather than a beginning. Fourteen years after the relief of Vienna – almost to the day – the last Turkish attempt to sweep back up the middle Danube lay shattered. The Sultan was left with virtually no army outside Asia.

Heavy rain saved Mustafa II from the immediate consequences of his defeat; Leopold I was not prepared to send his troops on a wintry expedition into the Balkans. More significant was the impact of Zenta on European diplomacy as a whole. England and the Netherlands sought to arbitrate, hoping to secure peace in the East so that the Habsburgs could concentrate on the struggle against Louis XIV's France: there was as yet no Eastern Question to perplex western statesmen, only a tiresome and distracting Eastern Sideshow.

Long negotiations ended in the last week of January 1699 with a peace settlement concluded at Karlowitz (now Sremski Karlovici). Emperor Leopold was well satisfied by the treaty. Clauses which offered trade concessions to Austrian merchants and confirmed the right of Roman Catholics to worship freely within the Sultan's lands might be imprecisely phrased, but they appeared to give the Habsburg Emperor a claim to intervene in internal Ottoman affairs. The territorial clauses of the settlement were almost deceptively straightforward: Hungary and all of Transylvania (except for a triangle of land around Temesvar) were in Habsburg hands when the peace talks began, and they remained so under the terms of the treaty; the Venetians had consolidated their hold on Dalmatia and the Peloponnese, and they retained them; the Turks had pulled back from southern Poland and the Ukraine, and they made no attempt to recover these lands from the Poles. Talks with Russian emissaries went on even longer, but a compromise was reached in June 1700; the Treaty of Constantinople confirmed Tsar Peter's possession of Azov and a stretch of the lower Dniester, provided that all Russian fortifications in the region were dismantled.

No signatory of these treaties regarded the redrawing of frontiers as final. The contest for mastery of the Black Sea was only just beginning and it seemed likely that the distant possessions of a decaying Venice would soon slip from the Republic's grasp. In one region, however, the Peace of Karlowitz lastingly changed the map. Until 1683 the

'Military Frontier' across western Hungary and Croatia had formed a defensive wall against Islam; after 1699 the Frontier stretched as far east as Transylvania, looming so aggressively over the Balkans that the Austrian Habsburgs seemed poised to throw the Turks back into Asia, just as their Spanish kinsmen had expelled the Moors of North Africa a century before. Yet this was an illusion. The new Military Frontier, like the old, proved essentially defensive, if only because of Habsburg preoccupation with the grand designs of the French, and the problems of Germany, Poland and the Italian peninsula. Prince Eugene fought one further successful campaign in the east, adding lustre to his reputation at Temesvar in 1716 and Belgrade a year later; but, although the Banat of Temesvar never returned to Ottoman rule, by 1739 the Turks had recovered Serbia, and it was another century and a half before a token Turkish detachment finally lowered the last crescent flag to fly over Belgrade. An Austrian march on Constantinople – a real threat at the time of Karlowitz – never took place. Apart from two decades in the early eighteenth century, the Sava and Danube rivers continued to mark the boundary of the Habsburg Monarchy until the empires were swept away at the end of the First World War.

Karlowitz was not, as some writers maintain, a disaster for the Ottoman Empire.[10] The Peace enabled Turkey to parry the challenge from the West, ready to meet the great threat from the North and new dangers in Asia, too. For three years after Karlowitz the last Grand Vizier of the Köprülü family, Amcazade Hüseyin, undertook vigorous reforms, in the system of levying taxes, in the organization and training of the army, and in developing a sail-powered fleet to replace the traditional oar-powered galleys. Hüseyin's reforming zeal intruded into many cherished preserves. Inevitably it offended the conservative *ulema*, still led by the Sultan's nominee as *şeyhülislâm*, Feyzullah Effendi. Had not a fatal illness forced him to resign in September 1702, Hüseyin would almost certainly have fallen a victim to his political enemies.

Over the next eleven months events followed a familiar pattern. Feyzullah Effendi, though vigilant and alert at the start of the reign, soon succumbed to the seductive venality of office. By the turn of the century he was amassing a considerable fortune and exercising nepotism on a grand scale. Rumour said that Sultan Mustafa and Feyzullah were planning to move court and capital back to Edirne, a decision which would have destroyed the livelihood of hundreds of traders in Stamboul and along the shores of the Golden Horn. In July 1703 four companies of Janissaries, their pay heavily in arrears, led a mutiny in Stamboul, winning support from other soldiers and religious students. The rebels marched on Edirne, where the Sultan and the *şeyhülislâm* were in residence. Although Mustafa II hurriedly exiled Feyzullah and his kinsfolk, he could not avoid his father's fate. The Viziers deposed him on 22 August; and dropsy carried off yet another victim in the *kafe* at the end of December.

Once again an Ottoman prince, fetched from the Fourth Courtyard of the Topkapi Sarayi, was girded with the sword at Edirne rather that at Eyüp. Here, however, a slight change crept into an otherwise familiar scenario. Unusually, the twenty-nine year old Ahmed III was a brother, rather than a half-brother, of his predecessor; their Cretan mother, Rabia Gulnus, was in her early sixties at Ahmed's accession and she enjoyed some influence as *Valide Sultana* until her death twelve years later. Yet for a few months it seemed as if the Ottoman dynasty itself was under notice to quit. Ahmed was forced to pay out a larger amount of Accession Money than any predecessor, satisfying the mutinous Janissaries with funds confiscated from the discredited Feyzullah Effendi and his circle of intimates. Even so, the Sultan could not distribute an equal sum to every unit of rebellious troops, and there was widespread discontent in Rumelia and south-western Anatolia.

A hostile army gathered at Silivri, where the road to Edirne turned inland from the Sea of Marmara. If at that moment the commanders could have agreed on a nominee for the Sultanate from one of the other leading families, the Ottoman Empire might well have fallen apart, dissolving into a loose confederation of khanates. But Ahmed, and the Empire, survived. He was prepared to use the Janissaries as protectors of the dynasty. At their approach the rebels fled from Silivri, many becoming brigands in eastern Thrace and the Rodopi Mountains. The threat of civil war receded.[11]

For the first half of his twenty-seven-year reign, Ahmed III showed a political guile which occasionally rose to shrewd statesmanship. In retrospect, the years 1703 to 1718 form a period of weak government; thirteen Grand Viziers followed one another with disconcerting rapidity; and control of the outlying provinces was so poor that in 1711 there were seventy days of bloodshed in Cairo, as six military corps collaborated in the 'great Insurrection' against Janissary pretensions. But in the imperial capital Sultan Ahmed used these years to consolidate his position on the throne, playing off rival viziers and 'Lords of the Divan' while advancing his own nominees to key posts in the army and at Court. The policy of modernizing the army and navy, begun by Hüseyin, was cautiously continued and met with some success. While no Ottoman commander could outwit Prince Eugene, the Russians were checked on the river Pruth in 1711, Peter the Great himself narrowly avoiding capture. But the most striking achievements of this period were in southern Greece. The remarkable speed with which the Peloponnese was recovered testifies to the effectiveness of the redesigned fleet. It also provides a significant commentary on the status of Ahmed III's Greek Orthodox subjects.

Over the centuries Ottoman Sultans appropriated many churches as mosques, but they never sought to enforce conversion on the whole Christian community.[12] Mehmed II recognized his Orthodox subjects as a religious 'nation' (*millet*); they had to pay heavy taxes and accept discriminatory laws – no proselytizing of Muslims, no church processions, no riding of a horse, no carrying of arms, etc. – but they were permitted self-government in spiritual and secular church affairs under the leadership of the Greek Patriarch in Constantinople, who was given high Ottoman rank: a Pasha with three horsetails. Later Sultans used Greeks widely in government service; almost invariably, for example, the interpreter (dragoman) to a foreign envoy would be a Greek. But it was from commerce that the Greeks grew wealthy. A Greek quarter – which included the walled residence of the Patriarch – survived in the Stamboul district of Constantinople around Phanar (Fener), the old Byzantine lighthouse above the Golden Horn. By the early eighteenth century these 'Phanariot' Greeks formed a mercantile aristocracy, active not only at the heart of the Empire but throughout Rumelia and the Levant as well. Their greatest commercial rivals had long been the Venetians and, to a lesser extent, the Genoese. The Phanariots presented Ahmed III with a series of appeals from Greeks under Venetian rule in the Aegean islands of the Peloponnese imploring the Ottomans to come and liberate them from Latin domination. This influential pressure group was supported by Sultan Ahmed's Cretan-born mother, who did not die until November 1715. Military and naval action against the Venetian Republic would be more popular in Constantinople than any campaign on the lower Danube.

By 1710 a quarter of a century of Venetian administration was bringing prosperity back to the Peloponnese after many years of neglect. The population had increased rapidly, assisted by colonization from north of the Gulf of Corinth, and in the less arid districts farming was flourishing for the first time since the Classical Age. But, despite this rising standard of living, Venetian rule was unpopular with the Greeks themselves. When the French traveller Aubry de la

Moutraye landed at Methoni in the summer of 1710 he found that the people deeply resented trade restrictions which, they said, favoured Venetian merchants.[13] The Greeks complained, too, of the coming of an Italian priesthood and of Roman Catholic attacks on the Orthodox Church; they thought their co-believers enjoyed greater freedom of worship in the lands still within the Ottoman Empire. This Greek Orthodox hostility to intrusive Latin rites, together with Phanariot hopes of crippling Venetian trade, ensured that the proposed war was warmly supported along the Golden Horn. Early in December 1714 occasional exchanges of fire between Ottoman and Venetian vessels in the Aegean gave the Sultan an excuse to declare war on the Republic of St Mark.

The campaign began in the following summer, when the Grand Vizier's army advanced into the Peloponnese. The invaders met little resistance from troops in Venetian pay and found they could count on ready support from the Orthodox clergy. At the same time Ottoman forces captured the last Venetian strongholds in Crete, at Spinalonga and Kalami, and in the Cyclades they took Tenos – Venetian for the past five hundred years, strongly Roman Catholic, and not yet the centre of Orthodox pilgrimage which was to make the island famous in the nineteenth century. With the assistance of ships provided by Pope Clement XI and the Knights of Malta, the Venetians tried to mount a counter-offensive in 1717 at a time when the Ottoman commanders were reeling from a succession of blows struck by Prince Eugene in the Banat. But this final assertion of Holy League solidarity was little more than a gesture. By the summer of 1718, when peace was made at Passarowitz, Venice had agreed to abandon the Peloponnese. Although the Republic held the Ionian islands, Kithira and four small harbours on the coast of Epirus for almost eighty more years, they were retained for commercial purposes, not as strategic bases to support a forward policy in the Aegean and the Levant.

Even though the settlement went almost unnoticed in western Europe, the Peace of Passarowitz marked the close of an epoch in Mediterranean history. The Ottomans had gained a final strategic victory, checking the earliest of the maritime challenges from the West. Never again would the lion of St Mark roar across the waters off Lepanto or break the mournful silence of Soudha Bay. Yet as a sign of sustained Ottoman recovery, these events in the Peloponnese were unconvincing. They were made possible by an identity of interest between Muslims and Orthodox in defeating papal endeavours to proselytize the eastern Mediterranean. Relations between the thirty

Sultans and more than a hundred and fifty Patriarchs who followed the fall of Byzantium were based on a mutual abhorrence of the Latin religious practice and the hope of mutual respect for the office which each dignitary held. This hope was not always realized; two out of every three Patriarchs were deposed upon Ottoman insistence after relatively minor deviations in policy; six more grievously offending Patriarchs were hanged, drowned or poisoned. Yet both the Sultanate and the Patriarchate were naturally conservative institutions, not entirely blind to reform, but instinctively suspicious of beliefs which might disturb the delicate balance of authority between them. Neither consciously promoted nationalism: the Patriarch maintained the Byzantine tradition of universalism within an ecumenical church; the Sultan ruled a multinational empire of which 'Turks' were only one component, the socially underprivileged Turcoman Anatolian peasantry. The war to recover the Peloponnese showed that the two institutions could achieve an operational partnership against the Latin church. It remained to be seen how their relationship would respond to any show of missionary crusading zeal among Orthodox believers beyond the Ecumenical Patriarch's spiritual jurisdiction.

That challenge was closer to hand than either Sultan Ahmed or the Patriarch realized. After rebuffing the Russians on the Pruth in 1711 Ahmed and his Viziers affected a careless contempt for Tsar Peter, who had vainly attempted to stir up a Balkan Christian revolt. To underestimate what was happening in Russia was a mistake. Within three years of the Peace of Passarowitz, Peter sought to elevate his status by assuming the title of Emperor of All the Russias; and in the same year, by his 'Spiritual Regulation', he subjected the church of Muscovy to a state control more binding than that imposed by any other European sovereign on a religious hierarchy. Soon new Russian agents, emissaries of Holy Church as well as of an imperial State, began to infiltrate the Sultan's Balkan lands where they encouraged a latent patriotic sentiment, especially in the districts which had shown the greatest hostility to Venetian rule. With Holy Russia assuming the role of militant guardian of the True Faith, it became increasingly difficult for Orthodox believers within the Ottoman Empire to maintain their passive acceptance of second-class citizenship under the Sultan's rule. In 1452 a Byzantine official, critical of his Emperor's attempts to reunite the Eastern Church with Rome, is said to have remarked, 'It would be better to see the royal turban of the Turks in the midst of this city than the Latin mitre'; and in 1710 that view still prevailed among most Greek churchmen.[14] But, however much they might mistrust the Latins, respect for the turban was wearing thin. By the second half of the century there were many Greeks who hoped that the finest of their dreams would soon become a reality: to hear the Holy Liturgy sung once more in Constantinople's domed Basilica of the Divine Wisdom no longer seemed an impossibility.

CHAPTER 3

Tulip Time and After

The decline of the Ottoman Empire was neither rapid nor continuous. By 1700 the age of Islamic conquest in Europe was over; frontiers had contracted after lost or indecisive campaigns; and peripheral provinces, acquired somewhat haphazardly in North Africa and the Yemen, would soon be slipping into virtual independence. From the closing years of the seventeenth century outsiders predicted the collapse of the Sultanate time and time again. Yet, against all expectancy, the Ottoman Empire outlived imperial Spain, republican Genoa and republican Venice, the elective monarchy of Poland, British colonial America, the vestigial Holy Roman Empire, Bourbon and Napoleonic France, and the temporal power of the Papacy; it even survived by a few years the Habsburg and Romanov empires, so long its apparent residuary legatees, and the Hohenzollern empire which had aspired to overtake France as its chief creditor.

It is easier to identify signs of decay in the Ottoman Empire than to discover why it became such a durable institution. Undoubtedly one source of vitality was a conviction within the ruling élite and the *ulema* that the Ottoman Empire *was* Islam. The prestige of the Caliphate, whether held legitimately or by appropriation, enhanced the secular power of a Sultan after he was girded with the Sword of Othman at Eyüp, however feeble his personality might be. 'May it be known to His Imperial Majesty that the origins of good order in kingship and community and the guarantee of a stable foundation for the faith and the dynasty lie in a firm grasp on the strong cord of the law of Muhammad,' the Ottoman counsellor Mustafa Koçi Bey wrote in 1630 in a famous treatise which he presented to Murad IV; and later memoranda to several of Murad's successors similarly stressed the wisdom of basing public and private life on Holy Islamic Law (the *şeriat*).[1]

But there remained in the structure of the Ottoman state an innate conservatism which was always restorative and reformist in character rather than narrowly obscurantist, as some members of the *ulema* wished. This is a thin distinction, but an important one: provided outward forms looked familiar, the military and naval techniques of western Europe might be adopted and changes of practice introduced into the day-to-day business of government. Already, under the Köprülüs, the Grand Vizier had acquired an official residence, in a road skirting the outer wall of the Topkapi Sarayi, and from 1654 he retained there an administrative staff in the residence which because of its lofty gate became known as the Sublime Porte (*Bab-i Ali*) and remained the recognized seat of government until the fall of the Empire. There were several periods in both the eighteenth and the nineteenth centuries when a Sultan or a Grand Vizier cautiously experimented with westernization, seeking to introduce a European style to the well-worn fabric of Ottoman rule.

The earliest and most original innovator was Ibrahim Pasha Kulliyesi, who became Ahmed III's Grand Vizier in 1718, after two years as *kaimakan* (deputy Grand Vizier).[2] Foreign observers portray Ibrahim as a sybaritic impresario, with an aesthete's eye for the beauties of landscape, and great intellectual curiosity. But he was also a shrewd diplomat and a skilled manipulator of palace politics, able to remain Grand Vizier for twelve years, at a time when fourteen months had become the norm. He survived by playing off his enemies against each other, by close marriage links with the dynasty, and by constantly keeping the Sultan amused, entertained and free from all cares of state.

Ibrahim married the Sultan's eldest daughter; and he is generally called Damat ('son-in-law') Ibrahim to distinguish him from the many namesakes whose ambition never carried them so high. Like his imperial master, he was greedy for wealth and personally extravagant. Yet, despite his many failings, Damat Ibrahim cut an impressive figure, showing broader vision than any of his predecessors. He was the first Ottoman minister to send envoys to the greater European capitals: in 1719 to Vienna; in 1720–1 to Paris; and in 1722–3 to Moscow. As well as negotiating trade agreements, they were to serve as observers, reporting back to the Grand Vizier on aspects of life and culture which might be 'applicable' to conditions in the Ottoman Empire. The instructions to Çelebi Mehmed, the envoy to France, have survived. He was to visit 'fortresses, factories, and see generally the products of French civilization'. This task he performed diligently. Reports were sent to the Grand Vizier describing the French court, Parisian street scenes, hospitals, military training grounds and schools. Above all, Celebi lavished praise on the spread of books in libraries and the wonders of printing – a skill to which the envoy's son, Mehmed Said, gave particular attention.[3]

The two visitors to France were cultural missionaries. They helped dispel the legendary suspicion of the 'cruel Turk' and stimulated a fashionable interest in *turquerie*, even to the extent of introducing kebabs to western Europe. But their main influence was on court life in Constantinople. Although the Blue Mosque was completed in 1616 and the Yeni Cami 'new mosque' in 1663, the classical period of Ottoman-sponsored architecture had long since ended. During their half-century of campaigning in Europe the Sultans had favoured Edirne, a pleasantly relaxed city which was also a week's journey nearer to the battle fronts. But with the return of peace Ahmed III was prepared to burnish the fading glories of his imperial capital, if only Ibrahim could provide him with the funds.

Ibrahim did just that – and more. A property tax was invented and, at least in the centre of the empire, successfully levied. Emergency 'campaign assistance taxes' were raised regularly, even if there was peace along every frontier. On the Anatolian waterfront Ibrahim built a new villa, prompted by the first detailed reports from Celebi in Paris; and there he entertained his father-in-law throughout May 1721, looking out across the Bosphorus. Ahmed III's aesthetic sense was highly developed; he was interested in poetry, in painting and calligraphy, and particularly in horticulture. He was delighted with his Grand Vizier's villa and its gardens. The Venetian envoy reports that Ibrahim promptly presented it to him.[4]

But a new villa was not enough to satisfy Ahmed's cultural acquisitiveness. Celebi Mehmed's descriptions of Fontainebleau and, even more, of King Louis' compact château at Marly, fascinated him. In imitation of what he assumed to be French royal fashions – and with active encouragement from Damat Ibrahim – Ahmed III created Sa'adabad ('The Place of Happiness'), an exquisite summer palace above the 'Sweet Waters of Europe', beyond Eyüp, some four miles up the Golden Horn from the Topkapi Sarayi. The palace was built in 1722, with astonishing speed. The two streams which constituted the Sweet Waters, the Alibey Suyu and the Kagithane Suyu, were canalized, so as to give Sa'adabad a long, ornamental lake and feed fountains and cascades set in the grounds of the palace. Other members of the Divan sought to emulate their sovereign's example. A new waterfront palace went up for Damat Ibrahim at Kandilli, some five miles up the Bosphorus, where he sumptuously entertained the Sultan in 1724 and again in 1728, on both occasions for a fortnight. Foreign architects were invited to Constantinople; small waterfront villas, often of timber or moulded plaster rather than the more expensive marble and stone, went up along the Anatolian shore of the Bosphorus as well as at the head of the Golden Horn.

> The pleasure of going in a barge to Chelsea is not comparable to that of rowing upon the canal of the sea here, where, for 20 miles together, down the Bosphorus the most beautiful variety of prospects present themselves. The Asian side is covered with fruit trees, villages and the most delightful landscapes in nature; on the European stands Constantinople, situated on seven hills, . . . showing an agreeable mixture of gardens, pines and cypress trees, palaces, mosques and public buildings, raised one above another, with as much beauty and appearance of symmetry as you ever saw in a cabinet adorned by the most skilful hands.

So the 29-year-old Lady Mary Wortley Montagu wrote home to Lady Bristol in April 1718, describing the city where her husband was in residence as King George I's ambassador.[5] But she was writing before the Sa'adabad craze swept the Court. Had she returned to the Bosphorus five or six years later, she would have seen her symmetrical 'cabinet' embellished with Rococo extravagance. The French envoy, Louis Sauveur de Villeneuve, commented particularly on two aspects of court life – the Imperial Progresses from palace to palace, and the liking of the Sultan and his ruling class for festive illumination in the night sky.

Soon after his arrival in Constantinople, Louis de Villeneuve wrote back to Paris:

> Sometimes the court appears floating on the waters of the Bosphorus or the Golden Horn, in elegant caiques, covered with silken tents; sometimes it moves forward in a long cavalcade towards one of the pleasure palaces . . . These processions are made especially attractive by the beauty of the horses and the luxury of their caparisons; they progress, with golden or silver harnesses and plumed foreheads, their coverings resplendent with precious stones.[6]

And one night, looking across to Stamboul from the hill of Pera (now Beyoğlu), Villeneuve was fascinated by 'the domes of its mosques, rising from within crowns of fire, while an invisible apparatus strung between the minarets made it possible for verses from the Koran to be inscribed in the sky by letters of fire.'[7]

The Venetian envoy (*bailo*), less surprised by processions of boats or by carnival chains of slow-burning resin lamps, commented as early as February 1723 on the wealth of decoration brought by the Sultan's leading officials to the pavilions or kiosks they had erected in the tree-festooned parkland of Sa'adabad.[8] Every visitor seems to have been impressed by some particular novelty in these socially giddy years: a *halvah* fête, perhaps, with dishes of sesame seed and honey available to all comers; or the painting of portraits, in defiance of the Islamic inhibition against the representation in art of the human figure; jugglers and wrestlers and midgets; parrots and exotic caged singing-birds; confectionery made to look like palm trees or, at the wedding feast of three of the Sultan's daughters, a sugar and candy garden seventeen square metres in area. To many foreign envoys it seemed a toy world of frivolous inconsequence, fascinating in itself but in startling contrast to the realities so often exposed along the lower waterfront of the Golden Horn, where non-Muslims suffered the bastinado or gasped for death after they had been impaled, or left to hang with a meat hook inserted under the chin.

'Let us laugh, let us play, let us enjoy the delights of the world to the full,' proclaimed the principal court poet, Ahmed Nedim, boon companion to the Sultan in his later years.[9] This was a happy philosophy for an empire allegedly in decline. But it was not an utterly hedonistic way of life. New Muslim schools were founded and old ones, fallen into neglect by misappropriation of their endowments, received support either from individual viziers or from the Sultan and his chief minister. Books had been printed in non-Turkish languages by Jews and Christians in Constantinople ever since the closing years of the fifteenth century, and on Mehmed Said's return from Paris, Damat Ibrahim encouraged him to set up the first Turkish language printing press, with technical assistance from Ibrahim Muteferrika, a Hungarian-born convert to Islam. Despite complaints from the *ulema* that the printing of the Koran and other Islamic sacred works was blasphemous, and strong hostility from scribes and calligraphers fearing for their jobs, Muteferrika brought out the first Turkish printed book in 1729, a treatise on historical geography. Twenty-three more volumes were printed over the following thirteen years; among them, in 1732, Muteferrika published his own study of magnetism, *Fuyuzot-i minatisiye*.[10]

Ahmed III was the most sophisticated and cultured Sultan for more than a century and a half. His companion, Nedim, was more than a gifted poet; he took charge of the library which Sultan Ahmed founded, and which may still be seen to the west of his *turbe*, outside the Yeni Cami at the Stamboul end of the Galata Bridge. Elsewhere, too, Sultan Ahmed's beneficence as a patron of art and learning continues to delight visitors to modern İstanbul: there is no lovelier chamber in the private apartments of the Topkapi Sarayi than Ahmed III's dining-room, with its intricate gilt-patterned ceiling and lacquered wood panels bright with painted flowers or bowls of fruit; and there is no finer roofed street fountain than the huge *çeşme* he erected between St Sophia and the Topkapi Sarayi. Across the Bosphorus, outside the mosque beside the old ferry landing-stage in Üsküdar (Scutari), is another fine fountain which, in 1726, Sultan Ahmed commissioned to be placed where the Sacred Caravan set out each year on its fifteen-hundred-mile pilgrimage to Medina and Mecca. And the two slim minarets at Eyüp have stood elegantly flanking the historic mosque ever since Ahmed's progresses passed that way on their journeys to his dream palace at Sa'adabad.

It is, however, as a lover of flowers that Ahmed III is best remembered. Historically his reign became *Lale Devri* (Tulip Era). Tulips had followed the Turks westwards from Anatolia, where they were wild flowers; a Habsburg ambassador in the sixteenth century took them back to the Low Countries, where from the 1560s onwards the Dutch began to cultivate the bulb, producing more than twelve hundred different varieties at a time when the flower was no longer of great interest in Constantinople. Ahmed's father, Sultan Mehmed IV, restored the bulb to imperial favour, first at Edirne and later in the Topkapi Sarayi. But for Ahmed the tulip was an obsession. His palace gardens were planted with row upon row, each variety given a separate bed. New specimens were ordered from the West and from Persia. One autumn the Venetian *bailo* thought it worthwhile to inform the Doge that a ship had just arrived in the Golden Horn from Marseilles with a cargo of 30,000 bulbs for the Sultan's gardens. A little later in the century an acerbic French merchant, Jean-Claude Flachat, commented that the Turks set less value on human life 'than on a horse or a fine tulip'.[11]

Decorative tiles, lacquered panelling, the binding of books for the new libraries and many other forms of artistic expression made use of the tulip motif, as did the court poets. Every April the Sultan held a tulip festival in the lower terraced garden, beyond the Fourth Courtyard, of the Topkapi Sarayi – the 'Grand Seraglio', as foreign envoys called the palace. The festival was timed for two successive evenings, coinciding with the full moon. Turtles (or tortoises) with slow-burning candles on their shells moved around the tulip beds to provide illumination at ground level. On shelves around the wall of the garden were ranged vases of tulips, carefully chosen so that their colours were in harmony when lit by candles in glass bowls among them. Ahmed III received homage, enthroned in state outside the Sofa Köşkü pavilion, to the accompaniment of the twittering of song birds in an improvised aviary suspended from the branches of the overhanging trees. The second evening was always set aside for what was virtually a springtime party to entertain the ladies of the harem. The evening might include a treasure hunt for confectionery or, if the Sultan was in a generous mood, for jewelled trinkets hidden in the garden.

'The favour of the Grand Vizier increases every day,' reported the Venetian *bailo* in January 1724.[12] Damat Ibrahim had taken advantage of internal discord in Persia to occupy huge areas of the country on the cheap, militarily speaking, and rich booty and reward were flowing back to Constantinople, lessening the burden of war taxation and encouraging free-spending extravagance at court. But intervention in Persian affairs was rash; feeling against the Ottomans rallied dissident Persian groups, sometimes acting with Afghans who had moved into Persia from the west. By the winter of 1726–7 it was clear to outside observers that Damat Ibrahim was desperately trying to distract his sovereign from a mounting crisis in the East, as well as from constant unrest in Cairo and the difficulties of raising taxes in outlying provinces, some of which were suffering from acute famine. 'What can be expected of a Sultan lost in the idleness of the Palace, a Vizar who has not seen the face of War, a *Kapitan* Pasha [admiral] who has never left the castles [defensive forts on the Bosphorus]?', wrote *bailo* Dolfin impatiently to the Doge in March 1727; and he added, 'It is still possible to reverse the situation. The Empire lacks the head, not the arm.'[13]

Rather surprisingly, Damat Ibrahim survived that crisis. He believed that he remained in touch with the public mood in the capital. Ordinary townsfolk in Stamboul and Galata had benefited from the coming of cheap coffee houses, from the shoring-up of long neglected buildings and the provision of more fountains, and from the institution of the first Ottoman fire brigade, set up in 1720 by Ahmed Gerçek, Louis David by birth, a French convert to Islam. Across the Bosphorus, too, Damat Ibrahim courted popular favour. In March 1729, when he was returning from further palace building at Kandilli, famished peasants at Üsküdar begged him to help find them food. Next day, an ample supply of free bread arrived from the Stamboul bakeries; and the hungry of Üsküdar

38

gave thanks to Allah for the ready response of such a charitable Grand Vizier.

But in the autumn of 1730, after twelve years in office, Damat Ibrahim misread all the signs of popular discontent. Rumour reached the capital that he had accepted a compromise truce with the Persians which involved the surrender of Sunni Muslim villages to the Shi'ites. On 28 September 1730 Patrona Halil, an Albanian-born ex-Janissary who had become a second-hand clothes dealer, began haranguing worshippers outside the Bayezit Mosque; five close companions supported him in denouncing the constant violation of Holy Law by the Grand Vizier and the Sultan's closest advisers. From the mosque an angry crowd of demonstrators surged towards the Topkapi Sarayi, collecting dissidents from the Janissary barracks as they went. The Janissary mutiny turned a demonstration into an insurrection.[14]

Damat Ibrahim seems to have thought that the crowd could be easily dispersed. He had forgotten – or did not know – that the most reliable troops were encamped at Üsküdar, on the Anatolian shore, ready to set out eastwards on a further Persian campaign. He also placed unjustifiable confidence in his imperial father-in-law. For when Ahmed III heard that Patrona's rebels were demanding the heads of the Grand Vizier, the Grand Admiral, and one other 'westernized' minister, he obliged them. All three were, as was the custom, swiftly strangled before decapitation; the executioners disturbed the Grand Admiral in his waterside villa as he was transplanting his tulips, totally unaware of any political crisis in downtown Stamboul.

If Ahmed III thought that by sacrificing his ministerial cronies he could save his throne, he was mistaken. Along both banks of the Golden Horn there followed two days of rioting, arson and looting – a sudden show of cultural xenophobia towards anything thought to be 'Frankish' (western). On 1 October Ahmed abdicated, under threat of deposition, making obeisance to his 34-year-old nephew, Mahmud I, who had been confined in the *kafe* ever since his seventh birthday. Back to the *kafe* went the 'tulip king', spending the last six years of his life only a few hundred yards from the pavilion where he had sat in floral majesty each April. His daughter Princess Fatma – Damat Ibrahim's widow – was imprisoned a year later for plotting to restore her father, and it is possible that Ahmed's death, in his sixty-third year, was hastened by poison, although no Sultan since Suleiman I had survived into his sixties.

Ahmed III had reigned for twenty-seven years. Against all expectancy, his nephew remained on the throne for twenty-four. For thirteen months after his accession, foreign envoys looked on Mahmud as a mere puppet of Patrona Halil and his bully boys, rebels who set fire to most of the exquisite palaces and kiosks of the Tulip Years. Their leader grew rich very quickly, as boss of a city-wide protection racket. Momentarily it seemed he might find an even broader field in which to peculate; on 24 November 1731 the Sultan invited Patrona Halil and his chief supporters to come to the palace in order to discuss plans for another Persian War. No such discussion took place. Soon after their arrival in the Topkapi Sarayi, Patrona Halil and his associates were seized, and strangled on the spot. Mahmud could now rule in his own right, entrusting the administration to Grand Viziers sympathetic towards westernizing reform, but more cautious than Damat Ibrahim and less tenacious of office.

Much survived the Patrona Terror, most notably Muteferrika's printing press. There was even an imperial tulip festival each spring, albeit trimmed down to economy size. Like Ahmed III, Mahmud showed an interest in books and education, at least in his capital city: a small library outside the Mosque of the Conqueror and a primary school attached to the mosque of Ayasofya are still standing. He also completed a project, abandoned in the previous reign, for supplying water piped from outlying reservoirs to Pera, Galata and the northern shore of the Golden Horn; the octagonal water distribution centre (*taksim*), erected on the Sultan's orders, is still at the top of İstiklal Caddesi (modern İstanbul's Regent Street or Rue de Rivoli) and has given its name to Taksim Meydani, which it is tempting to call İstanbul's Piccadilly Circus.

These projects belong mainly to Mahmud I's later years, as also does the patronage he extended to the building of Stamboul's first Baroque mosque, the Nurousmaniye Cami, next to the Bazaar. He had begun his personal rule by giving urgent attention to defects in the methods of tax collection; a new law improving the efficiency of the *timar* system was issued as early as January 1732. Later in that same year Ibrahim Muteferrika presented the Sultan with a printed edition of his own treatise, some fifty pages long, an inquiry into the science of ruling the nations, *Usul ul-hikem fi nizam al-uman*. He described the types of government existing in other states, urged the sovereign to relate external policies to the geographical structure of neighbouring lands, and suggested how the Ottomans might learn from the military science and discipline of infidel armies – towards whom Muteferrika dutifully showed a tactful contempt.[15] Mahmud I was impressed; and, like many later Sultans, he turned for advice to a foreign expert. The

Comte de Bonneval would, he hoped, modernize the Ottoman army, making it once again the conquering vanguard of Islam.

Claude-Alexandre, Comte de Bonneval, a French general from the Limousin, had every confidence that he could live up to what he assumed to be the Sultan's expectations. He was fifty-two when in 1727 he entered Ottoman service, having fought for and against Louis XIV and served under Prince Eugene against the Turks before falling out with his commanding general and spending a year in prison. The Venetian Republic had nothing to offer him and so he travelled down to Ragusa (Dubrovnik), crossed into Bosnia, accepted conversion to Islam, and made ready to fight for the Sultan. After a few months observing the Ottoman army, he prepared a memorandum for Mahmud I, explaining how he would create new fighting units of infantry and artillery, to be trained by young hand-picked officers; and how he would restore the Janissaries as an élite fighting force by grouping several *orta* in the corps into regiments, thus giving officers a regular ladder of promotion on the model of the French and Austrian armies which he already knew so well. Foreign-born military advisers – German, Austrian and Scottish officers, in particular – had played a considerable role in modernizing the Russian army: one in four of Peter the Great's senior commanders was a non-Russian, and the new guards regiments founded by his successor, Empress Anna, were almost entirely raised and trained by foreigners. To assist him, Bonneval knew he would have three somewhat younger French officers who had converted to Islam, together with some Irish and Scottish soldiers of fortune and, possibly, some Swedes. On paper there seemed no reason why 'Ahmed' – as Bonneval was now known – should not give the Sultan a fighting force to match the army of his northern neighbour.

The vicissitudes of Bonneval's career well illustrate the difficulties facing any reformer at the Sultan's court. In September 1731 the Grand Vizier Topal Osman invited him to modernize a single section of the Sultan's army, the *kumbaraciyan* or bombardier corps, responsible for making, transporting and firing all explosive weapons (mortar bombs, grenades, mines) on land or aboard a naval vessel. He was provided with a training ground and barracks outside Üsküdar, consulted over the construction of a cannon foundry and musket factory, and asked to draft a memorandum for the Sublime Porte on foreign policy. But six months later Grand Vizier Topal Osman was replaced by an Italian-born convert, Hekimoğlu Ali, who was so dependent on the conservatively-minded Janissary leaders that he dared not support army reform until he had been in office for some two years.

By the autumn of 1734, however, Bonneval was back in grace: on his recommendation a military engineering school was set up in Üsküdar; and in January 1735 he was made a high-ranking dignitary, entitled to two horsetails.

For the last twelve years of his life Claude-Alexandre became Kumbaraci Osman Ahmed Pasha. He could not, however, rely on Mahmud's continued support. Yet another Grand Vizier came into office in July 1735, and a year later the Pasha was exiled from the capital to Katamonu in northern Anatolia; funds for the bombardiers and the new army institutions were at once cut off. Somehow, in 1740, he slipped back to Üsküdar, but Janissary suspicion and jealousy made certain he never again enjoyed great influence. His grandiose plans for modernizing the army were ignored, although he was allowed to continue running his military engineering school until his death at the age of seventy-two. 'A man of great talent for war, intelligent and eloquent, charming and gracious', commented a French envoy; 'very proud, a lavish spender, extremely debauched and a great philanderer.'[16]

Bonneval's reforms contributed to the success of Ottoman armies in the sporadic campaigns from 1736 to 1739 against Russia and Austria. Sultan Mahmud's armies recovered much of Serbia, including Belgrade, and strengthened the Ottoman hold on Bosnia. Throughout Mahmud's reign the Sublime Porte had to look defensively to the east, as well as to the north and west, for in Persia the ruthless Khan Nadir Afshar seized power and in 1737 was recognized as Shah. Mahmud and Nadir exchanged gifts: an ornate oval throne, plated with gold and adorned with pearls, rubies and diamonds, was presented by the Shah to the Sultan; while Mahmud in return sent to Nadir a golden dagger, with three large emeralds in the hilt beneath another emerald which covered a watch. But despite such costly diplomatic courtesies, Sultan and Shah were at war for most of Nadir's reign, fighting largely indecisive campaigns in Mesopotamia, although the Persians gained some success in the southern Caucasus. The danger receded with the assassination of Nadir in 1747, an event which enabled the Sultan to recover the golden dagger he had presented. Both gifts are on show in the Topkapi Sarayi treasury, the dagger having (in 1964) featured in *Topkapi*, a film based upon Eric Ambler's thriller *The Light of Day*.

Shah Nadir's murder came at the start of an unexpected interlude in Ottoman history. Between 1746 and 1768, the Empire was at peace. Never before had twenty-two years passed without war along at least one frontier; and the country was to enjoy no comparable respite until the Kemalist Revolution and the proclamation of a republic. Yet as the Ottoman Empire was essentially a military institution, the 'long peace' proved curiously debilitating. Only one Grand Vizier – Koça Mehmed Ragip, in the late 1750s – tried to arrest the decline of effective government; he dispatched troops to stamp out banditry in Rumelia, Anatolia and Syria; and he appointed supervisors to check corruption in the *evkaf* and ensure that the revenue from religious endowments was applied to pious or charitable work.[17] But despite Ragip's efforts three familiar abuses soon crept back into the administration: the sale of offices; nepotism; and the taking of bribes. Instead of building on the reforms of the past quarter of a century, the Janissaries sought to put the clock back. Turkish printing virtually ceased, to the great relief of the professional scribes and calligraphers who had feared competition. After Ibrahim Muteferrika's death in 1745 only two volumes were published in eleven years, and the press thereafter stood idle until 1784 when Sultan Abdulhamid I issued an imperial edict on the need to re-establish Turkish printing. A similar halt was called to all efforts at army or navy reform. Bonneval's military engineering school only outlived its founder by three years; and almost two decades passed before any further attempt was made to modernize the Ottoman army.

During the 'long peace' it is doubtful whether the Sultans or their viziers in Constantinople were fully aware of the extent to which the empire was falling apart. The North African lands, from Libya westwards, were by now no more than nominal vassal states. In 1711 Ahmed III had recognized the hereditary rule of the Qaramanli family in Tripolitania and the Husaynid dynasty as beys of Tunis, as well as accepting the right of local Janissaries to nominate a governor in Algeria who would share power with three provincial beys. In Cairo a rapid succession of Ottoman viceroys had proved ineffectual: Egypt was virtually 'governed' – a euphemistic verb in this context – by rival Mameluke princes, working sometimes with and sometimes against the resident Janissaries. The chronic civil war permitted Bedouin to encroach on the fertile lands of the Nile delta, gravely hampering cultivation; there was a major famine in Cairo on four occasions during the reign of Egypt's nominal sovereign, Sultan Ahmed III. The famines were almost as bad in Mesopotamia, where Bedouin incursions brought the desert back to a fertile region on the Tigris north of Baghdad. In Mosul, Baghdad, Aleppo, and Damascus by the middle of the century, the *vali* was, in effect, a hereditary governor-general, his family forming an embryonic local dynasty safeguarded by a private army. Syria forwarded to Constantinople no more than a quarter of the revenue claimed by the imperial government as tribute money; and other outlying provinces were no better. Even the few imperial duties laid on local governors were sometimes disastrously neglected. The most notorious incident was the failure of local notables who had secured the hereditary governorship of Damascus from the Sultan to protect the pilgrim caravan from attack by Bedouin horsemen on its way to Mecca in 1757; on that occasion the raiders left 20,000 devout Muslims dead, among them a sister of the spineless Sultan, Osman III – who died from apoplexy soon after news of the raid reached his capital.[18]

Osman's successor, his cousin Mustafa III, much admired Frederick the Great's generalship; and in 1761 a treaty of friendship with Prussia, sweetened with trade concessions, held out prospects of a new twist to the European alliance system. Unfortunately Mustafa attributed Frederick's success to the alleged attention given by the king to his astrologers. This misunderstanding of the Prussian way of government led Mustafa to decide that if the stars were said to favour a Sultan's ambitions, the 'long peace' must end. With such calculations helping to shape policy, it is hardly surprising that in October 1768 a war party at court had no difficulty in convincing Mustafa of the need to challenge Catherine the Great's Russia.

Predictably, after years of military neglect, the Ottomans fared badly. Three Russian squadrons sailed from the Baltic to the Mediterranean. A protest to the Doge for allowing ships from the Baltic to enter the Adriatic at Venice suggests a basic ignorance of Europe's geography. Naval intelligence was low, too. A curious strategy which used the ships of the fleet as anchored forts in Çeşme harbour enabled the Russians to win an easy naval victory and put troops ashore near Smyrna (İzmir). Within a month the Russians gained a striking victory on land, too, when an army moving southwards into Moldavia scattered Ottoman troops at Kagul, on the river Pruth. By early 1772 Empress Catherine's armies controlled much of the Crimea and all of Moldavia and Wallachia, the heartlands of modern Roumania.

In tactics and strategy, it was a dull war. Until the last months neither belligerent produced a commander who showed tenacity or initiative. 'The Turks are falling like skittles,' ran a contemporary Russian saying, 'but, thank God, our men are standing fast – though headless.' At last, in the early summer of 1774, a brilliantly executed thrust by the Russian general Alexander Suvorov threatened to carry the war into Bulgaria. Mustafa III had died from a heart attack in the preceding January; the new Sultan – his 48-year-old brother, Abdulhamid I – was a realist. After six years of war, and with Austria threatening support for Russia in the field, the Sublime Porte wanted to end the fighting, if only to provide a respite in which the new Sultan could build up his army and his fleet. On 21 July 1774 peace was concluded at Kuchuk Kainardji, a Bulgarian village south of the Danubian town of Silistria and now known as Kainardzhi. *Küçük Kaynarca*

The Kuchuk Kainardji settlement is historically far more important than the war which preceded it. 'The stipulations of the treaty are a model of skill by Russia's diplomats and a rare example of Turkish imbecility,' reported the Austrian envoy, Franz Thugut.[19] If Abdulhamid I merely wanted a pause between rounds in a long contest, there is no doubt his negotiators served him poorly, since there was about the territorial settlement a sense of finality. Just as the Peace of Karlowitz in 1699 pushed back the frontier of Islam in central Europe, so Kuchuk Kainardji seventy-five years later acknowledged the dwindling of Ottoman power around the northern shore of the Black Sea. The Sultan gave up Ottoman claims to suzerainty over the Crimea and the Tatar steppe land, acknowledging the independence of the Muslim 'Khanate of the Crimea' (absorbed in Russia nine years later). At the mouth of the river Dnieper the Turks ceded to Russia a relatively small section of the Black Sea coast which supplemented the cession of the port of Azov. The Russians also acquired the fortresses of Kerch and Yenikale, which controlled the straits linking Azov to the wider waters of the open sea; and, further south, they were accorded special rights in Wallachia and Moldavia (although these 'Danubian Principalities' remained within the Ottoman Empire).

These territorial changes were a humiliating recognition of Russia's new status in a region where the Ottomans had enjoyed two and a half centuries of almost unchallenged mastery. But the Russians gained an even greater concession – freedom for their merchant vessels to trade with the ports of southern Europe and the Levant. For the first time since the Turks secured control of the Straits, the vessels of another country were allowed to trade in the Black Sea and to sail out through the Bosphorus and the Dardanelles into the Mediterranean. At the same time, Empress Catherine and her successors were promised the right to maintain a permanent embassy in the Ottoman capital, like the Austrians and the French, and also to establish consulates in every major port of the Sultan's empire. This concession made it easier for the Russians to send agents to disaffected provinces in south-eastern Europe, notably to Greece.

If, as many writers believe, Franz Thugut was referring to the religious clauses of the settlement rather than to its territorial and commercial aspects, his judgement is open to question. Confusion over their precise character has sprung from inconsistencies between the original versions, in Russian, Turkish and Italian, of the treaty, intensified by later translations into French, the common language of eighteenth- and nineteenth-century diplomacy.[20] It was long assumed that the religious Articles curtailed the rights of the Sultan, thereby hastening the decline of his empire: in reality they enhanced his authority by giving him wider personal responsibilities than any previous treaty had acknowledged. For the first time the Ottoman assertion of universal Islamic leadership received international recognition: Article 3 stipulated that 'as supreme caliph of the Mohammeddan faith . . . His Sultanian Majesty' retained spiritual jurisdiction over the Muslim Tatars when they gained political and civic independence. This claim was based upon the totally unsubstantiated tale that in 1517 the Caliphate had been formally transferred from the Abbasids to Sultan Selim I. Although effective jurisdiction over the Tatars survived for less than a decade, Article 3 had a lasting significance, for it confirmed the pontifical status assumed by the Sultans after being girded with the sword upon their accession. Over the following century and a half, respect for the spiritual pretensions of the Ottoman Caliphate increased as the territorial extent of Ottoman sovereignty contracted.

Even more controversial were Articles 7 and 14, relating to Orthodox Christendom. 'Henceforth Orthodoxy is under Our Imperial Guardianship in the places whence it sprang,' Empress Catherine proclaimed in a manifesto welcoming the treaty, eight months after it was signed; and many later Russian statesmen – and some Tsarist and French historians – were to insist that the settlement gave a Russian sovereign the right to protect Orthodoxy, its churches and its believers, throughout the Ottoman lands. This extreme interpretation of Kuchuk Kainardji led to the Eastern Crisis of 1853 and thus, indirectly, to the Crimean War. But Article 7 is specific in according 'firm protection of the Christian faith and its churches', not to the ruler in Russia, but to 'the Sublime Porte'. Since the Article does not mention a particular religious denomination, the Sultan would seem to have possessed a protective obligation towards *all* Christian churches within his empire, not merely the Orthodox; and later Ottoman reformers – Sultans and their ministers – often supported an impartial Muslim–Christian equality of status under the law. The treaty does, however, authorize the building and maintenance of a public 'Russo-Greek' church 'in the street called Beyöğlu of the Galata district' (Article 14). It is to this building that Article 7 refers when it promises that the Sublime

Beyöğlu

46

Porte will 'allow ministers of the Russian imperial court to make various representations in all affairs on behalf of the church erected in Constantinople'.

No 'Russo-Greek' church was ever built in the 'street called Beyöglu'. It is still possible to walk down the old 'Grand Rue de Pera' and visit three Roman Catholic churches, one nineteenth-century Anglican church, and several former embassy chapels; other Christian religious institutions are mentioned in the older guide books; but there is no evidence that the building proposed by the treaty of Kuchuk Kainardji progressed even as far as a foundation stone. This is hardly surprising; had Russia erected a specific place of worship under the protection of the Sublime Porte, it would have become difficult to assert that the treaty gave 'ministers of the Russian imperial court' a generalized right to champion the interests of Orthodox believers in the Empire as a whole. At Kuchuk Kainardji the Ottoman diplomats may have surrendered more lands and more commercial concessions than Abdulhamid I intended. But they were not 'imbeciles'. Their legalistic minds defined religious rights even down to the naming of a street. They conceded far less than Catherine claimed. Where they failed was in underestimating Russian sharp practice.

CHAPTER 4

Western Approaches

Abdulhamid I responded to the challenge of Kuchuk Kainardji in what was, by now, accepted form: he ordered military and naval reorganization at the centre of his empire. Baron de Tott, a Hungarian *émigré* serving in the French army, was invited to raise and train a rapid-fire field artillery corps, with its headquarters on the Golden Horn. Close at hand were de Tott's new cannon foundry and his mathematics institute. Also on the Golden Horn were new shipyards where two French naval architects, with a small group of workmen from Marseilles, made certain that the Sultan would soon have a modern fleet to replace the vessels lost at Çeşme; and a naval academy was established beside the Bosphorus, to provide some basic skills in navigation. There was one big difference from past reform eras. Earlier advisers had been mostly renegades like Bonneval, with pressing personal needs to 'turn Turk'. But, as Abdulhamid did not wish to retain foreigners in his service, he never insisted on their conversion to Islam. Baron de Tott returned to France in 1776 and wrote his memoirs, and most of his companions in Constantinople also went home, full of sensational tales of the Orient; some, however, remained in Turkey for another twelve or thirteen years. Only de Tott's immediate successor, a Scottish officer named Campbell, became a Muslim. No one knows why he cut himself off from a famous clan, but the reasons must have been compelling as Campbell was even prepared to accept that for the rest of his life he would be called 'Ingiliz Mustafa' (Mustafa the *Englishman*).

Much westernization was superficial. Apart from the creation of a naval base at Sinope, the reforms were concentrated close to the capital. Foreign envoys remained unimpressed. Attempts in 1778 to support Tatar resistance to the Russians in the Crimea exposed the weakness of Turkey as a Black Sea power. Seven months elapsed between the Porte's decision to intervene and the embarkation of an expeditionary force from Üsküdar and the Bosphorus fortresses. After six weeks of idleness the Ottoman admirals decided that the winds would allow their vessels to sail into the Black Sea. For some eighteen days the ships, with troops still aboard, cruised pointlessly off the southern coasts of the Crimea until, in mid-September, the first gales swept down from the north and they ran before the wind to find refuge at Sinope. As winter set in, the fleet returned to the Bosphorus. No landing had been attempted; no aid reached the Tatars.[1]

The absurdity of this ineffectual exercise was in keeping with the chaotic character of administration in other parts of the empire. By 1780 the Ottoman structure was becoming corroded, rather like old feudal bonds in Henry VI's England three hundred years before. Although outwardly the traditional apparatus of government was still in being, effective authority even in the central provinces was in the hands of local notables, often the heads of families who raised their status by showing extortionate enterprise as acquisitive *timar* holders. Mere token acknowledgement of a Sultan's sovereignty, common for several decades among governors of the Maghreb dependencies in North Africa, the Hejaz and lower Mesopotamia, had spread closer to the capital. Southern Lebanon was already a cockpit of warring factions: long-surviving dynasties like the Shihbab and Jumblatt families con-tested control with the holders of military fiefs; and in the Druze districts the uniate Maronite Christian Church held out for landowners and peasants alike a prospect of order and stability lacking in the predom-inantly Arab communities.[2] Ahmed Djezzar, in origin a Bosnian slave, ruled the coastlands from Beirut to Acre for the last forty years of the century, surviving by the exercise of such ruthless brutality that, even in a land where bloody massacres were commonplace, he was known as 'the Butcher'.

In Anatolia the Ottomans could impose authority only between the Marmara coast, Bursa and Eskişehir and in the Karaman province, beyond the lower Taurus. Elsewhere western Anatolia was controlled by six 'feudal' families: the Paşaoğlu in the north-east, bordering Kurdish areas where the Sultan's power was minimal; the Çapanoğlu on the central plateau around Angora (Ankara) and Kayseri; the Jānikli in the mountains behind Trebizond; the Karaosmanoğlu in the south-west, based on Aydin and controlling the Menderes valley; the Yilanlioğlu around Antalya; and the Kuchukalioğlu in the Adana area.

A similar pattern prevailed across the straits in Rumelia, where there were four dominant 'feudatories'. Tirsiniklioğlu Ismail was master along what is now the Bulgarian bank of the Danube from Ruschuk (Ruşe) westwards to Nikopol. Dağdevirenoğlu controlled the Edirne region. Kara Mahmud of Bushat, who was lord of northern Albania by 1770, subsequently consolidated the hereditary pashalik of Scutari (now Shkodra), claimed by his father some ten years before. The most famous of all these warlords was Ali Tepedelenlioğlü, 'Ali of Tepelene', whose stormy career spanned more than half a century.[3] No one associates Ali Pasha with his birthplace, for Tepelene is a forgotten village at a river-crossing in southern Albania. He is best remembered as the legendary 'Lion of Ioánnina' (Janinà), the fortress town in Epirus which he seized in 1788, a few months after Sultan Abdulhamid rewarded his war service against the Austrians by appointing him Pasha of Trikkala. But already by 1770 he was lord of southern Albania, having made himself Bey of Tepelene when he was about twenty-eight years old. From this small Albanian power-base Ali advanced his career, until by the close of the century he and his sons were effective rulers over all Epirus, Thessaly and most of the Peloponnese as well.

Many provincial notables were capriciously cruel, although several – like the Sultans themselves – tempered a natural despotism with occasional gestures of benevolence. Modern Baghdad rightly recalls the firm and enlightened administration of the Mameluke leader, Suleiman Pasha 'the Great'. The eastern frontier had long been loosely held by poorly paid Ottoman garrisons and the Persians constituted a serious threat on several occasions, for four years occupying the rising river port of Basra (1775–9). Thereafter, however, from 1780 to 1802, Mesopotamia and most of present-day Iraq was ruled from Baghdad by Suleiman, who imposed an iron rule to curb the Bedouin and check the Persians. He was, however, too contemptuous of his imperial overlord in Constantinople to send anything more than a token annual tribute to the Sultan's coffers.

Some sixteen hundred miles away, along the European frontiers of the empire, individual beys observed an Islamic fanaticism more intensive than any fervour shown in the capital. In Bosnia, for example, a conservative landholding Muslim aristocracy subjected a Christian peasantry to heavy taxation, although little revenue found its way back to Constantinople; often the notables, with Sarajevo as their stronghold, defied successive governors in Travnik, the provincial capital, maintaining that they were dangerously innovative. Yet, in reality, both governors and notables had to stand on the defensive against a double threat. They faced, as ever, the risk of invasion from Roman Catholic Hungary; but they were also aware of a challenge from Montenegro, the neighbouring and fiercely independent mountain fastness whose Orthodox ruler, Prince-Bishop Danilo, had celebrated Christmas in 1702 by ordering the massacre of every Muslim in his principality. Eighty years later Danilo's great-nephew, the wise and able Vladika Peter I – Prince-Bishop in Cetinje from 1782 to 1830 – began to westernize his principality as part of the long struggle to keep the Turks away from the Black Mountain, whose villages they had sacked on three occasions; and at last, in 1799, Vladika Peter duly secured from the Sultan formal recognition that the 'Montenegrins have never been subjects of our Sublime Porte'.

This assurance to the smallest of the Balkan principalities was an inexpensive gesture of appeasement, given at a time of protracted crisis. Throughout the last two decades of the eighteenth century the Ottoman system was shaken by a succession of challenges to its corporate existence. By 1781–2 the evident decay of centralized administration, the anarchy in many outlying provinces, and the threat of erosion along distant frontiers, had begun to tempt the Sultan's most powerful neighbours into behaving as if the Empire were under notice to quit. Catherine the Great, influenced by her favourite Prince Potemkin, exchanged letters with the Habsburg Emperor, Joseph II, proposing an alliance: Austria would acquire large areas of modern Roumania and Yugoslavia while Russia would absorb Turkish lands around the Black Sea and establish autonomous states in Rumelia, eventually setting up a new Byzantine Empire under the sovereignty of Catherine's grandson, the infant Grand Duke Constantine Pavlovich (1779–1831). When, in April 1783, Catherine proclaimed annexation of the Tatar khanate of the Crimea as a first step towards realization of this secret 'Greek Project', there was widespread indignation at Constantinople.[4] But no declaration of war was made; the Sultan and his viziers were pessimistic about their chances of success without a powerful ally, and none was forthcoming.

Yet it became increasingly difficult for Abdulhamid to ignore Russian provocation. His chief concern was the persistent Russian advance in the Caucasus, following the establishment in 1783 of a protectorate over Georgia. But there were other acts of aggravation, too: the encouragement given to visits by Greek Orthodox churchmen to the court at St Petersburg; the incitement of unrest by Russian consular officials in Bucharest, Jassy and several Greek islands; the rapid building of a river port to handle Black Sea trade at Kherson, on the

Dnieper, where 10,000 people were settled by 1786; a triumphal progress by the Empress through her newly acquired Crimean lands. Abdulhamid was physically strong and mentally alert, the father of twenty-two known children, but by 1785 he was ageing rapidly and growing morbidly suspicious of palace intrigue. In the spring of that year he connived at the fall and execution of Halil Hamid, a reforming minister who had trimmed down the Janissary Corps by some sixty per cent. In January 1786 the Sultan appointed Koça Yusuf as Grand Vizier. He was a Georgian convert to Islam who as governor of the Peloponnese had been inclined to see Russian agents lurking on every quay in his province. In August 1787 Koça induced the ailing Abdulhamid, although still without an ally, to declare war on Russia.

This renewed conflict with imperial Russia began a half-century in which the Ottoman Empire was intermittently at war with foreign powers for twenty-four years. During the same period the Sultans were also forced to mount fifteen repressive campaigns against insurrections in outlying provinces, the most serious of which developed into wars of national liberation. These military and naval demands checked the economic growth of the Turkish heartland and limited the character of the reforms undertaken by Abdulhamid's two strong-minded successors, Selim III and Mahmud II. At the same time, they brought the Sublime Porte into the European diplomatic system, posing an Eastern Question to which the only possible solution ultimately proved to be the dissolution of the multinational Ottoman Empire itself.

At first, in the early autumn of 1787, Koça Yusuf's war seemed reluctant to come to the boil. Even when Joseph II became Catherine's ally, six months later, little happened. On land, the Austrians lumbered into Bosnia and crossed from the Bukovina into northern Moldavia, while the Russians eventually took the fortress of Ochakov, commanding the approach to the Bug and the Dniester; and in June 1788 two naval engagements were fought amid the mudflats of the Dnieper estuary, where a Russian flotilla led by the American hero John Paul Jones exposed the weakness of the newly revived Ottoman navy. There was little co-ordination between Russia and Austria, both empires being distracted by threats elsewhere in Europe. Habsburg victories in Serbia went unexploited by the Russians until Suvorov won his ten-hour battle at Focsani in August 1789; but by the following summer, when Suvorov and Kutuzov stormed the Turkish defences around Izmail, Austria was already negotiating for a separate peace. The Ottoman envoys secured good terms from the Habsburgs at Sistova in August 1791; and joint British, Prussian and Dutch mediation enabled the war with

Russia to be ended before Catherine's armies swept south of the Danube delta. Even so, the Peace Treaty of Jassy (January 1792) was yet another humiliation for the Porte in what had so long been reserved as the Ottoman's maritime lake: the Sultan recognized, not only Catherine's annexation of the Crimea and the protectorate over Georgia, but the southern advance of the Russian frontier to the line of the lower Dniester. It was in this region that, in August 1794, the first stones were laid of the port of Odessa, soon to give the Turks a more formidable competitor for Black Sea trade than up-river Kherson.[5]

Abdulhamid I, like his predecessor in an earlier conflict with the Russians, succumbed to apoplexy at the height of the war. His nephew Selim III acceded in April 1789, that momentous month when George Washington became the first President of the United States and deputies converged on Versailles for Louis XVI's opening of the States General. Events in America mattered little to Selim; but what happened in France was of considerable interest. Even during his years of nominal confinement in the *kafe*, Selim had been in touch with Louis. A trusted friend, Ishak Bey, served as Selim's personal emissary, travelling to Versailles in 1786 with a plea that France, as a long-term friend and ally of the Ottoman Empire, should provide aid in modernizing the army and support policies aimed at the containment of Russia. But the Comte de Vergennes, Louis' foreign minister for the first thirteen years of his reign, had himself served as ambassador in Constantinople: he was sceptical over the prospects of reform in Turkey and strongly opposed to any enterprise which might lead to a Franco-Russian conflict. Louis' reply to Selim was guarded and patronizing. 'We have sent from our court to Constantinople officers of artillery to give to the Muslims demonstrations and examples of all aspects of the art of war', Louis wrote in a letter dated 20 May 1787, 'and we are maintaining them so long as their presence is judged necessary.'[6]

Throughout the war with Russia French officers continued to give advice to cadets on the Golden Horn. Translations of military manuals were turned out by the excellent private press attached to the French embassy: aspiring Turkish gunnery specialists could therefore study the treatises from which the young Bonaparte profited at the academy in Brienne. Of course, none of these benefits were in themselves sufficient to change the military balance along the shores of the Black Sea. Whatever his sympathies and inclination, Selim was able to do little to reform or improve the Ottoman state during the first three years of his reign, when day-to-day reports of the war with Russia determined the behaviour of sultan and viziers alike. Nevertheless, in the autumn of 1791 Selim ordered twenty-two dignitaries, both secular and religious, to draw up memoranda on the weaknesses of the empire and the way to overcome them. When, a few months later, the Jassy settlement gave the Ottoman Empire a respite from war, the Sultan resolved to press ahead with a policy of westernization. He hoped that the preoccupation of European statesmen with events in Paris would, at the very least, enable him to ensure that his army and navy should catch up the armed forces of the West in training and equipment.

These good intentions look tediously familiar, but Selim's plans went further than any reforms contemplated by his predecessors. The twenty-two collected memoranda encouraged Selim to seek a 'New Order' (*Nizam-i Cedid*), thereby virtually imposing a revolution from above. Administrative changes included revised regulations to strengthen provincial governorships, the creation of more specialist secular schools to provide training in the ancillary subjects essential for military and naval command (including the French language), control of the grain trade, the institution of regular ambassadorial diplomacy with the major European Powers, and improvements in methods of ensuring that provincial taxes reached a new central treasury, which was given the right to impose taxes on coffee, spirits and tobacco. Earlier Sultans had given their somewhat erratic support to the building of modern ships of the line and the reform of new light and heavy artillery units; Selim III instituted a form of conscription for the navy in the Aegean coastal provinces, tightened discipline in the artillery and other specialist corps and, amid widespread consternation, announced the creation of new infantry corps, organized and trained on French lines and equipped with modern weapons. The Janissaries, suspicious as ever of innovation, had their arrears of back pay settled, and were promised more money for active service, and regular pay-days. But the new barracks for young Turkish recruits above the Bosphorus and at Üsküdar seemed a direct challenge to the entrenched status of the Janissaries. Sultan Selim's other reforms were soon forgotten, and the term 'New Order' became applied solely to the regular infantry battalions which the *Nizam-i Cedid* brought into being.

Selim was well informed of events in revolutionary Paris.[7] In June 1793 Citizen Marie Louis Henri Decorches – the Marquise de Saint-Croix in less egalitarian times – arrived in Constantinople as representative of the French Republic. On *quatorze juillet* two French ships rode at anchor off Sarayburnu (Seraglio Point), impartially flying the Ottoman crescent, the stars and stripes, and the tricolor; they fired a salute, while a 'tree of liberty' was solemnly planted beside the Bosphorus. Some eight weeks later the Sultan sent a detailed inventory to Paris, listing the type of technicians and instructors he wished to recruit from France for temporary service in his army and navy. Despite pressing concerns around France's frontiers, the Committee of Public Safety gave careful attention to the Sultan's requests: an Eastern Front on the lower Danube or an aggressive naval presence in the Black Sea would distract the rulers of Austria and Russia from the activities of republican armies along the Rhine or in northern Italy. And Selim's advisers, for their part, were pleased to encourage the revolutionaries in Paris: 'May God cause the upheaval in France to spread like syphilis to the enemies of the [Ottoman] Empire', the head of the Sultan's personal secretariat wrote early in 1792, when war between France and Austria seemed imminent.[8]

But Selim was too shrewd to commit his empire irretrievably to an unholy alliance with Jacobins. When he decided to modernize his diplomatic system, accrediting resident ambassadors to other courts rather than sending envoys on special missions, he chose London rather than Paris as the first destination of an Ottoman representative. For this decision there were three sound reasons: the hostility shown by William Pitt, the Prime Minister, to Russian aggrandizement in the Black Sea, and especially to the fortification of Ochakov; the absence, as yet, of any apparent British desire to acquire Ottoman possessions; and a passing acquaintance with the ways of the British aristocracy gained from Sir Robert Ainslie, whose eighteen years as George III's ambassador in Constantinople were drawing to a close. Soon afterwards Selim sent resident ambassadors to Berlin, Vienna and St Petersburg. Only then did he choose a permanent envoy for the French Republic.

It was more natural for Selim to establish links with Paris than with any other capital. Some of his officials were already familiar with the language, and the Sultan encouraged the teaching of French, although he does not seem to have spoken or read it himself. Among European writers, only in eighteenth-century France was a rational attempt made to anatomize systems of government and administration, providing blueprints for peoples whose institutions were shaped by other traditions.[9] It is interesting that, when a French-language library was set up to serve Selim's specialist military and naval academies, among the works shipped out from Marseilles was a complete set of the *Grande Encylopédie*. But far more general than these touches of rarefied learning were the commercial contacts, many of them long-established, especially in Syria and the Levant. More recently, French trade at the centre of the Empire had increased threefold in eighty years, with a sizeable community settling in Smyrna. The influences of one culture upon another were, of course, two-way. At the start of the century while fashionable society in Paris and Versailles amused itself with *turquerie*, Constantinople discovered French furniture, French ornamental gardens and French decorative design.

'Frankish' customs had cost Ahmed III his throne, and Selim must have realized it was rash for a Sultan-Caliph to turn so often towards Paris while every Janissary around him was turning towards Mecca. A persistent legend ascribes the intensity of Selim's francophilia to his delight in the company of Aimée Dubucq de Rivery, a young creole who disappeared while sailing between Marseilles and Martinique.[10] She is supposed to have been captured by Barbary pirates, sent from Algiers to Constantinople as a placatory gesture from the corsairs to Abdulhamid I, and then to have lived happily ever after as the 'French Sultana' and the mother of Selim's cousin, Mahmud II – who was born at least three years before Aimée went missing. There is no authentic evidence that the unfortunate young woman reached Algiers, let alone Turkey. But even supposing she did become one of the Favourites in the imperial harem, how could she have enlightened the Sultan on the politics and pursuits of the French? She was too young to know much about them herself. Not every girl from Martinique became so worldly-wise in the ways of Paris as Aimée's distant kinswoman, the future Empress Josephine. For Sultan Selim the fascination of France was never personal; it remained political and military. He was convinced that he would find there a key to unlock for his empire the science of modern war.

It seemed, briefly, in the autumn of 1795, that the lock might be opened for the Sultan by Brigadier-General Bonaparte. On 20 August Napoleon, whose career had made little progress over the past fifteen months, wrote to his brother Joseph: 'If I ask for it, I shall be sent to Turkey by the Government, with a fine salary and a flattering ambassadorial title, to organize the artillery of the Grand Turk.' Ten days later a note was left at the War Ministry: 'General Buonaparte, who has won a certain reputation during his command of the artillery of armies in difficult circumstances, particularly at the siege of Toulon, offers to accompany a government mission to Turkey. He will take with him six or seven officers, each an expert in some particular branch of the art of war. If, in this new career, he can make the Turkish armies more formidable, and the fortresses of the Turkish empire more impregnable, he will consider he has rendered signal service to his country; and when he returns he will merit her gratitude.'[11] He appears to have been issued with a passport in mid-September; but before he could set out, the legendary 'whiff of grape-shot' against a mob marching down the rue Saint-Honoré on 5 October carried 'Citizen Buonaparte' into French history. He never saw Constantinople – 'the centre of world empire', as he was once to call the city.

Napoleon's non-mission to Turkey is a fascinating minor 'might-have-been'. It is tempting to assume that his genius would, in some way, have arrested the military decline of the empire. But why should a relatively unknown Corsican of twenty-six achieve more than Baron de Tott before him or Major von Moltke forty years later? Opposed to all westernizers were four centuries of tradition and prejudice, intensified by the narrowly selfish interest of privileged office-holders. Only if Bonaparte had entered Constantinople as a conqueror and a convert to Islam might he have reshaped the Sultan's empire, and for a few months in 1798–9 this eventuality seemed not impossible.

Ever since the mid-1760s a pressure group of Marseilles merchants had urged successive governments to seize Egypt and establish a colony there. Choiseul briefly favoured such a project but Vergennes, with his long experience of Ottoman rule, argued that French commercial interests would be better served by continuing the traditional policy of good relations with the Sultans. The earlier revolutionary regimes followed this line, but the Directory wavered. Repeated memoranda from Bonaparte, his great Italian campaign by now behind him, convinced the Directors of the advantages of sending an expedition to 'the Orient'. In April 1798 it was agreed that Bonaparte would embark an army for Egypt, consolidate French control over the Levant to the discomfiture of the English and, while destroying the corrupt power of the Mamelukes in Cairo, impose good and beneficial government in the name of the Sultan, whose treasury would thereafter be able to rely on the arrival of the annual tribute. The basic directive for the expedition emphasized that respect must be shown towards the Muslim faith. In order that the Porte should be left in no doubt of the Directory's good will, it was decided that Talleyrand – who became Foreign Minister for the first time in July 1797 – should travel to the Golden Horn and explain to Sultan Selim the finer subtleties of French policy. This interesting encounter never took place. General Bonaparte, with some 38,000 men, duly sailed for Egypt in the third week of May; but Talleyrand did not set out for Constantinople. It was never his intention to do so.[12]

For four or five months the Directory backed the Egyptian expedition. All at first seemed to go well. Bonaparte defeated the Mameluke forces at the 'Battle of the Pyramids' (fifteen miles distant) on 21 July and entered the capital in triumph three days later. His civil administration became a model of good government, the wisest known in Egypt for many centuries. Despite the state of war, irrigation projects were begun, new mills and hospitals built, conditions in the markets improved, tax-collection made efficient. All the reforms which a benevolent Sultan might profitably have introduced in Constantinople were embodied in decrees signed by the conqueror of Cairo. Apart from an irreverent tendency to use minarets as king-size flagpoles, Napoleon made every effort to please the Muslim faithful, speaking to the *ulema* of his deep respect for Islamic teaching, hinting that he might himself accept conversion. In each town and village entered by the French, printed proclamations in Arabic were posted. They listed the blessings of liberation – of which, it was confidently hoped, those who could read would inform those who could not:

> People of Egypt . . . I come to restore your rights, to punish the usurpers; I respect God, His Prophet and the Koran more than did the Mamelukes . . . We are the friends of all true Muslims. Have we not destroyed the Pope, who preached war against the Muslims? . . . Have we not through all the centuries been friends of the Imperial Sultan (may God fulfil his desires) and enemies of his enemies! . . . Let everyone thank God for the destruction of the Mamelukes. Let everyone cry 'Glory to the Sultan! Glory to his ally, the army of France! A curse on all Mamelukes! Happiness to the People!'.[13]

This rhetoric provoked a sour response from Constantinople. Not only did the Sultan decline to recognize the French army as his ally; in September he formally declared war on the French Republic. A month later a firman proclaimed the jihad, a Holy War against the 'infidel savages' who were holding Egypt.

The Directory was no longer interested in Egypt, however, for Nelson's naval victory at the mouth of the Nile on 31 July had cut the links between Marseilles, Toulon and Alexandria. On 4 November Talleyrand informed Bonaparte that he might, if he wished, seek to march on India; or he could remain in Egypt, organizing the province as a French dependency, as in his transformation of northern Italy; or he could advance through Palestine, Syria and Anatolia and seek the capture of Constantinople. These grandiose instructions did not reach Napoleon's headquarters until 25 March 1799; and by then, working out his own grand strategy, he had struck northwards and was besieging Acre.[14] There it became clear that Bonaparte's expedition was bringing an expedient cohesion to the Ottoman Empire. Selim was by no means displeased to see the Mameluke usurpers humbled, but he was not prepared to allow the French to seize a potentially rich province of his empire. The factious feudatories of Palestine and Syria collaborated with the Sultan's nominal governor in Damascus to confront the invaders. Ahmed Djezzar 'the Butcher' was capable of raising an army of 100,000 men to check Bonaparte's thrust northwards and, with the assistance of a British naval flotilla under Commodore Sidney Smith, resisted French assaults on Acre for seven weeks, until a convoy brought from Rhodes a contingent of Selim's 'New Order' troops to reinforce the garrison.

With bubonic plague spreading among his troops, Bonaparte abandoned the siege of Acre. General Kléber defeated the *sipahi* cavalry at Mount Tabor on 16 April and, on this victorious note, the French retired from Syria to Egypt. With British and Russian naval backing, a convoy of sixty vessels brought 15,000 'New Order' troops and Janissaries to the Egyptian coast in mid-July; they landed at Abu Qir (Aboukir) without waiting for the arrival of their horse transports, and threatened the French base at Alexandria; but they could not prevent the infiltration of their lines by the battle-hardened French infantry, and were scattered by Murat's cavalry. French reports of their victory emphasized the folly of the Janissaries, who showed greater interest in securing 'trophies' by decapitating wounded prisoners than in regrouping to meet the enemy's next assault.

Napoleon never again fought personally against Ottoman troops. By mid-October he was in France; a month later he became First Consul. As the Ottoman Empire had joined the Second Coalition, the war continued after Bonaparte left Egypt. In March 1801 an Ottoman army, with British military and naval backing, landed successfully near Alexandria and, in a seven-month campaign, forced the capitulation of the hard-pressed and deserted survivors of the *Armée de l'Orient*. A peace treaty was signed at Amiens in the following summer.[15]

It had been a bitter war, especially so long as Napoleon still aspired to become 'Emperor of the East'. His troops broke faith and committed atrocities at Jaffa; and, after two rebellions in Lower Egypt, he ordered the execution of Muslim hostages in Cairo. Selim III, for his part, had assumed a proper anti-French stance. He confiscated French property; he even worked with the Russians, allowing a fleet to pass through the Straits, while a Russo-Turkish military condominium replaced the pro-French regime set up in the Ionian Islands on the fall of the Venetian Republic. But at heart Selim remained a francophile, eager to turn to Paris for aid and advice at the earliest opportunity. It is tempting to speculate on what might have happened in 1798–9, had Talleyrand gone on his projected mission to Constantinople and achieved such diplomatic success that the 'Sultan and French army' alliance of Bonaparte's proclamation was a reality before the *Armée de l'Orient* set foot in Selim's Egyptian lands.

CHAPTER 5

The Strange Fate of Sultan Selim

As soon as the peace treaty had been signed at Amiens in June 1802, Selim III seemed to slip easily back into the traditional friendship with France. Confiscated property was restored, the favourable commercial concessions which had facilitated the growth of a richly rewarding trade in the Levant were renewed, and the French were assured of access for their merchantmen to the Black Sea ports. Yet there remained deep suspicion and mistrust. French policy was devious. General Horace-François Sébastiani was sent on a mission to Syria and Egypt in the autumn to reassert French influence in a troubled area, either openly or subversively. At the same time, to show respect for the Sultan, the First Consul appointed a distinguished soldier as ambassador: General Guillaume Brune, a one-time revolutionary poet and law student, had fought at Arcola and Rivoli, and in 1799 had repelled an Anglo-Russian invasion of Holland. Selim's choice of emissary to Paris was stranger: Mehmed Said Halet Effendi was a Muslim fanatic, ashamed to be sent to the evil capital of so hateful a land of infidels.

The return of peace put an end to Selim's collaboration with the feudal notables in Syria, the Lebanon and Anatolia. Yet, despite Sébastiani's intrigues, from Egypt there came at first a firm assertion of the Sultan's suzerainty and a steady flow of tribute money. In part this was a legacy of good French rule, but it owed more to the perception and carefully calculated loyalty of Muhammad Ali, a tobacco merchant from Kavalla born in the same year as Napoleon, who had arrived in Egypt as a junior officer in an Albanian regiment and won rapid promotion by defeating two Mameluke leaders who were seeking to recover their old ascendancy. The Sultan appointed Muhammad Ali provincial *wali* (governor) in May 1805: but as early as 1803 he was grafting 'New Order'-style reforms on to the framework of a Bonapartist administration. This creation of a westernized autocracy in Egypt was to take Muhammad Ali some thirty years.[1]

Less gratifying to Selim were reports from the western Balkans, where Ali Pasha had hoped to add the Ionian Islands and the old Venetian enclaves along the coast to his growing dominions in Albania and Epirus. The uneasy Russo-Turkish collaboration in Corfu checked Ali's ambitions, but he continued to rule from Ioánnina in great state, establishing his own diplomatic contacts with European Powers, inviting foreign experts to train his troops and, when it suited him, ignoring orders and decrees from Constantinople. Further north, the line of the Danube along the present Bulgarian-Roumanian frontier was controlled by two veteran warlords, Osman Pasvanoğlü Pasha of Vidin in the west, and Tirsiniklioğlü Ismail further east. Both were dead by the summer of 1806, and effective military power was then exercised by Mustafa Bayraktar ('the standard bearer'), nominal commander of the Sultan's troops on the vital eighty-mile sector between Rushcuk and the fortress of Silistria, in reality the master of much of Bulgaria. Across the Danube, the Principalities of Wallachia and Moldavia had enjoyed considerable autonomy since the Treaty of Kuchuk Kainardji; they were ruled by Christian hospodars appointed by the Sultan, Constantine Ypsilantis and Alexander Maruzzi. Both were regarded by the more reactionary members of the Divan as virtual agents of the Tsar.

In Serbia Selim III's reign opened with a period of mild administration. The Serbs were even allowed to raise their own national militia in order to protect themselves from Pasvanoğlü's marauders. But the advance towards autonomy was abruptly halted when the Sultan sought the backing of the war-lords to hold the line of the Danube. In February 1804 five years of exploitation and misrule by the Janissaries stimulated a national Orthodox Christian rebellion in the wooded hills of the Šumadija district, between the rivers Drina and Morava. The Serbian leader, Karadjordje Petrović – once a pig-dealer, and an ex-sergeant of the Austrian army – insisted that he was fighting to secure acceptance of Sultan Selim's reforms by the Janissaries and the local beys; and there was some truth in this assertion. Selim was at first more troubled by Ali Pasha's pretensions than by the Serbian revolt, even though Karadjordje gained control in December of Belgrade and the towns of Smederevo and Sabac. Only in 1805, when the Russians began giving the Serbian movement active support, did Selim awaken to the full danger of recent events in the Šumadija.[2]

No umlaut

The wide disruption in so many outlying provinces increased the importance of the diplomatic power game being played out in the capital. From where would the Sultan gain the strongest support? British naval power was of little help in keeping order along the Danube or in the Balkans. Should he look to the French army, or risk the invidious embrace of the Russian bear? His inclination had been to preserve his independence by insisting on neutrality when Europe went to war again in 1803 and Pitt began to build a Third Coalition. But the weakening power of Ottoman rule was spread over too many sensitive areas for there to be any real hope of peace. Wiser emissaries than Brune and Mehmed Effendi might have resurrected the Franco-Turkish alliance, but in Paris the Sultan's envoy was regarded as a bad joke, while Brune was at least as poor an ambassador as Bernadotte had been six years earlier in Vienna.

General Bernadotte could, when he chose, exercise a certain charm of manner. General Brune could not, for he had none. He irritated the Divan and the Porte by his arrogance, and by insisting on courtesies due to his rank and that of his master in Paris.[3] Although Selim III had accepted the beheading of a French king without protest and the planting of a tree of liberty on Turkish soil, he reacted strongly against the assumption of an imperial title by a commoner-soldier. He saw no reason to acknowledge the former invader of Egypt and Syria as 'Emperor of the French', nor to recognize the high status accorded to Brune in May 1804, when Napoleon made him the ninth senior Marshal of the Empire. Brune, convinced that Selim needed French backing for his army reforms, complained of an insult to his sovereign and demanded his passports, confident that the Porte would give way and apologize. But the Grand Vizier indicated that Brune was perfectly free to return to Paris. Twice the ambassador delayed his departure, vainly hoping for a change of mood in Stamboul. By the autumn, when he at last accepted failure and sailed back down the Dardanelles, French influence counted for little, despite Selim's personal inclinations. More was at stake in this curious quarrel than mere temperament or prestige. In the previous year almost a quarter of the grain from southern Russia had found its way to Marseilles through the Straits, much of it in fifteen vessels flying the tricolor flag.[4] That trade was now at an end.

French discomfiture was to Russia's benefit. The Tsar's ambassador, Alexander Italinskii, had upstaged Brune ever since their arrival on the Golden Horn in the same week in December 1802. Although Italinskii's requests were unwelcome at the Sublime Porte, they were generally supported by convincing evidence. Russian consuls reported the infiltration of the Peloponnese by French agents, and French encouragement, not only of Ali Pasha and his family in Ioánnina, but of Wahhabi fundamentalist trouble-makers beyond the fringe of the Syrian desert. Reluctantly Selim turned towards an alliance with the Tsar. Russian vessels moved steadily through the Straits, enabling Admiral Dmitri Senyavin to concentrate a flotilla of five ships of the line and several thousand troops on Corfu.

Napoleon, for his part, believed that half the Divan was in Russian pay. So, indeed, he told Selim, in a peremptory personal letter sent from Paris at the end of January 1805. 'Have you, a descendant of the great Ottomans and emperor of one of the greatest of world empires, ceased to reign?' Napoleon asked. 'How do you come to allow the Russians to dictate to you? . . . Are you blind to your own interests? . . . I am writing to you as the only friend France still has in the Seraglio . . . Rouse yourself, Selim, make your supporters ministers . . . The Russians are your true enemies, because they wish to control the Black Sea and cannot do so without having Constantinople, and because they are of the Greek religion, which is the faith of half your subjects.' It was a powerful plea to 'France's most ancient ally'. In effect, the letter told the Sultan to be his own master and restore cordial relations with France, or else face Napoleon's wrath '. . . and I have never been a feeble foe'.[5]

The unfortunate Selim had not 'ceased to reign', but his power was more circumscribed than any outside observer realized. At the very time Napoleon was drafting his letter, Selim was seeking to raise more troops for his 'New Order' army by ordering a general levy throughout the Balkan provinces. This measure would have deprived both war-lords and Janissaries of recruits and necessitated the transfer of some Janissaries to the new regiments. There were skirmishes between Janissary and New Order units in several districts of Rumelia; enlistment and training at Edirne was made impossible, for the Janissary commanders and local notables cut off supplies and imposed military 'picket lines' to exclude recruits from the city. Weakly Selim capitulated, fearing a march on the capital by insurgent forces.

Beyond the frontiers there was a dramatic shift in the balance of power during these months of internal crisis for the Ottomans. More than 50,000 crack Austrian troops were forced to surrender to Napoleon at Ulm in October 1805; on 13 November the French entered Vienna; and on 2 December the Austrian and Russian Emperors were defeated in the decisive battle of Austerlitz. By the Treaty of Pressburg, three weeks later, the Austrians surrendered to France all the one-time Venetian lands in the Adriatic, theoretically making Dalmatia part of metropolitian France, and giving Napoleon a common frontier with the troubled Ottoman province of Bosnia. Soon afterwards Senyavin's squadron from Corfu seized Cattaro (Kotor), partly to prevent the surrender of this fine natural anchorage to the French, but also to give the Russians contact with the Montenegrins and insurgent Serbs. Sultan Selim hesitated no longer. He refused to ratify the latest proposed alliance with the Tsar and, in February 1806, belatedly accorded Napoleon his recognition as Emperor. On August 9 yet another soldier-diplomat, that arch-intriguer General Sébastiani, arrived in Constantinople as ambassador. A military mission accompanied him, once more raising Selim's hopes of creating the westernized, modern army he had sought for nearly twenty years.

Sébastiani's instructions, which the Emperor personally dictated, differ remarkably in tone from the letter sent to Selim eighteen months earlier.[6] The instructions fall into two sections. The first lays down the qualities necessary for an ambassador to ensure that France is 'treated as the most favoured Power': 'tact, subtlety and trust rather than arrogance, force or intimidation'; 'no support of any rebel against the Porte . . . , in Egypt, Syria or any Greek island'; 'the instilling of a feeling of confidence and security'. The second section shows what role Napoleon was prepared to assign to a westernized Sultanate. Significantly, like every later plan drafted in foreign chancelleries, it assumed that the Ottoman Empire would survive solely by grace of Europe's sufferance.

> My unswerving objective in policy is to make a triple alliance between myself, the Porte and Persia, aimed directly or indirectly against Russia . . . All our negotiations must seek these points: (i) closure of the Bosphorus against the Russians . . . ; (ii) forbidding Greeks from sailing under the Russian flag; (iii) arming every fortification against the Russians; (iv) subduing [anti-Ottoman] rebels in Georgia and re-asserting the Porte's absolute rule over Moldavia and Wallachia. I do not want to partition the empire of Constantinople; even were I offered three-quarters of it, I should refuse to do so. I wish to strengthen and consolidate this great empire and to use it, as it stands, against Russia.

A Franco-Ottoman-Persian alliance would not merely protect the right flank of Napoleon's armies as his empire thrust deeper into eastern Europe: it would provide a corridor to the Caucasus and the frontiers of India. So intent was Napoleon on completing this grand strategic plan that a Persian envoy travelled to his headquarters in a remote Polish castle, while General Gardane was sent off on a diplomatic mission to Teheran.

Napoleon's grand strategy brought seven years of conflict to Russia and Persia and six years of war between Russia and the Ottoman Empire, fought mainly in modern Roumania, or down the Black Sea littoral of Georgia. No French troops participated in these campaigns. To Napoleon they were diversions. But the fate of the Ottoman capital was another matter for him: 'Who is to have Constantinople? That is the crux of the problem', he remarked, in slightly varied words, more than once.[7] Paradoxically, in posing the Eastern Question in a broader form he aroused for the first time a British strategic interest in the Ottoman heartlands. In the short term, this diplomatic manoeuvring of arch enemies was to have a dramatic effect on events in Constantinople and on the fate of the Sultan.

Selim was personally heartened by the Sébastiani mission. The General, a Corsican training for the priesthood when the Revolution secularized his thoughts and ambition, could claim an achievement denied any Ottoman commander: he had led cavalry into Vienna. Perhaps for this reason he was honoured as no ambassador before him, becoming the first non-Muslim envoy permitted to wear a sword in the Sultan's presence. Of more practical value was the freedom he enjoyed to spread propaganda. The embassy printing press turned out *Grand Armée* bulletins in both Turkish and Arabic and, on Napoleon's personal insistence, circulated them to ports throughout the Levant. The news, in mid-November, that the renowned Prussian army had been defeated at Eylau and scattered, made a deep impression. It strengthened Selim's conviction that the French cause was invincible.

Sébastiani's coming had already led to swift changes in Ottoman policy.[8] Within four days of the ambassador's arrival the Sultan dismissed the allegedly pro-Russian hospodars in Wallachia and Moldavia. A month later he closed the Straits to Russian warships; and he went ahead with plans for doubling the number of 'New Order' troops. The Tsar's ambassador, Alexander Italinskii, warned St Petersburg that the Turks had gone over to the French side; and under threat of an immediate Russian attack on the Bosphorus, Selim wavered, even reinstating the deposed hospodars as a gesture of appeasement. But this came too late to change Russian policy. In the last week of November 1806 Moldavia and Wallachia were overrun and on 16 December the Sublime Porte declared war on Russia. At that moment General Sébastiani achieved an ascendancy at the Porte unmatched by any previous foreigner. He seemed to possess greater influence on Sultan Selim than the *şeyhülislâm*. He even succeeded in persuading Selim that to imprison an ambassador when declaring war on the sovereign whom he represented was a barbarous custom. Largely thanks to Sébastiani, Italinskii escaped incarceration; he found refuge with his family aboard HMS *Canopus*, an 80-gun line-of-battle ship which had been at anchor in the mouth of the Golden Horn for three weeks.

It was on the initiative of the British ambassador that *Canopus* was lying off Galata. Charles Arbuthnot – better remembered in middle age as 'Gosh' Arbuthnot, the close friend of the Duke of Wellington – had been in residence for the past two years. Like so many of his compatriots, he was certain that nothing would so effectively concentrate a Sultan's mind on essentials as the sight of warships flying the White Ensign above the waters off his palace. A couple of months before Sébastiani's arrival Arbuthnot had assured the Foreign Secretary (Charles Grey, Viscount Howick) that Selim III 'would prefer a French war in Bosnia to an English one off the Seraglio Point'. His reports confirmed the predilection of the Foreign Office and the Admiralty for a show of strength at Constantinople similar to the action off Copenhagen in April 1801, when Admirals Hyde Parker and Nelson used some fifty ships to intimidate the Danes. At the end of the second week in November, Howick notified Arbuthnot that naval reinforcements would soon be sailing from Plymouth for the eastern Mediterranean. Meanwhile the ambassador was to demand Sébastiani's departure, on the grounds that the General's activities were a breach of Ottoman neutrality.[9]

But Arbuthnot was already shaping British policy long before the messages from London reached Constantinople. He sought armed mediation in Turkey's quarrel with Russia; and it was to give weight to his diplomacy that at the beginning of December he induced Rear-Admiral Louis to bring *Canopus* and the 44-gun frigate HMS *Endymion* up through the Dardanelles – the Hellespont of ancient times – into the Sea of Marmara. While Sir John Duckworth was bringing a more powerful squadron from Gibraltar to the Aegean, Arbuthnot tried to convince the Porte of Britain's indignation at Sébastiani's privileged position, but he made little impression. Louis took *Canopus* back down the Hellespont, carefully studying the Turkish forts on the way; as yet, no fleet had attempted to force its way through the Straits in the face of Ottoman resistance.[10]

At the end of January 1807 tension in Constantinople became explosive, and Arbuthnot was warned by his spies to leave Pera. He invited the British merchants in Constantinople to dine with him aboard *Endymion* on 29 January; once they were aboard, the frigate slipped quietly away and headed for the Dardanelles. If Arbuthnot had hoped to find a powerful naval force awaiting him at the mouth of the Straits, he was disappointed; there was only Admiral Louis in *Canopus*, with two other ships. The Admiral told Arbuthnot the French were helping the Turks to improve the defences of the Dardanelles, belatedly modernizing the sixteenth-century fortresses of Sedd-el-Bahr and Kilid Bahr and siting new batteries on the Asian shore. Louis had sent a fast vessel to Malta with a request for ten line-of-battle ships and troop transports to provide landing parties to spike batteries on the Gallipoli peninsula and across the Narrows. Meanwhile the four ships waited in Besika Bay, off Tenedos (Bozcaada).

A swift naval passage up the Dardanelles, with all the panache of the Nelson touch, might have speedily toppled Sébastiani from his eminence. But ten days elapsed between *Endymion's* reunion with *Canopus* and the arrival of seven line-of-battle ships in Admiral Duckworth's squadron. For nine more days the wind blew directly down the Dardanelles, keeping the squadron in the lee of Tenedos. At last, on 19 February 1807 – for the first time in the history of the Royal Navy – British warships began to force the Dardanelles. Heavy cannonades came from the forts and from some of the older Ottoman ships, off Maidos; several were sunk by return fire; no British vessels were seriously damaged. By the following evening Duckworth's small fleet had crossed the Sea of Marmara – not, however, to threaten Sultan Selim in the Topkapi Sarayi, for winds and current down the Bosphorus were too strong to approach the moorings Louis had used in December. HMS *Royal George*, Duckworth's flagship, dropped anchor some eight miles short of the city, off the island of Prinkipo (Büyükada).[11]

For two days pinnaces and caiques plied across the waters, as Arbuthnot sought to negotiate from strength. The arrival of the ships, outwardly unscathed, caused consternation – until it was noted that they were lying well off shore. Despite a heavy sea *Endymion* reached the mouth of the Golden Horn, but was withdrawn when an envoy from the Porte warned Arbuthnot that feeling was running so high, the presence of the frigate might precipitate a general massacre of foreigners. At 11.20 in the morning of 22 February Duckworth ordered his ships to prepare to sail close in and bombard the city, but almost immediately he cancelled the order: constant squalls and strong head-winds saved Constantinople from the fate of Copenhagen.

While armed diplomacy faltered and stuttered, General Sébastiani resumed his military career. The French mission supervised the siting of artillery around the city. Civilians were mobilized to strengthen the defences: even the Greek Patriarch, staff in hand, was seen exhorting a thousand Phanariots to help build new fortifications. The strong winds straight down the Bosphorus continued until the last day of the month. By then some 300 guns were in position, commanding the waters between Prinkipo and the Golden Horn. They were not called into action. Duckworth, fearing that his ships might be bottled up in the Sea of Marmara, sailed the squadron down the Straits and into the Aegean. On this occasion the fire from the forts at the Narrows was more accurate; masts and rigging on several vessels were shot away.[12]

Back in the lee of Tenedos Duckworth's chastened captains were joined on 8 March by a Russian force under Admiral Senyavin. Briefly Arbuthnot and the two Admirals considered forcing the Straits and bombarding the capital; but to what purpose? Without troops, there was no prospect of striking a militarily decisive blow. Moreover, the British were by no means convinced it was in the national interest to help the Tsar become master of Constantinople. On Friday, 13 March, the allied squadrons sailed off across the Aegean. The first British naval demonstration in the Dardanelles had proved a fiasco.

It was not the only one. On Saturday, 14 March, 6,000 British troops were landed seven hundred miles way at Alexandria, in an attempt to wrest Egypt from Ottoman suzerainty. Had their transports been attached to Duckworth's squadron, the show of strength off Selim's capital might well have achieved all Arbuthnot desired. As it was, the Egyptian expedition, too, was a blunder. Five months of determined resistance by Muhammad Ali, backed by an energetic French consul-general, confined the invaders to a few hundred square miles of swampy shore around Alexandria and Rosetta. An orderly evacuation followed in September. From the Bosphorus to the Nile delta, British prestige stood at rock bottom.[13]

On paper, Duckworth's failure vindicated Sultan Selim's policies. As the British ships sailed away from Prinkipo Island there was wild rejoicing in Stamboul and Galata. A shower of rich gifts testified to the Sultan's high regard for Sébastiani and the French military mission. The Grand Vizier prepared to strike at Turkey's other enemy. Early in April 1807 the main Ottoman army left the capital for Edirne in preparation for a summer offensive against the Russians in the Danubian

Principalities. The fleet, too, prepared to seek Senyavin in the Aegean. The more modern ships were undamaged by Duckworth's guns, having wintered up the Bosphorus; and on 10 May the Ottoman navy left the Golden Horn, sailing southwards through the Dardanelles a few days later. After the big military and naval concentration around the capital in the first quarter of the year, Constantinople was relatively denuded of troops.

Selim felt sufficiently sure of his standing and popularity in the capital to resume his policies of westernization, but this proved a grave miscalculation.[14] Coffee-house rumour maintained that he invited French actors to perform in his palace and that, contrary to the teachings of the *ulema*, his rooms were decorated with imported paintings from Western Europe which depicted the human body. Once again, as in the last years of Ahmed III's reign, there were complaints from the sober-minded that 'Frankish' (European) manners and customs were permeating society in the capital, and seditious ways of thought undermining Holy Law. Rather strangely, Selim failed to identify, amid this mounting unease, the stern disapproval of the *şeyhülislâm*, the 'Chief Mufti' as foreign ambassadors generally called him. The Sultan even sought his advice.

Not that Selim had any intention of abandoning his cherished reforms. To pay for modern weapons he needed ready money. He therefore resumed a process, begun several years earlier, of converting *timar* fiefs into crown land, which would then be leased out to tax-farmers who had no feudal military obligation and who were permitted a dangerous freedom in choosing the methods by which they might raise money from their tenants. Not surprisingly, these *iltizam* leases were unpopular with the peasantry, whom unscrupulous tax-farmers ruthlessly exploited; better the old system than any 'new order'. At the same time, the constant debasement of the coinage caused hardship and despair in the trading communities, not only around the Golden Horn but in Smyrna, Adana and Salonika as well. Even so, a fortnight after the Ottoman fleet had sailed into the Aegean, and while Mustafa Pasha Bayraktar was leading an army northwards across the Danube, Selim went ahead with the next stage of military reform. The young Janissary auxiliaries (*yamaks*), mostly Albanians or Circassians, were to be reconstituted as New Order regiments, wearing French-style uniforms: red breeches, tightly cut, and blue berets. Or so it was intended. But in the fort of Rumeli Kavak, out beyond Sariyer and nearly at the mouth of the Bosphorus, the *yamak* auxiliaries mutinied, rather than be issued with the infidel dress. On 25 May 1807 they murdered a New Order officer and threatened to march on the capital, some fourteen miles away.

At this point Selim showed again that wretched weakness of character which had so nearly cost him his throne during the Edirne disturbances two years earlier. Instead of sending loyal French-trained officers from the New Order barracks against the Rumeli Kavak mutineers, he consulted the 'Chief Mufti', who urged him not to precipitate a civil war but to discover the nature of the *yamak* grievances. It was fatal advice, as no doubt it was meant to be. Over the following two days discontent spread through the Bosphorus forts until, on the morning of 27 May, six hundred *yamaks* from Büyükdere, a camp three miles south of Rumeli Kavak, landed by boat at Galata, carrying the contagion of unrest to the capital. Thousands of Janissaries joined them, as well as religious students meeting in the At Meydani, the 'square of horses', encompassing the Byzantine Hippodrome, less than half a mile from the inner apartments of the Topkapi Sarayi. Desperately the Sultan played for time; was he, perhaps, still hoping for 'a whiff of grape-shot' from French-trained gunners? It seems unlikely, although Sébastiani had some experience in such matters; eight years earlier, he had commanded the 9th Dragoons, supporting Bonaparte at St Cloud on 18 Brumaire.

But Selim was no Napoleon. In his panic, he was prepared to sweep away his one prop: the New Order regiments would be disbanded, he announced. He then sent some of his westernizing ministers out of the palace to meet their death, next day appointing reactionaries to the Divan in their place. None of these gestures satisfied the At Meydani mutineers; they suspected that, if Selim remained on the throne, today's announcements would be rescinded once he could bring back loyal troops from the Danube Front. Lest Selim should fail to get their message, the mutineers seized his personal secretary in the outer First Court of the palace and hacked his body to pieces. The dead man's head was then borne into the throne room and laid before Selim, as a dog might drop a bone at his master's feet.[15]

'May a Sultan whose behaviour and enactments work against the sacred teachings of the Holy Koran continue to reign?' the *şeyhülislâm* was asked next day – a somewhat loaded question. The answer was never in doubt. The only problem was who should succeed to the throne; though Selim III had taken eight wives, none had borne him a boy; and of Abdulhamid I's thirteen sons, only two had survived infancy. The eldest of these, Prince Mustafa, was mentally unstable; the younger, Prince Mahmud, was said to be influenced by the fashionable

French heresies of his uncle. The rebels and the *ilmiye* had no hesitation in requiring the natural order of succession to be observed. A *fetva* was issued: Selim III was deposed on 29 May 1807 in favour of Mustafa IV; and while the At Meydani mutineers, Janissary commanders and Chief Mufti imposed reactionary rule through judicial murder, the *kafe* apartments of the Topkapi Sarayi gave sanctuary to the most enlightened incumbent ever to return to their seclusion.

French diplomats and soldiers in Constantinople and the neighbouring forts, fearing for their lives, could do nothing to influence Ottoman policy in this crisis. Sébastiani was recalled to France, soon to resume his active service in Spain. The events in the capital, and especially the suppression of the New Order regiments, abruptly halted the offensive on the lower Danube, where Bayraktar was forced to abandon the siege of Russian-occupied Bucharest. Mustafa Pasha Bayraktar himself was politically conservative, long convinced that Selim was reckless in pushing through reform. But he was also a competent general, anxious to get on with a campaign that had begun well, and he possessed too stern a sense of discipline to accept months of anarchy, as in the days of Patrona Halil. Briefly he hurried back to the capital, and restored a semblance of discipline. But he found it impossible to collaborate with the *ulema* and the new Divan, and he soon returned to the war zone in the Danubian Principalities.

Then suddenly, less than a month after Selim's fall, the chessboard of diplomacy was overturned by a Russo-French armistice and the meetings of Napoleon and Tsar Alexander I at Tilsit. Within a fortnight treaties, public and secret, bound the recent enemies in uncertain partnership. Napoleon did not entirely desert his Ottoman allies, however much their new rulers might rail at 'Frankish customs'. The Treaty provided for Russian evacuation of Moldavia and Wallachia and the conclusion of a Russo-Ottoman armistice, which was signed at Slobodzeia on 24 August, in the presence of a personal envoy from Napoleon. The Emperor was as determined as his British enemies that the Russians should not secure control of Constantinople; but he was prepared to discuss with Alexander the future partition of the Ottoman Empire – largely an imaginative exercise in hypothetical map-making. Both sovereigns showed a fine lack of embarrassing precision. They had no choice. What would happen next on the Golden Horn was anyone's guess. How far would the Sultan's effective sovereignty extend by the end of the decade?

With the francophile Selim deposed, the British hoped they might recover some influence at the Porte. Sir Arthur Paget, for the past five years a skilled negotiator in Vienna, arrived in Constantinople late in August on a special mission. But he achieved little. Rival secular and religious pressure groups were in bitter conflict. Although all loathed the 'abominable customs' of the French, Paget was puzzled by the Porte's apparent determination to remain, so far as possible, under Napoleon's protection.[16]

Sultan Mustafa IV was a puppet of the reactionaries, though it was never clear at any one moment who was pulling the strings. Increasingly, the discontented – including many frustrated opportunists – drifted away to provincial cities. Most went north, crossing the Bulgarian lands to Ruschuk, the walled ferry-town where Mustafa Bayraktar had his headquarters, looking out over the Danube and the Wallachian plain towards Bucharest. There, a secret 'Ruschuk Committee' planned a counter-coup. Agents in the palace would convince the pliable-minded Mustafa IV that the only way he would be able to rule in his own right would be to follow the example of Mahmud I and shake off the fetters imposed on him by those rebellious Sultan-makers, the Janissary commanders and the devious *şeyhülislâm*, Ataullah Effendi.

The Committee's agents did all that was expected of them. On 19 July 1808, on the invitation of Mustafa IV, Bayraktar arrived back in Constantinople at the head of his army and obliged the Sultan and his Grand Vizier by getting rid of the more overbearing Janissary commanders and of Ataullah Effendi, whom Bayraktar replaced with a less ambitious Mufti. But having accomplished the task for which he had been summoned south, Bayraktar showed a strong reluctance to take his army back to stand guard yet again along the lower Danube. Spies reported to Mustafa IV that the Pasha intended to secure his deposition and restore Selim III. Mustafa, however, reasoned that if both Selim and his own half-brother Mahmud were killed, he would be the sole surviving male member of the Ottoman dynasty, and therefore his life and his possession of the Sultanate would be secure. On 28 July 1808 Sultan Mustafa therefore sent executioners into the Fourth Courtyard to have his kinsmen killed in their *kafe* apartments.

Confusion persists over what happened where inside the Topkapi Sarayi on that Thursday.[17] Selim certainly resisted the executioners, and it is probable that he burst through into the throne room before dying in the Sultan's presence. It is also clear that he was not quietly and efficiently strangled, for Bayraktar found the blood-stained corpse when his troops burst into the inner courtyard later in the morning: 'The Bayraktar was touched and confused. They say he wept tears,' a Dutch diplomat reported two days later.[18] The Grand Admiral wanted to avenge Selim's death by having Mustafa killed on the spot. But the execution of two Sultans on one morning might have been regarded as excessive. Moreover, as Mustafa had calculated, it seemed probable that if he were killed the Othman line would be extinguished, for there was still a grave doubt over the fate of Prince Mahmud. No ambitious competitor for high office wanted a struggle for the succession between rival notables, with private armies converging on the capital from various provinces. A civil war of this character would have broken up the Empire for all time.

The 23-year-old Mahmud survived. He appears to have heard the commotion as the executioners burst in upon his cousin, Selim. A long tradition maintains that Mahmud, helped by his mother the *Valide Sultana* Naksidil, escaped to the roof of the harem while Naksidil's slave-girl, Cevri Khalfa, prevented the killers from mounting a staircase in the colonnaded corridor of the outer harem which would have enabled them to seize the Prince. One report says that Bayraktar found the young man concealed beneath a pile of carpets and that, having secured a *fetva* of deposition against Mustafa IV, he thereupon proclaimed the accession of Sultan Mahmud II. An equally probable tale says that the Prince had the good sense to remain in the shadows of the forest of chimneys on the palace roof until swords were sheathed below. At all events, within a fortnight his accession was acknowledged in solemn ceremonial at the Eyüp mosque – and Mustafa Pasha Bayraktar became Grand Vizier. The wretched Mustafa IV was back in the *kafe*, again heir-apparent in a dynasty into which no child had been born for almost twenty years.

The cycle of palace revolutions was still not complete. Bayraktar tried to resume the policy of army reform. He raised, not 'New Order' regiments – for the term was discredited – but 'New Keepers of the Hounds' (*Segban-i Cedit*), reviving the name of a bodyguard once acceptable to the Janissaries. Yet, since he gave command of these troops to former New Order officers, the reactionaries were far from placated. Moreover, Bayraktar made the mistake of feasting with his *Segban* guards at the meal which marked the end of Ramadan, a time of stress, when old resentments easily fray fiery tempers. The Janissaries brooded on their grievances overnight. Next morning (15 November 1808) they attacked the Grand Vizier within the Sublime Porte itself. Bayraktar took refuge in a neighbouring small stone building, which looked solidly defensible. Unfortunately it was a powder magazine; and as the fighting went on around it there was a sudden massive blast which killed the

Grand Vizier, his bodyguard, and several hundred of the attacking Janissaries.[19]

The fighting and the explosion were some distance away from the Topkapi Sarayi, allowing Sultan Mahmud to act swiftly. His favourite Sultana, Fatma, was several months pregnant (she died the following February, giving birth to a princess who did not survive infancy: a tragedy which could not, of course, have been foreseen that November) and Sultan Mahmud, oddly confident of a male heir, took the decision which Bayraktar had rejected in July: his half-brother, the ex-Sultan Mustafa IV, was strangled forthwith. At the same time Mahmud called out from their barracks other *Segban* units under training, and appealed for help to the warships in the Golden Horn, whose officers loathed the Janissaries. For two days there was a highly destructive civil war in Stamboul, with large fires in some of the oldest parts of the city. Eventually the *ulema*, horrified by the damage to the mosques and the *evkaf* pious foundations, secured a cease-fire and a compromise. The *Segban-i Cedit* had to go, at least as a separate institution, and the Janissaries were promised the restoration of their barracks, virtually destroyed in the bombardment. But Mahmud II remained on the throne: he was still Sultan thirty years later.

Selim III – that 'Most Exalted, Most Excellent, Omnipotent, Magnanimous and Invincible Prince' (the salutation is Napoleon's) – had promised much and accomplished little. In the end, prejudice and convention triumphed over his will to reform. In one sense Selim was a would-be saviour of the Empire, rejected by his people because they could not understand him. Perhaps his main achievement was negative, a warning to later Ottoman reformers how not to refurbish their inheritance. Yet in two respects the dramatic climax to Selim's reign possessed lasting significance. It showed the revived importance of the Bosphorus and Dardanelles as vital strategic guard-posts of the Empire, essential to be kept in good repair and held by troops whose loyalty was beyond suspicion. And it also emphasized the oddest feature of Ottoman rule in these years of arrested decline: the extent to which, as in an older Mediterranean civilization, nominal government of a vast empire in three continents still depended upon the mood of a single city. With the politics of Constantinople counting for so much and the Sultan's distant subjects receiving so little attention in the capital, it is hardly surprising if movements for local autonomy, which even before Selim's accession had cost the Ottomans direct sovereignty over many outlying provinces, were becoming clearly defined expressions of separatist sentiment.

Mustafa Pasha Bayraktar perceived the danger, for he had spent much of his life consolidating a virtual satrapy along the lower Danube. During his sixteen-week Grand Viziership he summoned the powerful notables of the empire to the capital for a conference to discuss reform.[20] In the last days of September 1808 the heads of over-mighty families arrived from inner Anatolia, from Karaman, Aleppo and the Lebanon, and from southern Rumelia. Of those who did not care to travel so far from their power base, most sent deputies. Yet, sound though the idea of such a conference was in itself, once again little was achieved. The notables pledged loyalty to the Sultan and respect for the Grand Vizier as his sovereign representative, but they safe-guarded their local rights so jealously that Mahmud II rejected their agreement. In retrospect, the greatest interest of the gathering is in noting those who thought themselves so independent that this first initiative of Sultan Mahmud's reign was of no concern to them. From Bayraktar's conference there were two outstanding absentees. There was no Ali Pasha of Ioánnina: the lord of southern Albania and the Greek mainland did not even send one of his sons, but was represented by a single frightened nominee, attended by his own bodyguard. Most significantly, from Muhammad Ali in Cairo there came no one at all.

CHAPTER 6

Mahmud II, The Enigma

Over a century and a half after his death, Mahmud II remains the most puzzling of the thirty-six Ottoman Sultans. We know what he looked like because his enlightened views allowed artists to paint several portraits. All show a vigorous, broad-chested man, haughtily conscious of his sovereignty; a well-trimmed dark beard emphasizes the paleness of his face. Most of all we notice the 'large black peculiar eyes which looked you through and through and which were never quiet', as a Scottish traveller, Charles MacFarlane, commented – and as Byron, too, observed on the one occasion he was admitted to the audience chamber.[1] But, although we may recognize him framed on a wall, the inner man eludes us. Was he a despot or a reformer, a capricious betrayer of trust or a dedicated ruler of vision, a muddler who plunged into disastrous wars or a shrewd statesman who preserved his Empire from rapacious neighbours? Should we think of him as the 'Infidel Sultan' who imposed European ways on the Islamic faithful, or as *Mahmud Adli* ('Mahmud the Just'), like Turks today? The contrasts seem endless. Mahmud is one of history's more enigmatic figures; he defies over-simplified docketing as a 'good' or 'bad' ruler.

Yet the attempt has been made. Harold Temperley, writing shortly before the fall of the Ottoman Empire, thought he was 'the greatest sovereign since the days of Suleiman', a Sultan who, acceding when 'all was chaos at Constantinople', ensured by percipient statecraft that 'the marvellous vitality of the Turkish Empire was soon to reassert itself'. From across the Atlantic later historians, too, pay tribute to Mahmud 'the determined reformer', 'the Ottoman Westernizer'.[2] And in İstanbul the epitaph on the Sultan's *turbe* in Yeniçeriler Caddesi recalls 'A great Sovereign, just and wise, the sun to his empire, He who opened the gate of the East to new life'.

77

Contemporaries were more critical. Stratford Canning, later Lord Stratford de Redcliffe, the most famous of British ambassadors, remembered Mahmud as 'in temper and policy a despot and a caliph', a ruler whose 'natural abilities would hardly have distinguished him in private life. He had no scruple of taking life at pleasure from motives of policy or interest.' Adolphus Slade, a British naval officer who spent many years at Constantinople, complained of Mahmud's stubborn inflexibility; reform, Slade argued, removed natural checks on a Sultan's despotism, 'accomplishing the entire subversion of the liberties of his subjects'; and, after four years in Ottoman service, the great Prussian soldier Helmuth von Moltke considered Mahmud's qualities as essentially destructive: he would 'raze to the ground any other authority within the compass of his Empire', and yet he lacked the skill to 'set up his own building in its place'. Moltke scorned the analogy often drawn between Mahmud's services to the Ottoman Empire and Peter the Great's achievements in Russia: while the Tsar acquired strategically valuable land to expand his empire north and south, Mahmud lost historic possessions in two continents.[3]

Yet, whatever their reservations, contemporary critics and later commentators agree that from his accession until the last weeks of his life Mahmud recognized the need for change in the Ottoman state. Romanticists like to believe he was introduced to the concept of enlightened despotism in his youth by the 'French Sultana' said to have been his mother, Aimée Dubucq de Rivery. More plausibly, it seems possible that he was influenced by the unfortunate Selim III in the months the fallen Sultan and the heir-apparent spent confined together in the *kafe*. Mahmud's first years on the throne were certainly overshadowed by memories of Selim's fate, and by a fear of renewed violence in the capital. He showed no inclination to live in the Stamboul palace where he had so narrowly escaped death at the hands of his half-brother. It remained the Grand Seraglio, the formal residence of the Court, but Mahmud dined and slept in a smaller and more defensible palace, across the Golden Horn at Beşiktaş. From there an imperial caique carried the Sultan in state to the Topkapi Sarayi for official ceremonies.

For four years after his half-brother's death Mahmud was still the only male member of the dynasty. In December 1812 an Ottoman prince was born in the palace, after a lapse of more than a quarter of a century, but the child was sickly and died in infancy. The Sultan's continued good health therefore remained essential in order to ward off that old bogey, an empire disintegrating in a power struggle between rival notables. Mahmud faced a double task: he had to safeguard his position, while not offending powerful sections of the community; and he had to convince the other powers that the Ottoman Empire was still an effective unitary state. Small wonder that after those critical days in November 1808 he moved cautiously. Outwardly he seemed to abandon all pretence of westernization, restoring the traditional corps of the Ottoman armies and ignoring the recent improvisations of Selim and Mustafa Bayraktar. But gradually, and almost imperceptibly, the Sultan placed his own supporters in key military and naval commands and in the principal offices of state, ready to revive the active rule of the sovereign. It was a slow process, spanning eighteen troubled years in which there were few signs of renewed vitality at the heart of the Empire.

The beginning of this period coincided with the arrival in Turkey of Stratford Canning, who by mid-century was the best-known of ambassadors to the Porte, 'the Great Elchi'. He reached Constantinople *Elçi* at the end of January 1809, less than three months after Bayraktar's death. At twenty-two he was beginning his diplomatic career as secretary to Sir Robert Adair, the envoy sent to re-establish links with the Ottoman Empire; and already, before their ship was allowed into the Sea of Marmara, Adair had concluded a formal peace treaty at the Dardanelles, secretly pledging British naval aid if the Sultan's Aegean and Adriatic possessions were attacked by France, Austria or Russia. Somewhat surprisingly, the improvement of Anglo-Turkish relations was soon entrusted to this young and inexperienced secretary, for within eighteen months Adair left for Vienna and Canning became 'minister plenipotentiary to the Sublime Porte'. In all, Stratford Canning – created Viscount Stratford de Redcliffe in 1852 – represented British interests at the Porte for twenty-three years (1810–12; 1824–7; 1831–2; 1841–6; 1848–58), and his opinions on Turkish affairs still commanded respect in London in the late 1870s, during the great Eastern Crisis. But at no later moment did Ottoman prestige abroad count for so little as in these early years, when it seemed as if the Empire must soon fall. 'Mahmud', Stratford later recalled, 'had everything to apprehend from the circumstances in which he was placed. Both morally and materially his empire was bordering on decrepitude.'[4]

After two years of uneasy truce, hostilities with Russia were resumed in December 1809, and the Ottoman army fared disastrously. Sultan Mahmud's commanders suffered a series of defeats; their ill-equipped troops were forced back from the Danubian fort of Izmail southwards across Bulgaria into the main Balkan mountain range. To Stratford

Canning's intense fury, although the Sultan could no longer count on help from Napoleon, the French encouraged the Turks to carry on fighting against the Russians. The French embassy, he informed the Foreign Secretary, contained 'the vilest scum that ever fell from the overboilings of the pot of Imperial Jacobinism', and he spent much of his first eighteen months as ambassador finding honeyed phrases to flatter the Grand Vizier and counter a series of French intrigues.[5] It was clear to all outside observers that, as Franco-Russian relations deteriorated from the high point reached at Tilsit, Napoleon would use every means to prevent Tsar Alexander from concentrating his armies in Poland.

In October 1811 Stratford Canning's persuasive attempts at mediation seemed close to success: Russo-Turkish peace talks opened in Giurgevo. But, as so often, the clash of Turkish pride and Russian obstinacy made the discussions drag on inconclusively. Eventually, in May 1812, the imminence of a Napoleonic invasion induced the Russians to accept terms, and a peace treaty was at last signed at Bucharest, generous to the defeated Ottomans. Although Bessarabia became a Russian province and limited autonomy was promised to insurgent Serbia, the Sultan's authority was confirmed in the Danubian Principalities (subject to the restoration in both Moldavia and Wallachia of the traditional hospodar administration).

The Bucharest settlement pleased Canning: the Turks had won concessions unattainable seven months before. He was well satisfied by the way the Sultan's emissaries had extricated their master from the Russian imbroglio. So, it seemed, was Mahmud; he declared himself 'much gratified' by the 'English minister's interest . . . in my royal affairs.' But when the *Grande Armée* crossed the river Niemen and thrust relentlessly forwards into Russia, the Sultan had second thoughts. In the autumn of 1812, with Napoleon in Moscow and the Tsar's armies apparently beaten, Mahmud decided that his emissaries had conceded far too much, and he took vengeance on them: two Phanariot brothers employed as translators and intermediaries during the peace talks at Giurgevo were executed, while the plenipotentiary who signed the Treaty of Bucharest was sent into exile. By then, however, Stratford Canning had left Turkey and was home in England.[6]

Over the following three years the map of central and western Europe was dramatically redrawn through the collapse of the French Empire and the peacemaking of the Great Powers at the Congress of Vienna. But, apart from the establishment of a British protectorate over Corfu and the seven Ionian islands, there were no significant changes in the Balkans or around the eastern Mediterranean. The Bucharest settlement, together with Tsar Alexander's Grand Design for a lasting European peace, thrust Ottoman affairs temporarily into the background: Mahmud II could face the immediate problems of his Empire without the risk of intervention from formidable neighbours beyond the Danube. No help came to the Serbs when, in 1813, the convergence of three Turkish armies on their nascent principality crushed the nine-year rebellion and forced Karadjordje Petrović to flee to Hungary. And little interest was taken by the European Powers in what was happening at the opposite extremity of the Empire, in Mesopotamia, where the ruthless policies of Halet Effendi ensured a restoration of direct Ottoman rule. So impressed was Mahmud by Halet Effendi's success in Baghdad that, from 1813 onwards, he accepted this arch-traditionalist and former envoy to Napoleon's court as his most trusted adviser.

For the moment, too, the Sultan was left to deal in any way he might wish with the ambitious Governor of Egypt, Muhammad Ali. Here, however, the western European Powers had interests to protect. During the closing stages of the Napoleonic Wars the British replaced the French as the principal western European traders in the Levant; they therefore showed some concern over what was happening in Alexandria, Cairo and Beirut. But their needs were relatively straight-forward: the maintenance of good order in the ports and free movement of goods. It made little difference to London merchants that they were carried mainly in Greek-owned vessels. Nor did it matter to foreign traders whether government in Egypt and the Levant was exercised directly by the Sultan, or by his appointed representative, so long as it was efficient. There was no open conflict between Mahmud and Muhammad Ali during the difficult period of readjustment which followed the eclipse of French influence in the Levant. So changed was the character of gubernatorial administration that it became customary to speak of Muhammad Ali as the 'Viceroy of Egypt'. Yet Mahmud continued to find him dutiful and accommodating: he liquidated the last of the Mamelukes (1811), paid to the Sultan his regular annual tribute, placated the *ulema*, and – at Mahmud's request – sent well-trained Bosnian and Albanian troops to suppress rebellions in Arabia.

Ali Pasha in Ioánnina posed a more immediate problem. His diplo-matic contacts, first with the French and later with the British, made him a considerable power in Balkan politics. He was establishing a dynastic authority which, to Halet Effendi, seemed a greater threat to the Ottoman hold on Europe than the Serbian rebellion. In 1820 hit-men sent by Ali to Constantinople sought to assassinate a personal enemy in a house adjoining the imperial palace. Halet Effendi induced the Sultan to dismiss Ali and his sons from their official posts and to prepare land and sea expeditions to recover the Epirus and end Ali's half-century of rule. His autonomous despotate crumbled with astonishing rapidity and by August 1820 Ioánnina was invested, the thriving commercial centre suffering as much from Ali's scorched-earth policy as from the rigours of a siege. Even so, for more than a year the old Lion held out in the citadel, fleeing at last to his small fortified island villa in the Lake of Ioánnina. It was not until the closing days of January 1822 that treachery enabled the local commander to have him slaughtered there. The corpse was decapitated and Ali's head exposed outside the Topkapi Sarayi to celebrate the triumph of Mahmud's armies over a chieftain who had defied the authority of five Sultans.[7]

The collapse of Ali's authority allowed the Ottomans to recover military control of land routes on either side of the central Pindus range, southwards to the Peloponnese. By now this region was of vital strategic significance. With the imminent fall of the despotate, a new and more serious challenge had begun to threaten Ottoman rule in the Balkans. Ioánnina had never been simply the lair of an almost sophisticated brigand. Henry Holland, visiting the 'inland city surrounded by mountains' in 1812, commented both on the widespread continental connections of the Greek merchants there, and on the high level of cultural life: 'The Greeks of Ioánnina are celebrated among their countrymen for their literary habits', he wrote, somewhat surprisingly.[8] Ali never permitted local communities to take any political initiative, nor was he interested in their spiritual well-being, whether Islamic or Christian. But, though a Muslim Albanian himself, he had allowed the Greeks to assert their cultural national identity, in so far as it existed in the first decades of the nineteenth century. Moreover, he had personal contacts with influential Greek emigrants in Vienna during the Congress. In the last resort, in May 1820, Ali called on the Greeks of the despotate to join him in resisting the Turks. They failed to respond to this appeal. Leading Greek patriots, however, both in the Peloponnese and among emigrant communities abroad, sought to take advantage of Ali's protracted last stand. Accidentally, he advanced the timing of the national rebellion: it was no coincidence that the Greek War of Independence began in 1821 while Ottoman troops were still heavily engaged around Ioánnina.

The Greek rebellion and its consequences shaped Mahmud's policies, directly or indirectly, for the remaining eighteen years of his reign.

Yet the Greek awakening took the Sultan and his viziers by surprise.[9] Until the end of the eighteenth century there had been little awareness of any Hellenistic heritage among those subjects of the Sultan who spoke the Greek language – almost one in four of the total population of the empire. Officially, the Patriarchate in Constantinople sought to maintain the traditional status of the Orthodox Church as a recognized *millet*, and so too did the wealthy Phanariot aristocracy. But commercial links with France, and in particular with Marseilles, had helped to spread the ideas of the French Revolution on both the mainland and the islands of modern Greece. Greeks who had lived in France encouraged an ideal of Hellenism which stemmed from Classical Greece and had nothing in common with the nostalgic longing of Orthodox believers for the resurrection of a Byzantine Christian society. In combating these dangerous ideas, successive Sultans could therefore count on support from the Patriarchate. In 1798 a 'Paternal Exhortation', circulated in Constantinople in the name of Patriarch Anthimos of Jerusalem, emphasized the role of the Sultan as God's chosen protector of Christian life and denounced the 'teachings of these new liberties' as the work of the Devil. 'The Almighty Lord', it explained, 'puts into the heart of the Sultan of these Ottomans an inclination to keep free the religious beliefs of our Orthodox faith and, as a work of supererogation, to protect them, even to the point of occasionally chastising Christians who deviate from their faith, in order that they may have always before their eyes the fear of God.'[10]

Such ultra-conservative teaching, though effective at the heart of the Empire, carried little weight with the Hellenizing communities in Wallachia and Moldavia, who looked for support from Tsar Alexander I and from his Corfiot adviser, John Capodistrias. This was unrealistic. Despite Alexander's genuine religious zeal, the Tsar would not back any conspiratorial body and Capodistrias, knowing that Alexander had no wish 'to set the cannon moving again', treated all approaches from Greek revolutionaries with extreme caution.[11] Nevertheless it was in the rapidly growing Russian port of Odessa that, in 1814, three Greek merchants founded (or, possibly, revived) a secret 'Society of Friends', *Philiki Hetairia*, to support the liberation of the Balkan peoples from Ottoman rule. Three years later, with the connivance of Russian consular authorities, the *Philiki Hetairia* moved its headquarters to Constantinople. Soon it could count on the support of the principal Greeks in the Mani, on the sympathy of Metropolitan Germanos (Bishop of Old Patras), on the chiefs of certain Christian bandit groups (*klephts*) in the Peloponnese, and on some distinguished

Phanariot officers serving in the Russian army. In March 1821 it was one of these officers who sought to set the Balkans ablaze. General Alexander Ypsilantis, an aide-de-camp of the Tsar, led a handful of Greek patriots from across the Russian frontier in a raid on Bucharest and Jassy.

Ultimately Ypsilantis's raid proved a tragic failure, for the general wrongly counted on the rapid spread of national revolutions against the Sultan throughout Ottoman Europe, a crusade of Orthodoxy which the Tsar would enthusiastically lead. Ypsilantis proposed an alliance with Miloš Obrenović, who in the spring of 1815 had led a second Serbian rebellion against the local tyranny of Janissary commanders and gained considerable autonomy for Serbia from Sultan Mahmud, who saw in Miloš a shrewdly competent vassal. The wily Miloš, hoping for recognition as hereditary Prince of Serbia, had more to lose than to gain by supporting Ypsilantis against the Sultan. The peasantry of Moldavia saw no reason to exchange remote Ottoman sovereignty for a more immediate Greek–Russian rule, and they therefore remained hostile to Ypsilantis's appeals, while the Tsar disowned his aide-de-camp almost immediately. Within three months the Ottoman forces had restored order in the two Danubian Principalities, and Ypsilantis was a fugitive in Austria.

Yet the ill-considered raid had grave repercussions for the Sultan. In the Peloponnese it precipitated the war of independence, symbolically dated from the blessing accorded by Metropolitan Germanos on 25 March to a sacred banner in the monastery of Aghia Lavra. More immediately, the raid led to a panic reaction in Constantinople. The Ottoman army was campaigning, not only against Ali Pasha in Epirus, but also – with little credit – against the Persians along the ill-defined border between Mount Ararat and Lake Van. Mahmud feared lest, at this moment of Ottoman weakness, the Turks should lose Stamboul and Pera. On the last day of March 1821 the British embassy noted the issue of an order for every 'Turk' in Constantinople to procure arms and keep them in his home in case the Greeks should attempt to seize the city by insurrection.[12] At the same time, the Janissary barracks made weapons available for over 12,000 men of the Corps, should they be needed.

Confirmation of the rising against the Ottomans in the Peloponnese was conveyed to the Porte by Lord Strangford, the British ambassador, in a dispatch drafted by his consul in Patras.[13] The news seems almost to have unhinged Mahmud. He was convinced that he was the intended victim of an Orthodox Christian conspiracy, backed by the Russians.

He at once sought a *fetva* from the *şeyhülislâm* proclaiming a Holy War against Greek Christians. But the *şeyhülislâm* was a man of probity. He discussed the crisis with the Ecumenical Patriarch, the septuagenarian Gregorius V, and, to his credit, refused the Sultan's request, a courageous act which almost certainly hastened his supercession before the end of the year and his eventual execution. Gregorius returned from his meeting with the *şeyhülislâm* hoping for a compromise. Already, seven Greek bishops had been imprisoned on the Grand Vizier's orders. On Palm Sunday the Patriarch issued a solemn Anathema, signed by himself and twenty-two other prelates, formally condemning the *Philike Hetairia* and excommunicating Ypsilantis and his principal agents; all 'prelates and priests' were commanded to 'concur with the Church' in opposing the rebellion under penalty of suspension, dispossession and, ultimately, 'the fires of hell'.[14]

Ten years later Mahmud might have shown wiser statecraft, exploiting the formal Anathema to divide his enemies. But, as an Ottoman official told Strangford a few weeks later, the Sultan experienced 'a fit of violent anger and indignation' over the following days, becoming convinced of the Patriarch's complicity. Had not Gregorius been born in the same village as Germanos of Patras, and had he not befriended the rebel Metropolitan when the two dignitaries were both in Constantinople five years earlier? There seemed no doubt to the Sultan that Gregorius was corresponding with insurgent leaders in the Mani and had received letters from Ypsilantis. The news that Greek and Serbian families, technically under the Patriarch's guardianship, had fled the city and boarded ships sailing to Russia, appears finally to have sealed Gregorius's fate.

On Palm Sunday the Anathema was printed and published. On the following Saturday afternoon – 10 April by the Orthodox calendar, 22 April by the Gregorian calendar of western Europe – the Patriarch was officiating at the Liturgy preceding the Solemn Easter Vigil when armed soldiery burst into the patriarchal church, in the Phanar district of Stamboul. As the service ended, they seized the Patriarch and the officiating bishops and priests, still in their robes, and threw ropes around their necks. Gregorius was dragged to the gate of the Phanar quarter, hanged from the staple above the entrance, and allowed slowly to choke to death. For three days his body was left suspended from the gate, his hastily-elected successor having to push it aside before going to the palace to seek confirmation from the Sultan of the dignity bestowed upon him. Three other bishops and two eminent priests were hanged elsewhere in Stamboul. To humiliate the Orthodox

Christians even further, the Sultan finally ordered Gregorius's body to be handed over to a group of Jews, who dragged it by the legs 'through a very dirty market' and cast it, weighted with stones, into the waters of the Golden Horn. 'It is impossible to carry anger, indignation and cruelty to a higher pitch', commented Bartolomeo Pisani: as Strangford's principal dragoman he was the ambassador's chief informant about all that was happening in the city during this terrible Easter week, when inflamed mobs roamed the streets, looting Greek churches and even destroying the patriarchal throne.[15]

'The Councils of this Empire are now directed by a spirit of relentless fanaticism from which the most dreadful results may be expected,' Strangford reported to the Foreign Secretary, Castlereagh, three days after the Patriarch's execution. But the ambassador's mood soon changed. Unlike his Russian and Austrian colleagues, he was consistently sympathetic to Sultan Mahmud. He explained to Castlereagh that the Greeks were being punished as rebels, not as Christians; that 'the Greek clergy were the principal agents and promoters' of the rebellion; and that the Sultan had brought troops into Constantinople to check the wrath of the mob, whose mood Strangford likened to the anti-papist Gordon rioters in London half a century before. Three months after the Patriarch's execution, Strangford was insisting that earlier reports had been much exaggerated: 'Out of a number of 76 churches and chapels in the city and neighbourhood of Constantinople, but one was utterly destroyed and only 13 injured or plundered by the mob.' As evidence that all was now in order, the ambassador commented on the 'disarming' of Turkish children: 'Little miscreants under seven years of age, and armed with daggers and pistols, had till now the privilege of robbing, shooting and stabbing with impunity,' he explained.[16]

Stratford Canning, always confident of outmanoeuvring any Russian diplomat, had regarded the French as the great intriguers at Constantinople; his successor concentrated his mistrust on the Tsar's emissaries. Strangford became the first British ambassador to accept 'the Russian bogey' implicitly, as an article of faith. In this conviction he was grossly unfair to his Russian colleague, Alexis Stroganov, who throughout the Greek crisis showed remarkable restraint. The Holy Synod of the Russian Orthodox Church constantly urged the government in St Petersburg to avenge the insults to the Church by a new war against the Turk. But Tsar Alexander I remained resolutely set against embarking on any expansionist policy so long as his Empire was weakened by problems left unresolved following the

Napoleonic upheaval, and in his relations with the Sultan's ministers Alexis Stroganov skilfully interpreted the Tsar's wishes.[17] He protested strongly against the widespread attacks on Christians in Constantinople, reminding the Porte of the protective rights accorded to his sovereign by the Treaty of Kuchuk Kainardji, and he made ready to leave for Russia; but he chose his words carefully. The Ottoman authorities were left in no doubt that the Tsar deplored rebellion against legitimate government, be it Christian or Muslim. So long as Alexander remained on the throne, Mahmud II discounted the Russian bogey. He was convinced the Greek revolt would be short-lived. Although the coasts of the Peloponnese and Attica and the more prosperous islands might be controlled by Greeks, the rising was ill-coordinated and there was intense rivalry, both between the rebel leaders themselves, and between different regions in the Greek lands. Without Russian intervention it seemed to Mahmud that within a few months his armies would reconquer the Peloponnese and restore order by ruthless repression. Consistently the Ottomans underrated their insurgent opponents.

The Sultan fatally miscalculated in failing to recognize the long-term significance of the Easter killings. In sanctioning the execution of the Patriarch and the vilification of his remains at such a moment in the Church's calendar, Mahmud alienated a quarter of his subjects. The Orthodox Christian *millet* was thrown into permanent opposition to the Sultanate, thereby weakening the Ottoman Empire throughout the last century of its existence. Moreover, Gregorius V continued, in death, to trouble the Ottomans. The Patriarch's body did not decompose in the murky waters of the Golden Horn. Shortly before dusk on one evening in that Easter Week of 1821 it floated to the surface, close to a grain ship trading with Russia. The corpse, and what remained of the vestments, were recognized by a refugee from the patriarchal household who was already aboard the ship. To the Orthodox faithful this reappearance of their martyred Patriarch came as a sign of Divine beneficence. Unobtrusively the Greek master of the vessel recovered the body before sailing for Odessa. There Gregorius was accorded a martyr's funeral. By June he had become the symbol of that Hellenic awakening which he publicly deplored throughout the last troubled months of his life.

Half a century later, when the Russians wished to emphasize the interdependence of the Orthodox churches, Gregorius's bones were translated to his Greek homeland, and his remains have been revered for over 120 years in a tomb still standing near the entrance to the

Metropolitan Cathedral of Athens. However, in the summer of 1821 the religious demonstration in Hetairist Odessa merely confirmed Mahmud II's hostility towards every aspect of the Russian Church. 'The Turks', Bartolomeo Pisani reported, 'consider it a further proof of the uniformity of sentiments, in religion as well as political matters, prevalent between the Russians and the Greeks.'[18] The Sultan, in his anger, threw caution to the wind. He personally ordered all vessels sailing through the Straits to be searched. When he refused to allow the passage of grain ships, it seemed to the diplomats in Constantinople as if another Russo-Turkish conflict was inevitable. Hastily both Strangford and his Austrian colleague intervened: the embargo on the Odessa grain ships was lifted.

By the autumn the crisis in the capital was over. Although Stroganov was recalled to St Petersburg in July, Russia did not declare war on the Ottoman Empire for seven more years; and by then the Eastern Question was posed in an entirely different form. The intermittent clashes of Ottoman troops and Greek rebels were merciless encounters, each side perpetrating acts of cruelty long and bitterly remembered. In July 1822 it seemed as if the Greeks would soon be subdued: at Peta, three miles to the east of Arta, the army which had disposed of Ali Pasha earlier in the year gained a striking victory, restoring to Ottoman rule all of western Greece except for Missolonghi; and at the same time 20,000 of the Sultan's best troops sought to cross the isthmus of Corinth and advance on the Greek strongholds in the Peloponnese. But, to Mahmud's fury, his commanders could make little headway. By the spring of 1823 there was complete stalemate: rival insurgent leaders fought among themselves, but the Sultan could not take advantage of these divisions, for the Greeks had command of the islands and the sea.

At this point Mahmud took a gambler's risk: he turned for help to the most efficient and most ambitious of his vassals, Muhammad Ali. Over the preceding ten years the Viceroy of Egypt had gone from strength to strength, creating in this historic Ottoman dependency the Europeanized-Islamic New Order which Selim III had vainly sought to impose at the heart of his empire. At Sultan Mahmud's request Muhammad Ali had sent disciplined troops to crush Wahhabi revolts in Arabia, ensuring that his army controlled the Holy Cities of Mecca and Medina, in the name of the Sultan-Caliph. Another army, trained by Napoleonic veterans, thrust southwards along the Nile, swelling its number with slaves and in 1822 founding the city of Khartoum. The Viceroy could give his Sultan a well-drilled and disciplined army, a good navy, and an able commander to restore order in Greece as in Arabia. In return, Sultan Mahmud offered Muhammad's son, Ibrahim, considerable power as both Pasha of Crete and Governor of the Peloponnese. The Greek seamen assumed that, although Ibrahim might establish himself in Crete, he would not attempt a sea crossing in winter. They were wrong. In February 1825 Ibrahim landed some 10,000 men, with horses and artillery, at Modon, in the southern Peloponnese. A co-ordinated grand strategy ensured that, at the same time, the Greeks were attacked from the north by the regular Ottoman army.[19]

At first it seemed as if Ibrahim would gain a speedy victory. In the Peloponnese only Nauplion successfuly resisted the Egyptian assault. But in western Greece Missolonghi defied a siege by a predominantly Turkish army until April 1826, when Ibrahim himself crossed the Gulf and took the town where Byron had died two years earlier. The legendary association of Missolonghi with those last heroic months of 'the noblest spirit in Europe' made it certain that Ibrahim's intervention would revive old prejudices in Britain and in France, where philhellenic sentiment was growing rapidly. Reports from merchants and consuls in the Peloponnese emphasized the devastation caused by Ibrahim's 'inhuman barbarians' as they set fire to villages and small towns along their line of march. As early as July 1825 the Greek provisional government had asked for British protection, relying on the apparent sympathy of the Foreign Secretary, George Canning, and on the influence of the City of London, where a Greek loan of £800,000 had been floated nine months before. The long-disputed Ionian Islands had passed under British protection in 1815 by agreement among the four Great Powers. A unilateral assurance of protection for the whole of Greece was more than any British statesman could give, but the Foreign Secretary was unwilling to stand aside and leave the fate of the Greeks to be decided in Constantinople – or St Petersburg. Accordingly, in the winter of 1825–6 the British and Russian governments – though at heart mutually suspicious – came gradually to accept the need for joint mediation between the Sultan and his rebellious Christian subjects. The Duke of Wellington, in Russia for the funeral of Tsar Alexander I, signed an agreement with Count Nesselrode in early April 1826 which provided for mediation 'in the contest of which Greece and the Archipelago are the theatre', and for the creation of an autonomous Greek state within the Ottoman Empire. At the same time George Canning sent his cousin Stratford back to Constantinople as ambassador, but with instructions to pursue

in 1824 ?

a devious policy. 'Exaggerate, if you can, the danger from Russia,' 'Stratty' was told.[20]

Yet, so far as Mahmud II was concerned, by the spring of 1826, the Greek rebellion was at an end. Muhammad Ali's modernized military machine brought the victory which had so long eluded the traditional Ottoman regiments and the Janissaries. The Sultan was therefore faced with two urgent – and inter-related – tasks: to free himself from dependence upon his Egyptian vassals, father and son; and to emulate Muhammad Ali's example in Cairo by imposing a series of drastic reforms on the imperial capital. He sought to consolidate central authority and, at the same time, to sweep away the archaic institutions which hindered westernization by their vested interest in retaining obsolete practices. But, to avoid provoking the reaction which had frustrated the efforts of earlier reformers, he had to move with caution. As a preliminary step to ensuring success Mahmud wooed the *ulema*, hoping to silence any doubts over his zeal for the faith. New mosques were built, and religious establishments which had fallen into decay were revived. In November 1825 Mahmud secured the appointment of the energetic and personally loyal Mehmed Tahir Effendi as *şeyhülislâm*. He was a natural reformer, a Grand Mufti who had no intention of allowing local imams to behave as though they were Janissary commanders at prayer.

The Janissary Corps remained the greatest obstacle to Europeanization. When Byron and his friend Hobhouse arrived in Constantinople in 1810 they found themselves residents of a Janissary-ordered city. Foreigners lived, for the most part, in the derisively nicknamed 'Pig Quarter' of Pera, the district where foreign Christians might eat pork; and in Pera every ambassador had an *orta* (battalion) of Janissaries assigned to his service, providing – on paper – a body of 200 delegated protectors for his nationals. In reality, as Hobhouse wrote, 'there are not more than four or five in constant attendance.'[21] But the *orta* would assemble speedily 'upon any requisite emergency'. Even the fire brigade was under Janissary control. Most blazes in the capital were blamed on Janissary arsonists, who were alleged to start fires in order to secure payment for extinguishing them. From being the 'formidable foes' of Christendom in the seventeenth century, the Janissaries had degenerated into a privileged social menace. When in late May 1811 the Janissaries mustered for what became their last campaign against a foreign enemy, 13,000 men reported for active service at the barracks in Stamboul, and like their predecessors over so many years duly marched out of the city along the road towards

Edirne and the theatre of war. But by the time the Corps reached Silivri – a mere 35 miles away – they were down to 1,600 men. Some 11,400 deserters had dropped out. Ten years later, when the Greek Revolt began to shake the heart of the empire, the Janissaries had become little more than a body of licensed bandits. 'Time and again the Sultan had passed the pen of pardon over the page of their wrong-doing,' one of Mahmud's court propagandists later explained, in a semi-official chronicle of the most momentous event in his reign.[22]

During the winter of 1825–6 Sultan Mahmud increased the strength of the artillery corps in the capital and in the forts along the Bosphorus. At the same time he planted his own nominees at the head of the Janissary Corps: the first sound disciplinarian – Kara ('Black') Hüseyin – commanded the corps for only eight months in 1823, for the Sultan had hurriedly to remove him to commands in Bursa and İzmit to prevent a Janissary uprising which he was not yet ready to contain; but Kara Hüseyin's successor, Celaleddin Mehmed, prepared the ground more carefully. Hüseyin remained in the vicinity of the capital, and in April 1826 was described by the British ambassador as 'the Pasha of the Bosphorus'. He 'has manifested his energy by a most unsparing execution of refractory Janissaries,' Stratford Canning commented.[23]

Mahmud was determined to avoid his predecessor's mistake of 1807: having provoked the Janissaries to insurrection, Selim found he lacked the armed might to keep order in the capital. By May 1826 Mahmud was confident that most senior officers were sympathetic to reform, and at the end of the month he required the Corps to accept a European code of drill, European uniforms, and training in the use of rifles. For over a fortnight resentment at this new attempt to impose order and discipline smouldered in the ranks, but the natural rebels within the Corps had no leaders, nor any plan of resistance. On 5 June the Grand Vizier appeared at a parade in the braided jacket and tight trousers which were accepted dress among officers of the European armies. It was announced that the Sultan would review the Janissaries, in their new uniforms and drilled in westernized form, on 18 June, a Sunday. Drilling for the parade finally exasperated the Janissaries. On the Wednesday evening the junior officers of five Janissary *orta* gathered in At Meydani, the old Hippodrome, a time-honoured place of assembly. They demanded the immediate withdrawal of the army reforms. Their troops in the neighbouring barracks were encouraged to overturn the soup cauldrons, a traditional signal of revolt.

'I had not long been in bed when my sleep was interrupted by the sudden appearance of a dragoman, who announced that the Janissaries "were up",' Stratford recalled in later years.[24] Despite Mahmud's precautions it seemed at first as if the Janissaries would soon secure control of Stamboul. But Mahmud was at Beşiktaş rather than in the old palace when the revolt began, and Kara Hüseyin was able to bring considerable reinforcements and twenty-five cannon down the Bosphorus to command the approaches to the Topkapi Sarayi. Moreover, whereas on earlier occasions the Stamboul mob had invariably backed the rebels, in 1826 the mass of the population failed to respond to the usual xenophobic appeals, probably because the *ulema* were solidly behind the Sultan. Only poorer artisans, afraid of losing their meagre livelihood from ancient crafts if 'westernization' continued, supported the Janissaries. They were strong enough to attack the Porte itself, but the threat of Kara Hüseyin's cannon halted them short of the old palace. By Thursday noon the Janissaries had fallen back on their At Meydani barracks.

'The weather was hot, and we dined at an early hour,' Stratford recalled some years later, describing the scene from the Pera embassy; 'My seat at table fronted the windows which commanded a view of Stamboul beyond the Golden Horn, and I had scarce taken my place when I observed two slender columns of smoke rising above the opposite horizon. What could they mean? I asked, and the reply informed me that the Sultan's people had fired the barracks of the Janissaries, who had no resource but to fly.' In a thirty-minute bombardment of the barracks and the old concourse of the Hippodrome, many hundreds of Janissaries perished. Others, taken prisoner, were swiftly executed. 'The mere name of Janissary, compromised or not by an overt act, operated like a sentence of death,' Stratford wrote. Summary executions took place throughout the Friday, too. Hüseyin's gunners escorted the Sultan to the weekly *selamlik* prayers, trailing through the filthy streets captured soup-kettles and Janissary flags and emblems. 'Things continue in a violent combustion, or rather a merciless inquisition, for every corner of the town is searched,' Bartolomeo Pisani reported that day. 'No quarter is given to anyone.'[25]

Out in the provinces most Janissaries prudently chose to conform rather than to resist the new Ottoman march of progress, although cannon were brought into action against dissidents in both İzmit and Edirne. On Saturday, 17 June 1826, the Janissary Corps was formally abolished. So limited and localized was the resistance of the Janissaries that in retrospect it seems extraordinary that no previous sultan had turned the cannon on them. Mahmud's success came not merely from his employment of the ruthless Kara Hüseyin, but from the skill with which he had already isolated the Corps from the *ulema*, who in the past had so frequently stirred up the mob in the capital.

There are wild variations in the estimates of the dead in the Empire as a whole. The Sultan promised life pensions to Janissaries wise enough to have kept out of trouble during these momentous days, but so many applicants were speedily killed on trumped-up charges that those with a sure instinct for survival preferred to forgo their claims. Eight executioners were kept fully employed throughout the second half of June. Stratford Canning thought about 6,000 had perished; he was probably right, although several sources put the figure far higher. Contemporary Turkish writers, recognizing the liquidation of the Janissaries as a landmark in Ottoman history, gave these events a euphemistic respectability by referring to them collectively as 'The Auspicious Incident', an episode which held out a promise of future success for the Sultan. But to foreign residents on the Bosphorus the blood-bath of June 1826 came as a dramatic end rather than an auspicious beginning. 'The sanguinary measures . . . have struck a panic throughout the nation,' wrote the British ambassador. 'A main source of the greatness and glory of the Ottoman Empire' had gone, he reported; and he added, without too much conviction, 'The Sultan must show that he can sheath the sword when justice is satisfied.'[26]

CHAPTER 7

Egyptian Style

With the Janissaries no longer threatening any ruler who 'opened the gate of the East to new life', the Sultanate enjoyed a rare sense of security. Soon Mahmud II felt able to impose the changes in administration, government and society which he had sought since his accession, and the last thirteen years of his reign stand out as an era of reform. He died, however, bitterly frustrated. Unresolved problems in the Eastern Question and the growing menace of Muhammad Ali's Egypt halted his revolution from above when it had completed no more than its first quarter-turn towards the West.

Yet the list of Mahmud's achievements in these years still makes impressive reading. Both the army and navy were modernized; an official Court Gazette was published, regularly in Turkish and occasionally in French (*Le Moniteur Ottoman*); new government departments (embryonic 'ministries') were set up – Justice, Civil Administration, Finance, Trade, and Religious Foundations among them. The Sultan himself appeared in westernized uniform – 'Egyptian style', as Stratford Canning interestingly described it, for there was no doubt that Mahmud continued to follow trends set by Muhammad Ali, however much he might mistrust his ambition.[1] Fluency in French became essential for those who sought advancement in Ottoman service, civil or military. It was not only the soldiery who changed their appearance: for court functionaries and civil servants a frock coat, black trousers and fez replaced the flowing robes and turban of the past. Soon the particular cut of the frock coat ensured that it had a name of its own, the stambouline, identifiable in Paris and in London.

Some changes sprang directly from the liquidation of the Janissaries. There were fine pickings from the Corps' properties, enabling the Sultan to reward the most loyal of his supporters. Mehmed Tahir

Effendi was given the former home of the Janissary *Aga* as an official residence for the *şeyhülislâm*. Kara Hüseyin was accorded the courtesy title of Aga Pasha and appointed Commander-in-Chief (*serasker*) of the new Ottoman Army, which was proleptically honoured with the name *Asakir-i Mansure-i Muhammediye* (Victorious Soldiers of Muhammad). The *serasker*, too, received an official residence: Beyazit, the first palace the Ottomans had built after capturing Constantinople. Once modernized, it served as the Ministry of War until the fall of the Empire. Soon after taking up office Hüseyin received Mahmud's permission to build there the marble tower for fire-watchers still prominent on the İstanbul skyline.

There was, of course, in many of these reforms, an element of window-dressing. But other changes went to the heart of Ottoman society. It was logical to follow the destruction of the Janissaries with the abolition of the last feudal obligations, and in 1831 the *timar* system – which Selim III had drastically modified by his creation of *iltizam* leases – was finally swept away, with some 2,500 military fiefs becoming imperial domain and being leased out to tax-farmers. The *sipahis*, as antiquated a fighting force as the Janissaries, were either pensioned off or embodied in the new army, where they provided four squadrons of cavalry. More radical were Mahmud's sustained attempts to 'nationalize' the *vakif* so as to ensure that revenue from the *evkaf* pious foundations was supervised by the state. This reform, possible only so long as the Sultan-Caliph and the *şeyhülislâm* worked together in close co-operation, remained incomplete, although Mahmud did extend governmental intrusion into *vakif* affairs by setting up his Ministry of Religious Foundations.[2]

Mahmud II was also conscious of the need to stimulate the economic life of his empire, particularly in the provinces which constitute present-day Turkey. Towards the end of his reign he established a Council of Agriculture and Trade, which he intended should discuss ways of developing subsistence farming into a productive industry and of promoting the export market. In the early years of the reform era his main concern was, by a secure system of communications, to safeguard internal trade from brigandage. Traditional routes were repaired until they resembled roads, and an embryonic Ottoman postal service was set up. It linked the capital with İzmit and soon afterwards with Edirne, along specially protected 'postal roads'. But overland communication was difficult before the age of railways, particularly in Anatolia. An empire which possessed some five thousand miles of shoreline and a multiplicity of small natural harbours had long accepted coastal shipping as the principal form of commercial transport, to the great benefit of the Phanariots. From 1826 onwards Sultan Mahmud encouraged the building of a merchant fleet which would no longer depend upon Greek seamanship.

Briefly the Sultan hoped his Turkish subjects would pioneer steamships in home waters. On 20 May 1828, amid great excitement from astonished onlookers, the first steam-boat chugged confidently up-current to anchor off Galata.[3] She was a British vessel, the *Swift*, and – together with another London-built ship – was soon purchased by the Sultan, who retained the English officers to train Turkish crews in steam-navigation and engineering; but this experiment was not a success. By the end of the reign British steam tugs plied the Bosphorus, British and Austrian steamships ran a joint service between Constantinople and Trebizond, and in the last fortnight of May 1837 regular and competing Austrian and French steamships linked Constantinople with Trieste (in fourteen days) and Marseilles (in ten). Although these contacts – and shorter inshore voyages by British, Italian, Greek and Russian ships – improved the empire's foreign trade, little of it was carried in Turkish vessels, despite the Sultan's early patronage. The Ottoman coastal steamship line, for which Mahmud had enthusiastically purchased several vessels, did not begin a regular service until five years after his death. As so often in his reign, he saw what needed to be done, but his subjects lacked the skills to attain what he asked of them.

Yet in foreign affairs Mahmud II was not so clear-sighted. His reform era coincided with a succession of defeats in statecraft more humiliating than any predecessor had sustained. The Greek revolt, which the Sultan believed to have been ended in the spring of 1826 with Ibrahim's entry into Missolonghi, was far from over; and the ambitious Muhammad Ali was prepared to turn Ibrahim's army against the Sultan if the Ottoman state showed signs of beginning to slip into quick decline.

After the fall of Missolonghi the Greek revolt became a klephtic war, the local variant of guerrilla resistance. Patriot groups in the mountains would launch raids on Ottoman positions, their leaders seeking and securing temporary truces whenever the situation began to look desperate. Isolated Greek garrisons still held out – Athens until the summer of 1827, for example. Ambitiously-named 'national assemblies' met in towns or islands beyond the reach of Ibrahim's troops: the best-known of these assemblies met at Epidaurus in the early spring of 1826, while during February 1827 there were rival assemblies at Kastri, in the eastern Peloponnese, and on Aegina. But the most active resistance came from groups of philhellene volunteers, many of them French or British although coming from some ten other countries, too. Occasionally, serving British and French naval and army officers stretched neutrality into an unauthorized co-belligerence. It was a curious situation, puzzling to the rival combatant forces and exasperating to the statesmen of the Great Powers who, since the Congress of Vienna, had been seeking to introduce a disciplined orderliness into the conduct of international diplomacy.

Both Greeks and Turks exaggerated the influence of these phil-hellenes on their governments in London and Paris. Yet it could not be discounted. George Canning – who shaped British diplomacy from September 1822 to August 1827 as Foreign Secretary and, for the last three months of his life, as Prime Minister – was not prepared to rush into war on behalf of the Greeks. But he was alarmed by rumours that Ibrahim intended to exterminate the Greek population in the Peloponnese and set up Muslim military colonies there, and he was aware of strong 'anti-Turk' prejudice among his liberal Tory sup-porters, a curious blend resulting from classical learning, commercial interest, and the deeply-rooted conviction that Ottoman troops on the march were, and always had been, a marauding horde of plunderers and incendiarists.

Canning recognized that the Russians held the key to any solution of the Eastern Question, for only the Tsar could put both military and naval pressure on the Porte. At the same time, to restrain Russia it would be better to work with Nicholas I than against him. Canning therefore wished to implement as soon as possible the St Petersburg Convention of April 1826, which had accepted the need for Anglo-Russian mediation to create a Greek autonomous state. But it was by no means clear that the Tsar was still interested in Greek affairs. Throughout the summer of 1826 Russian and Ottoman diplomats held talks in Akkerman, a small town near Odessa, now named Ovidiopol to honour an earlier resident. The resultant Convention of Akkerman (7 October 1826) gave Russia greater control over the internal adminis-tration of the Danubian Principalities and concessions along the disputed frontier in the Caucasus. It also reaffirmed the right of the Serbs to autonomy, but it made no reference to Greece. Mahmud seems to have hoped that, in settling other problems, the Convention would rule out a Russian crusade on behalf of the Orthodox Greeks. Here he miscalculated: the Convention enabled Nesselrode to concen-trate solely on the Greek Question in long negotiations with the British and French. In July 1827 a new Treaty of London committed Britain, France and Russia, not only to recognize an autonomous Greece, but to induce the Sultan to accept an armistice by concentrating a combined fleet in Greek waters.[4]

Never before had warships of these three Great Powers collaborated as allies: never again did they do so until 1915, at the Dardanelles. Not that George Canning thought the guns need open fire: the naval presence was a deterrent, and armed diplomacy would ensure a settlement rather than prevarication. A secret emissary was sent to Cairo to talk to Muhammad Ali directly, in case the Sultan's ministers played for time. But all these plans were thrown into confusion by George Canning's death on the day that news of the treaty reached Constantinople. When the Porte scorned the proposed allied mediation, Stratford Canning encouraged the naval commander to exercise a freedom of action which his cousin had never envisaged. On 20 October 1827 Vice-Admiral Sir Edward Codrington led twenty-four British, French and Russian warships into Navarino bay, where eighty-one Turkish and Egyptian vessels rode at anchor off Ibrahim's main supply base in the Peloponnese.

Responsibility for what happened next remains uncertain.[5] In Britain it has long been maintained that Codrington wished to persuade Ibrahim to embark his troops and sail off to Alexandria while the allies imposed an armistice, and that the battle of Navarino began only when a fireship was sighted bearing down upon the allied squadron. Ottoman historians claim that Codrington had sought for many days to lure the Turco-Egyptian fleet into battle on the open seas, and that the fireship was intended to scatter ships which had established an illegal blockade along the Greek coast. But whatever the immediate cause of the battle, the allied bombardment was decisive. Within three hours two-thirds of the Ottoman-Egyptian fleet was sunk, with the loss of 8,000 lives. Navarino was therefore an even greater disaster for the Sultan's navy than Çeşme in 1770, although the impact was lessened by the fact that Codrington destroyed mainly old and decaying warships: Mahmud's ambitious naval reform programme had been launched only four weeks before. By cutting off supplies from Crete and Egypt, Codrington ensured the eventual triumph of the Greek cause. French troops landed in the Peloponnese and supervised the evacuation of Ibrahim's army; and when, thirteen weeks after the battle, that stormy petrel John Capodistrias reached Nauplion as Greece's first President, he came ashore from one of Codrington's ships, HMS *Warspite*, which was symbolically escorted into Greek waters by a Russian and a French veteran of Navarino.

Wise statecraft might have secured Mahmud a compromise settlement after Navarino, enabling him to anticipate and avoid new challenges to the survival of the Ottoman State. But, as at Easter 1821, the Sultan's hot temper led him into another act of folly. The Muslim faithful were called to arms in order to resist the combined onslaught of the Russians and the Greeks and, shortly after Capodistrias reached Nauplion, the Sultan ordered the closure of the Straits to all foreign ships. The long-anticipated Russo-Turkish War followed at the end of April 1828, even though Mahmud and his ministers knew how limited were their resources. The new Ottoman army, 'The Victorious Forces of Muhammad', was still in training; and Mahmud could not rely on further help from Muhammad Ali, who had received little reward for the great expenditure incurred by Ibrahim's expedition to Crete and the Peloponnese. In declaring war on the Ottoman Empire, Tsar Nicholas convinced himself that a spring campaign in the Balkans would ensure rapid victory.

He was mistaken. His armies advanced into eastern Anatolia, took Kars, and were welcomed by the Armenian Christians as liberators from Muslim rule. In the Balkans three Russian columns reached the Danube south of Bucharest, but they encountered strong resistance around Silistria and Ruschuk and it was not until the following summer that they penetrated the Balkan mountains. August 1829 was a black month for Sultan Mahmud: in the east one Russian army had taken Erzerum and threatened Trebizond, on the Black Sea; and, less than 150 miles from his capital, a second Russian army captured Edirne after a three-day siege. Some cavalry units even reached the Aegean coast. Hurriedly the Porte sought the mediation of the Great Powers; and it was at Edirne on 14 September 1829 that a peace treaty was signed (generally known as the Treaty of Adrianople, the city's Byzantine name).

A senseless war, which a Sultan of less pride and greater moral courage need never have waged, was followed by a peace settlement which left the core of Ottoman lands intact.[6] The Treaty of Adrianople allowed the Russian frontier to creep southwards in the Caucasus to include all Georgia, but Erzerum and Kars were evacuated and in Europe the Tsar pulled back his troops north of the river Pruth. The Sultan at last accepted the Anglo-Russian proposals for an autonomous Greece, although with its boundaries as yet undefined. In a show of Slav solidarity, the Russians secured concessions for their Serb brethren. Although an Ottoman garrison remained in Belgrade,

Serbian autonomy became a reality; Miloš Obrenović was invested as hereditary Prince of Serbia by Mahmud II eleven months later and the administration was handed over to the Prince's nominees. The harshest clauses required payment over ten years of an extremely high war indemnity, equivalent in total to twice the annual budget of the whole Ottoman Empire. Moreover, although the Russian armies were to evacuate the Balkans, the Sultan had to accept demilitarization of his frontier along the Danube and the Pruth, a provision which would ensure a rapid return of Russian troops in the event of any renewal of the war. Tsar Nicholas was satisfied that the peace settlement gave Russia the choice of preserving the Ottoman Empire or of breaking it into fragments. Already, in the last weeks of the war, he had set up a six-man committee in St Petersburg to map out the future course of Russo-Turkish relations.

The committee reported to Nicholas I two days after the peace treaty was signed: to destroy the Ottoman Empire would be to invite Austria, France and Great Britain to secure footholds in the Balkans and the Levant, thereby (wrote Nesselrode) forcing Russia 'to plunge into a labyrinth of difficulty and complications each more inextricable than the other'.[7] The Tsar accepted the need to preserve the Ottoman Empire; only if it seemed about to collapse would Russia need (in his own words) 'to ensure that the exit from the Black Sea is not seized by any other Power'. Mahmud and his ministers knew nothing of these deliberations in St Petersburg, but they soon became aware that their traditional enemy was showing a rare benevolence; even the hated war indemnity was cut, in return for minor frontier concessions. Moreover, when the Navarino coalition decided on total independence for the Greeks, not merely autonomy, it was the Russians who insisted on negotiating the revised settlement, rather than imposing it on the Sultan under threat of force. In February 1830 the London Protocol set up a sovereign Greek kingdom guaranteed by Russia, Great Britain and France as Protecting Powers, although not until 1832 did a German prince (Otto of Bavaria) accept the Greek crown.

The new kingdom was small. The Ottoman frontier ran barely 130 miles north of Athens, leaving most of modern Greece under Mahmud's rule. Yet the creation of an independent state out of part of his empire was an ominous precedent. Moreover, though the Greek War was over, its aftermath frustrated Mahmud's attempts at westernizing his empire. Muhammad Ali expected territorial compensation for Ibrahim's long campaigns – Syria, perhaps? The Viceroy possessed natural shrewdness and coldly calculating gifts of patience. His son, a fine military commander, had none of these gifts; caution was to him a sign of weakness. In November 1831 Ibrahim crossed the Gaza desert and, with offshore support from a reconstituted navy, thrust northwards along Bonaparte's old line of march, taking Jaffa, Jerusalem and Haifa, until he reached the formidable bastion of Acre which, once again besieged, defied him for eight months. By mid-summer in 1832 the whole of Syria and Lebanon was in Egyptian hands; and by July, when the Viceroy persuaded his son to halt his advance, the invaders were approaching Antioch and Alexandretta (İskenderun).

Although Mahmud proclaimed Muhammad Ali and Ibrahim rebels and traitors, the Viceroy insisted that he remained the Sultan's loyal subject and that he only sought compensation in Syria for the services he had rendered the Ottoman state. With the Egyptian army encamped in the plain of Issos – where Alexander the Great once defeated Darius – there was a flurry of diplomatic activity around the Porte and the Constantinople embassies. A compromise settlement would have permitted Mahmud to press ahead with the material improvements he sought at the heart of his empire: the building of new houses, bridges, roads and schools; and especially, in these later years, the reconstruction of Christian villages destroyed during the fanatical conflicts of the previous decade. But neither the Sultan nor the Sultanate had changed in character: three prominent ministers fell suddenly from favour, and were executed as swiftly and as mercilessly as Kara Mustafa a century and a half before; and Mahmud's personal pride and confidence in his new army made him unwilling to offer concessions to Muhammad Ali. The Sultan was, however, prepared to look abroad for support. Early in November 1832 Lord Palmerston, by then in his third year as Foreign Secretary, received a request from Mahmud for naval assistance against the Egyptians; but the Royal Navy was already more heavily committed outside the Mediterranean than Palmerston's cheese-paring cabinet colleagues thought desirable, and the Foreign Secretary took no action, apart from supporting a remonstrance urging Muhammad Ali 'forthwith to retire to Egypt and rest content with that fertile country'.[8]

Ibrahim, however, would neither withdraw nor wait any longer on events. He resumed his advance, penetrating the Taurus range. In December 1832 his troops routed an Ottoman force outside Konya, taking the Grand Vizier prisoner. By the first days of February the Egyptian vanguard was at Kutahiya, deep into Anatolia, and less than two hundred miles from the Bosphorus. Mahmud, desperate to defend his capital, sought aid from the most formidable of his neighbours: three flotillas of Russian warships were invited to sail down the Bosphorus to moorings off the Golden Horn. They were followed by a Russian expeditionary force which established advanced headquarters on the Asiatic shore of the Bosphorus at Hünkar İskelesi, a bay some twelve miles up the straits from Constantinople and generally transliterated as Unkiar Skelessi. By early April nearly 30,000 Russians were deployed in defence of Mahmud's capital, with a camp at Büyükdere on the European shore as well as at Unkiar Skelessi.

The Russian presence alarmed the *ulema*, producing the first serious grumblings of discontent with Mahmud's policies since the bloody suppression of the Janissaries seven years before. But the Tsar's intervention made it certain that the other Great Powers would soon take an interest in a crisis which they had tended to regard as an Ottoman domestic affair. British and French naval squadrons cruised off the Dardanelles in June. By then, however, the original crisis was over: Muhammad Ali accepted French mediation; Ibrahim's army would withdraw from Anatolia in return for confirmation of Muhammad Ali's status as Governor of Egypt and Crete, while Ibrahim would become Governor of Damascus, Aleppo and Adana. Both father and son remained technically the Sultan's vassals, Muhammad Ali having rejected Ibrahim's pleas to insist that the settlement should grant them total independence.

Throughout the early summer of 1833 the Russians remained military masters of Constantinople, for the only time in history. But Nicholas and Nesselrode showed moderation. The Tsar sent to Constantinople a firm, gifted and charming plenipotentiary, his personal friend Count Alexis Orlov, with instructions to seek a lasting treaty with the Porte. Orlov flattered the Turks, high and low alike: generous gifts at the top were matched by the distribution of 24,000 medals, each bearing the Tsar's portrait, to the Turkish soldiery in order to express his Imperial Master's admiration for the courage with which they would no doubt have fought had Ibrahim's army borne down upon them. At the same time, once the Egyptians had pulled back from Anatolia, the Russian fleet sailed away and the tents came down in the huge camp at Unkiar Skelessi. But before the last officer in the military mission left for Odessa an alliance treaty was signed, much to Mahmud's personal satisfaction, for he hoped it would dispel for all time the Russian bogey. Orlov's treaty of Unkiar Skelessi of 8 July 1833 was essentially a pact of mutual Russo-Ottoman assistance in case of attack, valid for eight years. A secret article gave

Russia the right to waive any request for Ottoman assistance, provided the Sultan closed the Dardanelles to 'foreign vessels of war'. Orlov told the Tsar he was perpetuating a Russian protectorate on the Bosphorus. He thought the Russians would be summoned back again within a few years. 'Thanks to our antecedents,' Orlov wrote, the Tsar's troops would be able to return 'without arousing suspicion and . . . in such a way as never to leave again, if need be.'[9]

Nicholas I, Nesselrode and Orlov all believed the treaty was a guarantee of stability and order in Constantinople. It enabled them to control Mahmud, firmly rejecting as early as 1834 the Sultan's attempt to secure Russian backing for a war of revenge against Muhammad Ali. But news of the treaty alarmed Palmerston and his French colleagues: they believed it contained even more drastic secret articles, giving the Russians the right to regulate the passage of ships through the Straits at any time. Palmerston convinced himself that the Tsar was planning the dismemberment of the Ottoman Empire. Russophobia remained rife in the Foreign Office throughout the decade, with fears of the Tsarist agents said to be active in Persia and Afghanistan. The Foreign Secretary had a curious conviction that a forward policy in Central Asia would, in some mysterious way, 'place the Dardanelles more securely out of the grasp of Russia'.[10]

Palmerston also believed in the imminence of another struggle between the Sultan and his vassals in Syria and Egypt. In this he was right; and it proved difficult to restrain Mahmud in 1835 and again a year later, when he sent a secret agent to London, hoping to win active British support for renewal of the war. The army's defeat at Konya had deeply shocked Mahmud, and he convinced himself that it was his duty to avenge an Ottoman defeat by the Albanian tobacco dynasty he had come to despise. Mahmud was only forty-seven at the time of the battle of Konya but he was a sick man, prematurely old from drink and dissipation; and in his last years he became obsessed with the need to complete the military reforms he had always sought. Prussian, Russian, British and French officers were invited to the barracks in Pera and Üsküdar, and to field exercises in Anatolia. By 1837 the Sultan could rely on some 40,000 good infantrymen and six regiments of cavalry, but with artillery weakened because guns of nine different calibres were in use. Most critical was the Sultan's total inability to chose good commanders.

In 1838 Mahmud instructed his ambassador in London to offer Britain generous concessions in a commercial treaty, hoping that the prospect of improved trade would tempt Palmerston into a formal alliance. By the early spring of 1838 it was clear that the British would not give him the support he sought. By now the Sultan, who had long suffered from tuberculosis, knew he could not live much longer, for he was also racked with pain from cirrhosis of the liver. He determined on one last quest for military victory. In mid-April 1839 he ordered Hafiz Pasha to lead an Ottoman army across the Euphrates towards Aleppo, calling on the Syrians to throw off Ibrahim's Egyptian yoke and welcome the Sultan's troops as liberators.

Cautiously Hafiz moved forward. With him were some Prussian advisers, the most senior of them being Major Helmuth von Moltke. At first Ibrahim made no response to the threat from the north; neither did the Syrians rise in rebellion. But Hafiz never reached the borders of Syria. From the town of Nezib (now Nizip) a cloud of dust heralded the approach of Ibrahim's army. Moltke advised Hafiz to await the enemy behind fortified trenches and solid town walls; the *ulema* declared that a rebel must suffer in the open plain. Hafiz listened to the mullahs, not to the future victor of Sadowa and Sedan.

The battle of Nezib – on 24 June 1839 – was short but decisive. The Ottoman vanguard was checked and turned back, throwing the troops immediately in the rear into confusion. The Prussians advised Hafiz to send forward a single unbroken column; he preferred to hack about him, cutting down his own fleeing fugitives in a paroxysm of anger. Every Ottoman field piece was destroyed, or abandoned by its terrified gunners. Ten thousand prisoners passed into Ibrahim's hands. Moltke was fortunate to escape. 'The army of Hafiz Pasha has ceased to exist,' the Prussian wrote contemptuously that night to Berlin. 'The Turks threw down their arms and abandoned their artillery and ammunition, flying in every direction.'[11] Nezib was an even greater disaster for the Ottoman army than Konya.

Fortunately for his peace of mind, Sultan Mahmud was spared knowledge of the defeat. No courier was in a hurry to take the bad news across five hundred miles of mountain to a sick man beside the Bosphorus. On 29 June, five days after the battle, Mahmud II finally drank himself to death. The first grim rumours of defeat were not confirmed until 7 July. By then Mahmud's eldest son, Abdulmecid, had been proclaimed sovereign and caliph. It was an inauspicious moment for a sixteen-year-old prince to accede to the throne.

CHAPTER 8

Sick Man?

Mahmud II's death was made public on 1 July 1839 and within twenty-four hours there was a minor palace revolution in Stamboul. The septuagenarian Mehmed Husrev Pasha seized the Grand Vizier's seals of office (literally) and induced Abdulmecid to confirm him as head of an emergency government. A sixteen-year-old ruler might have fared far worse: although a cynical French ambassador called Husrev the 'master-strangler', he could at least claim a long experience of the Ottoman administrative system.[1] As far back as 1801, Sultan Selim III had appointed him Governor of Egypt, the last before Muhammad Ali, and under Mahmud II he fought in the Peloponnese and against the Persians. For twelve years he was Grand Admiral of the Ottoman fleet and in 1827 he succeeded Hüseyin as *serasker* of the army, a post he held for another ten years. But age had made Husrev an arch-conservative, with many enemies. Like so many pillars of the Ottoman establishment, he had received generous gifts from Orlov at the time of the Unkiar Skelessi Treaty: now – six years later – one eminent rival, Grand Admiral Ahmed Fevzi, convinced himself that Husrev remained in Russian pay. So certain was he of Husrev's likely betrayal of Ottoman interests that he committed an even greater act of treachery himself. Even before news of the Nezib disaster could be confirmed in the capital, Fevzi sailed his fleet across to Alexandria. There he surrendered it to the Viceroy of Egypt, Muhammad Ali.

The odds were therefore stacked heavily against the frail young Sultan: no navy in the Mediterranean; no field army to face Ibrahim in Anatolia. Nor could he hope to find sound currency in the treasury, for that department of state was so troubled with chronic deficits that Mahmud had authorized debasement of the coinage on seventy-two occasions in a thirty-one-year reign. Yet, fortunately, Abdulmecid acceded with two great assets: his mother, the *Valide Sultana* Bezmialem; and a promise of loyal support from the most skilled of his father's westernizing reformers, Mustafa Reşid, who was a special envoy in London at the time of Mahmud's death.[2]

Bezmialem, a Georgian said to have been a bath-attendant before entering the imperial harem, was only fifteen when she gave birth to Abdulmecid. At thirty-one she was still young enough to despise and mistrust the elder non-statesman who had made himself chief minister. She advised her son to allow Husrev to incur the odium of seeking terms from Muhammad Ali but urged him to resist the Grand Vizier's attempts to advance his nominees to important offices of state. Abdulmecid duly played for time, awaiting Reşid's return from England before taking any major decisions on policy. His mother had given him sound counsel. So shrewd was her judgement of men and their motives that the *Valide Sultana* continued to influence the choice of ministers until shortly before her death fourteen years later.

Bezmialem recommended Reşid to Abdulmecid because she believed he understood what Mahmud had been seeking to achieve in his reform programme. But Reşid had qualities of his own, too. By 1839 his command of French was so good that he could converse with King Louis Philippe without an interpreter. He had met Palmerston in London and Metternich in Vienna, and he knew what Europe thought of the Ottoman Empire. Of equal value to the Sultan was a mission Reşid had undertaken to Egypt four years before, enabling him to see for himself the kingly authority Muhammad Ali exercised in Cairo and Alexandria. Abdulmecid appointed Reşid as Foreign Minister, retaining Husrev as Grand Vizier until June 1840. But it was Reşid who, with a sound instinct for cultivating goodwill in Westminster and Paris, persuaded Abdulmecid to allow him to make the first dramatic public gesture of the reign, the promulgation on 3 November 1839 of the Imperial Rescript of the Rose Chamber.

The occasion was described by several ambassadors and other foreign visitors to Constantinople.[3] All the higher dignitaries of Ottoman society, together with foreign envoys accredited to the Sublime Porte, gathered in the Gülhane ('Rose Chamber') gardens beyond the outer wall of the Topkapi Sarayi. There, in front of Grand Vizier Husrev, Reşid read out their sovereign's first 'Noble Rescript', with Abdulmecid looking down on the assembly from a window of the Gülhane kiosk itself. The 'Gülhane Decree' let the outer world know it was Abdulmecid's intention to reign as an enlightened Sultan. He would protect the lives and property of his subjects, introduce a code of justice asserting the

equal status of Muslims, Christians and Jews before the law, institute
a regular system of assessing and levying taxes; and he undertook to
enhance and respect the consultative legislative councils favoured by
his father, and to develop a fair method of conscripting his subjects for
service in a modernized army and navy.

The ceremony in the Gülhane gardens, with the westernizing Foreign
Minister prostrating himself twice before his Sultan and Caliph,
impressed the foreign observers as Reşid had anticipated it would.
'Theatrical' but successful, was the Russian envoy's verdict. 'A victorious answer to those who say that this Empire cannot be saved by its
ancient Government,' Lord Ponsonby, the British ambassador, commented two days later in a dispatch to Palmerston. An event 'fraught
with incalculable advantage', the Foreign Secretary replied early in
December; 'A grand stroke of policy, and it is producing great effect on
public feeling here and in France.'[4] Both Ponsonby and Palmerston
had in mind the mounting impatience of the Russians with their
Ottoman neighbour, and the inclination of successive governments in
Paris to back Muhammad Ali in building up a financially viable and
independent Egyptian state. Any move by the Sultan which indicated
renewed vigour at the centre of his empire was welcome. For another
three decades Ottoman decline was checked by a parallel process: the
imposition of westernizing changes upon traditional society at home;
and the bolstering of the imperial structure by other Great Powers
seeking stability in order to stave off drastic revision of the map of
Europe.

At first the renewal of war between the Sultan and Muhammad Ali
in the spring of 1839 had tempted Nicholas I to intervene with warships and soldiers. Surely, he argued, this provided the opportunity
Orlov had foreseen in 1833, the moment when a Russian expeditionary force would be hailed on the Bosphorus as returning guardians of
the Straits? Nesselrode was more realistic. Patiently, and with a cold
reappraisal of the imperial state debt, he persuaded the Tsar not to risk
all the uncertainty and expense of unilateral action. Thereafter Russia,
Austria, Prussia, France and Great Britain appeared to act in concert; on 27 July 1839 a collective Note from the ambassadors of the
five Powers indicated their wish to arbitrate in the Ottoman–Egyptian
War. This willingness of 'Europe' to impose a settlement in the Levant
came as welcome news for Reşid on his arrival home from London. It
enabled him to stiffen Abdulmecid's resistance to a peace party at court
which favoured accepting, as speedily as possible, whatever demands
Muhammad Ali might make.

Yet while the five Great Powers were prepared to recognize Muhammad Ali as the head of a new Egyptian dynasty, there was little cohesion among them.[5] Austria, whose policy was still shaped by Metternich (Foreign Minister since 1809), favoured the maintenance and strengthening of the Sultan's authority for two main reasons: a stable government in Constantinople would extend the trade concessions already enjoyed by steamship companies and mining concerns to other Austrian enterprises; while conversely, and of greater significance in Vienna, the disintegration of the Ottoman Empire would unleash Balkan nationalism, thereby threatening the existence of the multinational Habsburg monarchy. The Prussians closely followed the policy of their Austrian ally, although in the Berlin newspapers there was a certain grudging admiration for Ibrahim's victorious army.

French diplomacy backed Muhammad Ali. The happy coincidence that he had been born at Kavalla under the same zodiacal sign of the same year as Bonaparte at Ajaccio was duly noted; 'Napoleonic Legend' romanticism was in fashion that summer. More prosaically, Parisian bankers hoped they might turn Muhammad Ali's lands into a commercial satrapy dominating the Levant. For a variety of motives, the French therefore sought the inclusion of Syria and Lebanon – as well as the Arabian peninsula – in the territories of which he was overlord.

No other government agreed with the French. Palmerston feared that Muhammad Ali's efficient army would threaten the shortest route to India; and complained that his monopoly of trade in the vast area over which he asserted Egyptian sovereignty would deprive the City of London of advantages accruing from the Anglo-Turkish commercial treaty which Sultan Mahmud had accepted ten months before his death. Tsar Nicholas I – or, rather, State Chancellor Nesselrode – also mistrusted Muhammad Ali's ambitions. The Russians had good grounds for believing he was contemplating a grand alliance with the Persians, aimed at extending his empire into Mesopotamia in return for assisting the Qājár Shah in Teheran to undermine the Tsar's hold over the Muslims of the Caucasus and Turkestan. There was sufficient hostility to Muhammad Ali and his dynasty in both London and St Petersburg to foster an Anglo-Russian entente which was suspicious of the French and, since it was prepared to bolster up the Ottoman Empire as long as possible, could count on Austrian and Prussian support.

London now became a pivot for statesmen seeking to solve the Eastern Question. Nicholas I sent a special envoy with proposals for joint pressure on Muhammad Ali and for international agreement over closure of the Straits (the Dardanelles and the Bosphorus) to foreign warships in time of peace. At first the British cabinet disliked the idea of associating two dissimilar problems in a single agreement. But Nicholas persisted, and in July 1840 British, Russian, Austrian, Prussian and Ottoman plenipotentiaries concluded the Treaty of London, which closed the Straits to foreign warships in time of peace and presented a virtual ultimatum to Muhammad Ali.[6] He was required to submit to the Sultan's authority and settle for hereditary rule over Egypt, or else face joint intervention by the Great Powers. If he accepted these terms within twenty days he would also receive the right to administer Acre and southern Syria as Governor for life.

The Egyptians still had a formidable army: thirty-eight infantry regiments, more than ten thousand cavalry horses, and an artillery corps trained by Napoleonic veterans. It was spread over a huge area of the Levant and Crete, but Muhammad Ali also believed he could count on French naval support. Accordingly, he rejected the allied demand, thereby automatically forfeiting the offer of southern Syria. But he had gravely miscalculated the balance of forces. The French fleet did not intervene, leaving British and Austrian warships free to harry Ibrahim's vulnerable line of communications. They bombarded the Lebanese coast in September and October 1840, while British and Austrian marines and Turkish infantry supported Druze rebels in the hills north of Beirut. As Ibrahim's well-disciplined troops began to pull back towards the borders of Egypt, a British squadron bombarded and occupied Acre. Other ships blockaded the Egyptian coast.

The crisis was soon over. On 5 November Muhammad Ali concluded the Convention of Alexandria, which provided for the evacuation of Egyptian troops from Crete, Arabia and 'all parts of the Ottoman Empire . . . not within the limits of Egypt'. The Ottoman fleet, moored in Alexandria since the wretched Fevzi's defection, was allowed to sail back to the Bosphorus, and in February 1841 Sultan Abdulmecid formally published a decree which recognized Muhammad Ali as Viceroy for life, with his family assured of hereditary succession to the throne of Egypt. Ibrahim's army was limited by treaty to a mere 18,000 men – although within eight years their number had increased almost fourfold. The signatories of the Treaty of London, now joined by France, guaranteed the Egyptian settlement, and in the Straits Convention of July 1841 reaffirmed the principle of closing the Dardanelles and Bosphorus to foreign warships in time of peace.[7]

With the departure of Ibrahim's army from Anatolia and Syria, the Ottoman Empire was relieved from the only serious *Asian* threat to its existence prior to Allenby's offensive at the end of the First World War.

In London, Vienna and St Petersburg it was felt that an incompetent and decaying 'Turkey' had been saved, not by her own exertions, but by grace of the major European powers. This conviction sustained the fragile Anglo-Russian entente for several years; it prompted Tsar Nicholas to arrive unexpectedly in London at the end of May 1844, and to induce Nesselrode to go to England four months later, to press for concerted diplomatic action to forestall any future aggravation of the Eastern Question. As yet the Tsar was not prepared to put forward a partition plan (which would have aroused intense suspicion at Westminster), but from 1839 onwards he never wavered in his assumption that the Ottoman Empire was doomed, whatever palliatives might be proposed in Constantinople. The British, on the other hand, were prepared to wait upon events.[8]

These years saw Reşid waging a delicate campaign in the capital to persuade the Sultan to implement the promises implicit in the Gülhane Decree. Collectively the reform movement is known as the *Tanzimat-i Hayriye* (which might be translated 'Auspicious Restructuring', since the Turkish *tanzimat* is similar in meaning to the Russian *perestroika*). It was the most sustained attempt by any Ottoman minister to preserve the empire by centralizing authority and by secularizing, so far as possible, its autocratic character.[9]

As in earlier reigns, priority was given to reform of the army. The introduction of other changes depended, first and foremost, on military need; and the earliest stage of the *Tanzimat* may therefore be seen as emanating from what the old warrior Mehmed Husrev was prepared to concede as essential to building up an effective fighting force. The proposal to create a modernized army of a quarter of a million conscripts and to continue with earlier shipbuilding projects for a modern fleet required a full treasury, thus providing an obvious motive for reforming the system of taxation. But how could taxes be raised without closer administrative links between the capital and the provinces and without the improvisation of a new civil service? And good gunnery, accurate navigation, skilled accountancy, as well as efficient administration, all required better learning than the old religious foundations could give; hence the appointment in 1845 of a council of seven learned men who were to report on ways of developing a widespread secular educational system. On the other hand, the guarantees of property rights and of religious equality before the law, which had looked so impressive in the Gülhane Decree, held little appeal to the military mind. Where reforms of this character were even drafted, they remained ineffective – although, on paper, the new penal code of May 1840 looked an

110

impressive step forward. Constantly the reformers were anxious not to provoke the *ulema* by legal reforms which ran counter to the *şeriat*. The Islamic code, which had once provided Suleiman the Magnificent with so sure a foundation of government, continued throughout the century to constrain the advocates of a new model Ottoman autocracy.

The *Tanzimat* reform era remains a contentious subject of study. Even its precise dates are in dispute. Recent historians analyse a long and almost continuous process, covering the years from 1839 to 1876, when Abdulmecid's successor and half-brother Abdulaziz was deposed. Older commentators limited the *Tanzimat* to the 1840s, although they acknowledged a further phase of reform in the period after the Crimean War. They insisted that, even in the 1840s, there were interludes of 'reaction' – times when, in Temperley's revealingly reprehensive phraseology, no 'Englishman' was able 'to drive orientals along new roads'.[10] Reşid did indeed suffer setbacks, notably in 1841 when his plans for a system of provincial administration based upon the French model aroused such hostility from local tax-farmers and military governors that they were dropped, and he was sent off to Paris as ambassador. But he was back as Foreign Minister in 1845. Between September 1846 and January 1858 he was six times Grand Vizier.

Reşid did not foresee the problems of seeking to impose on a vast empire with poor communications changes to which the mass of the population remained indifferent. Much of his work was restricted to the area around the Bosphorus and the Golden Horn, and to towns having good sea links with the capital. An experiment in paper money (*kaime*) carrying interest, intended to relieve the treasury crisis of 1839–40, met with some success in Constantinople and Smyrna but caused new problems when shopkeepers began to hoard the notes so as to claim their eight per cent return each year.[11] Less progress was made in developing secular education than Reşid had hoped. Work on a much-heralded modernization of the university in Stamboul stopped when the walls were a few feet above the foundations, largely because of hostility from the *ulema* and the military authorities, alarmed by tales of student unrest in Germany and central Europe. A shortage of trained teachers outside the *ulema* hampered Reşid's plans for secondary schools (*rusdiye*) and only six, with a mere 870 boy pupils, were founded in the 1840s. In 1846, however, one of Reşid's first tasks as Grand Vizier was to give his patronage to a teachers' training college, appointing the gifted 24-year-old writer and scholar Ahmed Cevdet as first principal. It is significant that by the time of Reşid's death in 1858 the number of *rusdiye* had increased to forty-three, with 3,371 boy pupils.[12]

The appointment of Ahmed Cevdet, nineteenth-century Turkey's ablest educational and judicial reformer, was a typical instance of Reşid's gift for intellectual talent-spotting. His long ascendancy in government enabled Reşid to advance other westernizers whom he hoped would complete his work (though in later years several protégés became his rivals for office). Chief among them were the Stamboul shopkeeper's son Mehmed Emin Ali, and Kececizade Mehmed Fuad who, emerging from an *ulema* family background, worked for fourteen years at the Porte translating French laws and manuals on administration. This continuity of personnel has encouraged the modern tendency to treat the *Tanzimat* as a single span of active reform giving Ottoman institutions a vitality foreign diplomats were too prejudiced to perceive. But the number of reformers was small, a compact community able to find inspiration from the Code Napoleon. Moreover, there was no certainty that experimental reforms would be allowed to mature. Measures to which 'His Majesty the Most Noble, Most Powerful and Most Magnificent Sultan' had deigned to consent could, by the same superlative sovereign, be even more speedily rescinded.

Stratford Canning – back again as ambassador from January 1842 onwards – participated in what he once called 'the great game of improvement' for some nine years.[13] He could claim, with some justice, that he had sustained the impetus of reform during Reşid's virtual exile to the Paris embassy, browbeating Abdulmecid and exposing the corruption of the Finance Minister (probably the least desirable of the *Valide Sultana's* nominees for office). He helped secure laws against the slave trade and formal condemnation by Abdulmecid of the religious persecution of Christian believers, but he failed to have specifically Christian evidence declared admissible in the law courts, nor could he gain recognition of the right of Christians to serve in the Ottoman army. As ambassador he was concerned, not only with the effect of the *Tanzimat* reforms at the centre of the empire, but with the military expeditions which sought to impose respect for the authority of the Sultan far away from the capital, notably in the Levant and in the western Balkans.

The departure of Ibrahim's army from Syria and the Lebanon deprived four Ottoman provinces – Aleppo, Damascus, Tripoli, Sidon – of the most benevolent and effective government they had experienced for several centuries. Egyptian rule had brought considerable benefit to both Christians and Jews, particularly those engaged in trade or commerce. Basir II, who for almost half a century had sought to control the Lebanon from his palace of Beit-ed-Din much as Ali Pasha had ruled over Epirus from Ioánnina, collaborated closely with the Egyptians, and when they left he was deposed and sent to exile in Malta. His banishment gratified Muslim notables, out of favour during the Egyptian occupation; and at first they welcomed the return of Ottoman officials. By the spring of 1841, however, the whole region was in disorder, with armed resistance to the Ottomans coming from rival factions, many of whom remained bound in an almost feudal loyalty to the historic dynasties which had racked the same provinces in Abdulhamid I's reign. The Ottoman military commanders were forced to undertake punitive expeditions, at times showing a ruthless vengeance condemned by foreign observers – although, as in the Greek revolt, neither side possessed a monopoly of cruelty.

The European Powers, especially Britain, were more concerned by Syrian unrest than they had been by any earlier rebellion apart from the Greek. The Anglo-Turkish Commercial Treaty of 1838 provided new markets for British exports and gave British merchants favourable terms for the purchase of goods, raw materials and foodstuffs, thus stimulating the agricultural output of the Ottoman lands. Other governments soon concluded similar commercial conventions, making the Ottoman Empire more susceptible to the fluctuations of world trade while, at the same time, giving Europe a more immediate interest in the well-being of 'Turkey' as a whole. The restoration of the Sultan's rule in both Syria and the Lebanon was therefore carefully reported by local representatives of foreign governments and trading companies. The consuls offered protection to particular communities favoured in London or St Petersburg, Paris or Vienna: Orthodox Christians by the Russians; the Druze, and various Jewish and Protestant groups, by Palmerston; and the Maronites by the French and Austrians. But support for these groups varied widely from district to district, making generalization misleading. The journals and dispatches of the British consul-general in Beirut, Colonel Hugh Rose, show his personal willingness to protect Maronite convoys from attacks by the Druze, and his mistrust of the regular Ottoman troops. But they also complain of the extent to which his French colleagues stirred up Maronite unrest in ways 'detrimental to the interests of the Porte'.[14]

Peace of a kind was imposed in both Syria and the Lebanon in 1843 and again, after renewed fighting, in May 1845; but, despite the mediation of Stratford Canning and a visit to Beirut by Reşid in October 1846, there was little hope of an enduring settlement in a region where there were so many conflicts of interest. In 1848 and intermittently from 1850 to 1852 there were further risings against Ottoman attempts to impose military conscription and Arabicize the Fifth Army, the permanent garrison. Rather than be subject to a reformed and efficient central Ottoman government, local notables began to affect a particularist 'nationalism', especially in the Maronite districts around Mount Lebanon, a development of considerable significance for the second half of the century.[15]

Along the Ottoman Empire's north-western frontier, in Bosnia and Herzegovina, there was even more open hostility to the *Tanzimat* reforms. For the past fifty years the landowners – southern Slav in race and speech but conservatively Muslim in religion and outlook – had resisted every attempt at westernization made by successive Sultans. Mahmud II's formal abolition of feudalism finally destroyed the *Kapetanate*, the privileged caste of forty-eight beys who, when the Empire was at its zenith, had been entrusted with administering the subdivisions of Bosnia in return for raising *sipahi* detachments for the Sultan's cavalry. But the *Kapetanate* went down fighting, literally. Open revolt against Mahmud in 1837 was followed by an even wider rebellion when reports of the Gülhane Decree held out a promise of legal equality and social upgrading for Christians and Jews. Not until March 1850 did a powerful Ottoman army under Omer Lutfi Pasha finally suppress the Bosnian beys in a three-day battle beside the shores of Lake Jezero. Omer entered Jajce in triumph, having already routed the Herzegovinan Muslim notables outside Mostar.

As a historical figure, Omer Lutfi is more familiar under the name 'Omar Pasha', the renowned soldier of the Crimean War and the first eminent commander of a modernized Ottoman army.[16] He was born Michael Lotis (sometimes spelt 'Lattas') in Croatia in 1809 and became an Austrian army cadet, but while he was still under twenty he deserted and crossed the mountains into Bosnia. He was commissioned in the Ottoman army and, having apostatized, took the name of the second of the seventh-century caliphs. Mahmud II promoted him to the rank of major and appointed him military instructor of the boy-prince Abdulmecid. He gained an important victory over Ibrahim in the hills north-east of Beirut in October 1840, but was much criticized by the foreign consuls for the ruthless way in which he subsequently restored the Sultan's authority in the Lebanon. This rigorous maintenance of discipline Omer brought back to Bosnia, where he undertook operations in a terrain he had known since his boyhood. Inevitably he incurred the wrath of the Austrians, who regarded him as a renegade from Habsburg service.

During ten years of virtual anarchy in Bosnia the Austrians several times sent columns forward from Croatia, ready to advance their frontier if the Ottomans failed to re-establish effective government. There appear to have been at least three occasions in this troubled decade when Austrians and Russians discussed a hypothetical partition of the Ottoman Empire: Serbia, Bosnia and Herzegovina would fall to Austria, while Russia would establish client kingdoms in the eastern Balkans.[17] Yet these exchanges did not produce any clear-cut partition plan. If they show anything at all, it is Nicholas I's growing conviction that the decay of the Ottoman system of government could not be arrested by a fine-sounding programme of reform.

Not that Tsar Nicholas thought highly of Metternich's Austria, either. 'Sick, very sick,' he commented privately on the Habsburg monarchy early in 1846, thereby coining the metaphor he was later to apply more famously to another neighbour.[18] The Tsar's verdict on Austria appeared sound. The revolutions of 1848, beginning dramatically in France and the Italian peninsula, spread to the German-speaking lands and to the Danubian basin, outwardly destroying Metternich's Europe. No European government wished to see the Eastern Question posed at a time of convulsion in so many other parts of the continent. With tacit approval from Palmerston in London, as well as from Sultan Abdulmecid, the Tsar ordered his army across the river Pruth and into Moldavia and Wallachia to root out a suspected hornet's-nest of Roumanian patriot radicals in Bucharest. The consequent two-and-a-half-year Russian occupation of the Danubian Principalities aroused little protest in itself: no one seriously disputed Nesselrode's claim that the Russian move was justified by the treaty terms of both Kuchuk Kainardji and Adrianople. The revolutions did not spread into the Ottoman Empire.

What caused concern in London and Paris was the Tsar's failure to be content with occupying Moldavia and Wallachia. By July 1848 his troops were spread around the arc of the Carpathians, as if hovering over both the Habsburg and the Ottoman empires. There they might have halted, had it not been for the needs of the young Emperor Francis Joseph; in the early spring of 1849, four months after his accession, he sought Russian aid in restoring Habsburg authority along the central Danube; and Tsar Nicholas responded by sending two armies from the Principalities across the frontier into Transylvania to stamp out Kossuth's nascent independent Hungarian state.

Russian intervention in Hungary had two important consequences for the Eastern Question. In Europe as a whole it completed a diplomatic revolution: there was such widespread sympathy in London for Kossuth and his cause that the westward march of the Tsar's armies finally ended the fragile Anglo-Russian entente which had struggled on for nearly ten years. Britain and France began to act together, while Tsar Nicholas assumed he could count on close support from Vienna for his policies. Secondly, the suppression of the Hungarian revolution forced Kossuth himself, and four Polish generals who had fought for him, to seek asylum within the Ottoman Empire. In September and October 1849 the Sultan and Reşid, encouraged by Stratford Canning and the presence of a British naval squadron in the Dardanelles, stubbornly refused to surrender Kossuth and the Polish refugees to the Austrian and Russian governments. Not even the peremptory withdrawal of the Russian and Austrian ambassadors to the Sublime Porte made Abdulmecid waver.[19]

The crisis gave the *Tanzimat* ministers a diplomatic success. Mehmed Fuat travelled to Bucharest and on to St Petersburg, successfully negotiating with the Russians an agreement by which the Tsar would give up his demand for the surrender of the Polish refugee generals, provided that the Ottomans undertook to keep them away from the borders of the Russian Empire. The Austrians, too, abandoned their insistence that Kossuth should be handed over. Yet in both Vienna and St Petersburg there was some satisfaction that, even if the Sultan had refused to give way, at least Palmerston was prepared to acknowledge a breach of international law. He admitted that in taking his warships up the Dardanelles as far as Chanak (Çannakale) the British Admiral, Sir William Parker, had broken the Straits Convention – although Parker had, in fact, responded to an appeal for support from the British consul at the Dardanelles, Frederic Calvert.[20]

Admiral Parker's penetration of the Dardanelles set a bad precedent. It was the first in a series of provocative measures which culminated in the Crimean War. With one exception – a punitive campaign undertaken by Omer in Montenegro in 1852, halted under the threat of Austrian intervention – these actions were assertions of sea power by the rival European navies, generally to support intimidating demands on the Ottoman Government by overbearing envoys to the Sublime Porte; and it could be argued that naval power was also the principal issue at stake in the Crimean War itself, at least in Black Sea waters. But the protracted crisis which posed the Eastern Question in its most acute form was caused, not by battleship diplomacy, but by the revival of an old dispute: in May 1850 the Foreign Ministry in Paris ordered the ambassador in Constantinople to assert French rights to defend the privileges of 'Latins' (Roman Catholics) in Jerusalem,

Nazareth and Bethlehem, complaining that 'Greeks' (Orthodox monks protected by Russia) were excluding them from the Holy Places.[21]

There was nothing new in the French claim, which was based on a treaty concluded in Mahmud I's reign. Both Louis XVIII in 1819 and Louis Philippe in 1842 had sought electoral capital by backing 'Latins' against 'Greeks' in Palestine, and most foreign governments assumed that the latest ruler of France, Prince-President Louis Napoleon, would similarly lose interest in the Holy Places once his position at home was secure. But on this occasion the wrangle dragged on. Tsar Nicholas I remained intensely suspicious of Louis Napoleon, and the neo-Bonapartist system of plebiscitary government left the Prince-President needing support from the clergy-dominated French provinces, certainly until November 1852 when a referendum gave overwhelming backing to the return of Empire and he became the Emperor Napoleon III.

Sultan Abdulmecid wished to avoid antagonizing 'Latins' or 'Greeks'. In February 1852 he devised a compromise which offered concessions to the French over the vexed question of Latin access to the churches in Bethlehem but gave secret assurances to the Russians that there would be no change 'in the existing state of things'. The compromise was welcomed by Stratford Canning (now Viscount Stratford de Redcliffe), who four months later left Constantinople, 'perhaps' (as he thought) 'never to return'. But even before Stratford de Redcliffe reached England, there was renewed crisis in the capital. Both the Russians and the French suspected they had been duped by the compromise. Moreover, Louis Napoleon hoped that with the Great Elchi's departure for home a French diplomat might speedily acquire the influence at the Porte he had so long enjoyed. By chance the French ambassador, the Marquis de Lavalette, was in Paris for consultations. In June Louis Napoleon ordered him back to his post; and he was told to make so impressive a return to Constantinople that all the residents of the city, Turks and foreigners alike, should be well aware of his coming.

Accordingly, in mid-July Lavalette sailed up the Dardanelles and into the Bosphorus aboard the most formidable warship in the world, the 90-gun steam-powered *Charlemagne*. In penetrating the Straits the French navy committed a further breach of the 1841 Convention, but the Porte allowed this technicality to pass without complaint. The warship's presence greatly impressed the Ottoman authorities, as Louis Napoleon had anticipated: here, lying off the Sultan's palace, was a floating fortress able to master 'the most rapid currents of the Bosphorus by the sole power of the screw';[22] and supporting the *Charlemagne* in the eastern Mediterranean was a powerful squadron which, at the end of July, threatened to bombard the Lebanese port of Tripoli when the Ottoman governor refused to surrender French deserters. The apparent primacy of French sea-power ensured that, from July 1852 until his recall to Paris seven months later, Lavalette called the tune in Constantinople. His nominees became Grand Vizier and Foreign Minister; and in October and again in December 1852, instructions were sent to Jerusalem requiring the 'Greeks' to make concessions to the 'Latins' at Bethlehem.

No phase of the Eastern Question has provoked so much historical debate nor received such close attention in the West as the events of the following fifteen months – not least because the resultant conflict is the only occasion upon which French and British troops have fought together against the regular, organized army of a Russian state, Tsarist or Soviet. Yet during the winter of 1852–3 there were statesmen in both St Petersburg and London prepared to work for renewed Anglo-Russian collaboration, as in 1839–40, rather than fatalistically accept a drift into war. At Christmas in 1852 the Foreign Office and Stratford de Redcliffe (now in London) still sympathized with 'Greeks' rather than with 'Latins' over the Holy Places dispute. But Tsar Nicholas gravely misunderstood the mood in London. He believed that, like him, the British Government regarded the pusillanimous behaviour of the Porte as a sign of feeble corruption among Abdulmecid's ministers, despite the high-sounding intentions of the *Tanzimat* reforms. Nesselrode warned his imperial master that any discussion with the British of 'plans for an uncertain future' would be 'both dangerous and utterly useless', forcing London back into a suspicious hostility which it would prove hard to overcome.[23] Against Nesselrode's advice, Nicholas decided to sound out Lord Aberdeen's new Whig–Peelite coalition ministry over possible partition plans, should the Ottoman Government prove unable to resist foreign pressure or quell internal upheaval. On 9 January 1853, in a conversational aside to the British ambassador (Hamilton Seymour) as he was leaving a private concert, Nicholas I for the first time applied his anthropomorphic metaphor of 'sick man' to the Ottoman Empire: 'The country is falling to pieces – who can say when?' Nicholas said, according to the entry Seymour made in his diary that night.[24]

When Seymour wrote up the conversation two days later in a formal dispatch to the Foreign Office, he gave the famous metaphor a greater emphasis than in the entry in his private journal. And when in late January and early February the Tsar on four occasions received

Seymour in private audience, the ambassador faithfully reported Nicholas's words, catching precisely the melodramatic tone with which he tended to heighten all his pronouncements.[25] Inside the Winter Palace these remarks of the Tsar seemed in accord with the setting – like Rastrelli's masterpiece they were grandiose, over-elaborate and artificial enough not to be taken too seriously; but read dispassionately in Westminster in an ambassador's dispatch, they caused a stir. Nicholas seemed to be putting forward plans to carve up the Ottoman Empire: 'England' might receive possession of Crete and a free hand in Egypt in return for the creation of Russian satellite states in the Balkans.

Briefly it seemed as if the survival of the Sultan's empire depended on the European chancelleries. So at least it was assumed in London, where the significance of Nicholas's 'sick man' talks with Seymour was much exaggerated. Ever since Catherine the Great's 'Greek Project', hypothetical partition plans had from time to time enlivened Russo-Austrian diplomacy; they figured, too, in Franco-Russian exchanges during the Tilsit era. But the redrawing of maps on this scale was an unfamiliar pastime in Downing Street. The Aberdeen coalition cabinet – which contained more ministers skilled in foreign affairs than any other British government, before or since – was highly suspicious of this newest twist to Russian policy.[26] Why, the ministers wondered, did the Tsar prefer a 'gentleman's agreement' to a formal treaty? And was it Seymour's reporting, or Nicholas's imprecision, that clouded with such vagueness the 'commercial policy' Britain and Russia might pursue after the Ottoman Empire's disintegration?

British doubts were intensified by the Tsar's decision to send a special envoy to Constantinople. For Nicholas chose, not a seasoned and conciliatory diplomat like Orlov, but a turcophobe soldier, Prince Alexander Menshikov. His appointment worried Nesselrode, who warned Menshikov that 'the Ottoman Empire would dissolve at the first clash of arms', adding that Tsar Nicholas 'did not wish to precipitate this catastrophe'.[27] But the Prince's written instructions made it clear that Nicholas expected him to interfere in Ottoman affairs far more than had Orlov, twenty years before. He was given a threefold task: to secure the dismissal of the pro-French Foreign Minister, Mehmed Fuat; to conclude a treaty reasserting 'Greek' Orthodox privileges in Palestine; and to obtain formal acknowledgement of Russia's right to protect Orthodox Christians throughout the Ottoman lands. As a gesture of good will Sultan Abdulmecid might be told that, provided he rescinded every concession to the French, a secret defensive alliance would safeguard his empire and his throne.

Menshikov landed at Galata in great state on the last day of February, having reviewed the Black Sea Fleet at Sebastopol before embarking in an armed paddle-steamer, the *Gromovnik* ('Thunderer'). He speedily engineered the fall of the Foreign Minister by the simple expedient of refusing to deal with the Porte so long as Mehmed Fuad remained in office. With Lavalette back in Paris and Stratford de Redcliffe still in England, the interests of France and of Britain were in the hands of chargés d'affaires rather than ambassadors, and both were puzzled and alarmed by Menshikov's menacing manner. The British chargé, Colonel Hugh Rose (for ten years consul-general in Beirut), was served by a good intelligence service which informed him of Russian troop movements along the borders of the Danubian Provinces and naval preparations in Sebastopol. Rose thought war imminent. His French colleague, Vincente Benedetti, sent an urgent message to Paris requesting the dispatch of a French naval squadron. Rose, without reference to London, appealed directly to Admiral Dundas in Malta, sending him details of an anchorage in a bay near Smyrna to which he was at once to bring his fleet.[28]

The French squadron left Toulon for the Aegean on 25 March; but Admiral Dundas had no intention of sailing for Turkish waters without orders from the Admiralty, and these were not forthcoming. Instead of support from the Royal Navy, Colonel Rose was faced with the precipitate return, on 5 April, of Stratford de Redcliffe in person. At first the ambassador played down the crisis: Menshikov's tone was 'considerably softened', Stratford informed the Foreign Secretary, Lord Clarendon, on 11 April, adding that 'there was no question of a defensive treaty' between the Russian and Ottoman empires.[29] Yet the fears of Rose and Benedetti were justified. Tsar Nicholas had given serious consideration to plans for the Black Sea Fleet to land several divisions close to the mouth of the Bosphorus and surprise the Sultan and his capital before the other Powers could intervene. This project did not become known for another half-century, but the possibility of such a contingency was examined, with remarkable insight, by Captain T. A. Blakely, RN, in a report submitted to Stratford de Redcliffe a fortnight after his return to Constantinople. Another naval officer, William Slade, outlined means of defending the city against a Russian naval assault in a memorandum completed three weeks later.[30] Over the following five months the British ambassador was therefore able to provide the Porte with shrewd advice based not only upon his long acquaintance with Ottoman affairs but upon careful military and naval assessments as well. When on 21 May Prince Menshikov left for Odessa, furious with Abdulmecid for refusing Russia's protective patronage, he blamed the British ambassador for having 'bewitched' the Sultan and the viziers with his 'frantic activity'.

Menshikov, like so many of his contemporaries, exaggerated Stratford de Redcliffe's influence and his ascendancy over Ottoman policy. Even the British Foreign Secretary referred to him as 'the *real* Sultan' in a letter to a leading Scottish journalist that summer, and the historical legend which accused the ambassador of encouraging the Ottoman authorities to go to war persisted for more than a century, though the opening of the archives showed that in fact he favoured the maintenance of peace and worked to promote a settlement of the Holy Places dispute.[31] Stratford de Redcliffe did indeed stiffen Ottoman resistance to Menshikov's hectoring diplomacy, and he brought new heart to the *Tanzimat* ministers – for example, in mid-May he induced Abdulmecid to entrust foreign affairs once more to Mustafa Reşid. But the crisis was heightened by decisions taken in foreign capitals rather than by the Porte. The Aberdeen cabinet in London ordered Admiral Dundas to Turkish waters on 5 June in response to anti-Russian demonstrations in Britain; Stratford de Redcliffe did not ask for the dispatch of the warships.[32] And when Dundas's squadron sailed from Malta, their destination was not the Smyrna littoral – as Rose had suggested – but Besika Bay, an anchorage in the lee of the island of Tenedos (Bozcaada), barely twenty miles from the ancient Hellespont. To avid newspaper readers in Britain, the thought of a fleet off the Dardanelles was more gratifying than reports of a squadron inconspicuously at anchor over a hundred miles down the coast. Unfortunately, in Constantinople as in London and Paris, public feeling became dangerously excited by tales of foreign warships heading for the Straits in support of the Ottoman cause. Stratford de Redcliffe well understood this: Lord Aberdeen, Lord Clarendon and the Emperor Napoleon III did not.

Early in July the Russian army crossed the river Pruth and, as in 1848, occupied the Danubian Principalities. On this occasion Nesselrode made it clear that the troops would remain in Moldavia and Wallachia until the Sultan accepted Menshikov's demands. The Russian move infuriated the Austrians, whose trade would suffer if war came to the lower Danube, and an ambassadorial conference in Vienna produced a compromise intended to settle all disputes between the Russian and Ottoman empires by reaffirming the rights of Orthodox believers among the Sultan's subjects, while defining more closely the privileges accorded to Russia by the treaties of Kuchuk Kainardji and

Adrianople. Nesselrode was prepared to accept the 'Vienna Note', although with an 'interpretation' more favourable to the Tsar than the ambassadors had intended. Rather strangely, it was assumed in Vienna that Abdulmecid and Reşid would follow suit.

The Porte, however, was angered by the whole episode. Reşid regarded the ambassadorial conference as a double slight on the Sultan's sovereign authority: no Ottoman spokesman was consulted over the proposed compromise; and the Note was sent to the Tsar before being notified to the Sultan. The ambassadors in conference had 'taken upon themselves to draw up a Note without the knowledge of the party more immediately concerned', Reşid complained.[33] Stratford de Redcliffe persuaded Abdulmecid to offer to confirm, in general terms, the 'ancient privileges of the religion professed' by 'the Emperor of Russia'; but the Vienna Note remained unacceptable. To the British Foreign Secretary, writing to a friend, it was 'shocking' and 'incredible' that the 'horrible calamity' of war should threaten Europe because of 'two sets of barbarians quarrelling over a form of words'.[34]

Clarendon's indignation shows, yet again, the failure of the Europeans to appreciate the mood in Constantinople. The newspapers carried reports of mounting anger in the capital and the towns around the Bosphorus, where naturally xenophobic mobs threatened European lives and property; but no commentator saw these events as decisive for Abdulmecid personally. Yet in retrospect it is clear that the fate of the Sultanate was in the balance that summer. At the start of the century Selim III had sought to modernize the army; it turned against him. Mahmud II had continued the task; his reign ended in disaster at the hands of his Egyptian vassal. Abdulmecid had made the creation of a reformed conscript army the first object of the *Tanzimat*; and now, fourteen years after his accession, he was facing the great challenge of his reign. A victorious military campaign would finally silence the critics of westernization: appeasement of Russia would almost certainly cost him his throne.

In the second week of August the Sultan's policies were strikingly vindicated, with proof of the renewed vitality they had brought to his empire. Modern Egypt's founder-Viceroy, Muhammad Ali, and his soldier son Ibrahim had died within a few months of each other in the winter of 1848–9, and in 1853 the reigning Viceroy was Muhammad Ali's grandson, Abbas Hilmi. In politics and religion Abbas was conservative, prepared to travel to Rhodes in 1850 for a meeting with Abdulmecid, to whom he paid respectful homage as Sultan and Caliph.[35] In this role of faithful vassal Abbas dutifully raised an expeditionary force to fight for the Ottomans in any war with Russia; and accordingly, on 12 August, a powerful Egyptian fleet reached the Golden Horn, bringing 35,000 well-trained and disciplined men to augment the Sultan's army. Soon, with a nice touch of historic irony, the Egyptians were at Unkiar Skelessi and Büyükdere, their green tents pitched where Mahmud's Russian minders had encamped in 1833 after Ibrahim's victory at Konya. The presence of the Egyptian force convinced the Sultan's subjects in his capital that Abdulmecid was a worthy successor of Selim I and Suleiman, sovereign of an Islamic empire that still stretched from Danube to Nile.

By early September Stratford de Redcliffe knew he might delay the coming of war, but could hardly prevent it. Throughout that month there was much lawlessness in the capital: religious fanaticism inflamed public opinion against foreigners, while hotheads among the *ulema* called for the proclamation of a Holy War (jihad) against Russia. Eventually on Tuesday, 4 October, the ambassador received instructions from London authorizing him to summon Dundas's squadron from Besika Bay to protect Constantinople from a Russian assault, or to keep order in the city if grave rioting undermined the Sultan's authority. Stratford, however, delayed summoning the ships up to the Bosphorus, knowing that their presence would encourage still further the more bellicose of the Sultan's ministers.[36]

It was too late to save the peace. Already the Sultan had girded himself with the Sword of the Prophet as a pledge of war against the Infidel; and, on that same Tuesday, Omer Pasha as Ottoman commander on the Danube sent an envoy to Russian headquarters in Wallachia with an ultimatum demanding an immediate evacuation of the Principalities. For three weeks nothing happened, to the anger of fiery russophobes in the capital; renewed rioting at last induced Stratford de Redcliffe to summon the fleet from Besika Bay on 20 October – the anniversary of Navarino, as he wryly remembered.[37]

Three days later Turkish and Egyptian troops made surprise crossings of the Danube near Tutrakhan and attacked Russian outposts thirty miles south of Bucharest. When news of Omer's initiative reached Stamboul, there was wild rejoicing. With a modernized Ottoman army north of the Danube, huge camps of reinforcements on either shore of the Bosphorus, and French and British warships off the Golden Horn, what could go wrong? The 'sick man' had sprung suddenly to life.

CHAPTER 9

Dolmabahche

At first the momentum of Omer Pasha's offensive held promise of early victory. In the Principalities the Russian commander on the lower Danube, Prince Michael Gorchakov, was forced to fall back to new defensive positions around Bucharest, while from the southern Caucasus Prince Vorontsov complained that his armies were below strength; it would be impossible, Vorontsov warned the Tsar, to hold the foothills of the Georgian mountain chain the next spring if the Turks were able to ferry men and munitions to the Caucasus.[1] But the buoyant mood of elation in the Ottoman capital did not last more than a few weeks. The coming of winter froze all activity along the battle fronts in Europe and in Asia; and before the end of the year, the naval balance in the Black Sea had swung decisively in favour of the Russians.

On 24 November Admiral Nakhimov's flotilla from Sebastopol was cruising along the Anatolian coast when it sighted the masts of the main Ottoman fleet in harbour at Sinope. The Russians sailed away again, back towards Sebastopol, only a hundred miles across the Black Sea. But Nakhimov's sortie convinced the Turkish commander, Osman Pasha, that a Russian fleet would soon return in strength. He therefore sent a fast frigate to the Bosphorus, seeking reinforcements. But Sinope was three times as far from Constantinople as from Sebastopol, and disaster struck before any help could reach Osman. A wise commander would have put to sea: Osman, ignoring the lessons of Çeşme and Navarino, remained close inshore. His prediction, however, was perfectly correct. Six days after his reconnaissance, Admiral Nakhimov returned; and this time he commanded a squadron so powerful that it could concentrate 720 guns on the Turkish fleet and the shore batteries around Sinope. Most of the Ottoman vessels were sunk or, like Osman's flagship, ran aground while manoeuvring to give battle, and were captured. Fires, fanned by a strong inshore wind, spread from the stricken warships to envelop the straggling town. Only one Ottoman vessel, a steam-powered auxiliary under an English captain, escaped destruction. Forty-eight hours later this sole survivor sailed up the Bosphorus, bringing news of the disaster to Sultan Abdulmecid and to the commanders of the Anglo-French fleet at anchor off his palace. If Nakhimov decided to exploit his victory, only the allied squadron could give Constantinople an outer shield of protection. But to do so the allies would have to break precedent, and sail out into the Black Sea.

Sinope was a legitimate act of war, effectively postponing an Ottoman offensive in the Caucasus. In Britain, however, Nakhimov's masterstroke was misrepresented by press and public opinion, becoming 'the massacre of Sinope'. 'The English people are resolved that Russia shall not dictate conditions to Europe, or convert the Black Sea, with all the various interests encompassing its shores, into a Russian lake,' an editorial in *The Times* declared. 'To stop the aggressor with a blow' was as 'plain a duty towards humanity' as to 'send succour to Sinope', commented the *Morning Chronicle*.[2] By the end of the first week in January 1854 ten British and nine French ships of the line had sailed up through the Bosphorus. Any Russian vessel, warship or merchantman, should be 'required to return to Sebastopol', Stratford de Redcliffe was informed by the Foreign Office. Soon afterwards four British warships began convoying Ottoman troops from Sinope to Trebizond. Few people doubted that war between Russia and Turkey's Western allies would follow in the spring. It came on 31 March.

The vanguard of a French and British expeditionary force reached the Gallipoli peninsula within nine days of the declaration of war, later moving northwards to Varna. Originally the allies intended to join Omer Pasha's army on the Danube, advance through the Principalities to the delta, and eventually take Odessa. But Austrian mediation induced the Russians to evacuate Moldavia and Wallachia, which were then policed by Francis Joseph's soldiery throughout the war, a neutral buffer between the combatants. Thereafter the allied objective changed: the Anglo-French expeditionary force would capture Sebastopol and destroy the fleet responsible for the Sinope 'massacre'; the war against Russia became identified with the Crimea.

In this familiar tale of battle heroics and administrative confusion the role of Omer Pasha's army has often been overlooked. Yet 6,000 Ottoman troops took part in the initial invasion of the Crimea and it was an Ottoman outpost which reported the first Russian advance on the morning of Balaklava. Lord Raglan, the British Commander-in-Chief, thought highly of the Ottoman infantry. According to Colonel Hugh Rose, who was serving as a liaison officer at headquarters, it was Raglan's concern for the valiant Turkish defenders of Canrobert's Hill that sent the Light Brigade forward on their famous charge. 'We must set the poor Turks right again, get the redoubt back,' Rose heard Raglan say on that historic October morning.[3] 'Johnny Turk', as the British called their ally, remained in the peninsula until after the final assault on Sebastopol. Thirteen thousand Ottoman troops defended the allied base at Eupatoria from a Russian attack, others joined the British and French in raiding the eastern Crimea, while in August 1855 Ottoman gunners and infantry fought beside the French and Piedmontese on the river Chernaya.

Twice Lord Stratford de Redcliffe had to travel to the Crimea to ease relations between Omer and Raglan's successors, for the Ottomans were eager to withdraw from the peninsula. Omer insisted that the vital front for the Sultan lay in the Caucasus rather than in the Tsar's Crimean appendage. At the end of September 1855, with the ruins of Sebastopol in allied hands, Omer's troops were at last able to sail for the Caucasian theatre of war. It was hoped they would relieve Kars, where for seven months an Ottoman garrison and a handful of British officers had resisted a series of Russian assaults. But Omer moved too slowly. The Kars garrison, fated to suffer more deaths from starvation than from Russian guns, was forced to surrender on 25 November, giving the Tsar's troops their principal prize of the whole war.[4]

In both the Crimea and the Caucasus the fighting ended with news of an armistice, concluded on 28 February 1856 far away in Paris. Grand Vizier Mehmed Emin Ali – the *Tanzimat* reformer – served as the Sultan's principal plenipotentiary at the Peace Congress, which Napoleon III had hoped would settle the affairs of all Europe as well as finding a solution for the Eastern Question. It was the only occasion in the nineteenth century when an Ottoman spokesman sat among the victorious peacemakers after a war against Russia; and Ali did well.[5] He showed a patient fluency in French and a fine sense of tactful restraint in dealing with the Tsar's chief representative, that deceptively courteous veteran of diplomatic bargaining, Alexis Orlov. There were moments in Paris when there seemed a closer accord between French and Russians than among the wartime allies, and Ali took pains to convince the peacemakers of Sultan Abdulmecid's sincere determination to persevere with the enlightened reforms promised in the Gülhane

Decree of seventeen years earlier. Ali's task was made easier by Abdulmecid's decision to issue the second Imperial Rescript of the *Tanzimat* era exactly a week ahead of the Peace Congress's opening in Paris. This *Hatt-i-Hümayun* of February 1856 reaffirmed the principles of Gülhane by asserting, even more categorically, the full equality of Muslims and non-Muslims within the Ottoman Empire. At the same time, the Rescript foreshadowed further provincial administrative reforms, made practical provision for the direct collection of taxes in place of the discredited tax-farming system, and accepted the need for official decrees to be written in simpler Ottoman Turkish, rather than in archaic forms often borrowed from Persian or Arabic.

Orlov would have preferred to see the Imperial Rescript written into the final Peace Treaty, so as to safeguard the improved status of the Sultan's Christian subjects by an international guarantee. Napoleon III sympathized with the Russians over this point. But, as Palmerston wrote to the ambassador in Paris, the British had fought 'not so much to keep the Sultan and his Mussulmans in Turkey as to keep the Russians out of Turkey'; and, if Orlov wanted written guarantees of the Rescript, then it must surely be because he wished to preserve for the Russians that claim of interference they had asserted ever since Kuchuk Kainardji. The British, and the Austrians with them, eagerly seized on Ali's assurance of Abdulmecid's firm commitment to reform; and on 30 March 1856 the Peace Treaty of Paris gave Ali what he wanted. While Article IX noted the 'generous intentions' of Abdulmecid's Rescript, it insisted that the Powers had no right to interfere 'in the relations of His Majesty the Sultan with his subjects, nor in the Internal Administration of his Empire'.[6]

Tsar Alexander II, who had succeeded his father Nicholas I twelve months before, claimed the *Hatt-i-Hümayun* as a moral victory. An Imperial Manifesto, issued in St Petersburg on the day after peace was signed in Paris, told the Russian people that by solemnly recognizing the rights of the Sultan's Christian subjects the Rescript fulfilled 'the original and principal aims of the war'.[7] Yet it was impossible to deny that the Treaty undid the work of Catherine the Great and her successors. Kars and all other towns and villages in eastern Anatolia won by Russian arms during the previous two years were restored to the Ottoman Empire. The Tsar lost all claims to protect the Danubian Principalities of Moldavia and Wallachia which, though still technically under Ottoman suzerainty, were to acquire 'an independent and national' administration, authorized to raise its own army. Moreover, southern Bessarabia was ceded by Alexander II to Moldavia, thereby depriving Russia of any opportunity to control the Danube delta. Most striking of all the treaty's provisions were the clauses which provided for the Black Sea to be neutralized and demilitarized. The waters of the Black Sea were thrown open to merchant vessels from any nation but closed to all warships, apart from 'light vessels, necessary for the service of' the Russian and Ottoman 'coasts'. All military and maritime arsenals at the Black Sea ports were to close. To Alexander II the dismantling of the forts and dockyards of Sebastopol and Odessa was a humiliation too bitter for a proud sovereign to sustain for any length of time.

By contrast, it mattered little to Abdulmecid that Sinope should cease to be a naval base. On paper, 'His Majesty the Emperor of the Ottomans' did well from the peace settlement. The independence and territorial integrity of his lands were formally guaranteed. Kars was restored to him. He remained nominal sovereign of the two Danubian Principalities and overlord of Serbia, where he retained a right to garrison troops. At the same time, the Sublime Porte was formally admitted to what the Treaty called 'the Public Law and System of Europe', thereby enabling the Ottomans to look confidently to financial institutions in London, Paris and Vienna for aid which, it was believed abroad, would increase Turkey's economic strength. This was a false assumption. Over a twenty-year period the Ottoman Empire contracted fourteen foreign loans – and in 1875 the government was forced to issue a declaration of bankruptcy.

Yet at first the new status of the Ottomans within the Concert of Europe, together with the prospect of further reforms, seemed at last to have checked the Empire's decline. The Sultan's pledge of civic equality between Christians, Muslims and Jews attracted refugees from Hungary and Poland to settle within the Ottoman Empire. Many were modern craftsmen bringing new skills to the cities. Some converted to Islam and helped promote the new educational system favoured by the *Tanzimat* reformers. But there were farming communities, too; best known was the village founded in honour of Adam Czartoryski and still called Polonezköy, a few miles off the route from modern Üsküdar to Sile, on the Black Sea coast. Polonezkoy long retained its Vistulan Catholic character, with a cluster of dairy farms and cherry orchards and a flourishing pork trade, rare in Muslim Anatolia. The refugees brought not simply a new vitality to this particular region near the capital, but also much of the romantic nationalism which had stirred central Europe and the western Balkans in the past two decades and was, as yet, an alien concept in Anatolia.[8]

The Crimean War quickened the pace of life in the Ottoman heartlands. Two years of naval and military comings and goings had made
the Turks more familiar with European manners and customs than
any earlier incursion from the West. The newcomers were drawn from
all classes and both sexes: rank-and-file soldiers and naval ratings;
journalists; nurses; dignitaries of state and aspiring politicians from
both London and Paris; civil engineers; churchmen both Protestant
and Catholic; and specialists in railways, in the electric telegraph, and
in other facets of the new technology. There were instances of shocked
protest from the *ulema* in several outlying districts. Knowledge that
unveiled women were nursing sick and wounded soldiers within the
sprawling Selimiye Kislasi barracks at Üsküdar aroused real distress
among faithful Muslims. When on the last day of February 1855 both
shores of the Bosphorus were shaken by an earthquake, there were some
who saw in this seismic phenomenon Allah's indictment of 'women who
make display of their adornment'. Yet, in general, the presence of so
many foreigners in Stamboul, Pera and other towns seems to have
helped break down local resistance to westernization. It may therefore
have eased the task of the later *Tanzimat* reformers.

Of equal interest was the impact made by Ottoman society and
customs upon these outsiders from the West. Unlike earlier travellers,
they were for the most part men and women who had never expected
to find themselves beside the Bosphorus. Some, like Sister Sarah Anne
of an Anglican religious nursing order in Devon, had set out for Turkey
at three days' notice. When Sarah Anne reached Constantinople, on 4
November 1854, the day was so wet that Florence Nightingale complained, in a letter home, of 'the Golden Horn looking like a bad
daguerreotype washed out'. But Sarah Anne responded to this 'most
beautiful view in all the world' much as had Lady Mary Wortley
Montagu a hundred and thirty years before her: 'Giddy and confused,' she wrote home, 'we could hardly realise that these painted
houses, gay gardens and glittering minarets were not a vision or
panorama.'[9] For the remainder of the decade a succession of books
in English – many of them by women authors – sought to counter the
prejudice of centuries against the 'terrible Turk'. They portrayed
Imperial Constantinople as both a treasure-house of the past and the
living capital of an empire made viable by the reforms of its sovereign
and his ministers. For some twenty years this optimistic view of
Turkey's moral assets prevailed in London society, a dream-image
which in 1876 not even the flame of Gladstone's outraged conscience
could expunge entirely.

Not every visitor was so rosy-eyed as Sister Sarah Anne. 'I never was more disappointed with any town than with Constantinople,' Colonel Charles Gordon wrote to his father in May 1854. 'I could not have believed it possible that such a magnificent situation could have been so thrown away by any set of barbarians. It is quite time that some civilised nation should get possession of it and build a proper town.'[10] The recipient of the letter was the Prime Minister, Lord Aberdeen, who had himself spent some eight weeks on the Bosphorus half a century before and could therefore judge the value of his son's jaundiced comments. Filth and dust abounded in both Stamboul and Üsküdar, but the building of 'a proper town' was, at that moment, high among the cherished ambitions of the Sultan. In (mainly non-Muslim) Pera the *Tanzimat* reformers were creating a Parisian-style municipality; a nominated council in this 'Sixth Arrondissement' (*altinci daire*) was responsible for planning and naming new roads, for supervising restaurants, hotels and theatres, and within a year introduced the first gas-lighting of a Turkish street. In one respect the waterfront skyline had already changed dramatically between the visits of Lord Aberdeen and his son. Facing Colonel Gordon as he looked across the Bosphorus from Üsküdar was Abdulmecid's newest palace, the Dolmabahche, which became the Sultan's chief residence a few months before the outbreak of war. The palace was more than a home: it was a symbol of Abdulmecid's faith in a revived empire.[11]

The Dolmabahche is as characteristic a monument to the *Tanzimat* era as Garnier's Paris Opéra to the Second Empire or St Pancras Station to Victorian London. In four hundred years the Topkapi Sarayi had grown into a grimly functional complex, culturally enriched by the compact artistry of its cluster of state rooms. By contrast, from the day that the Sultan first went into residence there, the Dolmabahche stood out as a spectacular show-piece, Versailles gone Venetian. Its classical columns and porticoes were spread along the shore of the lower Bosphorus like the façades of the Winter Palace and the Hermitage beside the Neva, but while the Romanovs had settled for rust-red, Abdulmecid delighted in the pristine white marble splendour which the architects Nikogos and Kalabet Balyan conjured up for him. Yet the Balyans designed their palace, not as a backcloth for the Bosphorus, but in the form of winged pavilions projecting from a central throne-room which was larger than any other in Europe. Architecturally their palace was a microcosm of the centralized empire. And this was as Abdulmecid intended. The Dolmabahche affirmed his confidence in the future. Unlike earlier Sultans, he did not simply set about westernizing the

Ottoman past; he sought to endow his heritage with an imperialistic grandeur worthy of the newest Great Power patronizingly welcomed into the Concert of Europe.

The expense of building and maintaining the Dolmabahche Palace was so great that to most contemporary rulers it would have seemed prohibitive. Running costs mounted to £2 million a year. To this drain on funds could be added renovation of the adjoining 'domestic' palace of Çirağan and an imperial villa near Ahmed III's fabled Sa'adabad and, above all, the building of another Balyan-planned palace across the Bosphorus at Beylerbey. This newest folly was not finished until four years after Abdulmecid's death. Although far smaller than the Dolmabahche, Beylerbey displayed a similar Rococo ostentation. All this was too much for the *Tanzimat* ministers. They repeatedly deplored the extravagance of both Abdulmecid and his successor, Abdulaziz. In October 1859 the highly respected Mehmed Ali resigned as Grand Vizier in protest at Abdulmecid's continued appropriation of funds for the 'palace which must surpass all others in the world'.[12]

There is no doubt that the Sultan's prodigality absorbed much of the £3 million loan which, in the summer of 1854, Ali and Mehmed Fuad had succeeded in raising abroad. In practice, however, the money received by the Porte was little more than half the nominal amount, because of both a high interest rate and liberal commissions to several groups of underwriters. Accordingly a second, more favourable, loan for £5 million was contracted within less than a year. It was guaranteed by the French and British governments, but only on condition that the money should be spent on purposes connected with the Crimean War, and that the expenditure be supervised by a British and a French commissioner. This innovation set a precedent for later years, when the growth of European financial control over the Ottoman Empire severely curbed the Sultans' freedom of action. But not in Abdulmecid's lifetime; there were no commissioners to prevent him from digging deeply into a third foreign loan. It was this particular act of spendthrift recklessnesses which prompted Ali's resignation.

Yet not all the financial ventures showed such folly. The Ottoman government also made use of foreign capital to improve communications within the Empire. Railways came slowly; in the Balkans a strategic line from Varna to the Danube was begun in 1856; and soon afterwards work started on a line along the Menderes valley in south-western Anatolia to tap the agricultural wealth of the hinterland serving the port of Smyrna. More postal roads were built in these closing years of Abdulmecid's reign, but pride of place went to the electric telegraph, which was developed by the British and French during the Crimean campaign and enthusiastically backed by the Sultan himself. In September 1855 the first telegrams were exchanged between Constantinople, London and Paris, and before the Sultan's death in June 1861 there were cables between Stamboul, Bucharest, Belgrade and Salonika, and in Asia from Üsküdar to Baghdad. Abdulmecid welcomed links with Western Europe. Moreover, he recognized that the electric telegraph provided a means of projecting centralized power from the Porte to provincial governors, those tiresome beys who had so often vexed earlier Sultans by the cavalier independence with which they administered the more distant regions. The telegraph helped promote a sense of cohesive unity within the Ottoman Empire.[13]

By now, however, it was a smaller Empire. The range of the Sultan's authority had contracted considerably in the past half-century. Algeria was a French possession, Tunisia already dependent upon France; and, although the Ottomans had re-established effective rule in Tripolitania, the Bedouin of Cyrenaica followed the strictly puritanical Sanussi order which was led throughout the second half of the century by Sayyid Muhammad al-Mahdi. In Egypt the cordiality which had marked the relationship between the Sultanate and the Viceregal dynasty on the eve of the Crimean War soon waned; it did not survive the death of Abbas Hilmi in 1854 and the accession of his uncle, Muhammad Said, who had been Muhammad Ali's favourite son.

Said is sometimes represented as pro-French and anti-Ottoman. But these labels oversimplify. An amiably weak-willed ruler, Said preferred to let events take their own course. The Egyptian tribute of £360,000 a year to the Sultan's civil list continued to be paid regularly; on three occasions it provided the guarantee on which the Porte raised a foreign loan. Yet the growth of a flourishing cotton-based Egyptian economy went ahead without reference to Abdulmecid or Abdulaziz. Nor was Constantinople consulted when, within a few months of becoming Viceroy, Said authorized his friend Ferdinand de Lesseps to draw up plans for a canal from Suez to the new Mediterranean port that perpetuates the Viceroy's name. The canal project aroused fierce opposition in Constantinople. The British, always mistrustful of the French in Egypt, assured the Porte that the opening of a new waterway in the most prosperous of the Sultan's tributary dependencies might benefit entrepreneurs in Paris but would certainly lower the importance of the old trade routes from the Straits to the Euphrates and Persia. Yet the Ottoman government had no effective power of veto. So weak were the links between Sultan and Viceroy that work on digging de

Lesseps' canal had been in progress for almost seven years before, in March 1866, Sultan Abdulaziz at last gave his formal approval to the project.[14]

Along the Empire's European frontiers the main challenge to the Sultan's authority continued to come from the surfacing of long-submerged Balkan nationalism. By 1860 Serbia was already virtually lost. The maintenance of Ottoman garrisons in Belgrade and two other fortresses proved an expensive embarrassment, especially when during Ramadan in 1862 a fanatical Turkish commander bombarded the Christian quarters of the Serbian capital for over four hours; the Ottoman withdrawal in 1867 made good sense, politically and economically. But relations with Serbia remained strained: the Serbs were encouraging their compatriots outside the Principality, particularly in Bosnia and Herzegovina (where there was an anti-Ottoman revolt in 1857), and their fellow Southern Slavs in Bulgaria and Montenegro. In May 1858 a punitive Ottoman expedition penetrated Montenegro, only to be trapped and routed in the rocky defile of Grahovo. Unrest along this mountainous north-west frontier land continued throughout the following decade. As a British traveller drily observed, it was a region where fighting the Turk was looked upon 'as a pastime, or a superior kind of field sport'.[15]

'Latin' Roumania owed much to the patronage of the Second Empire at a time when the former French ambassador to the Porte, Édouard de Thouvenel, served as Napoleon III's foreign minister. French support ensured that the Danubian Principalities – long a granary for Constantinople and its dependent towns – slipped from the Sultan's grasp within a few years of the Congress of Paris, as indeed the terms of the peace treaty had anticipated. Moldavia and Wallachia came together under the same hospodar (Alexander Cuza) in 1859 and their formal union as the 'United Principalities of Roumania' was proclaimed in December 1861, a few months after Abdulmecid's death. Technically Roumania remained an Ottoman tributary state for another sixteen years; but as a Christian principality it showed even more political independence than Egypt, particularly after 1866 when Roumania's newly-elected Prince, Charles of Hohenzollern-Sigmaringen, began his forty-eight-year rule in Bucharest.

The heart of the Levant posed a different set of problems from the Balkan lands, Egypt or the Maghreb. Syria and Lebanon perplexed the *Tanzimat* ministers in the last years of Abdulmecid's reign, as at its beginning. Fighting between Maronite peasants and landowners in 1858 around Mount Lebanon sparked off another civil war between

Druze and Maronite factions which, by the spring of 1860, had spread to Damascus. In that year some 8,000 Maronites and 1,500 Druze were killed in communal fighting or died from starvation in Lebanon alone, and more than 5,000 Catholic Christians were massacred in Damascus. News of this massacre led Napoleon III to urge the dispatch of an international peacekeeping force to protect the Maronites. He proposed an expedition to Beirut and ultimately to Syria, with most of the troops supplied by the French. Neither the Ottoman authorities nor the British wished to see a predominantly French expeditionary force in the Levant; was not the official anthem of the Second Empire, *Partant pour la Syrie*, a marching-song composed by Napoleon III's mother in her girlhood for her stepfather, the great Bonaparte? The Ottoman Foreign Minister, Fuad, hastened to Beirut ahead of the international peacekeepers, stamping out disorder by the drastic expedient of executing Ottoman officials and army officers who permitted trouble to break out in any district for which they were responsible. The French argued, with some justice, that the Sultans' commissioners had attempted to keep the peace with an iron hand in previous troubled years and that as soon as their firm grip was relaxed, Lebanon and Syria reverted to anarchy, with murder and destruction sweeping yet again through rival towns and villages. Despite the solemn assurance of the Treaty of Paris that the Powers would not interfere in the internal administration of the Ottoman Empire, the French continued to urge some form of international supervision to ensure that the Sultan imposed fundamental reforms on the government of both the Lebanon and Syria. In January 1861 Édouard de Thouvenel, with Napoleon III's backing, summoned a conference to discuss the problems of the Levant. So essential was French financial support for Ottoman ventures that the Porte readily accepted Thouvenel's proposal and sent delegates to Paris.

Critics of the Second Empire argued that Thouvenel's conference set a bad precedent, threatening the integrity of the Ottoman Empire.[16] But the Sultan's representatives served him well. With British encouragement they effectively prevented all discussion of specifically Syrian affairs, but in the spring a wise settlement was reached for the Lebanon itself. It was agreed that most of the interior should become an autonomous province under a non-Lebanese Christian Governor, with an advisory council equally representative of the differing religious faiths and with administrative districts so arranged that each would represent a separate sect. Not until this new settlement was in operation did Napoleon III withdraw his troops. To the surprise of diplomats who had known the region in the past two decades, this Lebanese settlement proved effective. It survived until the Ottoman military authorities took advantage of the war crisis in 1914 to impose direct rule, thereby clumsily ensuring that the Lebanese sided with the Sultan's enemies. The 1861 settlement did not, as its critics feared, hamper the *Tanzimat* reformers in their attempts to create a modern unitary state. The merit of the settlement lay in its recognition of local variations, district by district, so that power could be shared on a communal basis rather than being imposed by a distant and remote sovereign. For other regions devastated by social and religious conflict, the Lebanese Agreement offered a model of just administration. Sadly, they ignored it.

Abdulmecid gave formal approval to the new regime in the Lebanon on 9 June 1861. It was the last administrative act of his reign. Within three weeks he was dead, from tuberculosis, still only in his thirty-ninth year. His successor, his half-brother Abdulaziz, was thirty-one, a bearded giant who weighed over sixteen stone and required a bed eight feet long (which may still be seen in the Dolmabahche). By nature Abdulaziz was autocratic, and even more extravagant than Abdulmecid. Attempts to curb expenditure at Court led to outbursts of furious temper. He won Queen Victoria's approval when he took her arm and escorted her in to luncheon at Windsor in 1867; she liked 'the true, splendid, soft, brown oriental eyes', as she wrote to her eldest daughter, adding that 'he never touched wine'.[17] But foreign dignitaries visiting Constantinople were less indulgent. Even allowing for fabricated rumours which exaggerated the Sultan's eccentricities, it soon seemed clear to them that Abdulaziz would readily shed the enlightened westernized practices of a reformed Sultanate in favour of the more sinister whims of a capricious tyrant.

Yet, until Ali Pasha's death in 1871, *Tanzimat* restructuring of the state continued, with the Sultan under pressure from the French, British and Austrian governments to carry through the reform programme. Changes in provincial government in 1858 were complemented six years later by the Vilayet Law, which extended the pattern of large provincial units (vilayets), with clearly differentiated administrative departments, to the Empire as a whole. In general, law reform closely followed French models, as practised under the Second Empire: a new Ottoman penal code in 1858 was followed by a commercial code, promulgated at the start of Abdulaziz's reign, and in 1869 by Ahmed Cevdet's civil code, the *Mecelle*, a masterly compromise allowing the Islamic *şeriat* tradition to be preserved – and even enhanced – within

a fundamentally Napoleonic concept of law. French influence persisted, too, in education. The Galatasaray Lycée (the Imperial Ottoman
School), a boys' secondary school in the heart of Pera, opened its gates
in September 1869. The *Mekteb-i Sultani* was founded in order to provide
servants of Empire for the Ottomans – much as did Eton and Harrow
in England or, more precisely, the Lycée Louis-le-Grand in Paris. The
boys, Muslim and Christian alike, received most of their tuition in
French and followed a western curriculum, even to the extent of learning Latin.[18]

There were, however, already signs of a reaction against *Tanzimat*.
In January 1865 a Press Law set up a special department of the Sublime
Porte which soon afterwards began to suppress newspapers whose tone
was considered 'hostile'. It is significant that in June of that same year
the first influential group of intellectual dissidents emerged in the
capital. They were inspired by the essayist and playwright Namik
Kemal and the writings of the older reformer Sadik Rifat. Like dissidents in the Soviet bloc during the 1980s they were strongly individu-
alistic, with no agreed panacea for the Empire's problems. Namik
thought the *Tanzimat* reformers too inclined to borrow ideas and institutions from the West without allowing for the Koranic traditions which
still shaped society, especially in the more remote provinces. One
splinter group, led by Ali Suavi, went even further than Namik, becoming Islamic fundamentalist in its total dedication to the priority of
şeriat teachings.[19]

At first these 'Young Ottomans' (*Yeni Osmanlilar*) received financial
backing from Prince Mustafa Fazil, son of that formidable warrior,
Ibrahim Pasha; and it is possible that the Prince saw himself as the
constitutional monarch of a federalized empire which would stretch
from the lower Danube to the Euphrates and the Nile. But the dissidents
were totally loyal to the Ottoman state. They preached an Ottoman
patriotism which, at least from 1870 onwards, began to emphasize
Turkish nationalism, a new concept. So, too, in the Ottoman lands
was their campaign in favour of a 'constitution', an experiment already
working in Tunisia and, from 1866 onwards, in Egypt. Namik Kemal
advocated the summoning by the Sultan of a parliament on the model
of Britain or France. The Sultan's capricious style of personal rule
ensured that the Young Ottomans' campaign for an elected chamber
received increasing attention among the intelligentsia in the greater
cities. In 1873 Namik was shipped off to Famagusta, where he was
imprisoned in close confinement, but his arrest scarcely checked the
momentum of the campaign. It increased the appeal of the Young

Ottomans' cause by giving them a heroic exile awaiting a summons home.

'European systems of government, European ideas, European laws or customs – no *honest* Turk will ever pretend to admire any of these,' Stratford de Redcliffe had remarked to one of his aides during the Crimean War. 'If ever Easterns (*sic*) get imbued with Liberal ideas of government their own doom is sealed,' he added.[20] Sir William Bulwer, Stratford's successor as ambassador in 1858, was also more concerned with efficient government than with 'liberal' government, for his sojourn in Pera coincided with the peak period of unrestricted encroachment on the Ottoman economy by foreign banks. When he retired from diplomacy in 1865 he broke with precedent by serving as agent in the Levant for a French banking institution. As ambassador he had always welcomed reforms which provided openings for financial credit.

The Imperial Ottoman Bank was established with French and British capital in 1863: the Director-General was French, and his deputy was a City banker from London. A smaller institution, the *Société Générale de l'Empire Ottoman*, was set up later in the same year, and followed in 1868 by the *Crédit Général Ottoman* and by a small Russian Bank.[21] Throughout the decade French funds flowed into government bonds and investments likely to promote trade. The opportunities for foreign bond-holders were so great that successive governments in London as well as political leaders in Paris and Vienna willingly deluded themselves that 'Turkey' had become a modern and reformed state. When the Ottomans suppressed the Cretan rebellion of 1866–7 there were far fewer protests in the West than during the earlier conflicts with Greeks 'struggling to be free'.

The seal of international approval was extended to Abdulaziz in 1867, when he was invited to Napoleon III's 'Great Universal Exhibition' in Paris in 1867. It was the first occasion upon which a Sultan visited a non-Islamic state except to wage war. The Sultan was received by Emperor Francis Joseph in Vienna and, after meeting Queen Victoria at Windsor, rode in a colourful procession through the streets of London, 'looking like a typical Turk', as *The Times* reported, searching none too assiduously for the fitting phrase. A fast train sped him to Portsmouth, where the Queen made him a Knight of the Garter. When not prostrate below decks, the Sultan saw the might of the Royal Navy pass in review off Spithead and was deeply impressed, despite being 'not comfortable' (the Queen's words).[22] Abdulaziz brought with him to the West his nine-year-old son and two nephews, the future Sultans Murad V and

Abdulhamid II. The Sultanate had shed the isolation of centuries. Rigid *kafe* immurement of princes was gone; or so it seemed.

The Ottoman Grand Tour had important social consequences. It intensified Abdulaziz's delight in palace extravagance, and filled him with desire for a fleet of ironclads, mostly laid down in British yards. Above all, it confirmed his love of railways, '*une véritable fièvre de chemin de fer*' as the Russian ambassador wrote in 1873, the year locomotive smoke was first seen blowing out across the Bosphorus.[23] In that summer of 1873 trains began running in Anatolia, though only as far as İzmit, some 50 miles along the coast from Haydarpaša, the terminus facing Stamboul. The railway was built by the French, who were also responsible for a short line opened in the same year from Mudania, on the Anatolian shore of the Sea of Marmara, inland to Bursa. Yet, while French and British concerns still dominated the Ottoman economy, the chief beneficiaries from Abdulaziz's railway mania were Germany and Austria–Hungary. In 1872 a German engineer, Wilhelm von Pressel, presented the Porte with a ten-year master plan to extend the İzmit line to Ankara and the Persian Gulf, a project which appealed to Abdulaziz, though little was done to fulfil it until long after his death.[24]

The Sultan was also attracted by plans for an Orient line drawn up by the Bavarian-born Baron Hirsch, whose banking interests were in Vienna and Paris. In 1870 it therefore seemed as if the Ottoman capital would soon be linked with the railway network of central Europe. Significantly, a year later, a *Banque Austro-Ottomane* and a *Banque Austro-Turque* opened offices in Constantinople. But all Austrian railway projects suffered from the collapse of the Vienna stock-market on Black Friday, 9 May 1873; and by the end of Abdulaziz's reign the Orient railway had made little progress. It linked Constantinople with Edirne and Plovdiv (Philippopolis), while a feeder line ran southwards from Edirne to the Aegean coast at Dedeağatch (now Alexandroúpolis). Legend insists that the apparent inability of the Plovdiv route to follow a straight line across flat and open country was due to a clause in Hirsch's contract which provided for him to be paid, not an overall sum, but a fee for each kilometre of track laid. This tale is probably apocryphal, but there is no doubt that corruption was widespread at every level during the railway craze.

Shock-waves from Vienna's 'Black Friday' shook the already fragile Ottoman financial system. Almost half the total resources of the government was absorbed by the need to meet annuities, interest payments, and the demands of a sinking fund on a dozen foreign loans contracted by the Sultans since the Crimean War. As the Treasury accounts made no distinction between the needs of state and the inroads of the sovereign, it is small wonder that, with less than one-tenth of the loans being spent on measures to increase the Empire's economic well-being, Abdulaziz's conduct of government should have exasperated a succession of ministers. When Emin Ali died in September 1871 he had completed five terms of office as Grand Vizier, effectively dominating the Porte for some eighteen years, even though he had often clashed with his sovereign. This relative continuity of government ended with Ali's death, for Abdulaziz resolved to rule as an autocrat. He sought pliant Grand Viziers, whom he would dismiss as soon as they began to form political groups of personal followers; and he also nominated provincial governors, choosing those whom he believed capable of speedily collecting taxes in their particular vilayet. Between September 1871 and February 1874 there were six different Grand Viziers; in the provinces there were so many changes at the top that the average length of term for a governor was little more than four months.[25] With Grand Viziers flipping in and out of office every seven months and provincial governors every four, the widespread frustration at persistent misrule was turned against the Sultan himself rather than against his ministers or officials. If the ousted viziers possessed any strength of character, they could count on support from the Young Ottoman dissidents.

Two of these transient Grand Viziers were powerful personalities. Ahmed Midhat had served as an enlightened provincial governor on the lower Danube and in Baghdad. He was appointed Grand Vizier in the last week of July 1872, soon after his fiftieth birthday. Within three months, however, Midhat was dismissed, having fallen foul of the Sultan on three counts: he aired the possibility of a federalized structure for the Empire; he set up an Accounting Department; and, most disturbing of all, he began to investigate corruption at the heart of the Dolmabahche itself. The second masterful Grand Vizier was Hüseyin Avni, who held office from February 1874 to April 1875. To foreign diplomats Hüseyin seemed more formidable than Midhat, but he was less intelligent: he had served as *serasker* (Commander-in-Chief) for four years. No one was better placed to organize a military coup; and it was therefore foolish of Abdulaziz to dismiss Hüseyin because he resented his attempts to divert funds from the palace to meet the needs of the army. It was also foolish of the Sultan, four months later, to make Mahmud Nedim his Grand Vizier, for Nedim was popularly believed to be in Russian pay. There was no doubt that he treated the Tsar's ambassador, General Nikolai Ignatiev, with a consideration similar to the exaggerated respect which earlier viziers had accorded to Stratford de Redcliffe.

By now Abdulaziz's behaviour seemed to justify the rumours of his mental instability. Paroxysms of fury became more violent and more frequent. The Sultan seemed incapable of checking his extravagance. He would still spend lavishly on the harem and his palace, especially a new pavilion at Yildiz in high parkland to the north of the Dolmabahche. Yet in October 1875 the wretched Nedim was forced to announce a suspension of payment of interest on the Ottoman Debt, thus virtually admitting state bankruptcy.[26] The financial chaos caused by twenty years of European bank loans and extravagant mismanagement left the Ottoman Empire dependent for survival on the good will of foreign governments.

The state bankruptcy could hardly have come at a worse moment. In June 1875 the Christian South Slavs of Herzegovina rose in revolt, their old resentments over taxation fed by intensive Panslav propaganda originating in Moscow (as distinct from official Tsarist policy, which was determined in St Petersburg). The rising soon spread from Nevesinje, near Mostar, into Bosnia and along the restless borderland with Montenegro. It was followed in the spring of 1876 by a Bulgarian rebellion in the villages of the Rhodope Mountains, beyond Plovdiv. While this rebellion was taking place, a riot in Salonika over a Bulgarian Orthodox girl – said (wrongly) to be a convert to Islam against her will – resulted in the murder of the French and German consuls, killed in a mosque by fanatics whom the Ottoman governor was powerless to restrain. The Salonika murders caused instant indignation in the European chancelleries. Worse was to follow. Throughout June graphic newspaper reports from Bulgaria shocked public opinion. Eyewitness accounts of thousands of Christian men, women and children found dead after six weeks of repression by local volunteer militia (*başi bozuka*) stirred humanitarian crusaders in the West and among the Orthodox faithful of Holy Russia. Assertions that rebels as well as militia had committed atrocities went unheeded. Governments could not check mounting popular anger against 'the Turk', however much the great financial institutions might deplore the reopening of the Eastern Question at such a time.[27]

Abdulaziz was deposed before news of the Bulgarian atrocities broke in the newspapers of the West. On 10 May thousands of Muslim students packed the squares in front of the mosques in Stamboul and along the Galata waterfront demanding the dismissal of Nedim and the *şeyhülislâm*. Their mood was fundamentally conservative, hostile to outside pressure, and sympathetic to their co-religionists in Salonika; they accused the Porte of abject appeasement of the Great Powers after the killing of the two foreign consuls. The unrest was exploited by Midhat, Hüseyin Avni and the inner directorate of the Young Ottomans. Abdulaziz dismissed Nedim. He reinstated Hüseyin as Commander-in-Chief. He even appointed Midhat, whom he hated, a member of the Divan. But he could not save his throne.

Within a fortnight of Nedim's dismissal Sir Henry Elliot, the British ambassador, reported that the overthrow of the Sultan seemed inevitable: the word ' "Constitution" was in every mouth'.[28] As Sir Henry was notorious for spending much of his time with a voluptuous Greek on a tranquil island in the Sea of Marmara, it is not clear where he observed these mouths shaping so rare a word: but the British, fearing grave riots in the capital, ordered the Mediterranean fleet to Besika Bay off the approaches to the Dardanelles, and Ignatiev fortified the Russian Embassy. In the small hours of 30 May, on Hüseyin's orders, the commandant of the military academy sealed off the Dolmabahche with two battalions of infantry, while warships moored off-shore trained their guns on the palace. The *serasker*'s bodyguard escorted Hüseyin into the throne-room, where on the previous evening Abdulaziz had staged a cock-fight to amuse himself.

There followed some minutes of high drama. Hüseyin was suddenly confronted on the ceremonial staircase by the massive figure of his Sultan, still in a night-shirt but wielding a sword as if determined to fight to the death. Behind him appeared his formidable mother, the 66-year-old *Valide Sultana* Pertevniyal, a tigress urging her son to defend himself (and her own privileged position). There was no bloodshed, however; both *serasker* and Sultan remained at heart traditional formularists; Hüseyin presented a solemn *fetva* of deposition, and Abdulaziz bowed to the inevitable. His state barge took him across the Golden Horn to the Topkapi Sarayi, passing on its short voyage the caique of his nephew, Prince Murad, coming reluctantly to assume the responsibilities of Empire under Midhat's watchful eye. The frightened Murad implored Midhat to remain in the Dolmabahche. He did so willingly.[29]

After a night in the old palace, Abdulaziz was rowed back to the Çiragan, where he was joined by Pertevniyal and members of his harem. On 4 June the deposed Sultan was found dead, his wrists slashed by scissors. Officially he had committed suicide, a verdict accepted by the ambassadors. But the doctor attached to the British Embassy was among physicians who were allowed to examine the corpse; he came to the conclusion that the cuts could not have been self-inflicted. The drama was not yet over. Eight days after Abdulaziz's death, his favourite young Circassian wife Nesrin died, apparently in childbirth. The tragedy unhinged Nesrin's brother, Çerkes Hasan, a young army officer who had served as an aide-de-camp in the imperial household. On 14 June he burst into a meeting of ministers, firing his revolver wildly. Hüseyin Avni and the Foreign Minister were assassinated as they sat in conference.[30]

These events were too much for the new Sultan, who may well have doubted the suicide verdict on his uncle. Murad V was a westernizer by upbringing, sympathetic to the Masonic movement and a member of the Grand Orient Lodge. His visit to Paris had taught him the delights of champagne, which he would fortify with good cognac. Palace politics, laced with murder, were not to his liking. Sir Henry Elliot reported to the Foreign Office that, on hearing of Abdulaziz's death, Murad fainted and then was stricken with fits of vomiting for the next day and a half.[31] He was, too, deeply affected by the fate of Çerkes Hasan, who was publicly hanged four days after running amok at the cabinet meeting. So strange was Murad's conduct in the first fortnight of his reign that the *kılıç kuşanmacı* – the coronation ceremony at Eyüp – was postponed. Murad V became the only Sultan since the fall of Byzantium never girded with the sword.

Nine weeks after his accession a skilled British newspaper correspondent described the 35-year-old Sultan 'as one possessed, sitting on his sofa, motionless and speechless, smoothing his thin moustaches and beardless chin with his right hand hour after hour the livelong day, meditating on his abdication and only wondering on which of his reluctant brothers may devolve the burden which is too much for his shoulders.'[32] That burden was becoming heavier with the passage of each week of crisis. By now the Ottoman Empire was at war with Serbia and Montenegro, whose princes had responded to a widespread demand among their subjects to support their compatriots rebelling against Turkish rule in Bosnia-Herzegovina. Although the local Ottoman commanders had little difficulty in holding the frontiers, the presence of thousands of Russian volunteers alongside the Serbs and Montenegrins made it likely that the conflict would soon spread. If so, the Ottoman soldiery needed a sovereign more resolute than the nervous wreck whom Midhat had pushed on to the throne.

On 17 August Sir Henry Elliot described the visit to the Dolmabahche of an eminent Austrian neurologist: the Sultan, it was said, 'was suffering from chronic alcoholism aggravated by the emotions he has gone through'; with total abstinence and rest his mind might well recover.[33]

But the constitution-seekers were in a hurry. A *fetva* was prepared justifying this second deposition in three months on the grounds of the Sultan's insanity. No violence was used. Murad's younger brother, Abdulhamid, had already assured Midhat of his support for reform. On 31 August 1876 Abdulhamid II was proclaimed Sultan. The deposed Murad was transferred to the Çirağan, where he was confined in a modernized *kafe* until his death, twenty-eight years later.

CHAPTER 10

Yildiz

Abdulhamid's subjects were able to acclaim their Sultan and Caliph a week after his accession. Some 100,000 people – men, women and children – lined the waterfront or watched from higher vantage points as, in the late forenoon of 7 September 1876, twenty-eight oarsmen of the imperial barge rowed the new Sultan up the Golden Horn, to be girded with the sword at Eyüp. Not that much could be seen of him: ships dipping their flags as the barge passed seemed to salute a crimson canopy rather than a person, for at thirty-four Abdulhamid would already hunch his cadaverous body into that sinister, brooding figure whom cartoonists portrayed in later years as 'Abdul the Damned'.[1] He looked more impressive astride the traditional white horse with a golden bridle, riding back to the city after the ritual of *kiliç kuşanmaci* was fulfilled; but even then an observer commented on the furrows of thought across his face and the 'profound expression of melancholy' in those dark and darting eyes. His hooked nose, pallid skin, chiselled cheekbones and luxuriant beard emphasized the mistrust and suspicion inherent in his character.

Psychologically, everything was wrong about Abdulhamid's childhood. His father Abdulmecid had offered the ugly little boy scant affection; his mother, a Circassian dancing girl from the Trebizond slave market, had died from consumption when he was ten; his brothers found him an eavesdropper and a spoil-sport. He grew up lonely but never alone, so often reproved that he retained into manhood an inner timidity which made him fearful of assassination and inclined to waver at the moment any policy initiative was put to the test. Yet he came to the throne strong-willed and determined: he would rule, not reign; the centre of authority was to lie in the imperial palace rather than at the Sublime Porte.

A week after the *kiliç kuşanmaci* ceremony the British ambassador sent back to London his considered opinion of the new Sultan. Sir Henry Elliot commended Abdulhamid's 'kindliness of disposition and enlightened views', but he doubted 'whether he will accept restrictions which the reforming party thinks necessary'.[2] Over the previous twelve months the Sultan had prepared himself seriously for his duties. He never liked the Dolmabahche; as often as possible in the last years of Abdulaziz he had absented himself from the palace. Sometimes he stayed with his foster-mother at her villa inland from Pera, but he preferred his summer pavilion ten miles up the Bosphorus, above the wooded bay of Therapia (now Tarabya). There he would sound out the opinions of an English businessman – 'Mr Thompson' – who had a house and land next to the imperial estate. Thompson kept Abdulhamid well-informed about Disraeli and Derby, and all the eccentricities of the British parliamentary system. Almost certainly, he was the anonymous 'Englishman' who, on the eve of Abdulhamid's accession, let Elliot know of the heir-presumptive's intention to introduce a 'totally new era' of government, in which competent and unsullied ministers would exercise 'rigorous economy'.

Abdulhamid gained some understanding of finance from his banker, Hakop Zarifi, an Armenian he consulted at his mother's villa and at Therapia.[3] He seems, too, to have trusted his physician, John Mavroyeni, from whom he learnt of the Phanariot attitude to the crises of the Empire, noting the scant sympathy shown by Greek Orthodox believers for Bulgarians, or any other group of their Southern Slav co-religionists. Throughout the first months of the reign Abdulhamid continued his practice of seeking to draw out opinions on current problems of government, while saying little himself. Yet when he received the Young Ottoman intellectual leader Namik Kemal in audience, he went so far as to hold out to him some prospect of a revitalized Sultanate; and in the first week of October Abdulhamid set up a commission authorized to prepare a constitution. Sixteen officials with experience of central government or administration, ten *ulema* and two senior army officers were to meet under the chairmanship of Midhat Pasha.

A preliminary constitutional draft was swiftly completed. It bore a close resemblance to the parliamentary monarchy established by the Belgian Constitution of 1831 which, in its turn, had borrowed from Great Britain and France. But Abdulhamid, backed by the army and by religious leaders, had no intention of seeing the Ottoman Empire transformed into a parliamentary Sultanate. He did not object to a bicameral legislature, with an elected Chamber of Deputies and a

Chamber of Notables ('Senate') nominated by himself; and he accepted some basic guarantees of human rights, even freedom of the press. Yet he ensured that the constitution was entirely dependent upon his whim: a late insertion into the draft secured recognition of the Sultan's right to declare a state of siege which would suspend the guarantees of the constitution during a grave emergency; and Article 113 authorized the Sultan to send into exile any person whom he considered dangerous to himself or to the empire as a whole.[4]

The Constitutional Commission completed its work in record time, a mere nine weeks. There was good reason for this speed. During the autumn the international crisis in the Balkans intensified, with Russia threatening to go to war in order to protect Serbia and Montenegro from Ottoman vengeance and secure reforms in Bulgaria and Bosnia-Herzegovina. Gladstone's pamphlet on *The Bulgarian Horrors and the Question of the East* had gone on sale in London on the day before Abdulhamid was girded with the sword at Eyüp: the pamphlet sold 40,000 copies in a week in Britain, while a translation printed in Moscow set up a record for Russia of 10,000 copies in a month. The famous appeal for 'the Turks' to 'carry away their abuses in the only possible manner by carrying off themselves . . . bag and baggage . . . from the province they have desolated and profaned' made welcome reading in Moscow and St Petersburg, although it was regarded as inflammatory by statesmen still hoping to limit the crisis to the Balkan peninsula. Yet the pamphlet and the meetings of protest in Britain and in Russia helped shape government policies. On 4 November the Great Powers accepted a British proposal for an international conference which was to gather in Constantinople and examine ways of granting administrative autonomy to Bosnia and Herzegovina. The conference would affirm the territorial integrity of the Ottoman Empire, while considering administrative reforms suitable to the Bulgarian provinces.[5]

Abdulhamid regarded the proposal for such a conference in the imperial capital as outside interference with the peoples whom Allah had so recently called him to protect. Never before had a Sultan been faced with so humiliating a proposal; and for a fortnight Abdulhamid prevaricated. On 14 November partial Russian mobilization – together with the continued need of the Ottoman state for financial assistance from abroad – induced him, with extreme reluctance, to accept the idea of the conference. With one exception the delegates comprised the ambassadors to the Porte, supplemented by professional diplomats whom the foreign ministries in Paris, Berlin, Vienna and St Petersburg regarded as experts in Balkan affairs. The exception was the principal

1. Selim III, Sultan 1789–1807

Topkapi palace: the Gate of Salutation, the entry to the 'Old Seraglio'

3. The giant Sultan,
Abdulaziz

4. The British doubt
Ottoman promises of
reform: *Punch*, 6 January
1877

Sultan Abdulhamid photographed soon after his accession in 1876

6. *Punch* deplores the Armenian Massacres, 1896. The cartoon carries the caption: 'The Unspeakable Turk, "Ha, ha, There's no one about! I can get to business again!" '

The Sublime Porte; the gateway to the Grand Vizier's residence which gave its
me to the Ottoman government in general

Crowds outside the Yildiz palace for Abdulhamid's last *selamlik*, 23 April 1909

9. 'Abdul the Damned', 7 August 1908. A wary Sultan observes his subjects, shortly after he has restored the constitution

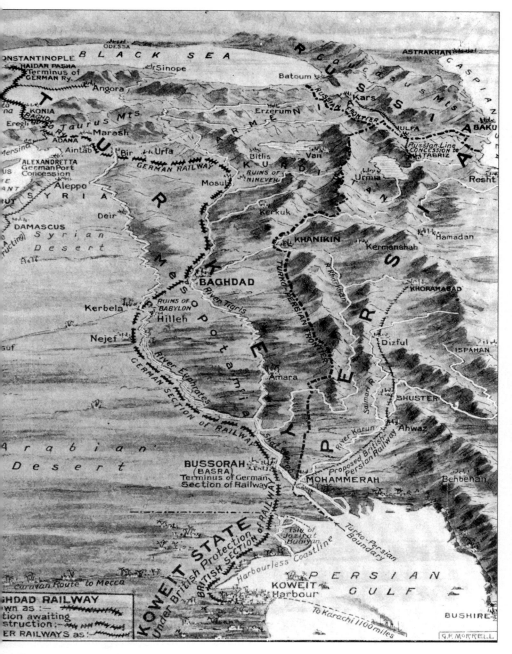

Railways to the Gulf: projected lines, as depicted in June 1913

11. and 12. Modernizing the Ottoman fleet: *above*, the battleship *Sultan Osman I*, built in England for Turkey but taken over on Churchill's orders as HMS *Agincourt*; *below*, the German battle-cruiser *Goeben* in the Bosphorus after becoming the Ottoman flagship *Jawuz Sultan Selim*

. General Liman von Sanders, head of the German military mission, with
ttoman officers at Haifa

. Constantinople from the air, 1918: *centre* St Sophia's basilica; *top left* Galata
idge; *centre left* the Blue Mosque, beside the old Hippodrome (Maydan). Above
Sophia's and to the right is the Topkapi palace

15. Enver Pasha listens to German advice while visiting the Caucasian Front in 1917

16. The Seyhulislam greets Kaiser William II in Constantinople, October 1917: Sultan Mehmed V is on the Kaiser's left, with Enver behind him

17. Allied warships moored off the Dolmabahche palace, 1919

British delegate, the Marquess of Salisbury, Secretary of State for India in Disraeli's cabinet. His six-week visit to the Ottoman capital was to have a far more enduring significance than the conference itself.

Lord and Lady Salisbury, and their eldest son, arrived at Constantinople on 5 December, three months after Abdulhamid's accession. No British cabinet minister had spent so many hours studying foreign affairs or written about them so extensively; and it is characteristic of Salisbury that he should have sounded out opinion in Paris, Berlin, Vienna and Rome before completing his journey to the Golden Horn. While the British prime minister and ambassador were turcophile, Salisbury already privately believed that the Crimean War had been a disastrous error of policy. These prejudices were confirmed by his hosts in the European capitals, who thought the Ottoman Empire had sunk into irreversible decline.

Nothing Salisbury saw in Constantinople caused him to revise his opinions. Abdulhamid received him in audience, showing those exquisite good manners which Elliot admired. But, to the ambassador's dismay, Salisbury remained unresponsive. He mistrusted the Sultan and all his ministers, despite the honours Abdulhamid bestowed on his guests. Not even the Order of Chastity (Third Class), so courteously awarded to the Marchioness, mollified her husband, although it amused him. 'A wretched, feeble creature, who told me he dared not grant what we demanded because he was in danger of his life,' Salisbury wrote in a private letter home to his third son that Christmas.[6] Such a comment from a career diplomat accredited to the Porte would be of little interest. But in 1876 Salisbury was the coming man of British imperial politics; as Foreign Secretary or Prime Minister (and generally as both) he was to shape British policy for almost half of the Sultan's thirty-two years on the throne. Never did he revise his conviction of Abdulhamid's worthlessness.

The conference was preceded by nine round-table sessions at the Russian Embassy, under General Ignatiev's chairmanship, intended to decide exactly how the Sultan should put his house in order. As if to prove his commitment to reform, on 19 December Abdulhamid appointed Midhat Pasha Grand Vizier. When, four days later, the conference held a first full session in the Ottoman Admiralty building beside the naval dockyard on the Golden Horn, the opening deliberations were suddenly disturbed by the booming of guns. Blandly the Ottoman Foreign Minister informed the delegates that the sound they heard was a salute honouring the proclamation of Midhat's constitution. With reforms promised for the peoples of the empire, the Sultan's representatives argued that the conference had become a superfluous irrelevancy. Well-orchestrated patriotic demonstrations by Muslim students denounced Panslavism and called for war against Russia; delegates noted that Greeks and Armenians were as vociferously anti-Russian as the Young Ottomans. These gestures of popular feeling strengthened the Sultan's resolve. Every proposal by the foreign delegates was rejected. On 20 January 1877 they abandoned the task. Their collective departure, planned as a dignified reproof, lost its effectiveness when the waterfront was lashed so severely by a gale that only an indignant Lord Salisbury braved the appalling weather.[7]

Abdulhamid was not displeased over the discomfiture of the foreign delegates who had assembled in his capital to dictate reforms. Nevertheless the failure of what the Turks, with a touch of derision, called the Dockyard Conference (*Tersane Konferansi*) kept Europe's money markets closed to the impoverished Ottoman state while bringing closer the prospect of war with Russia; and the Sultan, who hated Midhat, could therefore blame his Grand Vizier for having humiliated the foreign envoys. He also noted with sympathy the complaints of military and religious leaders at the Grand Vizier's attempt to have Christians accepted alongside Muslims as cadets at the War Academy. A fortnight after the conference broke up, Midhat was summoned to the Dolmabahche; he noticed as he arrived at the palace that the imperial yacht had steam up, though early February seemed an unlikely season for Abdulhamid to put to sea. But the Sultan was not even present at the Dolmabahche. An officer of the household informed Midhat that, under the emergency clause of the constitution (Article 113), the Sultan was ordering his arrest and banishment, as a danger to the state. He was put aboard the imperial yacht, which sailed at once for Brindisi. A minor bureaucrat, totally dependent upon his Sultan, replaced him as Grand Vizier. The diplomatic corps was assured that, although the architect of the 1876 Constitution might be in exile, the Sultan had no intention of abandoning the parliamentary experiment.[8]

Elections had already taken place in several provinces and were about to be held in the capital. They caused no excitement: the franchise was restricted, and the indirect voting procedure was regulated by a complicated pattern of electoral colleges. Among the more distant subjects of the Sultan, the prospect of parliamentary representation aroused little interest, except negatively in the Lebanon, where the Maronites refused to take part in any elections for fear that an all-Ottoman parliament would threaten the autonomy won fifteen years before. But in the third week of March 1877 the Sultan opened the

Meclis-i Mebusan (Chamber of Deputies) in an elaborate ceremony at the Dolmabahche attended by the diplomatic corps, the religious notables and all the dignitaries of state.

The Speaker was nominated by Abdulhamid, ignoring agreed procedures for election to the office by the Chamber itself; but the Sultan's speech was read to deputies by his palace secretary, Küchük Mehmed Said, who was to serve as Grand Vizier on seven occasions during the reign. The speech held promise of a programme of reforms which would improve administration, justice and farming. The deputies – 71 Muslims, 44 Christians, 4 Jews – then retired to the chamber set aside for them in Stamboul, a hall in a building near St Sophia, built in 1840 as a new university but subsequently housing government offices. There, over the following three months, the deputies discussed such topics as the composition of advisory councils in the provinces, a restrictive Press Law, and the need to cut the salaries of civil servants. *The Times* correspondent, attending one of the early sessions, was impressed by the multinational character of the *Meclis-i Mebusan*: 'We have counted in the Chamber 10 nationalities speaking 14 different languages,' he reported.[9] During the summer the Sultan appointed 21 Muslims and 5 non-Muslims to constitute a senate, the *Meclis-i Ayan* (Chamber of Notables). Abdulhamid allowed the two chambers no power and little initiative. The parliamentary session coincided with a mounting crisis, more threatening to the Ottoman Empire than any since Sinope; and yet the urgency of affairs rarely touched the work of the lower chamber. It was assumed, justifiably, that the deputies would approve any stand made by the Sultan and his ministers against external interference.

The failure of the Constantinople Conference was followed by a Russian diplomatic offensive in the European capitals which culminated in the Russian-inspired joint London Protocol of 13 March: the Sultan, the Tsar and the Balkan rulers would demobilize their armies, pending the introduction of reforms within the Ottoman Empire which would be supervised by the Great Powers. The Sultan would not accept dictation from Europe, and within ten days the Porte rejected the Protocol. The Russians, who had already made secret agreements with Austria-Hungary over the future of Bosnia and Herzegovina, concluded two treaties with Roumania allowing the Tsar's troops free passage to the borders of Bulgaria. Eight days later – on 24 April 1877 – Alexander II proclaimed a state of war with the Ottoman Empire and called on his armies to march 'for Orthodoxy and Slavdom'.[10]

This fourth Russo-Turkish war of the century lasted for ten and a half months. When the Russians crossed the lower Danube in June it seemed as if they would sweep all before them, for although the Ottoman soldiery fought bravely and had good artillery, staff-work was almost nonexistent. On the Caucasus Front the Russians swiftly seized several forts, forcing the Ottoman commander, Ahmed Muhtar, to concentrate his forces at Kars, the fortress which had been stormed twice by the Russians in the past half-century. Now Kars was again defended ably for five months. Despite initial Russian victories in the Balkans the former commandant of the War Academy, Husnu Suleyman, showed great enterprise in bringing an army by sea from Albania to Dedeagatch and launching a surprise counter-offensive which halted the invaders at the Shipka Pass, in the main Balkan chain. But the hero of the campaign was Osman Pasha. On 20 July, and again ten days later, his courageous generalship resisted wave upon wave of Russian assaults against the small fortified town of Plevna (Pleven), some eighty-five miles north of Sofia. A third attempt to take Plevna in mid-September cost the Russians even heavier casualties. Thereafter Plevna was meticulously invested by Russia's great military engineer, General Eduard Totleben. He would not storm the town; he would starve its defenders into surrender.[11]

Briefly, before the coming of winter, a mood of optimism prevailed on the Golden Horn. There was hope that fog, rain and snow would impose a stalemate on the battle fronts, making the Tsar seek peace: the long Russian supply lines were vulnerable to wintry conditions while Abdulaziz's expensive toys, the Ottoman ironclads, gave the Sultan naval supremacy in the Black Sea. At the same time, Abdulhamid raised morale by what, in retrospect, stands out as the earliest appeal to Panislamic sentiment. He countered the Tsar's invocation of 'Orthodoxy and Slavdom' by placing a new emphasis on his claims as Caliph. The sacred standard of the Prophet was solemnly borne out from the Topkapi Sarayi. With this Islamic oriflamme in his hands and with the backing of the *şeyhülislâm*, the Sultan-Caliph proclaimed a Holy War (jihad) against the infidel armies of the Tsar. As Alexander II had some 10 million Muslim subjects, a full response to the call of jihad would have provoked a grave rebellion within the Russian Empire. An agent of the Sultan travelled to Kabul to encourage the Afghan Muslims to open a new battle front in Central Asia. For the moment, however, a mass Islamic uprising remained unlikely. The immediate consequence of the jihad in the Ottoman heartland was an upsurge of patriotism, bringing recruits to the army and contributions to a war fund. Significantly, on 21 May the parliamentary deputies paid their sovereign the compliment of proposing that he assume the honoured title of *Ghazi* (warrior leader against the Infidel).[12]

During the summer the Sultan became increasingly hopeful of support from London. Four days before the Russian declaration of war, Sir Henry Elliot was succeeded as ambassador by Henry Layard, a turcophile archaeologist who had excavated Nineveh in the 1840s while serving as an attaché under Stratford de Redcliffe. Layard's public and private papers show the extent to which he modelled himself on Stratford, offering Abdulhamid the type of constructive criticism which the Sultan's father had accepted from the Great Elchi during the Crimean War. 'A man out of whom much might be made,' the ambassador wrote home patronizingly after his first audience with Abdulhamid; and at their second audience he was, he declared, 'even more favourably impressed' by the Sultan's qualities.[13] Prime Minister Disraeli (created Earl of Beaconsfield the previous summer) accepted Layard's judgements and warnings at their face value, although his Foreign Secretary (Lord Derby), his Indian Secretary (Lord Salisbury) and other cabinet ministers remained sceptical. In July, when the Russians seemed likely to break through to Edirne and the Gallipoli peninsula, Disraeli sent friendly assurances to the Sultan, indicating his willingness to order the British fleet through the Dardanelles to protect Constantinople from Russian occupation. Abdulhamid, however, had no desire to see the ironclads of the Mediterranean Fleet in the Sea of Marmara. The stubborn defence of Plevna and the failure to push Suleyman Pasha's troops back to Thrace relieved the threat to his capital, and the warships came no nearer than Smyrna.

Some of Abdulhamid's later hostility towards Great Britain sprang from misplaced confidence in his relationship with Layard during these months of protracted crisis. He knew that, while embassy telegrams necessarily went through the Foreign Office, Layard was also in direct personal correspondence with Disraeli. The Sultan treated both the ambassador and his wife with rare courtesy, inviting them to 'dine in a quiet way' with him on several occasions. He almost certainly suspected that Layard's news was passed on to a more august russophobe than the Prime Minister; at one audience that winter the Sultan, so Layard informed Disraeli, expressed the 'greatest admiration and affection for the Queen', 'spoke like an enlightened Christian', and 'referred more than once to Prince Albert and H.M.'s married life' as a fine example. Layard thought the conversation 'curious'.[14]

Winter did not, as the Turks had hoped, assist their defenders. The Balkan snows ruled out all possibility of relieving Plevna, which on 11

December at last surrendered to the Russians. Within a month the Tsar's troops were in Sofia, in time to celebrate there the great Orthodox Festival of the Epiphany. By 20 January 1878 they had taken Edirne and were threatening both Constantinople and the Gallipoli peninsula. This climax to the war coincided with the second session of the Ottoman Parliament, for which elections had been held in November and which the Sultan formally opened on the last day of the old year. The military collapse made this second parliament more vociferous than its predecessor, attacking the mismanagement of the war with detailed criticisms which, coming at a time when enemy artillery could be heard in the capital, made Abdulhamid fear that the religious patriotism he had encouraged earlier in the campaign would be turned against him personally. But, whatever the mood of parliament, the Sultan personally recognized the need for peace. On 31 January an armistice was agreed at Edirne.

The end of military operations left Abdulhamid exposed to three main dangers: the anger of the parliamentary deputies; the further encroachment of the enemy; and provocative actions by his would-be ally. The Sultan was not greatly troubled by the *Meclis-i Mebusan*. A fortnight after the Armistice he went in person to the lower chamber: one deputy complained that the elected representatives of the people were not consulted over ways to avert the military disaster; another deputy went so far as to propose a curb on the Sultan's personal expenditure. Abdulhamid listened impassively to all that was said. That night he issued a decree dissolving the chamber on the grounds that it could not carry out its duties effectively at such a moment of crisis for the Empire. The Sultan also authorized the arrest of the more outspoken deputies, but his Grand Vizier persuaded him to countermand this order, fearing the arrests would provoke a popular revolt. The deputies returned safely to their homes. Parliament, the Sultan subsequently explained, had not been abolished; it was suspended until the Empire should be ready for it. The chamber remained empty year after year. Three decades were to pass before Abdulhamid opened a third parliament.[15]

The Russians could not be sent about their business so simply or so swiftly. For three weeks after the Edirne armistice they threatened to enter Constantinople itself. To halt Grand Duke Nicholas's army the Sultan had been forced to make what was virtually an unconditional surrender. The armistice terms provided for the immediate withdrawal of the remaining Ottoman forces from Bulgaria; they also stipulated that the final peace treaty would include the imposition of a war indemnity, autonomy for Bulgaria, Bosnia and Herzegovina, total independence for Roumania, Serbia and Montenegro, and a revision of the Straits Convention to accord Russia new rights over the opening and closure of the Bosphorus and Dardanelles. If the Ottoman authorities evaded any of the armistice conditions, Grand Duke Nicholas reserved the right to order his troops forward. Some advanced units had already reached the Aegean coast at Dedeagatch, and the local Ottoman commanders insisted that the movement of Russian units had not ceased with the signing of the armistice. This was not so; the Grand Duke scrupulously observed the terms he had laid down. But rumour intensified the near-panic in Constantinople. On 5 February Layard telegraphed to London: 'Armistice does not stop Russian advance. Porte in great alarm.'[16] Two days later the Russians in Bulgaria cut all telegraphic lines between Constantinople and Western Europe, forcing Layard to send his messages by way of Bombay. This ominous development convinced Disraeli that the Russians were about to seize the Ottoman capital. On 8 February Admiral Sir Phipps Hornby, who had brought the finest battleships in the Mediterranean Fleet up to Besika Bay a fortnight earlier, was ordered to enter the Straits, return fire if necessary, and take up station off Constantinople.

Although Abdulhamid welcomed assurances of support from Disraeli, conveyed to him both by Layard and by his own ambassador in London, he was alarmed by British naval activity. 'The Sultan appears to have made up his mind that the entry of our fleet will lead to the loss of his life or at least of his throne, as it will bring the Russians into his capital, and a general massacre of the Mussulmans and destruction of their property will ensue,' Layard wrote to Lord Derby. 'I have scarcely been one hour, day and night, without having one of his Ministers in the house, or receiving a letter from them. They implore me to stop the approach of the fleet.'[17] Under no circumstances did the Sultan dare grant permission for the warships to enter the Dardanelles; but on 13 February Hornby entered the Narrows, in breach of the Straits Convention. Thirteen months were to pass before the British squadron sailed back into the Aegean.

As the Sultan had feared, the Russians regarded the arrival of the British ships as a hostile act. Their commander, Grand Duke Nicholas (the Tsar's favourite brother), ordered an advance to the Sea of Marmara, which his troops reached at San Stefano (now Yesilkoy, the site of İstanbul airport), six miles from Constantinople's outer walls. At this point, with Britain and Russia drifting into war, a compromise was agreed: the Grand Duke would take advantage of the new Orient Railway to move his headquarters from Edirne to San Stefano but would not send patrols closer to the city; Hornby's battleships would anchor eight miles south of the Golden Horn, off Prinkipo Island (Büyükada), where in 1807 Admiral Duckworth had brought his squadron after the first British naval passage of the Dardanelles. Tension continued. The British feared that the Russians would seize the Turkish fleet and, on 14 February, Layard was instructed to seek the immediate purchase of the four newest Ottoman ironclads.[18] But although the Ottoman Treasury was empty the Porte angrily rejected any such sale. Meanwhile, in San Stefano painful talks continued on a draft peace treaty.

It was an odd situation. No Russian commander had ever been so close to taking Constantinople as the (militarily incompetent) Grand Duke Nicholas. Among his staff captains in these frustrating weeks was Prince Alexander of Battenberg, whose brother Prince Louis was serving aboard the appropriately-named battleship HMS *Sultan* off Prinkipo Island. 'This morning I rode with the Grand Duke to the heights above San Stefano, and we saw Constantinople before us with St Sophia, all the minarets, Scutari, etc.,' Alexander of Battenberg wrote to his parents. 'Tears filled the Grand Duke's eyes. What satisfaction it must give him to stand at the gates of Constantinople with his army!'[19] During the uncertain weeks when Russian troops could see the masts of the British warships on the horizon, Prince Alexander was welcomed aboard HMS *Sultan* by his brother and by the battleship's captain. Here was a further instance of that royal kinship which made Anglo-Russian collaboration more natural than Anglo-Turkish: HMS *Sultan*'s commanding officer was Prince Alfred, Duke of Edinburgh, second son of Queen Victoria and husband of the Tsar's only surviving daughter.

'More Russian than the Russians' was Prince Alexander's verdict on the feelings of 'the ship's company' in a letter to his parents. A markedly different impression of the sympathies of Hornby's crews was conveyed to Abdulhamid by Layard and by his Phanariot physician, Mavroyeni.[20] At home British public opinion remained divided over the Eastern Crisis, with strong backing in the provinces for Gladstone's moral crusade on behalf of the Balkan Christians. In London, however, there was a renewal of russophobe patriotism, a mood popularized by James MacDermott's 'Jingo' music-hall song, with its raucous insistence, 'The Russians shall not have Constantinople'. A translation of MacDermott's heartening chorus was passed on to the Sultan by Mavroyeni. It is said to have brought a rare smile of satisfaction to those thin, cruel lips. He convinced himself that the British sailors in the ironclads off Prinkipo were Jingos to a man. However much he may have deplored their arrival, from late February 1878 Abdulhamid regarded Hornby's fleet as his lifeline to the West.

On 3 March a peace treaty was signed at San Stefano, based on the preliminary terms agreed at Edirne. It was a triumph for Panslavism.[21] As well as imposing a large indemnity, giving Russia considerable gains in eastern Anatolia, and confirming the independence of Roumania and of an enlarged Montenegro and Serbia, the treaty created a 'Big Bulgaria' as an autonomous principality under Ottoman tributary sovereignty. Never had a Sultan accepted such terms. Abdulhamid's one hope was that the Panslav settlement would prove unacceptable to Russia's rivals among the Great Powers.

Even before the treaty was signed Count Andrássy, the Austro-Hungarian Foreign Minister, had been alarmed by the boundaries proposed in the western Balkans, for they encroached on Austria's sphere of interest. He sought a new Congress of Vienna to patch up a more acceptable settlement; but the Russians would never allow their traditional rival in the Danube basin an initiative of this character. The most the Tsar and his ministers would concede was a Congress in Berlin later that summer, under German rather than Austro-Hungarian chairmanship. Although the German Chancellor and Foreign Minister, Otto von Bismarck, had little interest in Balkan affairs, he had equally no wish to see the whole continent plunged into war because of friction between Vienna and St Petersburg. At Bismarck's request, Andrássy sent out invitations to a Congress in Berlin during the very week the terms of San Stefano became generally known.[22]

Abdulhamid mistrusted Andrássy, not least because the Vienna stock-market crash five years before had weakened the credibility of any Habsburg minister. The Sultan placed more reliance on Disraeli. On the day the Treaty of San Stefano was signed he invited Layard to dine with him and discuss ways of revising the settlement. The ambassador spent the following week drafting a thirty-two page memorandum for the Foreign Office in which he set out the enormities of San Stefano.[23] He emphasized, not only the Balkan aspects of the treaty, but the advance of the Caucasian frontier which gave Russia control of the historic caravan route from Trebizond to Tabriz and Central Asia. Layard's memorandum intensified the hawkish mood in Downing Street. Cabinet discussion of the question of seeking a permanent 'place of arms' for Britain within the Ottoman Empire led Derby to resign as Foreign Secretary; and on 2 April Disraeli strengthened his government by appointing Lord Salisbury to succeed him. The new Foreign Secretary did not share his chief's romantic enthusiasm for the Sultanate as a historic institution, but he recognized the inherent dangers of a settlement which 'solved' the Eastern Question so decisively in Russia's favour. At the same time, Salisbury's independence of judgement made him more acceptable to the Russians than his predecessor, and by shrewd negotiations in April and May he secured from the Tsar's ambassador an acknowledgement that the peace treaty of San Stefano stood in need of revision.[24] Without Salisbury's patient preparatory diplomacy there would have been no redrawing of the Ottoman frontier at the Berlin Congress in late June and July.

Although Salisbury could never be convinced that the Ottoman Empire was 'a genuine reliable Power', he was prepared to negotiate a secret alliance guaranteeing the integrity of the remaining territories of the Sultan in Anatolia. But at a price. Disraeli insisted that fulfilment of the guarantee would be possible only if Great Britain had a base for operations in Asia Minor. What was required, he told the Queen in early March, was a base which would secure 'the trade and communications of Europe with the East from the overshadowing interference of Russia'. Serious consideration was given to Crete ('enormous advantages', but desire for union with Greece 'would infallibly produce political trouble'), the island of Stampalia (Astipalia) in the Dodecanese, and to the leasing of Mytilene or İskenderun. By May Disraeli had decided that 'Cyprus is the key to Western Asia'.[25] On 4 June the Cyprus Convention was signed in Constantinople: if Russia retained Kars, Batum or Ardahan, Britain would defend the Ottoman Empire in Asia against further Russian attack in return for occupying Cyprus, which would remain under the Sultan's sovereignty. Not until the fourth week of the Congress of Berlin did the Sultan issue the firman authorizing British troops to establish themselves on the island; and he did so then only after the British protested that the deputation he had sent to the Berlin Congress knew nothing of the Cyprus Convention.

At the Paris Peace Congress in 1856 Ali Pasha had impressed his fellow delegates by his statesmanship. Twenty-two years later the three Ottoman delegates to Berlin were nonentities: a Phanariot Greek who was once Minister of Public Works; a Turkish poet and palace official, with two years' experience of the Berlin embassy; and, more controversially, a Magdeburg-born convert to Islam who had deserted from the Prussian army and towards whom Bismarck saw no reason to show civility. Abdulhamid personally selected this sorry trio and briefed them verbally, giving them no written instructions. They were to save what they could in the Balkans, get the war indemnity scrapped and see that Varna, Batum and all Armenia were returned to Ottoman sovereignty.

Small wonder a Russian delegate noted in his diary of the Congress, 'The Turks sit and speak – like logs.'[26]

Their problems were compounded by doubts over what was happening in Constantinople. By the time they reached Berlin it was by no means certain that the sovereign who had entrusted them with such imprecise responsibilities would remain much longer on his throne. The Russian advance through the Balkans had forced thousands of refugees to flee to Constantinople, more than doubling the city's population. Food was short and there was no work for them. They were natural tinder for any demagogue seeking to kindle mob violence.

On 20 May Ali Suavi, once a Young Ottoman radical and now a hot-headed Islamic fundamentalist, armed a small group of these unfortunate refugees. He then led about hundred men into the Çirağan Palace and attempted to free the deposed Murad V, whom he intended to proclaim Sultan. The local police chief arrived, struck down Ali Suavi with his cudgel and, backed by the gendarmerie, killed or wounded half the raiders.

The whole incident lasted less than an hour.[27] It forms a trivial episode in the long tale of an empire in decline. But the abortive coup made a lasting impression on Abdulhamid's mind. Initially it threw him into a panic. For at least a fortnight he pursued uncertain policies, changing his ministers rapidly and giving orders which, within a few hours, he would countermand. A beneficiary of this vacillation was the deposed Sultan: Abdulhamid authorized his private execution but no action was taken, probably because Murad, a Freemason, was able to get a message to the Master of the Phanariot Masonic lodge, seeking help from Kaiser William I and the Prince of Wales. One night in that May Abdulhamid sent his secretary to the British Embassy to ask that HMS *Antelope*, the stationnaire assigned to the ambassador, should be moored off the Dolmabahche, ready to give the Sultan sanctuary in case of need. No sooner had *Antelope* taken up position than a second message to the embassy asked for the steam yacht to return to her old berth. Next morning the Sultan received Layard alone in the harem. He was, he said, in 'the greatest possible peril'; the army hated him; the people felt no affection for him; since his accession he had not enjoyed a single night of rest. He feared, not death, but immurement for life in the *kafe*. Would Layard protect his family if, in fighting for his throne, he was killed? A note on the following day, written by the Sultan himself, again stressed his sense of imminent peril. 'I grieve most sincerely for the poor Sultan, for whom I cannot but feel pity and even affection,' Layard wrote to Salisbury, six days before the Congress opened in Berlin. 'If however the safety of the state and our paramount interests require that he should be put aside, he must be sacrificed.'[28] No British ambassador – not even Stratford de Redcliffe in his prime – ever matched Sir Henry Layard as the would-be arbiter of Ottoman affairs during this summer of protracted crisis.

Abdulhamid was not 'sacrificed'. But his position remained uncertain for several months. At least two more conspiracies to restore Murad V were hatched by the Phanariot Freemasons and revealed to the Sultan by the growing network of police spies in the capital. The incompetence of the plotters seems to have helped Abdulhamid recover his nerve. Until the disasters of the war weakened his sense of mission he had been working towards the creation of a new autocracy; before the coming of winter in 1878 these despotic tendencies in his character began to reassert themselves. Ever since his accession he had chosen to live, not amid the Mecidian grandeur of the Dolmabahche Palace, but in the hillside summer pavilion at Yildiz which Abdulaziz had built over old cemeteries on a site looking out over the Çirağan Palace. Now Abdulhamid turned Yildiz into a tightly secure township, as intricate as the Topkapi Sarayi in the previous century and accommodating five or six thousand people, but more spacious than any earlier imperial Ottoman complex.[29] There was no single imperial residence. It was safer to move frequently from one small house to another, to confound possible assassins. Outwardly Yildiz was – as it is today – peaceful and attractive parkland, with shrubberies, lakes and fountains, gravel paths to chalet kiosks, and sudden panoramas of the Anatolian shore and of ships on the Bosphorus or out beyond the Stamboul headland. But Yildiz had, too, its own prison; it stood close to the menagerie in order, so it was said, that ambassadors and guests might hear the screech of birds and animals rather than of humans in captivity.

The two faces of Yildiz made the imperial township as much a symbol of Abdulhamid's reign as the Dolmabahche had been of his father's. Only trusted guards and intimates were allowed to work for the Sultan within the yellow-stuccoed walls. For nineteen years after his release from Russian internment the hero of Plevna, Gazi Osman Pasha, was head of Yildiz administration, responsible for security. Osman also served as chairman of a newly-established Imperial Privy Council, one of whose tasks was to root out corruption and inefficiency at the highest level of state, military or civilian. Until he became Grand Vizier in October 1879, the Sultan's secretary Mehmed Said organized the Yildiz bureaucracy, and the palace remained Said's power base throughout the reign; but Yildiz also had its own Press Department, Foreign Affairs office and Abdulhamid's personal financial secretariat, headed by Hakop Zarifi. The most sinister institution based at Yildiz was the *hafiye* (secret police), controlled for some twenty years by the Sultan's Circassian protégé, Ahmed Celaleddin. Subordinate to the *hafiye* were hundreds of informants (*jurnalcis*) paid to feed the Sultan with titbits of news, not only from his capital but from distant towns and villages as well. Arabs from Syria and Tripolitania – most of them influential members of the *ulema* – found a place in the *hafiye* secretariat alongside spies hotfoot from the labyrinth of the Kapali Carsi, Stamboul's grand bazaar. Many reports were fabricated, still more could not be verified, but all were carefully studied by Abdulhamid himself. The general effect on the Sultan of an overstaffed secret police force was disastrous; cumulatively, the scraps of information intensified his paranoia and sense of betrayal. For the remainder of his reign Abdulhamid's mind readily conjured up the bogey of imminent assassination. Guests entertained at Yildiz reported that the Sultan employed, not merely taster eunuchs who tested food before a meal passed his lips, but a first-puff eunuch to ensure that no one had poisoned his cigarettes.[30]

The dark suspicion of betrayal which so often clouded Abdulhamid's brooding mind was turned on ambassadors and foreign statesmen as well as on Ottoman ministers and bureaucrats. Layard soon fell from grace, despite his turcophile enthusiasm. Reports from Berlin and the other European capitals convinced the Sultan of British treachery. Shortly before the opening of the Congress *The Globe* newspaper in London published a leaked version of a secret Anglo-Russian protocol which proposed that the Russians should retain Kars and Batum while restoring the town of Bayazid and accepting the division of Big Bulgaria into two provinces. The secret convention also agreed that, as Britain had a special interest in Greece, the Great Powers should consult together over the future of Epirus, Thessaly 'and the other Christian provinces left under the Porte'. *The Globe*'s revelation had 'serious' effects on Britain's immediate standing at Constantinople: 'There is not a Turk or Christian, who is not now convinced that we have been playing Turkey and Europe false,' Layard wrote in a private letter to his predecessor, Elliot, 'that . . . we have been all along in secret agreement with Russia and Austria, to dismember the Turkish Empire and take our share of the spoils.'[31]

Fears aroused by *The Globe*'s revelations were confirmed when news of the final treaty terms reached Constantinople. Big Bulgaria was, indeed, destroyed, but the Sultan had to accept the creation of a Bulgarian Principality extending from the Danube to the Balkan range, and a province of Eastern Rumelia which, though directly under Ottoman rule, was to be given a Christian Governor and a special administrative system. Bayazid and the valley of the river Eleskirt were returned to the Sultan, as also was Macedonia south of Niš. Bosnia and Herzegovina remained Ottoman provinces but were to be occupied by Austro-Hungarian troops and administered through civil servants appointed in Vienna. No change was made in the Straits Convention, but the Ottoman Government undertook to introduce reforms in the remaining Armenian provinces and, once again, confirmed religious freedom throughout the empire. Montenegro more than doubled her pre-war size, while Serbia obtained Niš and some of the lands assigned at San Stefano to Bulgaria. Only over Greece were the provisions of the Treaty less exacting than *The Globe*'s revelations had led Abdulhamid to anticipate. British backing for the government in Athens was half-hearted, Disraeli even suggesting at the Congress that, as the Ottoman Empire had lost so much territory, it would be unwise to contemplate further redrawing of the map in the Balkans.[32] The Sultan was, however, required to authorize talks with the Greeks over frontier revision in Thessaly; he was informed that, should the two governments be unable to determine the new border, the Great Powers would mediate a settlement of the problem. Eventually, in 1881, the Sultan's troops evacuated Thessaly as far north as the river Pinios and the Arta district in southern Epirus, but the Porte continued to deny Greek claims to northern Epirus and Macedonia. Arta, Larissa and Trikkala became Greek: Ioánnina and the historic port of Salonika (Thessaloniki) remained firmly in Ottoman hands.

Abdulhamid's hope that the Congress would scrap the war indemnity was not realized. But it constituted less of a problem than he had feared, for the Treaty of Berlin made no reference to the indemnity, leaving the issue to be settled in direct bilateral negotiations. The Russians demanded some £32 million as a matter of principle, the Tsar's ambassador admitting privately to Salisbury that they attached little importance to the sum and thought payment would prove impossible. After four years of evasive talk the Porte undertook to pay Russia £320,000 annually (until 1982), the Tsar waiving all interest claims. But the Russians well knew that if the Ottomans remained in a state of chronic bankruptcy, their own economy would suffer; and they therefore rarely attempted to force their Turkish neighbour to pay the annual due. To assist the Porte to achieve some financial good order, it was agreed at Berlin that the seceding independent states would each take over a portion of the Ottoman Public Debt. At the same time the

Congress recommended to the Porte the creation of an international commission of financial experts who would safeguard the interests of Ottoman state bond-holders.

Abdulhamid's resentment of foreign interference made him resist as long as possible the establishment of any international commission. There was one moment at the Congress when the Russians went so far as to propose complete European supervision of Ottoman finances, backed by joint military occupation of the Empire until the economy was put on a sound basis; and a similar solution had been advocated a few months earlier by the nonagenarian Stratford de Redcliffe, although only as a last resort and strictly limited in time.[33] The idea of linking financial control and military occupation was received by the other delegates to the Congress with a cynicism bred of experience: once foreign troops had established bases, when would they withdraw again? Nothing more was heard of the proposal. But for Abdulhamid the abhorrent suggestion underlined the gravity of his financial crisis. He had begun his reign determined to avoid further foreign loans. His experience in the winter of 1877–8 confirmed the wisdom of this resolve, for the Ottoman Treasury's credit was so poor that wartime emergency borrowing in London and Paris brought in no more than three-fifths of the stipulated sum, the remaining two-fifths being absorbed by discount and interest. With the salaries of civil servants in Stamboul some four years in arrears and prices rising week by week, the Sultan knew there was a threat of rioting in the capital, still packed with indigent refugees. Understandably, he rated financial reform high among his priorities.

Fortunately, in his Armenian banker Zarifi, Abdulhamid retained a good adviser. An imperial decree in November 1879 set up a commission of Galata bankers who, with nominees of the Ottoman Bank, were to help pay off the public debt. At the same time the Ministry of Finance was reorganized, accepting responsibility for the empire as a whole and co-ordinating the collection of taxes from each province. The *Tanzimat* reform era, with its rationalization of the administrative structure, had left the bureaucracy top-heavy, with too many ministries employing too many officials in the capital. Economy was preached – and occasionally imposed – at the Ministries of the Interior and Foreign Affairs; a profits tax was instituted and, in theory, levied throughout the empire; and a Financial Reform Commission was created in order to scrutinize and trim all estimates of expenditure from government departments, although pleas of 'special interest' reduced the efficiency of this particular institution. Travellers' tales, backed by cautious comments from commercial attachés and consuls, suggest that behind an impressive façade corruption flourished. But the good intent was there.

Yet, if these changes convinced foreign ambassadors of Abdulhamid's sincerity, it soon became clear that a more powerful authority was needed to guard against any slipping back into the mismanagement preceding Grand Vizier Nedim's admission of state bankruptcy. At last, in December 1881, the Sultan accepted long-term supervision of Ottoman finances by European bankers. The 'Muharrem Decree' established the Ottoman Public Debt Commission, an institution which became virtually a separate and parallel Ministry of Finance, under an international directorate (French, Dutch, British, Italian, German, Austro-Hungarian, Ottoman) and employing some 100 foreign experts in a work-force of five thousand. The long-term effect of these changes was to raise state revenue by some 43 per cent in the course of Abdulhamid's reign, and the threat of imperial bankruptcy receded even though there remained an annual budget deficit. The probity of the Ottoman Public Debt Commission enabled Abdulhamid in his later years to attract European investment in public works projects, thereby stimulating the economy of the Empire as a whole. While French interests remained considerable, the British disposed of many holdings at the turn of the century, and Germany became the largest investor in Anatolia.[34]

In the aftermath of the war with Russia this last development seemed unlikely. Bismarckian Germany, taking its cue from the Chancellor himself, showed as yet little interest in the Ottoman Empire, and Abdulhamid's suppliant delegates, going fez in hand to the Congress, fared badly in Berlin. The definitive Russo-Ottoman Treaty of Peace of February 1879 confirmed the loss to Abdulhamid of some two-fifths of his empire and a fifth of his subjects. At Berlin the Ottoman Empire was relegated from the super-league to which it had won promotion at the end of the Crimean War. Effectively, it ceased to be a European Power, although Ottoman provinces straddled the Balkans from Edirne to the Albanian vilayet of Scutari on the Adriatic. But the Sultanate continued to bind together a vast multinational empire, even if in 1879 many outer bonds were slipping loose. Abdulhamid remained overlord of Syria, Mesopotamia, Arabia, Egypt and the Maghreb up to the Algerian–Tunisian frontier; and, though the frontier in the Caucasus had contracted, he was still sovereign of five vilayets in Armenia and Kurdistan as well as of the lands English-speaking geographers called 'Asia Minor'. Moreover, to a greater extent than his immediate predecessors, he was conscious of a moral authority as Caliph. Defeat at Russia's hands posed for Abdulhamid the problems of improvising a new concept of empire, and he accepted the challenge. It was fitting that the Sultan enjoyed a fuller panorama of Asia from the slopes of Yildiz than from the waterfront palaces down the hill.

CHAPTER 11

The Hamidian Empire

For the first ten years of his reign Abdulhamid II reluctantly accepted a constant diminution of Ottoman power and authority within Europe. The humiliations of San Stefano and Berlin were followed in 1880 by the enforced handing over to Montenegro of Ulcinj and a few miles of Adriatic coastline and, a year later, by the cession of Thessaly and the Arta district in Epirus to Greece. A convention signed with Austria–Hungary in April 1879 affirmed that Bosnia and Herzegovina were still Ottoman provinces, temporarily administered by the Austro-Hungarian Ministry of Finance. But it was a bitter blow to Ottoman pride when, in 1881, young Bosnians and Herzegovinians were conscripted to serve in Francis Joseph's army, as if they were already Austrian subjects. The subsequent foundation in Sarajevo of an Islamic *şeriat* law-school, with a delightful colonnaded portico and built from Habsburg government funds, was no doubt more gratifying to Abdulhamid as Caliph than as Sultan. Habsburg–Ottoman relations after 1878 remained coldly correct, with Vienna and Budapest insisting on exploiting every possible commercial concession, while the Sultan hoped for increased revenue from Austrian railway projects. The *sanjak* of Novibazar, the strategically important corridor which separated Serbia from Montenegro, remained under Ottoman rule; but for most of Abdulhamid's reign the Austro-Hungarian XVth Army Corps garrisoned four of the *sanjak*'s few towns.

To lay the ghost of San Stefano's 'Big Bulgaria' became an increasingly difficult task. Eastern Rumelia, the autonomous Ottoman province conjured up by the Berlin Congress, proved an unworkable creation. Although the province brought a steady revenue into the Sultan's coffers, misrule by his nominee as Governor – a Greek Orthodox bureaucrat from Samos – intensified Pan-Bulgarian feelings and in September 1885 provoked a revolt in Plovdiv whose leader, Stefan Stambulov, declared Eastern Rumelia united with Bulgaria. Over the following eighteen months the Ottoman authorities showed restraint and discretion, not least because Abdulhamid wished to avoid further accusations of 'massacring' Bulgars. He welcomed an ambassadorial conference in his capital, only to find in April 1886 that, in return for retrocession of a cluster of Muslim villages in the Rhodope mountains, the ambassadors required him to issue a firman confirming the union of 'the two Bulgarias' as a single tributary Principality. Technically, until October 1908 Bulgaria remained under Abdulhamid's suzerainty, and after his accession as Prince in July 1887 Ferdinand of Saxe-Coburg ensured that regular annual payments went from Sofia to Constantinople. But Bulgarian national ambition still sought an outlet to the Aegean. In practice, from 1885 onwards Bulgaria was as lost to its Ottoman suzerain as independent Serbia and Roumania.[1]

Briefly, in the early 1880s, Abdulhamid II considered the possibility of offsetting the empire's decline in the Balkans by reasserting Ottoman authority in Egypt. A few years earlier such an apparent reversal of history would have been out of the question; on at least two occasions Cairo had seemed about to cut all links with Constantinople and proclaim Egypt's full independence. During the protracted ceremonies which had accompanied the opening of the Suez Canal in November 1869 it was Ismail, the ruler of Egypt, and not his imperial master, who was host to the Empress of the French, the Emperor of Austria, the Crown Prince of Prussia and the Princes of Orange and Hesse. Empress Eugénie, Francis Joseph and the other foreign dignitaries might pay courtesy calls on Abdulaziz in Constantinople, as had the Prince and Princess of Wales a few months earlier; but in the Nile delta Ismail stood out as heir to the Pharaohs. He was responsible for giving Cairo an opera house to impress his guests and for commissioning *Aïda* from Verdi (for staging two years later). Proudly Ismail once assured an eminent foreign banker, 'My country is no longer in Africa, it is in Europe.'[2]

There is no doubt that the French-educated Ismail, who had succeeded his uncle Said as Viceroy in 1863, accelerated the pace of westernization, effectively separating Egypt from Turkey. He used the wealth of an expanding cotton trade to raise foreign loans and, until the European financial crisis of 1873, Egypt's economy prospered, with benefits from a good railway system and the highly profitable Suez Canal – of which, at its opening, Ismail was the largest single bond-holder. In the spring of 1866 Ismail struck the first of two bargains with his Ottoman suzerain: the annual tribute paid by Egypt was doubled in return for recognition of his rank as Khedive, with a right to increase the Egyptian army, to coin his own currency, and to confer titles and decorations without reference to the Sultan. After a state visit to Constantinople, in which he was lavish in distributing bribes to Sultan Abdulaziz and to influential courtiers, the Khedive secured even more generous concessions: a firman issued in June 1873 gave the Egyptian ruler virtual financial and administrative autonomy. Hitherto he had been able to raise money only by short-term credit; now he could seek long loans from foreign banks.

The concession was extracted from the Sultan too late. Four weeks earlier the Vienna Stock Exchange crash had shaken the confidence of European bankers. Credit sources contracted; and within two years Ismail found himself unable to pay the high interest on his short-term loans. His Suez Canal holdings passed to the British government, thanks to the enterprise of Disraeli and the ready funds of the Rothschilds. British and French experts sought to rescue the Egyptian economy, gaining greater control of public resources than the Ottomans had ever possessed. Hurriedly Ismail sought to please the Ottoman authorities: in 1877 some 30,000 Egyptian troops fought for the Sultan against the Russians. But the Dual Commissioners – the Anglo-French controllers of Egypt's finances – ordered drastic economies in the Khedive's army. They believed, though it is hard to agree with them, that Ismail was as reckless a spendthrift as Abdulaziz had been, and they made ready to bustle him off his throne. Desperately he appealed to Abdulhamid: a deposition imposed by foreigners in Cairo was an ominous precedent for Constantinople, he argued.

The Sultan was unimpressed. He was not sorry to see so staunch a champion of Egypt's independence pass into exile. On 26 June 1879, with the encouragement of the British and the French, he ordered Ismail's deposition. As overlord of Egypt the Sultan summoned to the throne Tewfik, Ismail's 27-year-old son. At the same time Abdulhamid imposed a top limit of 18,000 men on the Khedival army and cancelled the firman of June 1873, thereby effectively curbing Egyptian autonomy once again.

But this was not what the Dual Commissioners wanted. The Sultan had miscued his lines. They expected him to get rid of Ismail and cut the army down to size, but Tewfik was to be their puppet, not Abdulhamid's. Pressure from the ambassadors in Constantinople led two months later to publication of a revised version of the firman of deposition: Khedive Tewfik might exercise the same autonomous rights as his father, provided he paid the annual tribute to the Sultan and kept his army within the agreed limits. This restriction, however, intensified the Egyptian crisis. Which officers would keep their military careers, Arab-speaking Egyptians or the Turco-Circassians who were habitually promoted to the higher ranks? Over the following two years a xenophobic pressure group of Arab-speaking junior officers continuously threatened disorder in Cairo and Alexandria. Their leader was Lieutenant-Colonel Ahmed Orabi – conveniently known as 'Arabi Pasha' in Western Europe.

Abdulhamid believed he could handle Orabi as dexterously as he dealt with Midhat. He was prepared to use the Orabist mutineers to undermine Khedival authority, spreading such anarchy in Egypt that the Dual Commissioners would welcome direct Ottoman rule and give financial backing to the recovery of what was, potentially, the richest province of his empire. The Sultan's personal Egyptian policy was therefore extremely devious; while the Grand Vizier and other members of the Divan welcomed a British initiative which in June 1881 convened yet another ambassadorial conference in Constantinople, Abdulhamid refused to permit Ottoman participation in the talks and persistently turned down all requests for the dispatch to Egypt of an Ottoman expeditionary force. Instead, he summoned Orabi to Constantinople, while sending a personal emissary to Cairo for talks with Tewfik. At the same time, he secured from the ambassadors a curiously vague assurance that foreign troops would not intervene in Egypt 'except in case of unforeseen circumstances'.[3]

At first events played into Abdulhamid's hands. Riots in Alexandria – almost certainly spontaneous – led to looting and to the killing of some fifty Christians. British warships duly bombarded the city; a few weeks later, their guns covered the landing of an expeditionary force commanded by Sir Garnet Wolseley. On 13 September 1881 Wolseley destroyed Orabi's army at Tel-el-Kebir. The Sultan protested at the British action on two grounds: the invasion of Egypt infringed Ottoman sovereignty: and unilateral intervention made nonsense of the attempts at reconciliation which, as Ottoman emperor, he was sponsoring. He was not entirely mollified by British assurances that their military presence in Egypt was, like the Austro-Hungarian garrisoning of Novibazar, only a temporary exigency.

Abdulhamid's ambition of reasserting direct Ottoman authority in Cairo and Alexandria came close to success, at least on paper. Successive prime ministers in London did, indeed, have every intention of pulling out of Egypt as soon as possible. The continued military occupation was caused, in the first instance, by the need to contain the Mahdist revolt in the Sudan, safeguarding both the fertile regions of Egypt and the Red Sea ports against devastation from what was regarded as fanatic anarchy. But the decision to stay in Egypt was also an indirect consequence of an unexpected twist in Ottoman policies. Until 1887, and perhaps as late as 1894, the British envisaged an accommodation with the Sultan: Egypt would be governed by the Porte through a viceregal Khedive, with guarantees for foreign bond-holders and for unimpeded passage of the Suez Canal; if there were international pledges to observe Egypt's neutrality, British troops would be withdrawn. Sir Henry Drummond Wolff was sent on a special mission to Constantinople to persuade the Sultan to share in the administrative control of Egypt, and a preliminary agreement was speedily signed. It was followed in May 1887 by a formal Anglo-Turkish Convention: Great Britain would enjoy preferential rights in an Ottomanized Egypt, to be freed from military occupation within three years. For eight weeks Drummond Wolff waited in Constantinople while Abdulhamid had second – and third, and fourth – thoughts about the treaty. The French resented Britain's special status in Egypt and their ambassador received support from his Russian colleague; there was even a threat of war if the Convention were ratified. The ambassadors' strong words were intended to make the neurasthenic Sultan quail, and he took them seriously. It was not difficult for Abdulhamid to convince himself that the British were tricking him into signing away Egypt. In the rarefied isolation of the Yildiz Kiosk, he was highly receptive to the mystical revelations of Abul Hauda al-Sayyadi, a visionary prophet from Aleppo who viewed world affairs very differently from the Sultan's ministers and officials three miles away at the Sublime Porte itself.[4]

Ultimately Abdulhamid refused to ratify the treaty. The moment for such an undertaking was inauspicious, it appeared. The Sultan's hesitancy – or, as some believed, the generously greased palm of his Syrian soothsayer – allowed Egypt to slip from his grasp. An Ottoman High Commissioner resided in Cairo from 1887 to 1914 and each year tribute money of some £665,000 (about four per cent of the national revenue) was handed over to the Ottoman treasury. But, though lip-service was rendered to the Sultan's suzerainty so long as the world remained at peace, from 1883 until 1922 Egypt was enveloped in the British Empire as closely as an Indian princely state. Abdulhamid gained no advantage from his obduracy over ratifying the Convention, for successive British governments rode rough-shod over Turkish susceptibilities. Soon Egypt was to supersede the Straits in Whitehall's strategic planning. 'Cairo is . . . the gateway between Europe and Asia and between Europe and Australia,' a Foreign Office official patiently explained to his colleagues at the Treasury in November 1898; 'Recent events have made it also the gateway to a considerable portion of Africa,' he added.[5]

Twice Abdulhamid tried to rectify his error of policy, vainly seeking to secure a firm hold on that strategic gateway. In August 1894 his ambassador raised the possibility of a revised Drummond Wolff Convention with Lord Rosebery's Liberal government, and eighteen months later the Sultan persisted in efforts to persuade Salisbury to open new talks on Egypt, despite rebuffs from both the Foreign Office and the embassy in Pera. Marginally he preferred Salisbury and the Conservatives to the Liberals, among whom the formidable Gladstone continued to champion the rights of Christians under Ottoman rule until the autumn of 1896 (when he was approaching his eighty-seventh birthday). But Lord Salisbury never concealed his lack of confidence in the Ottoman will to survive. Nor, indeed, did most European statesmen of his generation. All seemed eager – to borrow Bismarck's metaphor – 'to pluck ripe fruit' from the Ottoman orchard. The French, who at the height of the Egyptian Crisis in 1881 grabbed 'the pear' of Tunisia, retained their political ambitions in Syria. Although official Tsarist policy was less committed to Panslavism than in the 1870s, the Russians remained a threat from the Caucasus; so, too, did Austrian commercial enterprise throughout the western Balkans. Even the Italians, who had looked covetously at Tunisia before the French established their protectorate, were showing an interest in Tripolitania and the Dodecanese islands. Only the Germans remained disinclined to stake an anticipatory claim to Ottoman spoils; and it was accordingly with Germany that Abdulhamid established the closest relations.

'The new element, the German, in Eastern politics deserves our grave consideration,' Layard had observed to Disraeli in 1877, soon after his arrival in Constantinople.[6] That particular warning was little more than a shrewd guess. Although Prussian officers had served in the Ottoman army for brief spells of duty from the later years of Mahmud II, only rarely was there close contact between Constantinople and Berlin during the Bismarck era; the Prussian consulate in Jerusalem, which had been established as early as 1842, was often more active than the embassy, safeguarding Lutheran religious rights and fostering farming settlements set up in Palestine by primitive Protestant sects. Even after Wilhelm von Pressel put forward his master-plan for Anatolian railways in 1872, little was done to win support for the venture in his homeland.[7] German financial institutions seemed wary of expansion. The prestigious Deutsche Bank, though willing to join the Stuttgart Bank in pledging money for an Anatolian railway in September 1888, had still not opened a branch anywhere in the Sultan's empire by the end of his reign. And when in 1899 the first German Ottoman bank was at last established, it was specifically a regional institution, the Deutsche Palästinanbank, with branches from Damascus southwards to Gaza. Seven more years passed before a Deutsche Orientbank began promoting German interests throughout the Levant and Egypt.

If the Sultan's subjects thought about Germany at all, it was as a military power rather than as a financial agency; bankers traditionally came from Paris, London and Vienna. Moltke, the most famous Prussian officer who had served Sultan Mahmud, continued to hold Turks in contempt throughout his later years as Chief of the Greater German General Staff; and when in 1882 Abdulhamid II sought a new team of military advisers, Moltke entrusted the mission to an obscure staff officer, General Otto Kaehler, rather than to a soldier of energy and initiative. Kaehler died within two years of reaching Constantinople, having shown himself to be a first-rate salesman for Krupps of Essen. It was Colonel Colmar von der Goltz, Kaehler's deputy and successor, who imparted to the Sultan's army the lessons of the three 'Bismarck wars' and won himself a European reputation – and eventually a Field Marshal's baton. Hundreds of heavy guns and field pieces were shipped to the Golden Horn from Hamburg, for Goltz made sure that modern artillery should defend the Dardanelles, while Krupps's specialists updated old forts along the Chatalja Lines to the west of the capital. Goltz's memoirs show that he despised Abdulhamid personally; he found him intensely suspicious of foreign influence at the War Academy, and so terrified of assassination that he imposed strict limitations on revolver practice in the capital; and, like other observers, Goltz noted how, as the years passed, the Sultan travelled less and less outside the Yildiz walls. His mission to Turkey remained frustrating. Attempts to create a smooth-running General Staff were hampered by the factious rivalry within the Ottoman high command, but Goltz did at least induce the Sultan to reorganize the military structure, thereby speeding up both mobilization and the transmission of orders from the high command to combat troops and distant garrisons.[8]

With remarkable patience Goltz, a witty member of a cultured family, countered *ulema* objections and persuaded Abdulhamid to send chosen officers to Potsdam for further training alongside the Prussians. Already, in the later years of Mahmud II, a few Turkish cadets had

gone to England to receive training at Woolwich, but the German con-
nection established by Goltz was more thoroughly organized than the
somewhat haphazard earlier experiment, and it continued until the First
World War. Although there were rarely more than twenty Ottoman
officers in Germany during any one year, some were seconded for long
periods. By 1889 when Kaiser William II paid the first of two osten-
tatious visits to the Sultan, Germany military influence was arousing a
lively interest in the embassies of other governments. In May 1890 an
intelligence assessment dispatched from Pera to the British Foreign
Office reported with some surprise (and slight exaggeration) that most
Turkish front-line infantry units were already equipped with high-
quality Mauser rifles.[9]

The employment of foreign specialists to modernize the army was, of
course, a familiar expedient favoured by all reformer Sultans, including
Abdulhamid I and Selim III as well as Mahmud II. Yet, uniquely,
Abdulhamid II modelled a newly-created cavalry corps on what was in
many respects an outdated concept. In March 1891 he established a
force of irregular horsemen reminiscent of the *akinji* outriders of the
seventeenth century or, more recently, of the *başi bozuka*, the notorious
'bashi-bazouks' whose bestialities were chronicled in every Western
European and American account of the Bulgarian atrocities. These
new battalions – *hamidiye*, as they were called – were recruited from the
nomadic Kurdish and Turcoman peoples of eastern Anatolia; they were
led by tribal chieftains, with Ottoman officers attached to them as
inspectors. It was assumed that their natural enemies were the Russians,
who seemed likely to thrust southwards from their Transcaucasian
possessions.[10]

At first the *hamidiye* were organized into thirty nominally disciplined
regiments of 600 men, although the force rapidly expanded; there were
63 regiments of between 800 and 1,150 men at the end of the century.
Superficially they resembled the Cossack troops maintained by the
Russians for over two hundred years; but while the Cossacks were
famous as a fighting horde before they became soldiers of the Tsars, the
Kurdish and Turcoman tribes had long thrived on brigandage, with
some six or seven chieftains only occasionally uniting in a loose con-
federacy, primarily to defend themselves against punitive expeditions.
Old habits died hard, and the circumstances in which local Ottoman
commanders employed the Sultan's 'tribal gendarmerie' did not
encourage their abandonment of traditional ways, especially in the
mountains around Erzerum. This development caused dismay among
the consular representatives of the Great Powers and intensified the

171

widespread abhorrence of 'Abdul the Damned'. If the Kurds used the weapons and regimental organization of the *hamidiye* to scourge the Armenian Christians around them in eastern Anatolia, their Sultan and Caliph was disinclined to check such bloody effusions of fanatical zeal. The Kurds, militant Muslims who had mistrusted *Tanzimat* westernization, served proudly in the *hamidiye*, which they accepted as a form of recognition of national identity bestowed upon them by their Ottoman sovereign. Tragically the *hamidiye* – like the 'Black and Tans' in Ireland – left a legacy of racial and religious hatred which survived the Ottomans and their immediate successors.

The creation of the *hamidiye* was characteristic of the reign as a whole. Earlier rulers had westernized Ottoman life: Abdulhamid sought to islamicize institutions they had imported from Europe. At the same time he became a champion of Arab causes they had neglected. Never before had Arabs from the Lebanon and Syria received such high advancement in Ottoman government as in the first half of his reign. They encouraged the assumption that, as Caliph, he had a right to protect Muslims living under British, French or Russian imperial rule; and he personally selected and approved religious dignitaries called to exercise spiritual authority in the Crimea and Cyprus, tributary Bulgaria and Egypt, and the Austrian-occupied western Balkans. It might be said that he harnessed, and effectively rode, the wild Panislamic sentiment which spread through much of Asia and northern Africa in a reaction to imperialism.

Abdulhamid's religiosity was not humbug. Unlike his recent predecessors, he emphasized the sincerity of his faith, scrupulously observing Muslim holy days and assigning money from his Privy Purse to restore mosques, spread Muslim schools and augment *ulema* funds. His subjects treated him with awed respect, hardly distinguishable from reverence. Sir Charles Eliot, a third secretary at the British embassy from 1893 to 1898, described the *namaz* prayers at the Yildiz mosque in the twenty-second year of Abdulhamid's reign:

Long before midday on Friday soldiers, and spectators, among which are hundreds of Turkish women, occupy all the available space . . . Ultimately a trumpet sounds . . . a victoria with the hood up comes slowly down the steep road. An old man in uniform, Field Marshal Osman Pasha, the hero of Plevna, sitting with his back to the horses, speaks with deep respect to some one seen less distinctly under the hood. The carriage stops at a flight of steps leading to the private door of the mosque. The hood is lowered by a spring, and he who sat beneath it alights, mounts the steps, and, in a moment of profound silence, turns and salutes the crowd. He has not come as the chief of a military race should come, on a prancing steed or with any dash or glory. There is no splendour in his dress or bearing, but for the moment that he stands there alone a solemnity falls over the scene . . . and we are face to face with the spirit of a great nation and a great religion incarnate in one man.[11]

Concern for the basic teachings of Islam inevitably strengthened the autocratic character of the Sultanate. Yet there was no Hamidian counter-revolution to the *Tanzimat* restructuring. The reform era continued: better public education; an agricultural bank to provide capital for the most widespread and least progressive of occupations; more municipalities, paved roads and gas-lit towns; and the standardization of procedure in both criminal and civil law courts – although, to his intense irritation, the Sultan was unable to abolish the special legal status enjoyed by foreign residents under the long-standing 'Capitulations' treaties. In one sense the Hamidian empire became more closely integrated in Europe, with the completion of Baron Hirsch's section of the railway into Serbia. On 12 August 1888 the first through-train from Western Europe reached Constantinople. From November it was possible for a traveller to leave Paris aboard the Orient Express at 7.30 on Wednesday evening and, after a 1,867-mile journey by way of Munich, Vienna, Budapest and Belgrade, to step down from the same carriage in Stamboul's 'elongated shed on a barren waste' at what the timetable cited as 5.35 on Saturday afternoon. The Sirkeci terminus was built soon afterwards and, across the Golden Horn, the Wagons-Lits Company opened a luxury hotel, the Pera Palace, in 'a thoroughly healthy situation, high up and isolated on all sides'. The coming of the trunk railway and an elegant hotel did not, of course, open up the shores of the Bosphorus to tourism, but they strengthened commercial contacts with western and central Europe, for good or for bad. The British ambassador believed that Abdulhamid was personally hostile to the new railway links. The arrival of the first train from the West went virtually unnoticed: 'The Turkish authorities had removed on the previous evening all flags and other signs of rejoicing and no Ottoman official was allowed to take any part in that important occasion,' the ambassador reported.[12] The Sultan's reactions continued to puzzle foreign observers, who were too ready to assume that the wearing of western dress made Ottomans occidental in thought and behaviour.

More than ever, the Hamidian Sultanate remained an empire of contradictions. The gas-lit streets of Pera and Stamboul offered the travellers a constantly changing peepshow, part European, part North African but, above all, richly Asian in cultural character and colour. Some outsiders were uneasy at the spectacle, disturbed as much by what was hidden from them as by what passed before their eyes. An astute and experienced British diplomat, returning to Constantinople in 1893 after an absence of ten years, was appalled at the degeneracy of a 'system rotten to the core'. He complained of a 'craze for money-making and speculation' among the 'men we deal with now . . . the products of a vitiated French education overlying the old (Turkish) stock'; and he contrasted the 'tawdry splendour of Yildiz entertainments' with 'the real Palace we don't see – the Sheikhs, and the astrologers and hole and corner intrigue, and all the dark doings and sayings.'[13] Yet, despite the cynical doubts of outside observers, a vein of Islamic piety ran not far beneath the surface. If, for example, a foreign visitor wished to relax in a Turkish bath (*hamam*) he would find that it constituted a 'religious foundation' (*vakif*); the *hamam* tradition implied cleanliness for the soul as well as for the body. More specifically Hamidian in character was the Sultan's encouragement of the holy language of the sacred Koran. Classical Arabic might have received an official status equal to that of Ottoman Turkish, had not the Grand Vizier persuaded him that patronage of even the purest Arabic would cause resentment in Stamboul, where there was already the first stirring of a narrowly Turkish national feeling.

That was a telling argument, for Abdulhamid was deeply sensitive to the temper of his peoples. He grew reluctant to ride through the streets of his capital, constantly fearing attempts on his life. So obsessed was he with the politics of murder that Ottoman newspapers were forbidden to inform their readers of the assassination of a foreign ruler or statesman: there was no suggestion that Tsar Alexander II, President Garfield, President Sadi Carnot, Shah Nasr-ed-Din or the Empress Elizabeth had met violent deaths. Once or twice a week Abdulhamid dared to emerge from Yildiz Park; occasionally he travelled up the Bosphorus, crossing to the Anatolian shore; but he was disinclined to venture deeper into his empire, least of all in Europe. Although he might possess visionary concepts of imperial and spiritual authority, the Caliph made himself as much a prisoner of his palace as, in those days, was the Pope in Rome. The directors of the Oriental Railway Company had presented Abdulhamid with a sumptuous royal coach. It remained unused until 1909, when it bore him into exile.

CHAPTER 12

Armenia, Crete and the Thirty-Day War

In the last decade of the old century three internal crises – in Armenia, Crete and Macedonia – alerted the European chancelleries yet again to what they assumed was the imminent collapse of the Ottoman Empire. Viewed down the avenue of history it is clear that the three problems were closely related to each other, in timing and in character. But it was not clear to contemporaries. The Armenian Massacres stirred humanitarian sentiment on both sides of the Atlantic even more profoundly than the Bulgarian Horrors twenty years before. In comparison with the sufferings of the Armenian people, the Cretan struggle for union with Greece and the tangle of nationalities in Macedonia were vexing variations on a far too familiar theme.

Most Armenians had been Ottoman subjects for some five hundred years.[1] Like Greeks and Persians, they were an ancient people, the first nation who collectively embraced the Christian faith – Gregory the Illuminator baptized their king, Tiridates III, some three hundred years before Augustine brought organized Christianity into Kent. By 430, however, the Armenian monarchy had disappeared, its lands divided between the Byzantine and Persian empires. The mountain ranges and high plateaux where the Armenians lived from earliest times passed under Ottoman rule in the fourteenth and fifteenth centuries, but large Armenian communities remained subject to Persia until 1828, when their lands were ceded to Russia. Despite the buffeting of history, bonds of language, literature and religion enabled them to retain a sense of national identity. At the time of the Ottoman conquest their 'Armenian Gregorian Church' had been, for more than a century and a half, united with Rome. Although they subsequently accepted most Orthodox dogmas and liturgical teaching, the Armenian hierarchy showed greater independence than other, numerically larger, Churches in eastern

175

Christendom; the Armenians continue, for example, to make the Sign of the Cross in a Latin manner rather than in the Greek. Under the Sultans they received a separate status as the Gregorian *millet*, with an Armenian Gregorian patriarch in Constantinople.

These spiritual leaders played no political role whatsoever until January 1878, when Patriarch Nerses Varjabedian was induced by some western-educated members of his community in the capital to travel to Russian headquarters at San Stefano and seek the Tsar's support for Armenian self-government in eastern Anatolia. But Alexander II – and even more his successor, Alexander III – mistrusted Armenian political ambitions. Neither at San Stefano nor at the subsequent Congress did the Russians press their cause. Lord Salisbury's concern for the Armenians in 1878 led to the appointment of eight British 'military consuls' who were to ensure that the Sultan carried out reforms in eastern Anatolia, but their activities – like the reforms themselves – were minimal. Their brief presence encouraged Armenian agitators to exaggerate the interest of successive British governments in their cause. Despite disappointment at the Berlin Settlement there was, from 1878 onwards, an active national independence movement among the Armenians, although the pace-setters were exiles rather than subjects of either the Tsar or the Sultan.

Unlike the Slav peoples within the Ottoman Empire, the Armenians remained a minority in every province they settled. There was a heavy concentration in Cilicia, around Adana, but most lived in the six eastern vilayets of Erzerum, Van, Bitlis, Diyarbekir, Sivas and Mamuret, forming a peasant population constantly in conflict with the nomadic Muslim Kurds around them. Intelligent or ambitious Armenians migrated to Constantinople, Smyrna and Aleppo. At the close of the 1880s there were about 150,000 members of the Armenian Church living in the capital, compared to 153,000 Greek Orthodox and 385,000 Muslims. Many Armenians became small shopkeepers. Some rapidly established themselves as merchants or bankers, often with notable success. Hakop Zarifi was accepted and trusted as Abdulhamid's financial agent long before he came to the throne; and in 1890 the Sultan was so impressed by a report on the oil potential of the Baghdad and Mosul vilayets submitted to the Ministry of Mines by a 21-year-old Armenian from Üsküdar that a firman ordered all petroleum revenue to be assigned henceforth to his Privy Purse rather than the Ottoman treasury. The percipient young Armenian was Calouste Gulbenkian.[2]

Not all belonged to the Armenian Gregorian Church. In Sivas and Diyarbekir many were Roman Catholics, having traditional links with

France; and from 1839 onwards American Protestant missionaries were active around Erzerum, winning converts and giving them a good schooling. It is a curious thought that, while Unionists and Confederates answered the call to the colours, a group of compatriots 5,000 miles from the Civil War battlefields were protecting a mission in Bitlis from marauding Kurds whose sheikhs remained hostile to all Armenian Christians, whether Protestant, Catholic or Gregorian. Thirty years later, when the Armenian Question was first posed, there were nearly a hundred interdenominational mission stations in Armenia. No US President before Woodrow Wilson paid much heed to their accounts of the Armenian struggle, but their presence in Anatolia ensured that they were able to arouse interest in the Armenian cause among newspaper readers on both sides of the Atlantic. By the early 1890s the Armenians could count on better publicity abroad than any subject peoples since the Greek War of Independence.

Throughout the previous decade there had been mounting tension in the eastern vilayets of Anatolia. In response to propaganda from their exiled compatriots the Armenians refused to pay legalized protection money to the Kurds, and complained of the rapacity of the Sultan's local representatives. Foreign consuls reported kidnappings and murder. The killings began in 1890 at Erzerum, where Armenian churches, homes and shops were wrecked in a spontaneous explosion of mutual hatred. They were followed by local massacres in the villages and by a hardening of attitudes on opposing sides. In 1891 the Sultan raised the *hamidiye* regiments among the Kurds. Two exiled groups took up the Armenian cause: the semi-Marxist *Hunchaks* ('Bell') movement, had been established in Geneva in 1887 and now an equally radical, but less Marxist, Armenian Revolutionary Federation (*Dashnagtzoutiun*, or 'Dashnaks') was founded in Tbilisi. Neither group had links with the Russian government, as Ottoman apologists claim; for seven years the Tsarist authorities had been seeking to russify their national minorities and they were even less inclined to tolerate an Armenian autonomist movement than during the great Eastern Crisis of the late 1870s. There is, however, no doubt that fanatical *Hunchak* agents encouraged hopes of an 'Armenian Revolution' in villages where there was deep resentment at discriminatory taxation favouring the Kurds. Moreover, it is difficult to understand the purpose behind a rising in the Sassun district south-west of Muş, during the autumn of 1894, unless it was to achieve martyrdom by provoking 'harsh reprisals' in order 'to make their case in Europe'. If it was this political calculation which prompted the rising in Sassun, the cynical planners did, indeed, fulfil their ghastly purpose. The *hamidiye*, well-primed before the rising began, wreaked a terrible vengeance: twenty-five villages were destroyed that autumn and more than 10,000 Armenians slaughtered. British consular officials had little doubt that the massacres were ordered by the local Ottoman authorities.[3]

Over the winter of 1894–5 the anti-Turk campaign of protest gained momentum abroad. In Britain the campaign transcended party divisions, with Liberals and Conservatives, Radicals and Unionists appearing on the same platform to uphold humanitarianism and the Christian faith of a martyred people. Reports of the Armenian massacres prompted speaker after speaker in Britain to demand punishment of 'Abdul the Damned' for permitting the condition of his Christian subjects to deteriorate rather than improve over the past decade. No British politician could hope for support from the electorate if he dared recall the Crimean alliance or the Jingo pledges to save Constantinople. In mid-April 1895, under pressure from Lord Rosebery in London, the British, Russian and French ambassadors drew up proposals for administrative improvements in the six vilayets of eastern Anatolia.[4] Abdulhamid, rightly suspecting that Paris and St Petersburg would not back their men on the spot with coercive measures, simply ignored the proposals.

At this point – the closing days of June 1895 – Rosebery's weak Liberal government gave way to a strong Conservative–Unionist ministry. Lord Salisbury once again became both Prime Minister and Foreign Secretary, and a month later enhanced his authority with a striking electoral triumph. The Eastern Question at once absorbed his attention. Turkey, he told the German ambassador, was 'too rotten' to last much longer; and he added that 'there would be no difficulty today if England had not committed the mistake of rejecting Tsar Nicholas's proposal to the British representatives before the Crimean War.'[2] These sentiments Salisbury repeated on other occasions. There is no doubt that he was convinced the Ottoman Empire would crumble into pieces within a few years. Yet it would be wrong to assume that he had, ready in his mind, any clear-cut partition plan. Over the following months he approached the Germans, French and Russians in search of a common policy, but met suspicion and misrepresentation.[5]

At first Salisbury believed he could coerce the Sultan by 'big words spoken in a loud voice' – and supported by a squadron of warships cruising in the approaches to the Dardanelles. The British were said to be planning the seizure of Lemnos or naval action off Smyrna or İskenderun. There was alarm at the Porte and unrest in the Stamboul streets: 'Let the Sultan judge the effect the fleet will have on other parts of the Empire by the effect he sees it has had on the feeling in Constantinople,' Salisbury telegraphed to Currie, the British ambassador.[6] Briefly this firm stance seemed effective. Abdulhamid shuffled his ministers, appointing Mehmed Kamil as Grand Vizier of a government of 'westernizers', and announced that he would accept the ambassadors' reform programme which he had resisted for six months. But mounting evidence of friction between Great Britain and Russia – together with a not unjustified suspicion that Kamil would work with foreign embassies to thwart Yildiz policies – induced the Sultan to change his mind, and Mehmed Kamil was dismissed after a mere five weeks in office. Little was accomplished. Consular reports described a reign of terror in the six vilayets of eastern Anatolia. By the end of winter in 1895–6 it was reported that over 30,000 Armenians had perished in the bloodshed of the past two years. These figures were disputed by an Ottoman commission of investigation; not surprisingly, they are challenged by historians who use the Yildiz Palace archives.[7]

Salisbury, like Palmerston earlier in the century, wished to give the ambassador 'discretionary powers' to call the fleet up to Constantinople in an emergency, without reference back to London. This proposal was strongly opposed by the First Lord of the Admiralty, George Goschen, who had himself been ambassador to the Sultan in 1880–1, and who argued that there was a risk of the fleet finding itself trapped in the Straits between a Russian squadron 'invited' by the Sultan to enter the Bosphorus and a French squadron, sailing eastwards from Salonika. So dangerous did the First Sea Lord think this strategy that he refused to discuss it. Although sarcastically speculating whether Her Majesty's capital ships were made of porcelain, Lord Salisbury accepted the verdict of the professionals.[8] Nevertheless, he encouraged contingency planning in case it became necessary to use force against the Sultan, and in the second week of February 1896 he received a secret memorandum from Colonel Chermside, the military attaché in Constantinople, which for the first time examined the prospects of landing troops to seize 'the south-western extremity of the Gallipoli Peninsula'. Chermside thought – and the commander of the Mediterranean fleet agreed with him – that marines landed from transports covered by the guns of the fleet would soon occupy the peninsula. Both the Director of Naval Intelligence and the Director of Military Intelligence strongly advised the cabinet against any such action, for which they claimed at least 20,000 men would be needed. The proposal was dropped; but, significantly, Chermside's report remained a top secret document, retained for future reference. Half a century later, when most nineteenth-century British archives were open, it was still not available for public inspection.[9]

On 11 February 1896 the First Lord of the Admiralty told Parliament that, as the Sultan had failed to carry out the promised reforms in Anatolia, 'we are free from any engagement as to the maintenance of the Ottoman Empire'.[10] This announcement was intended less as a direct warning to the Porte than as a sop to British public opinion, angered by continued reports of massacre from Armenia. The Foreign Minister, Ahmed Tevfik, showed some desire for reconciliation, but the Eastern Question rapidly increased in complexity during the early months of the year. In the third week of January 1896 the Consul-General in Salonika sent the Foreign Office clear evidence that Armenian revolutionaries were encouraging unrest among the Greeks in Macedonia.[11] By the end of February the ardently patriotic Greek community in Crete was in revolt against Ottoman rule. In the late spring there were rumours in Constantinople of British agents fomenting disturbances so as to give Salisbury an excuse for occupying the island, effectively absorbing it into the British Empire. This, however, was nonsense; the Cretan troubles embarrassed the British, especially as they coincided with phases of Anglo-American tension over Venezuela and Anglo-German tension after the Kaiser's tactless telegram to President Kruger. But the Cyprus Convention and the occupation of Egypt rankled with other governments, who noted the strategic value of Crete to a great naval power.

News of the Cretan rising had caused little surprise abroad. Insurrections in 1770, 1821, 1857, 1866–8, 1879 and 1889 left the islanders resentful of Ottoman repression; and they were increasingly angered by the harsh administration of Mahmud Jellaledin, a conservatively-minded *Vali*. Tension became acute in the late summer of 1894, after Jellaledin hanged four prominent members of the Orthodox Church on the island; although he was replaced by a *Vali* of Greek origin, acts of terrorism and counter-terrorism were reported from isolated villages over the following eighteen months. The most serious unrest came after riots at Khania in the last week of May 1896. At the same time reports were circulating in Stamboul and Pera of secret talks in Athens between Armenian revolutionaries, Cretan insurgents and the radical patriotic Greek nationalist movement, *Ethnike Hetairia*. Three Greek guerrilla bands were said (correctly) to have crossed the frontiers in Thessaly and Epirus. The governors of the Salonika, Monastir and Kossovo vilayets mobilized the *redif* (military reservists) in anticipation of an *Ethnike*

Hetairia rebellion throughout the remaining Greek provinces of the Ottoman Empire.[12]

Momentarily, in the summer of 1896, the diplomatic initiative passed to Count Goluchowski, the Austro-Hungarian Foreign Minister. Francis Joseph's ambassador to the Porte, Baron Calice, was also *doyen* of the diplomatic corps at Constantinople. In the first week of July Calice warned the Ottoman authorities that unless autonomy was conceded to the Greek majority in Crete, there would be such grave unrest throughout Thessaly, Epirus and Macedonia that the Powers would be forced to summon another Congress and impose a new order upon the Ottoman lands. At the same time Goluchowski asked Salisbury for the Royal Navy to join Austrian, Russian, French and Italian warships in a preventive international blockade of Crete, to stop Greek nationals coming to the aid of their compatriots. Salisbury refused: 'In view of the feeling which the cruelty of the Ottoman Government has excited in England we should have great hesitation in taking any step which would constitute us the ally of the Sultan against an insurgent Christian population,' he explained to the Permanent Under-Secretary at the Foreign Office in the Note which formed a basis for his reply to Goluchowski.[13] This principle the British never abandoned so long as the Ottoman Empire remained in being.

By the second week of August 1896 the Sultan had 420,000 men retained indefinitely on a war footing, a terrible burden for a government still heavily dependent on foreign loans. His ministers urged Abdulhamid to settle the Cretan Question. Once again there was a Porte *versus* Yildiz tussle, with the 'second scribe', Ahmed Izzet, urging the Sultan to stand firm against all promptings for reform. But although the diplomats regarded the thirty-two-year old Izzet as the current 'power behind the throne', Abdulhamid was at that moment more impressed by independent pressure from the German, French and Russian ambassadors. On 25 August he accepted a programme of reform in Crete, prepared by a commission from all the embassies at Pera: the Cretans would have a Christian Governor and a General Assembly with broadly autonomous powers and would be assured of two-thirds of the public offices, while the gendarmerie was to be reorganized under European commissioners. Although there were reports from the Van vilayet of a fresh wave of Armenian killings and terrorism, it seemed as if, in Crete, one deep-rooted grievance had at last been satisfied.[14]

Abdulhamid approved the Cretan reform programme on a Tuesday morning. Early on Wednesday afternoon – 26 August 1896 –

Armenian Dashnak extremists seized the headquarters of the Ottoman Bank in Galata (Beyoğlu). Their activities anticipated the methods used by numerous terrorist organizations in the Near East over the following century. They planted explosives in the building, took hostages, and demanded immediate reforms in the six eastern vilayets: they sought rights for the Armenians to match the concessions promised to the Cretans – even though, unlike the Greeks in Crete, nowhere did the Armenians form a majority of the population. For two hours there was shooting around and from within the Bank. Negotiations between the bank officials, the dragoman of the Russian Embassy and the terrorists made it clear that the chief Dashnak objective was to alert Europe to the plight of the Armenians; and in this they were eminently successful. In the small hours of Thursday morning the surviving terrorists were led from the building under safe-conduct to the bank director's yacht in the Bosphorus, and eventually into exile.[15]

They were the fortunate ones. Within thirty-six hours mob vengeance was to cause the massacre of some five to six thousand Armenians in the capital. During Wednesday night and the daylight hours on Thursday, Ottoman troops made no move to check the violence. British marines and Russian sailors were landed from the stationnaire warships attached to the embassies. On Thursday morning the ambassadors jointly asked the Sultan to issue 'such precise and categorical orders as will put an immediate end to this unheard of state of things, which is calculated to bring about the most serious consequences for Your Majesty's Empire.' When Abdulhamid protested that 'he had never heard such language in the twenty years he had been on the throne,' he was given an opportunity to hear even tougher talk from Baron Calice and from General Nelidov, the Tsar's ambassador. The Powers, he was told, would have to consider 'what remedy there could be for such great evils': failure to end the massacres would imperil both throne and dynasty. After prayers at the Friday *şelamlik* the Sultan at last took action: henceforth the faithful were 'forbidden to kill'.[16]

The Cretan rebellion had aroused little interest in Western Europe or the United States, but carnage in the streets of Constantinople was another matter. News of the massacre revived the agitation against 'Abdul the Damned', alias 'the Great Assassin' or, as Clemenceau in Paris preferred it, 'that monster of Yildiz, the blood-red Sultan'. To British statesmen, whether Conservative or Liberal, and to French radicals, there seemed little prospect of a stable, prosperous and well-governed Ottoman Empire so long as Abdulhamid remained on the throne. Even Kaiser William II, an appreciative and much-fêted guest

seven years earlier, wrote in the margin of a dispatch from his ambassa-
dor, 'The Sultan must be deposed'. Kaiser William encouraged the
British ambassador in Berlin to discuss the problems of alternative
Sultan-making with his Foreign Minister. But not, perhaps, too
seriously; within a few days the 'three emperors' (German, Russian,
Austrian) had agreed that 'if left alone from outside interference',
the Ottoman Empire could be preserved for many years to come.
Characteristically, the Kaiser thereupon sent Abdulhamid the latest
Hohenzollern family group photograph, duly autographed, as a per-
sonal gesture of good will.[17]

The Sultan did not entirely owe his survival to the deep mistrust
between the European Powers, but he continued to benefit from their
suspicion of each other's objectives in policy. Hardly had the Armenians
attacked the Ottoman Bank before the rival diplomats began posing
questions to which there could be no clear-cut answers. Who had known
of the raid in advance? Why did so many wealthy Armenians leave the
capital by steamer that Tuesday and Wednesday morning? Why, in this
week of massacre in the capital, did the Italians 'quietly' send warships
to Salonika and Smyrna, the other embassies speculated? Why did the
British Mediterranean Fleet sail from Malta to Lemnos, according to
operational plans drawn up some months before? And at the British
embassy there was a suspicion that the Russians were behind the raid,
for 'the present moment would provide a splendid opportunity for a
Russian *coup de main* on Constantinople'.[18]

Ambassador Nelidov did, indeed, return to St Petersburg two months
later. There he sought to win the backing of the young Tsar Nicholas
II for a project he had advocated for the past four years – a surprise
naval assault on the Bosphorus, with troops landing at Kilyos, Sariyer
and Büyükdere for a lightning advance on the Golden Horn. Nelidov
argued that Russia's traditional enemies on the Straits would not dare
support the Sultan at such a time. 'Turn the Bosphorus into a Russian
Gibraltar', he urged a Crown Council. Momentarily Tsar Nicholas
was attracted by the thought of Russian troops dominating the Straits
'for ever'. But Nicholas's closest advisers were more interested in
the Far East; they encouraged him to put the Near East 'on ice'. The
whole episode intrigued London, although it caused no adjustment
of policies. Intelligence reports from Odessa kept the Foreign Office
well informed of Russian plans and troop movements, but Salisbury,
who had discussed the Eastern Question with Nicholas II at Balmoral
in September, rightly discounted any precipitate Russian action. The
chief consequence of Nelidov's flurry of activity that winter was to

weaken the collective weight of coercion pressing the Sultan towards reform. Despite their deep mistrust of one another the ambassadors in Constantinople, responding to a British initiative, began six weeks of discussion at the end of December 1896, and by mid-February had completed a comprehensive programme of reforms for presentation to Abdulhamid. But there was no reason for the Sultan to bow to what he might, quite legitimately, regard as yet another instance of 'outside interference'.[19]

He could, too, by now cite the last series of reforms imposed upon him as a failure. Although the Cretans had accepted the settlement proposed in August, there were frequent clashes between Christians and Muslims on the island during the winter months, and early in February 1897 the Greek consul in Khania telegraphed to Athens, insisting that a massacre of Orthodox families was imminent, a claim never substantiated. In the mountains a committee of Cretan revolutionaries proclaimed the island absorbed into the kingdom of the Hellenes, and on 11 February a flotilla of torpedo boats commanded by the Greek king's second son, Prince George, sailed from Salamis to take possession of the island. Hasty diplomatic activity, including strong pressure from the Tsar, induced the Greek king to summon the flotilla home again two days later. No restraining orders from their sovereign could check the *Ethnike Hetairia*, however. Fifteen hundred armed volunteers embarked at Piraeus and sailed for Crete, determined to emulate the achievements of Garibaldi's Thousand redshirts in Sicily, the patriots who in 1860 made possible the speedy unification of Italy. Further north, armed bands of irregulars made provocative raids across the frontier into Thessaly.

Urgent appeals to the King and Queen of the Hellenes from their relatives in Western Europe and Russia failed to halt the drift towards war. Philhellene Liberals from Britain, in Athens that spring, also urged caution, for it was assumed that, with reservists, the Sultan could eventually put an army of a million men into the field. Their efforts failed. Canon MacColl, a persistent campaigner for the Christian nationalities under Ottoman rule, was told by the King of the Hellenes that, in the case of war, the Greeks would rise against their Turkish oppressors throughout the Sultan's empire; other nationalities would follow the Greek lead. In exasperation at the activity of the 'brigands', Sultan Abdulhamid declared war on Greece in the second week of April. No wave of insurrection shook the fabric of his empire.[20]

The mobilization plans perfected by General von der Goltz worked efficiently. An initial thrust by the Greek army on the Meluna Pass was halted by superior numbers of Turks based on Ellasona. Soon the Ottoman Army was advancing on Greek field headquarters in Larissa. 'In a few minutes the Army, from an organized and disciplined unity, was transformed into a seething disorganized mass of fugitives that sped helter-skelter across the plain, back to Larissa, a distance of almost forty miles,' Prince Nicholas wrote many years later, recalling his baptism of fire as commander of an artillery battery on 23 April, the fourth day of the war.[21] The Greeks rallied sufficiently to halt the invasion short of Thermopylae, while General Smolensky checked the Ottoman incursion in a valiant defensive battle at Valestino. But after thirty days of fighting King George I of the Hellenes reluctantly accepted an armistice, obtained from the Ottoman commanders through Russian mediation. All Greek combatants were withdrawn from Crete, which was policed by an international force drawn from the navies of Austria–Hungary, France, Germany, Great Britain, Italy and Russia. Across the main battle zone on the plains of Farsala and in Epirus an uneasy cease-fire was imposed while the ambassadors sought to improvise a peace settlement.

The Ottoman victory raised the prestige of the Sultan and the expectations of the Porte. In London, however, Salisbury was adamant that there must be no handing back of Christian towns to Ottoman rule; and he believed that the Tsar, as the greatest of Orthodox sovereigns, shared this conviction. Four months previously Salisbury had raised the possibility of a joint naval demonstration at the Straits with the Austro-Hungarian ambassador, only to be rebuffed in Vienna. Now he was willing to propose to Britain's traditional rival on the Straits collective naval coercion of the Porte. A telegram sent to Sir Nicholas O'Conor, the ambassador in St Petersburg, as the peace talks were beginning, showed Salisbury's belief that Abdulhamid, despite the victory of his army in the field, must accept a settlement dictated by Europe in concert:

If the Sultan remains obstinate in demanding the retrocession of Thessaly, the matter will require the most serious consideration of the Powers . . . No means of coercing him by land exist except at the cost of a difficult and extensive campaign. Very easy means exist of coercing him by sea . . . It is time for England and Russia to consider whether it is not possible for them to devise some form of agreement which shall enable them, in company with any other Powers who may wish to co-operate, to send a limited number of ships to anchor before Yildiz.[22]

No such naval demonstration was attempted, for the Russians were convinced – rightly – that Abdulhamid would treat the Greeks leniently,
thereby ruling out the need for coercion. The Salisbury Plan is of interest
as a historical might-have-been, a sign that he had abandoned the traditional policy of maintaining the Ottoman Empire as a barrier against
Russian expansion into the Mediterranean. Henceforth the Ottomans
would have either to stand on their own, using army and Caliphate to
concentrate on the Asian mission of the dynasty, or find from among
the European Powers another natural ally. The success of German arms
in the Thirty-Day War left little doubt in which direction Abdulhamid
would turn for foreign support.

First, however, a peace was patched up in the Balkans. Greece, close
to bankruptcy, had to pay an indemnity to the Ottoman Empire and
allow the free migration of Muslims to find refuge in Anatolia. There
was no major redrawing of national boundaries: the Greeks retained
Thessaly, apart from some twenty villages retroceded in a 'rationalization' of the frontier between Mount Ossa and the foothills of the Pindus.
Genuine autonomy was established in Crete, the island remaining
under Ottoman suzerainty but with a Christian Governor nominated
by the Sultan after consultation with Athens. In September 1898 the last
Ottoman troops were withdrawn from the island, after an affray near
Khania in which the soldiery killed many Greek Christians and eight
British marines. Two months later Prince George of Greece was
appointed High Commissioner in Crete, where he served as his father's
special representative for eight years. Russian, British, French and
Italian troops occupied the chief towns – an early and successful experiment in international policing of a troubled region.[23]

Outwardly the Ottoman hold on Macedonia seemed strengthened
by the defeat of the Greeks in the Thirty-Day War. *Ethnike Hetairia*
subversion was doused, even if anti-Ottoman resentment smouldered
on. Other Balkan states, ready to stake a claim to parts of Macedonia
had the Ottoman army faltered, stood aside and for two or three years
there was relative calm in the province. Yet, potentially, Macedonia
remained a more dangerous problem than either Crete or Armenia,
for its mixture of peoples attracted interference from neighbouring
governments. Greeks might constitute the most literate and articulate
Christian minority in the province as a whole, but both they and the
genuine Turks were heavily outnumbered by Southern Slavs, susceptible to propaganda from Bulgaria or Serbia, while there was also a
great concentration of Jews in Salonika itself, and in several districts
a Kutzo-Vlach minority, geographically scattered and only occasionally

remembered by their kinsfolk in Bucharest. British consular reports stressed the threat from the Bulgarian terrorist secret society IMRO (Internal Macedonian Revolutionary Organization), active from 1893 onwards, although the Sultan was able to exploit IMRO's rivalry with the rabidly Bulgar-nationalist 'Supremists' (alias EMRO), who were controlled directly from Sofia. Warmest champions of Abdulhamid's sovereignty were the Muslim Albanians; their resentment of foreign interference and Christian proselytizing was so strong that, early in 1899, they held a meeting of clan notables at Ipek (now Pec, in Montenegro) where they agreed to set up an Albanian League, pledged to defend the Sultan's lands and uphold the Caliph's authority against the Infidel.

Although Abdulhamid took the initiative, setting up a Rumelian Provinces Reform Commission and linking Salonika, Kossovo and Monastir in a single province, the *Vilayet-i Selase* ('The Three Vilayets'), more was required than administrative paper reforms if Macedonia were to stay under Ottoman rule.[24] High among the needs were changes in land-ownership for, apart from the immediate vicinity of Salonika and Serres, where Greek Christians owned big estates, the predominantly Slav peasantry remained in almost feudal subjection to the whims, caprices and farming methods of Muslim beys.

The British ambassador in Constantinople soon recognized the significance of the Thirty-Day War for Abdulhamid's reign. Early in June 1897 Currie told Salisbury:

A reform movement had made progress among the Turks, provoking strong measures of repression on the part of the Sultan, and the dissatisfaction with the arbitrary rule of the Palace was gaining ground. The Ambassadors were only waiting for the instructions of the Governments to press the reforms upon the Sultan. The state of things has now been entirely changed by the Greek War. Prompt mobilisation and good organization have brought about a reaction. The victories in Thessaly have restored the prestige of the Sultan and of his Mussulman subjects and have to a certain extent repaired the breach between them.[25]

All this was true, although foreign military assessors observed that the war had not continued long enough to prove whether the army commanders possessed the skill to improvise, modifying agreed plans should determined resistance jeopardize their success. The war gave notice to the European chancelleries that the Ottoman Empire was not so close to disintegration as they had assumed ten months earlier, when mob rule in the capital seemed to foreshadow a speedy foreign intervention.

The Thirty-Day War had one strange consequence, which passed unnoticed at the time. In February 1897, when Greek volunteers sailed from Salamis and Piraeus to help the Cretan insurgents, the ambassadors in Constantinople were attending conferences to discuss ways of safeguarding the Sultan's Armenian subjects from repression and massacre. The war crisis put a sudden end to these meetings; and the Armenian Question, so recently the cause of such deep feeling abroad, remained unanswered. The incidence of killings in the six vilayets died down as the Armenian nationalist groups quarrelled among themselves. An uneasy truce prevailed, until in 1909 there were further reports of massacre around Adana. By then a few Armenians held administrative posts, especially in the Ministry of Finance. Many wealthier Armenians from the capital and the greater trading cities considered themselves fortunate to be alive, and no less fortunate to emigrate. They brought their wealth and skills to Britain, America, Egypt and France, while their compatriots still within the Sultan's lands became once more a historic people, half-forgotten by the West.

Half-forgotten, yet half-remembered, too. As the Armenian crisis receded, one folk image remained firmly set in popular prejudice. In January 1896 the *Punch* cartoonist Lindsay Sandemann created a bogey figure, whom he dubbed 'The Unspeakable Turk': a sinister Sultan, caressing the edge of an unsheathed scimitar as he stands outside a ruined house of death; glancing diabolically up a deserted path, he exclaims: 'Ha, ha! There's no one about. I can get to business again.' Each fresh challenge to Ottoman rule brought 'The Unspeakable Turk' back to haunt the pages of the popular journals. The Sultanate could never shake off the odium of the Armenian massacres.[26]

CHAPTER 13

Ancient Peoples and Young Turks

Despite the abhorrence with which he was regarded in so many foreign capitals, Abdulhamid II could still count on backing from the most vociferous of Europe's sovereigns. Briefly, in August 1896, Kaiser William II had thought the Sultan would have to be deposed, but he soon rallied to his support and was gratified by the success of the German-trained troops in the war against Greece. Within two years William was contemplating a second visit to the Ottoman Empire, an 'expedition to the Orient' which would be more extensive than the customary cruises in the imperial yacht.[1] No Christian ruler had entered Jerusalem since the Hohenstaufen emperor Frederick II captured the Holy City during the Sixth Crusade. Now, six and a half centuries later, a Hohenzollern emperor would go to Jerusalem and Damascus as an emissary of peace and Christian good will, a pilgrim counting on the benevolent protection of the Sultan-Caliph. First, however, he conceded that it was essential to pay a courtesy call on Abdulhamid in his capital.

On 18 October 1898 the steam yacht *Hohenzollern*, gleaming white in the crisp autumn sunshine, moored off the Dolmabahche Palace, allowing the Kaiser to begin his second state visit with a display of naval showmanship watched by thousands of his host's subjects. In 1889, when an earlier *Hohenzollern* first brought the German imperial couple to Constantinople, the Germans were building up their influence in Turkey, and the Sultan's guests responded enthusiastically to Ottoman hospitality: 'just like something out of the Arabian Nights,' the Kaiserin noted at the time. Now the prize for Germany lay in Asia Minor rather than on the Bosphorus. The final decision had still to be taken by the Sultan over the vital rail link from Konya eastwards through Mesopotamia to the Gulf. As the first reports of rich oil deposits around Mosul were at that moment exciting British and Dutch companies, it seemed essential for Germany to secure agreement to complete this last sector in the vaunted Berlin–Baghdad railway project. European governments had long acknowledged the strategic value of such a railway across Asia Minor, which would reduce the journey time between Constantinople and Baghdad from twenty-three days to forty-eight hours. The oil rumours revived interest in the project, for it was assumed that a railway concession would carry exclusive oil and mineral rights for several miles on either side of the track. A 'Trade and Resources Map of Asia Minor', produced by enterprising printers in Halle, went on sale in Germany while the *Hohenzollern* was still in the Aegean. It sold with astonishing rapidity.[2]

Already, in 1897, William II had emphasized the importance of his Pera embassy by appointing as ambassador Baron Marschall von Bieberstein, head of the Foreign Ministry since the fall of the Bismarcks seven years before. Now the Kaiser included in his suite aboard the *Hohenzollern* Marschall's successor as State Secretary for Foreign Affairs, Count von Bülow, the future Chancellor. Together Bülow and Marschall sought out the Sultan's ministers and favourites, determined to consolidate Germany's commercial hold on Anatolia. Good arguments were persuasively supported with lavish baksheesh; Ahmed Izzet, in particular, fared well.

Abdulhamid himself was too shrewd, too proud and too suspicious to fall for such enticement. He needed German diplomatic backing, German finance and German technical skills. But not in a hurry. He had no wish to make his Empire a Hohenzollern dependency. Although by nature parsimonious in minor matters, if imperial presents were to be exchanged then he, too, would be generous, and he spared no expense in his determination to impress his visitors: a sober estimate by a French diplomat at the end of the year claimed that the Kaiser's visit had cost the Ottoman Treasury some thirty million francs, of which six million were spent on gifts.[3] Yet no treaty concessions were signed while the German visitors remained in the Ottoman Empire. In a symbolic gesture Sultan and Kaiser crossed the Bosphorus to the Anatolian shore and formally opened an impressive railway terminus at Haydarpaša, while Abdulhamid let it be known that he was prepared to lease port facilities around the terminus to the German directors of the Anatolian Railways. In November 1899 the Sultan at last made clear his willingness to accord Germany a further concession, but there was then a delay of almost three and a half years before the formal grant was signed and sealed. In the first week of March 1903 a German-controlled syndicate was authorized to complete the construction of the Baghdad

Railway, covering 1,280 miles from Konya to Basra. At the same time the syndicate gained, as anticipated, oil rights extending for twenty kilometres on either side of the track.[4]

The Kaiser was convinced that his 'journey to the Orient' significantly boosted German trade and investment in the Ottoman Empire; and perhaps he was right. In Berlin the Baghdad Railway Project became a matter of national pride, not simply a business enterprise. But the value of the concessions was never fully realized. Engineering problems, together with political harassment from the Russians, French and British, delayed contruction of the railway through the Taurus and Amanus mountains. The line was still not complete when, in October 1917, William paid a final visit to the Ottoman capital.

Whatever his later feelings, in 1898 the Kaiser resented suggestions that he had gone to the Ottoman Empire as Germany's principal sales representative. He accepted that political necessity dictated his visit to Constantinople itself, but he claimed that his intention was to bolster effective government within the Ottoman lands at a time when the authority of the Sultan had been diminished by the propaganda of terrorists in foreign pay. More than thirty years later, in exile in the Netherlands, William II peppered the margin of a German edition of Harold Nicolson's *Lord Carnock* with a defence of Abdulhamid, seeking to explain 'why the Sultan acted so severely' against the Armenians when the Ottoman Bank was seized.[5] He recalled 'the new bombs which I saw myself' seized from 'Armenians rounded up by the police' and 'brand new, shiny British pounds in gold'; and he developed an elaborate argument that the Armenians in the capital had been ordered by exiles in London 'to stage an insurrection so that the British government would be able to use it as a pretext for military intervention'. But, so the ex-Kaiser maintained, 'the red coats stayed away, and the Armenians waiting for them were killed. Thus England betrayed the Armenians, who had risen upon her instigation.' What he was shown in Pera and Stamboul convinced him that western denunciation of 'Abdul the Damned' was hypocritical. By contrast, the ruler of Germany would offer a hand of friendship, not only to Abdulhamid, but to all loyal Ottomans, irrespective of their faith and nationality.

To this theme of protective friendship the Kaiser repeatedly returned during his pilgrimage to the Holy Land. The planned itinerary provided for the *Hohenzollern* to sail southwards to Haifa, enabling him to travel up through Palestine, Syria and the Lebanon in a conducted tour, organized by Thomas Cook and Son. Had the *Hohenzollern* anchored off Jaffa rather than Haifa it would have been possible for the Kaiser to go by train to Jerusalem, for as early as 1892 a line had been opened down to the coast. But 'The journey from Haifa to Jerusalem was . . . on horseback or by carriage, and this pleased us all,' Count Bülow later explained. 'A railway . . . really did not suit the scene.'[6] Bülow did not add that the Jaffa–Jerusalem line was completed and run by a French, rather than a German, company.

The ostensible reason for this imperial Cook's Tour was to allow the German Emperor to be present at the dedication on Reformation Day (31 October) of a new Lutheran church in Jerusalem, the *Erlöserkirche* (Church of the Redeemer). But Germany's Roman Catholics were remembered, too. From his friend the Sultan William had obtained possession of the site of the Dormition, the traditional resting-place of the Virgin Mary, which he presented to the Catholic 'German Association in the Holy Land'. Most of all, the Kaiser sought to impress the Sultan's subjects with his stature as a world ruler. His entry into Jerusalem, astride a black charger and wearing white ceremonial uniform, his helmet surmounted by a burnished gold eagle, projected the might and grandeur of the German Empire, as if to awe a troubled city which Abdulhamid was too scared to visit.

Like Bonaparte in Egypt, William was attracted by Islam. 'If I had come there without any Religion at all I certainly would have turned Mahometan,' he wrote to the Tsar.[7] He was also influenced by con-sular reports showing how the growing Panislamic movement might be harnessed to serve Germany's needs. Accordingly, at Damascus, a week after his entry into Jerusalem, William laid a wreath on Saladin's grave, and it was there that he responded to a welcome from the *ulema* by giving 'His Majesty the Sultan and the three hundred million Muslims who . . . revere in him their Caliph' a pledge 'that the German Emperor will ever be their friend'. The Kaiser could offer such an assurance knowing that, in contrast to other world empires, his colonies contained few Muslim believers.[8]

The Germans made cultural and material gains from their sover-eign's expedition among these 'ancient peoples', as he chose to call them. In material terms, Turkey's imports from Germany rose from 6 per cent in 1897 to 21 per cent in 1910, to the cost of Britain and France in particular. Apart from occasional months of suspicion and strain (notably in 1908–9), official relations between Berlin and the Porte remained cordial. Religious groups and educationists spread the Ger-man language and German ideas in Asia Minor and the Holy Land. One Protestant organization, the *Jerusalems-Verein*, maintained eight schools in Judaea, while the Catholic *Palästinaverein* was active over a bigger region and the *Deutsche Orient-Mission* 'poached' Armenian districts earlier served by the Americans. Yet the three main German influences in Turkey remained armaments salesmen, bankers and railway engineers. In sixteen years German industry provided 200 locomotives and some 3,500 passenger coaches or freight waggons for the Anatolian Railway and its Baghdad offshoot, as well as steel rails for the tracks themselves. A Saxon engineer, Heinrich Meissner, was entrusted with construction of the Hejaz Railway, laid between 1900 and 1908 from Damascus southwards to Medina. Orders went to Germany for another hundred locomotives and some 1,100 coaches, built specifically for this narrow-gauge 'pilgrim railway'.[9] The Haydarpaşa concession for quays on the Anatolian shore of the Bosphorus attracted further German investment, although French firms continued to control the harbour works on the European shore of the Bosphorus as well as in Smyrna, Salonika, and Beirut, the most profitable ports of the Ottoman Empire.

At the time when Kaiser William II visited the three vilayets which geographically constituted Palestine, the Arab population outnumbered the Jewish by about ten to one. But Jerusalem was, of course, sacred to the most ancient of biblical peoples as well as to Christians and Muslims, and he was well aware of feelings aroused by the Jewish problem, in both central Europe and the Levant. On the day after his arrival in Constantinople he had received a five-man deputation of non-Ottoman Jews headed by Theodor Herzl, who had formally established Zionism at a World Congress in Basle twelve months before. The possibility of affording German imperial protection to Zionist settlement in Palestine held the Kaiser's interest, for one in ten of his subjects was Jewish, many of them wealthy and influential in business. 'Your movement, with which I am thoroughly familiar, is based on a sound, healthy idea,' he told Herzl. But when, nine days later, Herzl sought a second audience of the Kaiser – on this occasion outside Jerusalem itself – he found William far less receptive. Abdulhamid's representatives travelling with the imperial party had made it clear to their guests that the Sultan was thoroughly alarmed by Herzl's talk of the Jewish need for 'a publicly and legally assured home in Palestine', and the presence of Herzl and his companions in Jerusalem was an embarrassment. When, in 1901, Abdulhamid agreed to receive Herzl in audience at Yildiz, he made no attempt to conceal his hostility towards incipient Zionism.[10]

Jewish aspirations had never posed acute problems for the Ottomans.

By the turn of the century Jewish believers made up about 230,000 of the estimated twenty million men and women directly under the Sultan's rule, almost three-quarters of whom were Muslim. Jews had fared better in the Ottoman Empire than in Russia and many other parts of Eastern Europe. From 1868 onwards at least two Jews sat as regular members of the *Tanzimat* Council of State, helping to draft laws for the empire as a whole. The Jewish *millet* had long possessed a similar status to the Greek Orthodox and Armenian *millets*: the Chief Rabbi of Constantinople was on an equal footing in the Ottoman social structure with the two Christian patriarchs, although the largest concentrations of Jews were far distant from the Ottoman capital – in Salonika, on the north-western shore of the Sea of Galilee, and in Jerusalem itself. The Russian pogroms of Tsar Alexander III's reign posed a challenge for the Ottoman administration, as for so many other governments faced by the exodus of a persecuted people. In Palestine the Jewish population increased from a mere 24,000 in 1880 (barely half as many Jews as in London) to 49,000 in 1903 and to 90,000 by the outbreak of the First World War, when in the same region there were reckoned to be half a million Arabs. In 1882, as soon as large-scale immigration began, the Ottoman authorities took steps to prevent the landing of Jews from Russia and other parts of Eastern Europe at the ports of Latakia, Beirut, Haifa and Jaffa. Six years later Jerusalem – under Ottoman rule from 1516 onwards – became the centre of a special administrative unit, the *Mutasarriflik*, which stretched from the Dead Sea to Jaffa and Gaza and was governed directly by the Porte.[11]

Control of immigration along the Palestinian coast made political and economic sense to the Ottomans, and indeed to foreign consuls in the region. In contrast to other Arab lands in the Levant, and despite inner Jerusalem's cosmopolitan character, Palestine at the turn of the century was unusually homogeneous, its peoples overwhelmingly Sunni in faith. For the most part they were good, loyal Ottomans, and Sultan Abdulhamid was inclined to listen with especial sympathy to their representations, advancing some educated Arabs to positions of trust at Yildiz. In the Holy Land the Arabs, too, were an ancient people, like the Jews; they could claim descent from communities living there for ten centuries or more, perhaps even from the Biblical Canaanites. If thousands of poor Jewish peasants from Russia converged on so sensitive a region, the Ottoman government feared they would provoke chronic conflict with the Arabs and become a burden on existing Jewish settlements, some set up more than thirty years before. When therefore in 1891 Abdulhamid received the first petition from Arab notables in

Jerusalem demanding a ban on Jewish immigration and land purchase, he gave their plea sympathetic consideration. Even before Herzl began his campaign for a Jewish national home, the Ottoman censorship had resolved that there must be no reference in newspapers or books to the Promised Land of the Jews, to the boundaries of Palestine, or even to the Covenant of Abraham. Arab raiders, who had begun to attack the pioneer Jewish agricultural settlements between Jaffa and Jerusalem as early as 1886, increased their activities while foreign attention was concentrated elsewhere, on the plight of the Sultan's Armenian subjects. It is a tribute to the tenacity of the settlers – many of whom were pre-Herzl and non-political Zionists – that, although often in conflict with a socially conservative rabbinate as well as with local Muslims, they persevered and confidently sought foreign funds in their resolve to scratch a living from a land sadly reluctant to flow with milk and honey.

Despite the obvious hostility of the Sultan towards Jewish penetration of the Holy Land, the German authorities gave occasional support to German Jewish charitable organizations within the Ottoman Empire, at least until the outbreak of the First World War. In 1904 the World Zionist Organization established headquarters in the Rhineland, moving to Berlin seven years later, but with mounting anti-Semitism in Germany and central Europe the WZO had no influence on decision-making in the Wilhelmstrasse. While the Ottomans thoroughly mistrusted Herzl and his successors in the WZO, they tolerated the aid given by Baron Edmond de Rothschild, head of the French branch of the banking dynasty, to finance pioneer settlements for Polish and southern Russian Jews. Labour on these model settlements was supervised from 1884 onwards by agricultural experts, mostly from France, and their success held out a promise of prosperity and further investment in a part of the Ottoman Empire which was still basically poor and backward. Baron Edmond himself instigated many improvements, such as the planting of vines and the introduction of grapefruit cultivation, and in 1900 he set up the Jewish Colonization Association, of which he remained President until his death thirty-four years later. So long as the Ottoman authorities hoped for loans floated in Paris, they dared not impose too rigid restraint on the Colonization Association's activities.[12]

Yet all these Jewish initiatives ran counter to Abdulhamid's apparent determination to boost Islamic unity and integrate the Arab lands more closely with the Turkish core of his realm. Moreover, as Ottoman rule contracted there was a refugee problem for the empire as a whole. The flight of Muslims from the Balkans, Russia and the French-dominated

Maghreb caused grave social distress in the capital and around Smyrna. The Hejaz Railway project, the brainchild of Ahmed Izzet, was in a sense an ideological counterpart to the Jewish settlements, linking faith with material gains, calling as it did for a million pounds to be raised in voluntary donations throughout the Muslim world to improve the transport of pilgrims from Damascus to Medina, and ultimately to Mecca. But troops as well as pilgrims could be moved into the heart of Arabia, and with the townships of Amman and Ma'an linked to the Syrian cities and Beirut there was a prospect of colonizing the vilayet of Suriyya as far south as Aqaba with dispossessed Muslim refugees. The Hejaz Railway, and the telegraph lines running beside it, gave the Sultanate an opportunity to reassert Ottoman control over provinces long since slipping from its grasp.

But were these 'prospects' and 'opportunities' attainable if Ottoman government remained handicapped by the dark suspicion and inconsistency in Abdulhamid's paranoic mind and his consequent refusal to delegate power? The Sultan was gifted with a quick intelligence, which enabled him to take advantage of ideas he only half comprehended. Thus he tried to exploit – often simultaneously – Panislamic propaganda, Greater Ottoman sentiment, and 'Turkism', an intellectual movement which elevated the (traditionally boorish) Turkic element in the cultural heritage of his empire. But his patronage was capricious: puzzling reports from inventive spies would douse yesterday's enthusiasms, leaving unfulfilled much that the Sultan had seemed to champion. Sir Philip Currie told the Foreign Office on several occasions of the widespread 'dissatisfaction with the arbitrary rule of the Palace' which was encouraging the growth of a secret reform movement.[13] Under Currie's successor in Pera, Sir Nicholas O'Conor, the protest movement became identified as 'Young Turk' soon after the turn of the century.

Turkish historians claim, with some justice, that the earliest Young Turk cell was established in May 1889 by army medical students in Stamboul, and that as early as the summer of 1896 more than seventy Young Turk officers and cadets were exiled to Tripoli, after being court-martialled for conspiracy.[14] There remain, however, three basic problems in tracing the early history of the movement: the simultaneous existence of cells in Ottoman garrisons, which were necessarily secret, and of Young Turk exile groups in Geneva, Paris and Cairo, which were so vocal that they attracted publicity; the rivalry and backsliding of would-be leaders abroad; and a tendency of conspiratorial groups to accept generic classification as 'Young Turks', though differing from each other in tactics, and often in long-term objectives. Much of the inspiration for the Young Turks came from the Young Ottomans of the *Tanzimat* era, but the new protest movement possessed a broader social basis. Its supporters had benefited from the educational reforms, especially the revival of the university in Stamboul and the sound teaching in the *lycées* and military colleges. Moreover, by 1900 the Civil Service School (*Mekteb-i Mulkiye*) which had opened in 1859 was providing the administration with a hundred graduates a year. Of twenty Young Turks who rose to prominence in the first decade of the century, six had passed out of the War College and seven came from the *Mulkiye*.[15]

Yet the most revolutionary faction leader in the movement could claim an almost impeccable dynastic lineage. Prince Sabaheddin, who in 1899 had passed into voluntary exile with his father and brother, was a great-grandson of Mahmud II, a grandson of Abdulmecid, and the son of Abdulhamid's half-sister, Princess Seniha. It was Sabaheddin who, in February 1902, presided over a Young Turk Congress in Paris which passed a resolution calling on the Great Powers, 'in the general interest of humanity', to ensure that the Sublime Porte honour its treaty commitments 'to benefit all parts of the Ottoman Empire'. This resolution, however, was deplored by an influential minority who declared that the Powers were guided by an 'interest not always in accord with that of our country'. As so often in congresses of political exiles, the will of the minority prevailed: however much the Young Turks might affirm a wish to see 'European civilization spread in our country', in practice they became patriotically protective of the empire's independence. The aristocratic Sabaheddin was left to lead a splinter group, the Ottoman 'League for Private Initiative and Decentralization'. It was a cumbersome name but, as a statement of intent, admirably specific.

The growth of the Young Turk movement was closely linked to the mounting anarchy within the largest remaining province under direct Ottoman rule in Europe. The brief lull in terrorist activity in Macedonia, after the Greek defeat in the Thirty-Day War, was followed at the turn of the century by a wave of terrorism inspired by the rival groups who sought a Big Bulgaria. The most sensational coup was the seizure by IMRO in September 1901 of an American missionary, Helen Stone, who was held hostage in the mountains around Lake Doiran and eventually released in Strumica after the US Government handed over $66,000 in ransom money. Miss Stone was so well treated by her comitadji kidnappers that on returning to Boston, Massachusetts she became a strong supporter of IMRO claims.[16]

This episode was not in itself of grave importance, but the kidnapping of a woman missionary inevitably received much publicity in the American, British, French and Italian Press, with the journalists emphasizing the apparent inability of the Turks to prevent rival Supremists and IMRO commanders from terrorizing village headsmen into support. Immediately after Helen Stone's release, the European Powers began the leisurely process of diplomatic discussions with the Porte over the need for further reform in Macedonia, and in Thrace, too. The diplomats were soon reminded of the urgency of the problem. In the spring of 1903 a series of bomb outrages shook Salonika itself: the Ottoman Bank in the city was blown up, and a few months later there was a sustained guerrilla campaign by Bulgarian comitadji in the mountains. Greeks living in Salonika perished in the bomb blasts; the Ottoman *vali*, Hassan Fehmi Pasha, kept order in the city with a firmness and impartiality remembered by the Greeks long afterwards. But in 1903 the immediate consequence of IMRO activity was a revival of Greek patriot groups in Salonika and the neighbouring towns and villages. The Greek Consulate became the centre of the new movement. A Greek historian recalls how 'conference after conference . . . took place within the Cathedral and it was there, many a time, that plans were laid down for the activities to be carried out by the various bodies' of armed men.[17]

Not only Bulgars and Greeks threatened to explode the Balkan tinder-box. The new aggressively nationalistic spirit which followed the restoration of the Karadjordjevic dynasty in Belgrade in June 1903 led to the revival of Serbian revolutionary cells, especially at Üsküb (Skopje) and Monastir (Bitolj). Within eighteen months a 'small army' of Chetniks, trained in Belgrade and Niš, was operating in the upper Vardar valley and around Lake Ochrid, only fighting regular Ottoman troops when attacked but constantly staking out Serbian claims to be made when the Turks withdrew. The racial, cultural and religious map of the whole area was remarkably variegated. In Üsküb, for example, where the *ulema* remained powerful and there was a Serbian Orthodox bishopric, the town's first theatre was opened by two Roman Catholic merchants, one an Italian and the other, Kole Bojaxhiu, a fez-wearing Albanian married to a Serb. A daughter was born into this typically cosmopolitan Macedonian family at the end of the troubled decade. Her vocation lay far away from the Balkans, among the destitute of India: Ganxhe Agnes Bojaxhiu, an Ottoman subject by birth, became Mother Teresa of Calcutta.[18]

For a future laureate of one of the then newly-instituted Nobel Peace

Prizes to emerge from such a welter of conflict would have seemed ludicrously improbable. By 1903 the Great Powers, already divided by imperial rivalries, were alarmed at the prospect of fresh crises in the Balkans. Events were unpleasantly reminiscent of Bulgaria in the 1870s or, more recently, of Armenia. No government wanted another campaign of mass agitation against 'The Unspeakable Turk'. Among British Liberals there remained a powerful pro-Bulgarian lobby, and in both London and Paris there was some support for the idea of an autonomous Macedonia, but most governments were prepared to see Ottoman rule continue in the province, with international control of an effective gendarmerie force. Only the British wanted Ottoman troops entirely withdrawn from Macedonia (as from Crete). In October 1903 Tsar Nicholas II and the Emperor Francis Joseph, accompanied by their foreign ministers, met at Mürzsteg, an imperial hunting lodge about a hundred miles south of Vienna. There they agreed on a pro- gramme of reforms which the two sovereigns would recommend to the Sultan: a Russian and an Austrian 'civil agent' to advise the Turkish governor; a European commander of gendarmerie; and division of the province into 'spheres of policing', each the responsibility of a Great Power.

In the last week of November 1903 the Sultan accepted the Mürzsteg Proposals, a threatened naval demonstration by the Great Powers inclining him to respond favourably to a programme which he was known to detest.[19] Abdulhamid was, however, a master of dissimula- tion and delay, and little was done to implement these highly compli- cated proposals. An Italian took command of the gendarmerie, and officers from the five Great Powers drew up provisional arrangements for policing the region. Two years later – after a further show of naval strength by Britain, France, Italy and Russia – the Sultan made a further concession: an international commission would be set up to supervise revenue and expenditure in Macedonia. Only the Kaiser and Marschall von Bieberstein, his skilful ambassador, abstained from intimidatory action. 'The Germans do me as much good as they are per- mitted to do, whereas the rest of Europe do me as much harm as they can,' Abdulhamid remarked sourly in private conversation.[20] What he failed to realize was that the younger generation of army officers could see little distinction between the French, British, Italians or Russians to whom the Sultan seemed markedly subservient, and the Germans who were visibly profiting from the commercial concessions he had accorded them. Moreover, German military instructors, like many previous experts from abroad, showed a patronizing arrogance intolerable to young men of pride and ambition. That strong resentment of *all* foreign influence, on which Ottoman movements of opposition had so often fed, was by 1905–6 dangerously close to surfacing once again – but this time, with a difference.

In Serbia, Bulgaria and Greece, junior army officers from families with no tradition of military service to their sovereign already constituted dangerous pressure groups which threatened to impose upon their respective governments nationalistic policies of their own devising. A similar development was reflected in the changing outlook of the Young Turk movement between the Congress of February 1902 and a second Congress, also held in Paris, in December 1907. To the consternation of Abdulhamid's secret police agents, there was evidence in 1906–7 of dissident cells in several of the Sultan's field armies. An Ottoman Freedom Society (*Osmanli Hürriyet Cemiyeti*), founded in Salonika in September 1906 by the postal official Mehmed Talaat, won support from officers of the Third Army Corps. Two months later Mustafa Kemal, a 25-year-old staff captain born in Salonika and educated mainly at Monastir, founded a secret Fatherland Movement (*Vatan*) among officers of the Fifth Army Corps at Damascus; *Vatan* soon established cells in Jaffa, Jerusalem and Beirut. By the following September the Ottoman Freedom Society had established links with Young Turk exiles in Geneva; and soon after the Second Paris Congress the leaders of this combined Young Turk movement adopted the name Committee of Union and Progress (CUP – *Ittihad ve Terakki Cemiyeti*), whose organization absorbed Kemal's *Vatan* and several other dissident bodies as well.[21] The common bond between the affiliated societies in the CUP was Macedonia. Most members were serving or had recently served in the troubled province, or had been born there. In 1908 Salonika, second city in modern Greece, acted as a powerhouse for the Young Turk Revolution.

The events of that summer followed no recognizable pattern, the most dramatic episodes taking place in so remote a corner of the empire that it seemed inconceivable they could rock the Ottoman throne. The military Mufti of the Third Army garrison in Monastir was a police agent, a Yildiz Palace spy. By chance, early in June, he stumbled across a CUP conspiracy involving Adjutant-Major Ahmed Niyazi, an officer of suspect loyalty stationed at Resne (now Resen), between Monastir and Ochrid. The Mufti was shot and wounded, to prevent his reporting back to the capital, but Niyazi decided to precipitate a revolt, seizing arms and ammunition during Friday prayers on 3 July and taking to the mountains around Ochrid in an act of armed rebellion. The CUP, fearing counter-measures, supported Niyazi and many junior officers joined him in the hills, the best-known of them being Major Enver, who was serving on the staff of the Inspector-General of Rumelia, Hüseyin Hilmi, himself sympathetic to the young Turks. At Niyazi's prompting the CUP contacted foreign consuls in Salonika and sent agents to all the principal towns in Macedonia, proclaiming a restoration of the 1876 Constitution. At first Abdulhamid played down the significance of the insurrection. He was, however, shaken by the assassination in Monastir of one of his most loyal generals, and subsequently by the mutinous mood of troops hurriedly sent from Anatolia to suppress the Macedonian rebellion. Reports reaching the capital showed how rapidly the garrisons of Rumelia were declaring themselves in favour of the Constitution. Exactly what they sought was obscure, although it was clear that in several districts the insurgents had support from the Albanians, and from some Bulgarian and Greek communities. There were echoes, too, of older struggles in greater cities: '*La Patrie, Liberté, Égalité, Fraternité*', the British vice-consul heard a young CUP officer proclaim in French in the small town of Drama.[22]

As morale declined at the Yildiz Palace, Sultan Abdulhamid made one last effort to recover the political initiative. Not for the first time in his reign, he decided to forestall the opposition. He dismissed Mehmed Ferid, Grand Vizier for the past five and a half years, and summoned back to office for the seventh time Küchük Mehmed Said, who had read the Sultan's speech to the *Meclis-i Mebusan* in that false dawn of Ottoman constitutionalism thirty-one years before. Within forty-eight hours, Said Pasha and his master had agreed to meet the first demand of the Macedonian revolutionaries. The Sultan – so he explained five months later – believed that the peoples of his empire were by now well enough educated to accept the workings of parliamentary government. An imperial *irade*, made public on 24 July 1908, announced that the suspended Constitution of 1876 would immediately be restored. A few days later a general amnesty for political prisoners and exiles was proclaimed. On 1 August a *hatt-i hümayun* confirmed the abolition of the secret police, freedom from arbitrary arrest, permission to travel abroad, equality of race and religion, and reorganization of existing governments. The charter also promised the summoning of an elected parliament within three months. Demonstrations of mass enthusiasm, supported by over a dozen nationalities, swept through towns and villages in Europe and Asia.[23]

The Hamidian era was over. The Young Turks destroyed autocracy without a shot fired nearer to Yildiz than Salonika. But there had been no change of Sultan-Caliph. On 31 August the longest and wiliest survivor for three centuries began the thirty-third year of his reign under the strange mantle of a constitutional monarchy. It lay uneasily across his hunched shoulders.

CHAPTER 14

Seeking Union and Progress

The sudden restoration of the Constitution took the Committee of Union and Progress by surprise. Its founder-members had envisaged a longer campaign before they could persuade the Sultan to resume the tentative experiments in representative government after a lapse of thirty-two years. It had seemed likely that, in partnership with sympathetic *ulema* dignitaries, the Young Turks would first need to devise a way of deposing the reigning sovereign. Instead it soon became clear that the imperial *irade* had transformed the existing relationship between ruler and ruled. On 31 July, the Friday after it was proclaimed, Abdulhamid ventured as far as the Ayasofya mosque for the weekly *selamlik*, the first time in a quarter of a century that he had mustered sufficient courage to cross the Golden Horn in order to pray in the ancient basilica of Byzantium. The carriage drive was a minor personal triumph; he was even cheered in the narrow streets where he most feared assassination.[1] It was with some reluctance that, early in August, he conceded it was still necessary for him to receive a CUP deputation and discuss the merits of their programme of reform.

This gracious accessibility of a not unpopular Sultan created problems for the would-be revolutionaries: who would go to Yildiz as their spokesmen? The CUP was not a political party: it was not even a nation-wide movement of protest. Outside Macedonia it lacked any co-ordinated organization and there was, as yet, no single person who stood out as leader. For Major Niyazi, Major Cemal, Major Enver or any of the junior officers to travel to the capital was dangerous; they might legitimately be regarded as rebellious mutineers. The most experienced CUP member in Macedonia was Dr Nazim, director of the Salonika Municipal Hospital and chief contact between the Young Turk conspirators and the exiles in Paris; but, though he became Secretary

General of the CUP's central committee two months later, Nazim always chose to remain out of the public eye. There was also Hüseyin Hilmi, a respected figure throughout Rumelia who had publicly proclaimed the Sultan's *irade* in Salonika amid great enthusiasm. Yet Hilmi, too, was unsuitable; while sympathizing with Young Turk objectives, he was loyal to the lost liberalism of an older generation. At fifty-five Hilmi could hardly serve as spokesman for officers and administrative officials more than twenty years his junior.[2]

Eventually the Committee chose three skilled bureaucrats: Mehmed Cavit (often transcribed as 'Djavid'), a Salonika merchant's son with a flair for economics; Mustafa Rahmi, who came from one of the wealthiest land-owning families in Rumelia; and Mehmed Talaat, who had helped set up the Ottoman Freedom Society in Salonika almost two years earlier. Talaat, born into an Edirne peasant family, possessed a powerful intelligence. While too self-made a politician to risk isolation through ready compromise, he was also too ambitious to limit his options by blind acceptance of a doctrinaire fanaticism. Over the following ten years it was Talaat rather than any of his more flamboyant colleagues who effectively transformed CUP resolutions into political action. Major Ahmed Cemal (or 'Djemal') and Major Enver, the two ruthless Third Army staff officers, became better-known abroad; but as the confused memoir material on the Young Turk movement becomes clearer, so Mehmed Talaat, the one-time telegraph clerk, stands out more and more as mastermind in this formidable triumvirate.

Even in his first audience with Abdulhamid, Talaat seems to have imposed his personality. On its arrival in the capital the deputation had been treated with contemptuous disdain by Said Pasha; Talaat and his two companions duly asked the Sultan to dismiss Said and appoint a more liberal ministry. Within four days Said was out of office and the anglophile Mehmed Kamil Pasha became Grand Vizier for a third time, bringing together a cabinet of reformers in which only the *şeyhülislâm* and the Foreign Minister had previous experience of office. The new-found confidence of the CUP led to the arrival in the capital of four other inner members, including Cemal and Enver. This inner committee resolved that it would not seek a takeover of government itself but would remain in being as a pressure group, influencing decision-making in the palace, the Porte and eventually in parliament, too. At the end of August Sir Gerard Lowther, a recent arrival as ambassador, patronizingly informed London that 'considering the country is being run by the Committee of the League, a collection of good-intentioned children, things are going pretty well.'[3]

Like earlier reformers, both Kamil's government and the CUP emphasized the need to convert the Ottoman Empire into a modern centralized state. Such a programme had been proclaimed at least four times in the previous century, with achievements on each occasion falling sadly short of that good intent which Lowther thought he once more saw around him. Yet while Kamil's proposed reforms looked extremely familiar, the CUP sought more drastic measures. Their ideal was a Muslim capitalist bourgeois society, proud of its Anatolian Turkish origins: all Ottoman subjects, irrespective of race and religion, should enjoy equal rights *and* accept equal obligations in service to a centralized state. There would be no more variations of law under the *millet* system and no more resort to the 'Capitulations', the privileged status in commerce and at law enjoyed by foreigners. The CUP also favoured agricultural reform and a fairer system of taxation. But even this new and vigorous programme of change provided one interesting instance of continuity with the past: the Young Turks called for the extension and completion of the *Mecelle*, the civil code which Ahmed Cevdet's commission had evolved forty years before.

The newly established freedom of the press and rights of political association favoured the growth of a multi-party system.[4] But, while there was a hard core of Islamic traditionalists and a small Ottoman Democratic Party in the field, the election of 1908 was contested by only two main groups: the CUP, though not yet organized as a party, campaigned as the 'Unionists' (*Ittihatçilar*); and in mid-September there was established a decentralist Liberal party (Ottoman Liberal Union, *Osmanli Ahrar Firkasi*), which included among its members the Grand Vizier and Prince Sabaheddin, who returned hurriedly from Paris to enter the political arena. The elections, conducted in November and early December again through an indirect electoral college system, gave overwhelming support to the Unionists. For the moment, however, the Mehmed Kamil government remained in office. On 17 December 1908 Sultan Abdulhamid once more braved the perils of Stamboul's narrow streets to open the third parliament of his reign in the government offices behind the Ayasofya mosque. A few months later the Çirağan Palace was converted for the use of both chambers of parliament; the palace had been vacant since August 1904, when the incarceration of the wretched ex-Sultan Murad V ended with his death from diabetes.

The development of an Ottoman constitutional monarchy was hampered by a succession of foreign crises. News of the Young Turk Revolution caused alarm in Vienna and Budapest. For thirty years

Francis Joseph's ministers and soldiers had treated the nominally Ottoman provinces of Bosnia–Herzegovina as a virtual colony. What would happen if the new regime in Constantinople challenged Habsburg authority by seeking the return of parliamentary deputies from Bosnia and Herzegovina? And what, too, if the Ottoman Parliament claimed representation from tributary states like Bulgaria? It was in the interests of the Sultan's neighbours to clarify and define the limits of his authority in the Balkans. Already, before the Young Turk revolution, Baron von Aehrenthal, the Austro-Hungarian Foreign Minister, had raised the ghost of traditional Balkan enmities by support for a projected railway from Sarajevo through the *sanjak* of Novibazar to Mitrovica and on to the port of Salonika, thus opening up Habsburg Croatia at the expense of independent Serbia. The CUP's activities spurred both Aehrenthal and the ruler of Bulgaria into action. In the first week of October 1908 Austria–Hungary formally annexed Bosnia–Herzegovina, and in Sofia Prince Ferdinand was proclaimed independent 'Tsar of the Bulgarians' (a title downgraded to 'King' when independence was recognized by the Powers six months later). Soon afterwards the Cretans sought formal acknowledgement of their freedom from Ottoman sovereignty and their union with Greece.[5]

The first effect of the crisis inside the Ottoman Empire was to strengthen the hands of the anglophiles. Two leading CUP officials, Dr Nazim and Ahmed Riza, travelled to London in the second week of November 1908 to seek an Anglo-Ottoman alliance, and were received by the Foreign Secretary, Sir Edward Grey. They explained to him that the CUP wished to change the character of the Ottoman Empire; potentially, so they claimed, 'Turkey was the Japan of the Near East.' Grey assured them of 'our entire sympathy in the good work they were doing in Turkey' and offered to lend 'men to organise customs, police, and so forth, if they wished them.' But he explained that there could be no close Anglo-Ottoman partnership since, except in the Far East, Britain still stood firmly outside the alliance system. It was an amiable but unproductive interview.[6] Although Grey and his principal advisers knew the importance of his two visitors, the Foreign Office seems to have been acutely conscious that they were technically private travellers rather than envoys from the Ottoman government. And there is no doubt that the Foreign Secretary himself rated lowly any prospect of a lasting Young Turk civilian administration. 'It may well be that the habit of vicious and corrupt government will be too strong for reform,' Grey had already written to Lowther ten weeks before meeting Nazim and Ahmed Riza. 'Out of the present upheaval there may be evolved a strong and efficient military despotism.'[7]

Yet it is hard to avoid a feeling of opportunities lost by the British during the Bosnian Crisis. With Germany, Austria–Hungary's staunchest ally, temporarily discredited at Constantinople, Grey might have welcomed a chance to recover Britain's lost influence at the Porte. Interests had, of course, changed over the last twenty years. No Foreign Secretary would wish to see European peace endangered by a scramble for land, as the Ottoman tide finally receded in the Balkans. But since the turn of the century, the Foreign Office – and, even more, the India Office – had been showing a greater concern for the Persian Gulf and the future of Mesopotamia than for the Straits; and the CUP was as alive to the importance of the Sultan's Asian lands as Abdulhamid himself. By 1899 skilled negotiations, conducted for the most part locally by agents of the Viceroy of India, had ensured that all the small Persian Gulf sheikdoms, including Kuwait, were in practice British protectorates, even if technically under the Sultan's sovereignty; and the London-registered Euphrates and Tigris Steam Navigation Company had a monopoly of port rights at Baghdad and Basra unchallenged until the Ottoman treaty concessions to Berlin in the Baghdad Railway agreements. Germany's discomfiture in the winter of 1908–9 should have given Grey an opportunity to safeguard trading interests in a region where the traditional Anglo-Indian commercial predominance was under threat. More was at stake than railway construction. By now oil politics, too, influenced decision-making at the Foreign Office and at the Porte. On 26 May 1908 – just nine weeks before the Young Turk Revolution – the first significant flow of oil in the Gulf region was reported from Masjid-i-Sulaiman, across the Persian frontier but barely 150 miles from Basra. Not surprisingly, one of the first actions of the Kamil Pasha government, under CUP pressure, was a decree which transferred oil revenue and property from the Sultan's Privy Purse back to the Ottoman State, thus countering Abdulhamid's swift initiative eighteen years before. Foreign bids for oil concessions and development, provisionally approved or subject to tentative bargaining under the old regime, had now to be resubmitted through the Ministry of Finance. Over such matters Ambassador Lowther's 'good-intentioned children' were precociously shrewd.[8]

The Bosnian Crisis absorbed the attention of Europe's chancelleries for some six months, and throughout this period the Ottoman Government continued to stress its desire for friendship with Great Britain. To a limited extent British diplomacy secured some compensation for the Young Turks: Grey persuaded his Russian Entente partners to postpone discussion of a revised Straits Convention, on the grounds that it was an 'inopportune' moment in Turkish affairs to raise so general a question; the presence of a British naval squadron off Crete emphasized Grey's insistence on ruling out any immediate transfer of sovereignty over the island to Greece; and in Anglo-Russian exchanges a curious bargain was struck by which the Turkish recognition of Bulgaria's independence won a renunciation by the Russians of forty Ottoman instalments of the 1878 war indemnity.[9] At the same time a British naval mission, headed by Rear-Admiral Sir Douglas Gamble, was sent to Constantinople to set in order, yet again, the Sultan's fleet.

All these face-saving gestures could hardly offset the sad reality that the coming of constitutional government coincided with a resumption of the old dreary round of territorial losses, after twenty years of Hamidian pride in empire. Muslim purists, already offended by the sight of unveiled 'modern' wives and daughters in the smarter streets of the cities, began to campaign against the reformers: a socially conservative Society of Islamic Unity was established, with the Sultan's fourth son, Mehmed Burhaneddin, as a member, and with rumours of financial backing from the palace. In the second week of February 1909 the CUP engineered the fall of the liberal Kamil Pasha and his replacement as Grand Vizier by their nominee, Hüseyin Hilmi. This political manoeuvre gave substance to Islamic Unity's complaint that the men from Macedonia were creating a new autocracy. Friction developed between the First Army, garrisoning the capital, and the officer politicians of the Third Army who had travelled from Salonika to direct the constitutional revolution. On the night of 12/13 April 1909 troops from the First Army barracks mingled with religious students in Stamboul, demanding the resignation of the government and the establishment of a Muslim fundamentalist regime strictly observing the *şeriat* code and respecting the authority of the Sultan as Caliph. Next morning a mob burst into the parliament building and killed two deputies. Abdulhamid willingly gave in to the demonstrators' demands and Ahmed Tevfik improvised a loyal coalition – which might be described as a 'Government of the Friends of Yildiz'. Foreign diplomats duly reported the restoration of imperial autocracy.[10]

Such an assessment was premature. The counter-revolutionary coup did not follow the traditional pattern; the demonstrators did not capture the CUP leaders, nor indeed did they detain – or kill – more than a handful of parliamentary deputies. There were, moreover, dissident officers who, though critical of many modernizing reforms, preferred the patriotic ideology of the Unionists to the uncertainties of Yildiz autocracy. Among these officers was the fifty-three year old general, Mahmud Shevket Pasha; he had spent nine years in Prussia co-ordinating the secondment of Ottoman officers to the German army, and was serving as Governor of Kossovo when the Young Turk Revolution began. The Pasha never joined the CUP, but he was entrusted by the new regime with crucial responsibilities as commanding general of the Third Army in Macedonia. When reports of events in the capital reached Salonika, Shevket Pasha ordered his divisional chief-of-staff, Adjutant-Major Mustafa Kemal, to organize the movement of the Third Army to the outskirts of the capital; and by 22 April a combination of Kemal's logistical planning and the benefits of a strategic railway enabled troops and guns to be concentrated at San Stefano. There Shevket's formidable army could offer protection to an assembly of parliamentary delegates who issued a manifesto formally condemning the Sultan's actions. After desultory fighting next day outside the Porte administrative buildings and the barracks in Taksim, Abdulhamid gave way and dismissed Tevfik's ministry. This time, however, the Sultan's swift change of heart could not save him. The CUP was determined his reign must end.[11]

Outwardly the conventions of law were observed. Under considerable pressure from Talaat, the *şeyhülislâm* sanctioned a *fetva* which provided for the removal of the Sultan from the throne; and on 27 April 1909 the 66-year-old Abdulhamid II was succeeded by his 65-year-old half-brother, Mehmed V. But in two respects this deposition differed significantly from the thirteen depositions which had preceded it. The request to the *şeyhülislâm* came, not from the viziers in council, but from representatives of parliament affronted by a ruler who 'swore to re-enter the path of righteousness, but broke his oath and raised a civil war'; and the Sultan was informed of his fate by a parliamentary delegation of two senators and two deputies who told him that 'the *Nation* has deposed you'.[12] Secondly, Abdulhamid was not to be immured in the *kafe* of an Ottoman palace. He was told parliament had decided he must be exiled to the provinces: a villa would be found for him in Salonika. On hearing of his destination, Abdulhamid fainted into the arms of his Chief Eunuch (an unfortunate who was soon to suffer a worse fate, being publicly hanged on Galata Bridge for cruelties perpetrated in his master's name in Yildiz's hidden cells). Abdulhamid's pleas and protests were in vain. Late that same night the ex-Sultan, two princes, three wives, four concubines, five eunuchs and fourteen servants set out on their twenty-hour train journey to the city where his troubles had begun.[13]

Apart from Abdulhamid's hated henchmen at Yildiz, there was no blood purge of yesterday's politicians, for in several instances the new regime needed their services. Ahmed Tevfik went to London as ambassador and stood aside from politics for the next ten years, declining to consider any inducements to hold office so long as the Unionists retained their grip on the reins of power. On 5 May Hüseyin Hilmi returned as Grand Vizier, heading the government until the closing days of the year, when he was succeeded by the jurist and former diplomat, Ibrahim Hakki Pasha. Two prominent Unionists held cabinet office under both Hilmi and Hakki, Talaat as Minister of the Interior and Cavit (Djavid) as Minister of Finance. Of the other CUP leaders, Colonel Cemal was successively military governor of Üsküdar and Adana, while Major Enver went to Berlin as military attaché. Four months after Abdulhamid was deposed Enver attended German military manoeuvres at Würzburg, where he made a considerable impression, not least upon his fellow guest, Winston Churchill.[4] If, over the next few years, statesmen and soldiers in Western Europe liked to assume that the handsome young Major was virtual ruler of the Ottoman Empire, then it was not in Enver's nature to disabuse them. There were moments when he believed it himself.

Yet who *was* 'lord of the Golden Horn' following Abdulhamid's deposition? Never again did the Ottoman Empire have a sovereign with pretensions to rule as well as to reign. Mehmed V was a benign dodderer. He ascended the throne physically and morally weakened by excesses of drink and sex, habits which for over thirty years were encouraged by his half-brother in the belief they would distract the heir-presumptive from political intrigue. Even had he been an ascetic monarch of quick intelligence, he would have found his powers trimmed by extensive amendments to the 1876 Constitution agreed by parliament in August.[15] Only the Grand Vizier and the *şeyhülislâm* should in future be chosen by the Sultan, who would therefore no longer appoint individual ministers or the presiding chairmen of the two Chambers (henceforth elected by their own members). Even the Sultan's personal staff was to be appointed by parliament – a provision intended to prevent the creation of another Yildiz inner government. Parliament had to meet from November to May in each year; ministers were responsible to the Deputies rather than to the Grand Vizier; and the Sultan was to possess no more than a delaying, suspensive veto on legislation initiated by either parliamentary chamber. Fundamental to all these revolutionary innovations was the amended Article 3 of the Constitution: sovereignty was vested in the head of the Osmanli dynasty only so long as he fulfilled an accession oath of loyalty to Fatherland and Nation, pledging observance of both the *şeriat* and the Constitution. Parliament therefore asserted an inalienable right to depose any sultan who infringed the basic codes of his empire.

On paper these constitutional amendments of August 1909 promised the Ottoman peoples a system of parliamentary government more widely based than in Tsarist Russia or Hohenzollern Germany. Reality, however, fell far short of the reformers' aspirations. The legislative record of the Young Turks in the first year of Mehmed V's reign was sadly repressive. The Vagabond Law (8 May 1909) treated persistent beggars lacking 'visible means of support' rather less generously than did the statutes of early Tudor England. The Law of Associations (16 August 1909) forbade the formation of political groups bearing the name of nationalities or races; this measure led to the closure of Albanian, Greek and Bulgarian clubs but imposed no restraints on the *Türk Denegli* ~~Dernegi ?~~ (Turkish Society), set up in the previous January, since it was argued that the word 'Turkish' implied a spoken language or popular culture and therefore lacked any political connotation. A 'Law to Prevent Brigandage and Sedition' (27 September 1909) provided for the raising of 'pursuit battalions' which would root out and suppress armed bands, particularly the Balkan comitadji. At the same time a Conscription Law introduced the new principle of military obligation on non-Muslims; this application of the CUP's professed abhorrence of 'distinctions of race and creed' rapidly lost the Unionists support from Christians and Jews. Other laws forbade the printing of books or newspaper articles likely to incite disorder; organizers of public gatherings were required to obtain police permits and ensure that only subjects notified in advance were discussed at their meetings.[16]

Municipal administration was improved; more schools were founded, particularly for girls; and work began on ending anomalies over the ownership of land, seeking to eradicate the last vestiges of the *iltizam* system. Yet, though the Unionists emphasized their hostility to the enjoyment by foreigners of special treaty rights, the Capitulations were not abolished. Despite the new regime's advocacy of Ottoman self-sufficiency, foreign experts were still encouraged to come to Constantinople and suggest ways of modernizing the administration: Sir Richard Crawford turned the experienced eye of a British civil servant on the Ottoman Customs service; M. Sterpin was brought from Brussels to direct Posts and Telegraph – Talaat had no high opinion of the efficiency shown by his old department; and Count Leon Ostrorog, already employed as an adviser on procedure to the judiciary, was given new authority as councillor responsible for reconciling Ottoman law with the major codes of Western Europe – a post from which, two years later, he resigned in disgust at the pressure exerted by traditionalist religious groups against whose obscurantism the more enlightened Young Turks had long railed.

It was assumed, both in the capital and abroad, that the reforms were directed by the collective leadership of the CUP, acting through the Grand Vizier and his chosen ministers, as the constitution required. This was a misleading impression. The CUP was mistrusted in the capital, its spokesmen accused of being irreligious self-seekers, steeped in Freemasonry and/or Zionism. Significantly, CUP headquarters remained in Salonika until 1912. Moreover, although both Hilmi and Hakki were technically Unionists during their terms of office, they did not have the last word in determining policy. The real power behind throne and parliament was General Shevket, and he remained outside the Union and Progress Movement.[17] His prestige as commander of the Third Army and instigator of the March on Stamboul enabled Shevket Pasha to impose a veiled military dictatorship on the constitutional Empire in the four years which followed Abdulhamid's fall. In May 1909 Shevket was confirmed as Inspector-General of the First, Second and Third Armies. A few days later he received wider powers as martial law administrator, thereafter maintaining for two years a virtual state of siege in towns where there was a risk of disaffection. Early in 1910 he entered Hakki's cabinet as Minister of War, observing such tight-lipped secrecy over the disposition of the armies and the purpose of his military budget that even Talaat and Cavit were never sure if he were friend or foe. Eventually Shevket emerged from the shadows, and for the first six months of 1913 served as Grand Vizier himself.

Disillusionment with the CUP, and more especially a mounting anger at its encouragement of narrowly Turkish nationalist groups, provoked opposition in several regions of the Empire, widely separated from each other. Resentment over the Law of Associations intensified the growth of secret conspiratorial societies, especially among the Arabs of the Levant. Muslims educated under French auspices in Syria and Lebanon funded a 'Young Arab Society' in Paris in 1911 as a direct challenge to Young Turk policies of centralization. More immediately serious was unrest in Albania. There had been fighting in the Lyuma district as early as May 1909, when attempts were made to levy new taxes, but a rebellion in the early spring of 1910 made a greater impression on the authorities, not least because it was concentrated in Kossovo, the region in which Shevket Pasha had so recently served as military governor. He over-reacted to what he regarded as a personal affront and sent 50,000 troops to restore order, authorizing public flogging of clan chieftains as a means of intimidating a fiercely proud people. The rebellion spread to include Christian as well as Muslim clans, forcing Shevket himself to lead yet another expeditionary force in April 1911, and two months later to encourage an official visit to the Albanian provinces by the Sultan-Caliph. And still the fighting dragged on.[18]

While the army was thus engaged at the north-western fringe of the Empire, the Armenian Dashnaks stirred up trouble once more in the north-east. At the same time, in the Sultan's far south-eastern lands, two Arab rebellions broke out, respectively under Sheikh Muhammad al-Idrisi in the Asir region south of Jeddah, and under the Iman Yahya Hamid-al-Din further south still, bordering Britain's Aden Protectorate. To meet these military emergencies at such distant extremities of the Sultan's empire, his Ministry of War sent to Arabia another 30,000 men, drawn from provinces where the Young Turk reforms remained as yet unchallenged. Accordingly transports sailed for the Red Sea, not only from Üsküdar and Smyrna, but from Tripoli and Derna in modern Libya, then at the south-western extremity of the Ottoman Empire. By the midsummer of 1911 the vilayet of Tripoli and the *sanjak* of Benghazi – the last North African lands directly under the Sultan's rule – were garrisoned by no more than 3,400 effective regular troops. This thin defensive force was spread along a thousand miles of Barbary coast, barely a night's steaming from the ports of southern Italy.[19]

Ever since the French had occupied Tunisia, Italian colonization societies had urged successive governments to show an interest in developing and acquiring Libya. In the early years of the century a new wave of French colonial activity from Morocco eastwards persuaded businessmen in Rome and Milan that if their government did not soon annex Tripolitania and Cyrenaica, the opportunity would be lost for good. There was, so their Foreign Minister later wrote, 'a general, vague desire to do something' among his compatriots.[20] As early as February 1911 the Ottoman ambassador in Rome expressed fears to the Porte that Italy was planning an attack, and in June he sent a further warning, which on this occasion was passed on to Shevket Pasha himself. There was, however, little Shevket could do – apart, that is, from sending 20,000 Mauser rifles and two million cartridges to Tripoli aboard a fast steamer, with orders that they should be distributed to the Arab tribesmen in the event of war. Despite Young Arab dissidents in Paris and revolts along the lower Red Sea littoral, Shevket knew that the invasion of Muslim territory by Italian Catholics would rally the tribesmen in support of their Sultan-Caliph against any Christian *giaours*.

On 27 September 1911 the Italians, complaining of Ottoman maltreatment of traders and merchants in Libya, delivered a totally unacceptable ultimatum to the Porte. War followed next day, with a naval sortie preparing the way for landings at Tripoli, Benghazi, Derna and Tobruk. The depleted Ottoman detachments could offer little resistance to an attack which, as well as bombardment from modern warships, also used aircraft for the first time, with small bombs dropped by hand from primitive biplanes. The Ottoman General Staff's improvised strategic plan worked well enough, however. Although the invaders seized the coastal towns, they could not penetrate the interior; their troops were untrained for desert warfare against skilled Arab horsemen and, in consequence, the rapid victory sought in Rome and Milan eluded the invaders. A naval blockade prevented Ottoman reinforcements reaching Libya from the Aegean or the Levant, but individual officers in mufti made their way through British-controlled Egypt and slipped across the frontier to help the resistance in Cyrenaica. Among these officers were Enver Bey and Mustafa Kemal, both of whom joined Ottoman regulars and Arab Sanussi tribesmen keeping watch on the Italian garrison at Tobruk. Enver Bey then travelled across the desert into Tripolitania while Kemal remained in the vicinity of Benghazi and Derna. By early November, when Libya was formally annexed by the Kingdom of Italy, the war had reached stalemate, with the 'conquerors' effectively holding no more than the coastal strip.[21]

When news of the loss of Tripoli, Benghazi and Derna reached Constantinople there was widespread anger. Hakki Pasha at once resigned as Grand Vizier; the CUP was blamed for weakening the army be seeking to indoctrinate the officer corps; and some months later Shevket resigned as Minister of War, complaining that it was impossible to modernize the Ottoman armies if differing factions of Young Turks and Liberals insisted on playing politics in the barracks of every garrison town.[22]

With the coming of spring in 1912 the Italians broadened the scope of the war. On 18–19 April Vice-Admiral Leone Viale's squadron of twelve warships bombarded the forts of the Dardanelles, but Viale was forced to abandon plans to escort a flotilla of torpedo boats up the Straits to attack vessels at anchor in the Narrows: Ottoman gunfire proved too accurate, and his activities were causing a sensation among the Great Powers – not unnaturally, the Turks at once closed the Straits to all commerce, a particular blow to the Russian Black Sea trade. When thwarted at the Dardanelles, Viale turned back into the Aegean and, with troop transports joining him at Stampalia, proceeded to occupy Rhodes and the remaining islands of the Dodecanese during the month of May.

Militarily the successive emergencies of the Italo-Turkish War showed clearly to foreign observers both the strengths and the weaknesses of the Ottoman Empire. Outside Europe well-armed Bedouin, supporting the Sultan's regular troops, could with shrewd leadership prevent a final victory, wearing down a conventional enemy force by raids and ambushes; and, nearer to the Ottoman capital, foreign artillery sited in strategic forts would repel any enemy assault. Although the Ottoman Navy had three modern cruisers, eight destroyers and fourteen torpedo-boats as well as some venerable battleships, it was of little account as a fighting fleet: Admiral Williams, who succeeded Sir Douglas Gamble as head of the British mission in 1910, found Turkish officers resented all attempts at reform; for purposes of prestige, they were more concerned with fitting out two newly purchased twenty-year-old German battleships than with manning their smaller warships adequately.[23] There were no manpower problems in the recently enlarged conscript army, but most recruits remained untrained in modern weapons. Moreover, while staff work was good for limited operations in a particular campaign, it was incapable of handling the logistical problems of a major war waged simultaneously on several fronts. Had the Young Turk reformers enjoyed five or six years of peace in which to impose genuine 'Union and Progress' on the empire, the Ottoman state might well have become militarily formidable once again. As it was, the crisis years 1911 and 1912 caught the constitutional empire at the weakest moment of partial transition, a time when there could be little hope of victory in defensive wars which no loyal subject of the Sultan-Caliph wished to fight.

Worse was soon to follow. The evident plight of their once powerful neighbour encouraged the Balkan states to come together under Russian auspices and make a determined thrust to expel the Ottomans from Europe after five and a half centuries. Despite rival ambitions in the rebellious Albanian lands and in Macedonia, during the summer of 1912 Serbia, Bulgaria, Greece and Montenegro came together in a Balkan League, with more precise secret military alliances following during the early autumn. The Balkan Wars began on 8 October when Montenegrin troops advanced into northern Albania and the *sanjak* of Novibazar.[24] The three larger Balkan kingdoms opened their campaign a day later, with a combined assault on Macedonia, a Bulgarian thrust into Thrace (which soon enveloped Edirne) and Greek naval operations in the Aegean. The Balkan allies could put more than 700,000 men into the field. Nazim Pasha, the ambitious general who took over from Shevket as War Minister in early June, could not hope to raise more than 325,000 men to oppose them.

Hurriedly, on 15 October, a peace was made with Italy. By the Treaty of Ouchy the Sultan accepted the loss of Libya in return for recognition of his religious status in the ceded provinces and an Italian undertaking – never fulfilled – to evacuate the Dodecanese islands and restore them to Ottoman administration. But there was no speedy way for Ottoman troops to be withdrawn from Libya and concentrated in Rumelia. It took Kemal and Enver over a month to return to the capital – in Kemal's case by steamer from Alexandria to Marseilles, by train to Bucharest and by steamer again from Constanza to the Bosphorus. By the time Kemal had completed his journey, in mid-November, Thrace was already lost to the Bulgarians; Kossovo, Monastir, Ochrid and Skopje were in Serbian hands; and the Greeks had won the race to seize the greatest of Macedonian prizes, the port of Salonika. The ex-sultan Abdulhamid was hurried back to the Beylerbey Palace aboard the German stationnaire guardship SMS *Lorelei* as Greek and Bulgarian forces converged on his city of exile.

Constantinople was by then crowded with less illustrious refugees, in pathetic flight from towns and villages which generations of their families had looked upon as their true home. The Bulgarian army, although still besieging Edirne, was also attacking the main defences of the capital, the Chatalja Lines, barely twenty miles from the old walls of Byzantium. Mehmed Kamil, appointed Grand Vizier on 29 October in the hopes that his anglophile reputation would win support from the British Government, appealed to the Great Powers to send their warships through the Straits to protect the city from occupation. At the same time he ordered the police to arrest several CUP activists, whom he suspected of plotting a coup. But by the third week of November tension had eased, both inside the capital and at the Front. The Chatalja Lines held firm, and morale was boosted by the exploits of the light cruiser *Hamidiye* whose commander, Hüseyin Rauf, slipped out through the Dardanelles and threatened Greek naval mastery of the Aegean. When the first snow swept westwards from Anatolia into Rumelia, the Balkan allies agreed on a cease-fire. The guns fell silent on 3 December. Within a week peace talks began in London under Sir Edward Grey's chairmanship.

Rumours that Kamil Pasha was prepared to accept humiliating terms in order to placate his English friends allowed the CUP to recover the political initiative.[25] The Grand Vizier was right to fear a coup. Talaat tried, in the first instance, to win support from General Nazim, but he remained so mistrustful of the CUP that he refused to be drawn into any conspiracy. On 23 January 1913 reports that Kamil was prepared to allow Edirne to become a Bulgarian city encouraged the Unionists to carry out the coup they had been planning for several weeks. Colonel Enver led a band of officers into the principal council chamber of the Sublime Porte building and forced Kamil's resignation at gun-point, while one of his companions shot dead General Nazim, who must have known more about the CUP's overt activities than was good for him. While the Young Turk general, Ahmed Cemal, took emergency powers as Governor of the capital, Enver went to the palace and browbeat the Sultan into appointing Shevket as Grand Vizier. Soon afterwards an Egyptian steamer left for Alexandria with Kamil aboard, a British diplomat having secured him a safe-conduct.[26]

'The Sublime Porte Raid', a dramatic episode which figures prominently in Young Turk legend, took place at a time when the peace talks in London seemed close to collapse, largely through Bulgarian intransigence. Fighting was resumed on 3 February, but hopes that the new Shevket government would pull off a victory in the field were soon dashed. On 6 March the Greeks at last captured Ioánnina, where Essad Pasha had maintained a valiant resistance throughout the winter in Ali Pasha's old lair. At the same time it proved impossible to loosen the Bulgarian hold on Edirne; shortage of food forced the city's surrender on 26 March after fierce fighting with heavy casualties. On 14 April another cease-fire was imposed; the peace talks were resumed, and by early June the Ottoman Government had to accept terms which recognized the loss of Crete, Macedonia, Thrace, Albania and most of the Aegean islands. Henceforth 'Turkey-in-Europe' would be limited to the hinterland of Constantinople, with the frontier running in an almost straight line from Enez (Enos) to Midye (Media), thus leaving Edirne more than thirty miles inside Bulgaria.

Even before the final collapse of the army, Ambassador Lowther's reports to the Foreign Office in London were anticipating yet another political coup during the summer months.[27] There is no doubt that the British authorities in Egypt hoped to restore Kamil, trusting him as a 'tried and convinced defender of the traditional friendship between Turkey and Great Britain'. But, though Kamil was smuggled back to Constantinople from his native Cyprus, he was hastily whisked away again, and it was the CUP who benefited from the next move in the ruthless power game. On 11 June Mahmud Shevket was shot dead in Beyazit Square as his car left the War Ministry for the Sublime Porte buildings. Cemal, as Military Governor, reacted swiftly. The murder was blamed on the political opposition, the Liberal Union Party, many of whose members were shipped off to Sinope under close arrest. Courts martial sentenced several Liberal leaders to death – often, as in the case of Prince Sabaheddin, *in absentia*. Now at last the CUP Young Turks seized power. The Committee's General Secretary, Mehmed Said Halim Pasha – one of Muhammad Ali's many grandsons – succeeded Shevket as Grand Vizier and was to hold office for more than three and a half years. But the real rulers of the empire were the famous triumvirate: Talaat, as Minister of the Interior; Cemal, as military governor of the capital; and Enver, who for the moment was content to enhance his authority by declining ministerial office, remaining a front-line soldier, and marrying the Sultan's niece, Princess Emine Naciye. At the time of Shevket's murder, the Princess was not quite fifteen years old.

Bulgarian folly, and his own boldness, completed Enver's ascendancy and consolidated the CUP's hold on power.[28] Resentment at Graeco-Serbian gains, especially in parts of Macedonia which they considered their own, led the Bulgarians to launch a surprise attack on their former allies on the night of 29–30 June, 1913. After six days of heavy fighting, King Ferdinand's troops were in a desperate position, made worse by the decision of Roumania on 11 July to seize the Dobruja, thus opening up a northern Front. Two days later the Ottoman army thrust westwards from the Enez–Midye line, encountering little resistance. As the army approached Edirne, Colonel Enver led his cavalry at the gallop ahead of the marching columns, and thus became the warrior-liberator of the city. He went at once to Sinan's masterpiece, the Selimiye mosque and, as a good Muslim who always carried a copy of the Koran in his officer's tunic, offered prayers to Allah for the city's deliverance. Although far from popular with many brother-officers, Enver's instinctive showmanship made him appear a hero-protector to some 200,000 bewildered refugees from the Balkan provinces who remained in or around the capital that summer.

Revised peace terms, settled in Bucharest, advanced the Enez–Midye frontier so as to return Edirne to Ottoman sovereignty. The CUP could thus claim some tangible fruits of victory in the Second Balkan War, an essential need if its propagandists were to rekindle the Young Turk enthusiasm of the 1908 Revolution. On paper, the achievements of five years of constitutional rule looked meagre. The Sultan's powers remained clipped, there were more schools, more effective policing and better urban sewerage (especially in the capital); and in the more enlightened cities the professional status of women was improved, giving them for the first time opportunities to become doctors, lawyers or civil servants. In this respect, and through tentative experiments in economic nationalism, the Young Turks continued the work of the *Tanzimat* era, while providing the republican reformers of the next generation with guidelines on what might be developed further – and what should be left well alone. These successes were offset by the repressive statutes enacted in the early months of Mehmed V's reign, and thereafter by a rapid diminution of parliament's influence. There was something symbolic about the fire of January 1910 which, sparked off by an electrical fault, swiftly destroyed the parliamentary chambers newly created in the Çirağan Palace and forced the deputies to develop their political skills in the cramped galleries of the Fine Arts Academy. Although the Sultan's male subjects were allowed to exercise their right to vote in the winter of 1913–14, military repression left the CUP as the only organized political party to contest the elections. By then Unionist candidates were narrowly Turkish in ideology, rather than advocating a racially egalitarian Ottoman commonwealth like many earlier Young Turks. Inevitably, in the absence of an alternative party, the Opposition (in so far as it existed at all by 1913) was also nationalistic in structure, with a large Arab group and smaller bodies representing the Greek, Armenian and Jewish communities. Most deputies had been vetted by the CUP before even seeking election.[29]

A pride in Turkish language and culture had shown itself before the turn of the century. It was intensified, however, by the disastrous loss of territories in the five years which followed the Young Turk Revolution. In 1878–9 Abdulhamid II had been forced to cede two-fifths of his lands. Between 1908 and 1913 another 425,000 square miles – or over a third of the total remaining area of the Empire – passed out of Ottoman sovereignty; and, even after the recovery of Edirne, the Sultan's foothold in Europe in 1914 still comprised no more than 4,500 square miles of what had for so long been the great imperial recruiting ground of Rumelia. If the CUP triumvirate was to prevent the crumbling away still further of the empire, it seemed essential to harness Turkish national pride to the service of the one institution which they understood, the Ottoman army. Shortly before his assassination Shevket had told the German ambassador that his country must have a special role in reshaping the Ottoman State: the army would be reformed 'under the almost dictatorial control of a

German General,' he declared.[30] Enver saw in the murdered Grand Vizier's professed intention a testament of faith in two armies which he, like Shevket, held in high respect. On 30 June 1913 Kaiser William II appointed General Liman von Sanders to lead a new military mission to Constantinople.[31]

CHAPTER 15

Germany's Ally

Familiarity with such epic legends as Gallipoli and Lawrence's Arab Revolt make it hard to appreciate that, even as late as midsummer in 1914, the Ottoman Empire remained outside the network of rival alliances, free to choose between the Central Powers and the Entente or to guard its neutrality. Throughout the July Crisis there was still no certainty which way Said Halim's government would turn. Relations with Britain and France had improved considerably in the preceding twelve months; and both countries were better trading partners for the empire as a whole than Germany or Austria–Hungary. Much progress had been made towards international collaboration in the management of the Turkish Petroleum Company, which was registered in London in 1911–12 and committed to developing the oil resources of the vilayets of Mosul and Baghdad (Iraq). So unruffled were Anglo-Turkish relations that, a fortnight after the Sarajevo murders, the British ambassador returned home on leave. As late as 21 July, Ottoman Bonds went on sale in London to finance British enterprises on the Bosphorus.[1]

Yet no one questioned that Germany's political influence there was considerable. Kaiser William II assumed that his empire still enjoyed a predominance which he, personally, was determined to uphold. In December 1913 he had urged the forty officers of General Liman von Sanders's new Military Mission to 'work unobtrusively . . . steadfastly and harmoniously' for 'the Germanization of the Turkish army';[2] and with realistic practicality he insisted that, while Goltz had managed with an annual 30,000 marks for baksheesh, Liman's fund 'to use as he thought fit' might creep up to a million marks a year in what was becoming a highly competitive and inflationary market.

Few ministers or officials in Berlin shared the Kaiser's confident enthusiasm for the mysterious East. Privately the German ambassador reckoned Turkey 'worthless as an ally'.[3] The Berlin–Baghdad Railway, which remained an obsessive interest of the Kaiser, could never serve as an axis of policy, for by 1913–14 the whole project was under strain. Completion of the line needed the injection of more capital, a grant of further privileges to its German investors, and the waiving of objections to its most southern route by the British (who, having settled disputes with the Ottoman authorities in August 1913, were unable to complete parallel negotiations with Germany until the following June). Nor could Berlin rely on constant support from the 'pro-Germans' in Constantinople. Although the Kaiser welcomed the appointment of Enver as War Minister in January 1914, within ten weeks 'Turkey's last hope' (as William had then called him) was quarrelling seriously with Liman. The hero-liberator of Edirne was infuriated by German attempts to secure key commands for Prussian gunnery experts in the forts of the Bosphorus. If Russian sources may be believed, already in March 1914 'German tyranny' was so deeply resented in the Ottoman officer corps in the capital that some thought was being given to expedient ways of removing Liman by assassination.[4]

The CUP leaders themselves would not have sanctioned so rash an act, though they never became the pro-German puppets depicted by Entente wartime propaganda. Talaat, from 1913 to 1918 the most influential figure at the centre of Ottoman government, at first favoured closer relations with Russia, believing that he could strike a good bargain with the Tsar's ministers alarmed by the mounting German military presence on the Straits. In February 1914 Talaat accepted Russian treaty proposals giving some protection to the Christian communities in the eastern Armenian vilayets; and in May he led an Ottoman delegation to the Crimea, where he was received in audience by Tsar Nicholas II at Livadia and tentatively put forward alliance proposals to the Russian Foreign Minister, Sazonov.[5] Talaat's colleague at the Ministry of Finance, Mehmed Cavit, favoured improved relations with France. Parisian nominees still dominated the Ottoman Public Debt Commission, and were ready to authorize a further loan, when bankruptcy again faced the empire. They shared control of the Ottoman Bank with the British, and gave shrewd advice to the Ministry of Finance; and French experts were also entrusted with organizing the gendarmerie in the capital and several other cities and ports. Nor was Cavit the only CUP leader to look to Paris. In the second week of July 1914 Ahmed Cemal visited the Quai d'Orsay, where he let it be known that, given the right conditions, the Ottoman government 'would orientate its policy towards the Triple Entente'.[6] Neither Russia nor France responded positively to these Young Turk initiatives.

While Enver inherited from Shevket's policy a new and powerful German military mission, Cemal as Minister of Marine inherited an equally strong commitment to seeking more and more British aid for refurbishing the Ottoman fleet. In the spring of 1912 Rear-Admiral Arthur Limpus became the third flag officer of the Royal Navy in five years to be seconded to the Turks as a senior adviser, and by August 1914 Limpus had more than seventy British naval officers attached to his mission (an almost identical number to the German army officers who came with Liman von Sanders, although the size of the German mission increased rapidly with the outbreak of war in Europe). Limpus's immediate predecessor, Admiral Williams, had already encouraged the purchase of a dreadnought, and the British-built *Reshadieh* was launched in September 1913, although it was some months before she could sail for Turkey. Before the end of the year Admiral Limpus scored two notable successes: Armstrong Whitworth and Vickers received contracts to build new naval dockyards; and Armstrongs also undertook to complete a second and even larger battleship, *Sultan Osman I*. Cavit and Cemal were certain they could raise the three and a half million pounds required for such prestigious symbols of imperial might as the two warships.

Public excitement over the new naval programme matched the equally well-orchestrated enthusiasm for the Hejaz 'pilgrim's railway' in the later years of Abdulhamid's reign. The CUP Clubs, set up in towns and large villages over the previous two years, supervised battleship fund-raising in local communities, emphasizing in reports for foreign consumption how even schoolchildren would bring in their contributions to so great a patriotic cause. A celebratory 'Navy Week' was planned on the Golden Horn, when it was proposed that the whole of the Sultan's fleet should escort the new battleships through the Dardanelles to inaugurate the era of Ottoman Naval Power.[7]

So quickly were the two ships completed in British yards that four hundred Turkish officers and seamen reached Tyneside in July 1914 to sail them to Gibraltar and across the Mediterranean on their commissioning voyage to the Straits. The men's arrival coincided with the mobilization of Britain's resources for war: on 1 August, before the crescent flag could be run up, both vessels were seized by the Admiralty and 'temporarily' commissioned in the Royal Navy. News of the Admiralty's action, telegraphed at once to Constantinople, caused dismay and consternation.[8] The anger of the Turks was fed by an anti-British press campaign, financed by the German embassy, which understandably made much of the British failure to offer immediate compensation. The seizure of the ships discredited sympathizers with the Entente in Said Halim's cabinet. For several weeks the 'pro-Germans' had argued that, if Germany and Austria–Hungary won a war from which the Ottomans stood aside, the victors would ruthlessly partition the Empire. Now the Entente Powers looked no less cynical: not only did they remain deaf to overtures for an alliance; they showed apparent contempt for the CUP's hopes of restoring Ottoman pride in the empire. On 2 August Said Halim and Enver concluded a formal alliance with Germany, so secret that Cavit, Cemal and most of their cabinet colleagues were kept in ignorance of its existence for several weeks. The alliance treaty provided only for military action against Russia – in which case it was accepted that Liman von Sanders would have 'an effective influence on the general direction of the [Ottoman] army'.

It has been claimed that the conclusion of the secret treaty 'was a supreme blunder, which brought down the Ottoman empire'.[9] Yet the alliance terms left the Porte with room to manoeuvre. Enver and Said Halim continued to press for definite promises of treaty revision in the Balkans before committing themselves to military action; Germany, they urged, should put pressure on Bulgaria and Greece to retrocede parts of Thrace and islands in the Aegean; but there was no response in Berlin. As late as the middle of August, the British ambassador was still emphasizing the pro-Entente dispositions of both Ahmed Cemal and Dr Nazim, and he urged the First Lord of the Admiralty (Winston Churchill) to send a 'sympathetic and friendly message to the Minister of Marine'. Churchill had already telegraphed an appeal to Enver, whom he knew and admired, counselling him to avoid entanglement with Germany. Now he sent a further message, setting out clearly the compensation which Britain would provide for the commandeered battleships: £1,000 a day, payable each week so long as Turkey remained neutral, was proposed. Enver formally declined to accept a message which, though pleasantly phrased, carried with it a distinct insinuation of bazaar bargaining.[10]

The Germans could offer more than a hiring fee and 'deep regrets'. They capitalized on Turkish resentment of Britain's naval rebuff. On the evening of 10 August the battle-cruiser SMS *Goeben* and the light cruiser SMS *Breslau* entered the Dardanelles, after evading pursuit by the Royal Navy from the Straits of Messina eastwards. *Goeben* had attracted interest and envy a few months earlier when she became the largest warship ever to drop anchor off the Golden Horn. Now the fine prize was to be handed over to the Sultan – on 12 August it was announced in Berlin that Germany had sold both warships to the Turks: *Goeben* became the *Jawuz Sultan Selim* and *Breslau* was renamed *Midilli*. Although they were not so powerful as the dreadnoughts seized by the British, the two warships had one inestimable advantage: they could put to sea at once under the Ottoman flag, with German officers and crews aboard and ready for action. The British naval mission officially ceased to function on 15 August, although Admiral Limpus remained in Constantinople until the Admiralty ordered him to Malta on 9 September.[11] By then Admiral Wilhelm Souchon, the 'droop-jawed, determined little man in a long ill-fitting frock coat' whose seamanship had brought *Goeben* and *Breslau* to the Dardanelles, was flying his flag as Commander-in-Chief of the Ottoman fleet; and the number of German workmen, sailors and coastal gunners on the Straits had risen to about eight hundred.[12]

In London it was assumed that the Ottoman Empire would soon enter the war as Germany's ally. There was, however, still some hesitancy in Said Halim's cabinet and, as if to remind ministers of their duty, the German-subsidized newspapers continued to emphasize the virtues of patriotism and self-sacrifice in service to the State. The effects of this press campaign were not always to Germany's liking. An intensive Turkish nationalism, active during the Libyan and Balkan Wars and associated especially with the sociological secularist writer Ziya Gökalp, reached fever pitch that autumn. Early in September the popular mood encouraged the Young Turks to announce the abolition of Capitulations: all foreigners in the empire would henceforth be subject to Ottoman civil, criminal and commercial codes of law.[13] Yet, although this move was intended in the first instance to penalize the British and French, it provoked a protest in Berlin since it also threatened the status of the increasing number of Germans serving within the Empire. Ardent Turks did not always bother to discriminate between one *giaour* and another. For the Young Turks in 1914, neutrality and reform would have been a wiser programme than the fulfilment of Enver's alliance treaty.

The scale of the German victory at Tannenberg convinced both the Grand Vizier and Enver that, whatever happened on other fronts in Europe, Russia would never again possess the resources to mount a sustained offensive along any distant borders of the Tsar's empire. The temptation to recover lost lands in the Caucasus was therefore almost irresistible. At the same time, the naval pressure from Russia's British ally was becoming intolerable; better to seek a speedy decision by force of arms than risk slow strangulation. On 27 September Royal Navy warships patrolling off the Dardanelles stopped and turned back a Turkish torpedo-boat seeking to enter the Aegean – a less high-handed action than it sounds, for there were several Germans in the crew.[14] The Turks responded by immediately closing the Straits and laying mines along the main channel. Trade between the Black Sea and the outer world at once came to an end, effectively closing the seaports of Bulgaria, Roumania, Russia and Turkey, except for coastal traffic. Thus, though Odessa and Constanza suffered from Turkey's self-imposed blockade, so too did Trebizond, Samsun and Constantinople itself. To offset the financial loss to the empire, Germany made available from 21 October onwards the equivalent of £200 million of gold bullion, stipulating that it would be handed over to the Ottoman Treasury as soon as the Sultan declared war. On 28 October Admiral Souchon, flying his flag in *Jawuz Sultan Selim*, led his ships into the Black Sea and shelled Odessa, Nikolaev and Sebastopol. This raid by Souchon was decisive. A Russian ultimatum on 1 November was rejected; so, too, were British and French ultimata four days later. By the end of the first week in November the Ottoman Empire was at war. Despite the growing secularism among intellectuals in his capital, Mehmed V observed the traditional responses of a Sultan-Caliph. On 11 November he proclaimed a jihad, or Holy War, calling on all Muslims in British, Russian and French territories to rise up and smite the Infidel.[15]

One sovereign responded immediately. At midsummer in 1914 Abbas Hilmi II, Khedive of Egypt since 1892, had gone into residence at the palace which his family retained on the Bosphorus. He was still there when war was declared, and at once he backed the Caliph's proclamation of a jihad: every dutiful Egyptian should rebel against British rule.[16] None did so; but the Khedive's call for action had far-reaching consequences. It cut the last constitutional links between Cairo and Constantinople, for Great Britain established a protectorate over Egypt on 18 December, deposed the unfortunate Abbas Hilmi II, and proclaimed his uncle Hussein Kamil 'Sultan of Egypt'. Wisely, London stopped short of annexing Egypt, although the island of Cyprus was formally absorbed into the British Empire on the day war broke out with Turkey. At the same time the Sheikdom of Kuwait, whose relationship with the Ottoman authorities had always been ill-defined, was constituted an independent government under British protection.

In London any lingering beliefs in the value of upholding the Ottoman Empire were jettisoned as soon as *Goeben* and *Breslau* anchored off the Golden Horn. Strategic interests were changing rapidly. It would now be better for the Russians 'to have Constantinople' than the Germans: the Tsar's empire was becoming increasingly dependent on British investment; and the possibility of satisfying historic ambitions on the Straits would reduce the risks of Anglo-Russian clashes in Central Asia and around Persia's oilfields. 'It is clear Constantinople must be yours,' King George V told the Russian ambassador within a week of Turkey's entry into the war; and at the same time his Foreign Secretary promised Russia an amicable settlement of the Straits Question once the Ottoman Empire sued for peace.[17] But there remained a strong feeling in the British Cabinet that it would better still to have an Anglo-French naval presence off the Dolmabahche and Yildiz, enabling London and Paris to shape the final partition plans of a fallen empire – always remembering, of course, the needs of 'our Russian ally'.

Early in September 1914 Winston Churchill as First Lord of the Admiralty, Lord Kitchener (the Secretary of State for War) and their principal naval and military advisers discussed a grand strategy for the war which they assumed would soon be waged against Turkey. High on their list of possible operations was the forcing of the Dardanelles by the powerful fleet already concentrated in the northern Aegean; if necessary, the Gallipoli peninsula should be seized in order to facilitate the passage of the warships. The complexity of this task was under-estimated. A preliminary bombardment of the forts at Cape Helles early in November, by both British and French vessels, silenced the guns at Sedd-el-Bahr, largely because one shell hit the magazine, causing an immense explosion; and six weeks later a British submarine torpedoed and sank a forty-year-old battleship at anchor in the Narrows. There was no further action in these waters until the New Year. By then defensive torpedo tubes, recommended by Admiral Limpus many months before, were in position at Kilid Bahr on the Narrows. Before the coming of spring Liman von Sanders planned to have six of the Ottoman Army's fifty divisions protecting the shores of the Dardanelles from invasion.[18]

Kitchener, with his vast experience of Egypt and the Levant, favoured swift action elsewhere, preferably against the Baghdad Railway. A week before Christmas a landing-party from HMS *Doris* went ashore north of İskenderun, covered by the light cruiser's eleven six-inch guns. So far from meeting resistance, the raiders found that the local soldiery raised no objections to the blowing up of locomotives, stores and rolling-stock, even helping naval officers to plant the charges which treated them to their big bang in the night sky. The episode, Churchill admitted two years later, strengthened the British assumption that their enemy was easy prey. 'What kind of Turk was this we are fighting?' the Admiralty wondered.[19]

The question was answered in the terrible battles for the Gallipoli peninsula. On 15 January 1915 the War Council in London finally agreed on a naval expedition 'with Constantinople as its objective' to open up a route of supplies to Russia, hard-pressed on the Eastern Front. But when, on 18 March, a third of the capital ships seeking to penetrate the Narrows were sunk, the whole concept of the campaign was changed: the 'Constantinople Expeditionary Force' – as, with a casual contempt for security, it was frequently referred to as it assembled in Egypt – was transported to Mudros, on the island of Lemnos in the northern Aegean. Five weeks after the naval bombardment British, Australian and New Zealand troops made a series of landings on the peninsula while a French Army Corps invaded what had once been the Trojan shore; but by then most of the Ottoman army – some 84,000 men – was on the alert. Inadequate planning, inter-service confusion, hesitant leadership, and all the unsuspected problems of the first amphibious campaign in modern warfare, worked together to turn an epic enterprise, imaginatively conceived and valiantly fought, into a tragedy of frustrated triumph. On 9 January 1916, almost a year after the War Council's resolution, the last British troops surreptitiously evacuated Cape Helles, leaving behind a network of shell-pitted trenches and enough food and equipment to sustain four Turkish divisions for four more months. Left, too, on either side of the Dardanelles, were the remains of 34,000 dead from Great Britain and her empire and 10,000 dead from France, metropolitan and overseas. Only one in four of those who perished have known graves.[20]

Gallipoli was the greatest defensive victory in Ottoman history. The tenacity of 'Mehmedchik' – the Turkish counterpart of 'Tommy Atkins' – won the empire of the Sultans a six-year reprieve. But the cost was frightful; although Turkish casualty figures in the campaign were never finally established, they must certainly have been twice as high as for the invading armies. Enver, as War Minister, claimed credit for the victory; more precisely, the strategic dispositions were ordered by Liman von Sanders while, at the tip of the peninsula, Essad Pasha and his staff successfully contained the inland thrust of the Anzacs. If a folk hero emerged from the campaign he was Mustafa Kemal, the colonel who inspired or cajoled the wavering fugitives of his XIXth Division into a valiant defence along the rocky ridges of Sari Bair and Anafarta. The official Ottoman War Ministry propaganda magazine wished to carry Kemal's portrait on its cover, but Enver personally intervened: there could be no public trumpeting of a contemporary whose military achievements were beginning to surpass his own. Kemal was given command of the Sixteenth Army, and sent to fight the Russians in Anatolia. Fourteen years later a British staff officer, writing the official history of Gallipoli, assessed Kemal's role in the defence of the peninsula objectively: 'Seldom in history can the exertions of a single divisional commander have exercised so profound an influence, not only on the course of a battle but perhaps on the fate of a campaign and even the destiny of a nation.'[21]

The fighting at the Dardanelles was forced on the Ottomans by their enemies. So, too, through much of 1915 and 1916, was the grim campaign along the old Russian frontier in Transcaucasia, where in mid-February 1916 the historic fortress of Erzerum fell suddenly to a surprise enemy assault, almost certainly thanks to information received by the Tsar's field commanders from Ottoman Arab officers incensed by the assertive 'Turkism' spreading through the Sultan's army. In contrast to these defensive campaigns at the Dardanelles and in eastern Anatolia were the attempts by both Germany and the Ottoman Empire to spread the jihad by fomenting rebellion. 'Our consuls . . . must inflame the whole Mohammeddan world to wild revolt,' Kaiser William declared. 'At least England shall lose India.'[22] So, it seems, Enver too believed. Before Gallipoli, he had invited Kemal to take command of three regiments and lead them across Persia to raise the Muslims of Baluchistan, Sind and the Punjab against the British Raj – an offer Kemal shrewdly rejected. Indian Muslims took little notice of the Caliph's proclamation, nor did Indian troops fighting alongside the British and Anzacs at Gallipoli respond to Turkish calls for mutiny.

Enver also gave his support to plans for saboteurs to cross the frontier from Mesopotamia into southern Persia and blow up the newly constructed Anglo-Persian Oil Company refinery at Abadan. Swift military action by the British frustrated this particular design, although the German agent, Wilhelm Wassmuss, later sparked off an anti-British rebellion over a wide area of southern Persia.[23] As a last resort Enver sent Young Turk officers into Libya to encourage the puritanical Muslim Sanussi sect to attack British outposts and, if Italy should again go to war with Turkey, to resume desert raids on the coastal towns of Cyrenaica. Here Enver had more success. Under Sayed Ahmed the Senussi fought loyally for their Caliph in the western desert until the empire's final fall. On the other hand, one prominent Ottoman agent, Jafar Pasha al-Askiri, who was captured by the British in a western desert cavalry skirmish, later supported the Arab rebellion in his native Mesopotamia and helped create the Iraqi army.[24]

At Germany's request the Ottoman High Command sought to implement a master design for 'the destruction of British rule in Egypt', developing a plan originally prepared in Berlin three months before Turkey became a belligerent. General Ahmed Cemal, abandoning ministerial office in order to return to active service, was appointed to command the Fourth Ottoman Army at Damascus in November 1914. Two months later he concentrated at Beersheba some 20,000 men, with artillery support, who were to mount an attack on the Suez Canal, 'the jugular vein of the British Empire'. With the Turks were some German specialist troops, and Cemal had a Bavarian colonel, Baron Franz von Kress von Kressenstein, as his Chief-of-Staff. Pontoon bridges, constructed in Germany and smuggled through neutral Bulgaria, were intended to allow the invaders to cross to the west bank of the canal. Both Cemal and Kress believed that a surprise raid in strength on the British positions would incite Egyptian nationalists to turn against the occupying 'colonialists' and welcome back Khedive Abbas Hilmi II. The raiders might hope to 'be joined by 70,000 Arab nomads', predicted Ernst Jaeckh, the German High Command's favourite Orientalist.[25]

Cemal's raid did not (as is often said) take the British by surprise: French reconnaissance aircraft had seen the columns advancing across the Sinai desert. From 3 to 10 February 1915 there was fighting to the north of Ismailia; a single Ottoman platoon successfuly bridged the canal before Cemal pulled his men back, disappointed at the failure of the Egyptians to welcome Ottoman liberation. While Cemal withdrew to Beersheba, Colonel Kress remained in the Sinai desert with a few battalions of infantry and a squadron of cavalry, as a standing threat to Egypt. German engineers supervised construction of a strategic railway linking Jaffa with Beersheba. Occasionally Kress's raiders would drop mines into the canal, until in the late summer of 1916 Anzac horsemen finally cleared the desert. Not until the end of the year did the British resolve to open up a new – and ultimately decisive – battle front in Palestine.[26]

As early as August 1914, some contact had been established between British Intelligence in Cairo and dissident Arabs serving with the Ottoman army in Mesopotamia. The principal emissary was Major Abdul Aziz al-Masri, who had founded in Baghdad a secret society known as *al-Ahd* (The Covenant), in which Iraqi officers pledged themselves to support any cause promoting Arab independence from Turkish rule.[27] The outbreak of war intensified British efforts to foment revolts in these outer Ottoman provinces. Here, however, there was a clash of interests between the Foreign Office and the India Office in London, and between Cairo and Simla, the headquarters of the British army in India; the Viceregal authorities opposed any encouragement of rebellion in the Ottoman Empire. They feared that the contagion of unrest would spread to the Indian subcontinent, where there were similar secret societies to those in the Arab lands.

There is no doubt that this cumbersome shared British responsibility for the Middle East helped the Ottoman High Command. While Cairo maintained political contact with the tribes of the Hejaz and southern Syria, it was the India Office which concluded the treaty of December 1915, recognizing the ambitious 35-year-old Abdulaziz Ibn Saud as ruler of Nejd.[28] The Viceregal administration in Bombay regarded the Gulf, Mesopotamia and the recently developed oilfields as falling within its sphere of interest – and also much of southern Arabia and Aden, where the British coaling-station was administered from 1839 until 1937 by military Political Residents appointed by the Government of India. And it was GHQ Simla which began the Mesopotamian Campaign with the dispatch of 'Force D' to the head of the Persian Gulf. The expedition landed at Fao on the second day of the war, brushed aside the local Ottoman garrisons and took Basra without much difficulty a fortnight later, thus safeguarding the oil installations in the Shatt-al-Arab. But instead of using Arab levies to harass the Ottomans, the British treated southern Mesopotamia as conquered territory: it was on this occasion that the 26-year-old Iraqi Arab nationalist, Nuri as-Said, was hurriedly deported to India.

Force D's hostility towards Arab nationalism, together with the arrival in Baghdad of Field-Marshal von der Goltz and a German mission, strengthened Ottoman resistance. Eventually General Townshend occupied the strategically important town of Kut-al-Amarah, 250 miles north of Basra, at the end of September 1915, and GHQ Simla at once urged him to advance on Baghdad itself. Townshend dutifully tried to accomplish all that was expected of him, but without Arab support any drive further into Mesopotamia was a rash undertaking, and on 22 November Goltz's improvised army, strengthened with a crack Anatolian division, defeated the invaders at Ctesiphon, less than twenty miles south of Baghdad. By 3 December Townshend's 17,000 men were besieged in Kut, together with 6,000 Arabs trapped in the fighting. Four attempts to relieve the town were defeated. Kitchener's confident ruse of offering Khalil Pasha, the Ottoman commander, at least a million pounds if he permitted the Kut garrison to go free was rejected

– and, for propaganda purposes, was treated with great contempt by Enver (who was Khalil's nephew). On 29 April 1916 the Kut garrison passed into a harsh captivity. As after the evacuation of Gallipoli three and a half months before, the Ottomans prided themselves on having routed an infidel invader. Momentarily the claim boosted morale at home.[29]

Like other governments in 1914, the Ottoman authorities had assumed that the war they were entering would soon be over. The economy could not stand the strain of long campaigns on several battle fronts. Although most towns and villages in the provinces were accustomed to feeding themselves, Constantinople had depended on grain imports from Russia and, to a lesser extent, from France and Italy. There was, in consequence, a severe shortage of food in the capital, even during the first winter of war; its effects were aggravated by an influx of refugees and the spread of typhus. Other regions, normally self-sufficient, suffered from the conscription of agricultural workers for service in the army and, in eastern Anatolia, from the devastation caused by an invasion. Famine in Syria and the Lebanon was caused in part by a prolonged drought, but also through an inequitable system of food distribution, made worse by the mobilization of railway rolling stock and track for military purposes. From October 1915, when Bulgaria entered the war as an ally of Germany, Austria–Hungary and the Ottomans, there was a direct rail-link once again with central Europe, giving the Turks a market for cotton, wool, leather, oil from the Mosul vilayet and other minerals. Without Germany's material backing the Sultan would have been forced to seek an early peace. As it was, official figures indicate that the cost of living in the capital quadrupled in the first twenty-five months of the war. Germany effectively subsidized its ally to the equivalent of a quarter of a billion pounds sterling in order to keep Ottoman armies in the field for four years.[30]

Politically there was no change in the character of Ottoman rule, although it was inevitable that censorship and police control should be strengthened. The Young Turks determined policy until the final weeks of war.[31] Said Halim remained Grand Vizier until February 1917 when Talaat, long the effective chief minister, formally succeeded him. At the same time Mehmed V continued to fulfil the duties of a constitutional Sultan. He welcomed Kaiser William II on his third state visit, presiding over a banquet in the Dolmabahche on 16 October 1917; and in the third week of May 1918 he was host during the only Habsburg State Visit to the Ottoman capital, entertaining Emperor-King Charles and his consort, Zita, with a splendour which taxed the resources of an empire threatened by runaway inflation. Seven weeks later – on 3 July – Mehmed V died and was succeeded by Abdulmecid's youngest son, the 57-year-old Mehmed VI Vahideddin, last of the thirty-six Ottoman Sultans. Five months earlier, almost forgotten amid the stress of war, their half-brother Abdulhamid had also died, not from an assassin's knife or poison as he had so long feared, but from heart failure in his bed at Beylerbey.

Although in some respects it seems astonishing, the Young Turks sought to maintain the momentum of their revolution throughout the first three years of war. In April 1913 decrees permitting judgments of the religious courts to be referred to the *Mahkfme-i Temyiz* (lay Court of Appeal) had asserted the primacy of the secular judiciary over the *ulema*; and this gradual toning down of the Muslim hierarchy's authority reached a climax towards the end of Said Halim's vizierate. From April 1916 the *şeyhülislâm* was no longer automatically a member of the cabinet, and in the next few months he was deprived of all his executive functions in what were now regarded as lay affairs, such as the administration of religious foundations and education. By the time of Mehmed VI Vahideddin's accession the *şeyhülislâm* was accepted as a solely religious dignitary, someone to be consulted and respected as an interpreter of Islamic teaching. There was also a series of measures which cautiously advanced the general emancipation of women: thus, in 1917 revision of the code of family law established that marriage was a secular contract, and recognized that a wife was entitled to divorce a husband who was a proven adulterer. Nevertheless, many social taboos remained rigidly enforced, especially in the countryside: and in the towns and cities all theatres, restaurants and lecture halls were still required to have a curtained-off area set aside for women.

Conservative disapproval of secularization lessened with the removal of the restraints on Muslim fanaticism which the Young Turks had imposed so long as they courted favour abroad. There was no longer any prospect of foreign inspectors-general operating in the provinces where Christian minorities complained of persecution. Renewed Dashnak activity in the city of Van, with the Russians now openly backing some form of Armenian autonomy on both sides of the old frontier, led to Ottoman fears that the Sultan's Armenian subjects would regard the Tsarist invaders as liberators and therefore assist their advance into Anatolia. Accordingly, in May 1915 the Ottoman authorities organized a mass deportation of Armenians from the eastern provinces to guarded settlements in northern Mesopotamia. As many as half a million Armenians may have died at this time from starvation, or from the sufferings of long marches through mainly Kurdish territory, or from massacres committed by the Kurds themselves, with the conniv- ance of local officials. Soon afterwards Armenian communities living in the countryside of northern Syria and Cilicia were similarly uprooted, and concentrated in central Syria. No one knows how many Armenians perished during the war. Official Turkish estimates put the total figure at about 300,000; maximum Armenian claims suggest a figure of some two million, killed during what is regarded as a systematic campaign of genocide.[31] Sadly, at least 1.3 million Armenian deaths seem probable. This estimate, if correct, means that in the war and its aftermath as many Armenians were slain as were soldiers serving the French Republic.

Inevitably, as the conflict began to drag out far longer than had been anticipated, individual CUP leaders began to assert an increasing independence of the Porte. Mustafa Rahmi, one of the three members of that first Young Turk deputation received by Sultan Abdulhamid in July 1908, was appointed *vali* of İzmir in 1915 and became such a powerful warlord in his province that he was able to protect both Armenians and Greeks from Muslim fury, occasionally putting out peace feelers to allied agents in Athens. Later in the war the Ottoman military commander in Syria, Ahmed Cemal Pasha, also showed an inclination to arrange separate terms with the Entente allies, but in the summer of 1915 he was still a pillar of the ruling triumvirate, convinced that the enemy would soon make a seaborne invasion in support of an Arab rebellion at some point between İskenderun and Haifa. Cemal therefore resorted to drastic repressive measures, intent on liquidating the Arab secret societies and other dissident groups. Eleven Arabs were hanged in Beirut on 28 August 1915 and arrests, executions and depor- tations continued in the Lebanon for eighteen months. The whole community suffered. Cemal saw no reason to distinguish too precisely between the likely treason of Arabs, Jews and Christians. As Lawrence wrote a few years later, Cemal 'united all classes, conditions and creeds in Syria, under pressure of a common misery and peril, and so made a concerted revolt possible.'[33]

Cemal was correct in assuming that an Arab rebellion was imminent. It had long been brewing. Shortly before the outbreak of war Emir Abdullah, the second son of the Sherif of Mecca, Hussein ibn Ali el-Aun, twice sounded out the British authorities in Egypt to see if he could win London's backing for a rising against Ottoman rule. Abdullah was familiar with political life in Constantinople as both he and his brother, Emir Feisal, sat in the Ottoman Parliament. Lord Kitchener,

British Agent and Consul General in Egypt from 1911 until the coming of the war, met Abdullah in Cairo and was impressed by evidence of the mounting Arab hostility towards the Young Turk regime. The Emir's father was not a natural rebel. He was an elderly conservative, alarmed by the coming of a westernized Ottoman governor to the Hejaz. As head of the Hashemite dynasty and thirty-seventh in direct descent from the Prophet, the Sherif of Mecca deserved the high respect with which Kitchener treated him and his emissaries. But the British may have exaggerated the status of the Sherif within Islam; they may, too, have attributed to him a desire to see the Ottoman Empire swept away, which he never possessed. After Kitchener became War Secretary in August 1914 he kept in touch with the Hashemite princes. 'It may be that an Arab of true race will assume the Khalifate at Mecca or Medina and so good may come by the help of God out of all the evil that is now occurring,' Kitchener wrote to Abdullah six days before Britain declared war on the Sultan.[34]

The jihad proclamation prompted the British to revive the idea of a Hashemite Caliphate. But by now Hussein was thinking of a crown. During the summer of 1915 Hussein exchanged letters with Sir Henry McMahon, Britain's High Commissioner in Egypt, seeking Cairo's support for the Caliphate, and for a Hashemite kingdom of Arabia, too. It would extend southwards from Cilicia (roughly the modern frontier of Turkey and Syria) down to the Yemen, and from the Mediterranean to the eastern limits of Mesopotamia. Ultimately, in a letter to Hussein dated 24 October 1915, Sir Henry McMahon agreed that Britain would 'recognise and support the independence of the Arabs within the territories included in the limits and boundaries proposed by the Sherif of Mecca', but with important reservations, notably the exclusion of regions considered not entirely Arab in composition or character. In the north both Mersin and İskenderun fell into this category. So too did 'portions of Syria lying to the west of the districts of Damascus, Hama, Homs and Aleppo' (in effect the eastern Mediterranean littoral). Other reservations included insistence on the acceptance of 'special measures of administrative control' throughout the vilayet of Baghdad and Basra to protect British interests, observance of British pledges to protect other Arab rulers, and a reminder that these promises concerned only 'those portions of the territories wherein Great Britain is free to act without detriment to her Ally, France'.[35]

McMahon's letter remains one of the most disputed documents in twentieth-century diplomacy. The weakness of his message lay not so much in its stated terms, imprecise though wartime conditions required them to be, as in its discreet omissions, and in particular its lack of any reference to Palestine, Jerusalem or the Jews. For several months Sherif Hussein continued his correspondence with McMahon, hoping to clarify the British offer and the meaning of that emotive word 'independence'. He had no success. But in December he received one more pat of encouragement: the Foreign Secretary, Sir Edward Grey, favoured 'Arab independence of Turkish domination', Hussein was told – provided, of course, that the Arabs themselves achieved it in revolt.[36]

There was good reason for this Foreign Office evasiveness. Doubts had arisen over what the 'French ally' would and would not regard as detrimental to her interests. In November 1915 François Georges-Picot, a former French consul-general in Beirut, arrived in London. Throughout December and well into the following year Georges-Picot held discussions with the much respected Arabist, Colonel Sir Mark Sykes. Together the two experts on the Middle East thrashed out proposals for the partition of the Ottoman Empire in the Levant, which in May 1916 were accepted as the 'Sykes-Picot Agreement'.[37] It envisaged the creation of two Arab states, one under French protection around Damascus, and another under British protection from Baghdad to Aqaba. The French would administer the Lebanon from north of Beirut to south of Tyre; the British would control Acre and Haifa; and Palestine would become the joint responsibility of France, Britain and (Tsarist) Russia. The Agreement has frequently been criticized as incompatible with the pledges already given to the Sherif of Mecca. It could, however, be argued that the Sykes-Picot Agreement amplified, clarified and complemented McMahon's proposals rather than invalidated them, and that later disputes arose rather more from the obligations assumed by the British in 1917 to the Zionist movement. Yet, whatever their importance for subsequent decades, within the context of the First World War the historical significance of the McMahon letters and the Sykes-Picot discussions is clear and unequivocal: they show that by 1915 the Entente allies were agreed on the disintegration of the Ottoman Empire, with help from a controlled explosion of Arab nationalism.

On 5 June 1916 Sherif Hussein began the Arab Revolt with a symbolic rifle shot fired at the Ottoman barracks in Mecca and a proclamation which was to serve as an Arab manifesto in the Islamic world. He denounced, in particular, the impiety of the Young Turks who had curbed the religious prerogatives of the Sultan-Caliph, having 'taken the religion of God as an amusement and a sport'.[38] At first the rhetoric was matched by deeds of arms, at least in the Hejaz. Mecca was soon cleared of Turks; the port of Jeddah was attacked on 9 June and, with offshore support from the Royal Navy, passed into Arab hands a week later; the town of Taif, an oasis forty miles south-east of Mecca, swiftly fell to Emir Abdullah, although Turkish troops continued to resist from behind the solid walls of the adjoining fort. Medina, however, could not be taken. The city housed not only the Prophet's sacred tomb, but the headquarters of the Twelfth Army Corps, commanded by the formidable and devout Fakhri en-din Pasha. Rather than see rebel Arabs in infidel pay enter Medina, Fakhri committed his garrison to a thirty-month siege. He was still defiant in January 1919, ten weeks after every other Ottoman army commander had accepted an Armistice.

Kitchener, who was drowned on his way to Russia on the day the Arab Revolt began, had always insisted on the need to prepare for a general insurrection, not simply an uprising in a particular vilayet. But other Arabs were slow to respond to the Hashemite call, and for several months it was questionable whether the fighting in the Hejaz posed a real military challenge to the Ottoman Empire. Not until the end of the year did Hussein's British sponsors, the 'Arab Bureau' in Cairo, begin seriously to co-ordinate the Revolt: Captain T. E. Lawrence, as head of the British mission to the Hejaz, secured the acceptance of Emir Feisal as effective leader of the Bedouin guerrillas, while the Ottoman veteran Major Aziz al-Masri trained regular Arab troops at Rabegh, where he was assisted by his fellow-Iraqi officer and conspirator, Nuri as-Said, allowed back from India.[39] Even during these essentially preparatory months, Enver, Talaat and Cemal could not ignore the threat to the Empire's southern flank, to the uncomprehending chagrin of their German advisers. For as long as the Hashemite rebel army was in the field – or, more accurately, in the desert – at least 30,000 Turkish troops were retained along the route of the Hejaz Railway and in Medina and the Yemen.

In the summer of 1917 the Hashemites went over to the offensive. On 6 July the Arabs captured the important port of Aqaba which, with British assistance, became the Emir Feisal's base for raids on the railway, seventy miles inland, and for an advance into Syria. Even before Aqaba fell, Ottoman complacency was shattered by a Bedouin raid on Baalbek, fifty miles *north* of Damascus, where on 11 June a bridge was damaged on the strategically important railway linking Syria with the heart of the empire. A British Intelligence assessment, reaching London from Switzerland some five weeks later, quotes a Turkish source as reporting that this revelation of unrest among the northern tribes caused the immediate transfer of six front-line battalions to

Baalbek in order to stamp out the embers of revolt in so sensitive a region.[40]

The Turkish concern was understandable, for the character of the war in the Middle East was changing rapidly. By carefully developing Basra as a military base and modernizing the port, General Maude had by January 1917 been able to concentrate an army four times as large as the forces of his Ottoman enemy; and on 11 March Baghdad was captured, for at least the thirtieth time in the city's long history. Enver, however, was unwilling to write off Mesopotamia as yet. With German backing, a new and powerful army group – code-named *Yildirim* (Lightning) – was concentrated in southern Anatolia during the summer months. General Erich von Falkenhayn, former Chief of the German General Staff and more recently the conqueror of Roumania, came to Constantinople and planned an offensive which would recover Baghdad and carry the Germano-Turkish Army through Persia and beyond, thus reviving the simplistic strategic goal of depriving 'England' of India. But 'Lightning' was soon forced to strike elsewhere. While Falkenhayn and Enver were planning *Yildirim* in Constantinople, General Allenby (newly arrived from the Western Front) was completing preparations for an offensive in Sinai, where in March and April the first two battles of Gaza had failed to breach the main Ottoman–German defensive system. By the autumn of 1917 Falkenhayn acknowledged that Palestine, rather than Mesopotamia and Persia, was the natural theatre of operations for *Yildirim*.[41]

Falkenhayn could oppose Allenby with fourteen Ottoman divisions and the nucleus of the German Asia Corps, some 6,500 specialist troops and staff officers. But Falkenhayn's army group was far less powerful than it appeared on paper. Mustafa Kemal – appointed to command the Seventh Army in Syria on 7 July – reported in September that in one of his divisions half the troops were so physically weak that they could not even stand on parade, let alone march against the enemy. Moreover, the Asia Corps' arrival in Syria was delayed by sabotage at Haydarpaša where, on 6 September, a huge explosion in the railway sidings destroyed rolling-stock, stores and munitions. There was, too, a fundamental flaw in the command structure: Falkenhayn himself despised and mistrusted all Turks. 'He had a stubborn, selfish streak in his character,' his best-known staff officer, Franz von Papen, was to recall.[42] So arrogant was the General's manner that Enver had to travel down to Damascus and seek to mediate between Falkenhayn and the two experienced Ottoman army commanders, Cemal and Kemal. Enver failed. Rather than attempt to carry out the German's battle plans, Mustafa Kemal obtained permission to go on long sick-leave early in October. Ahmed Cemal retained his command in Syria, but he remained incensed against Falkenhayn.

Allenby, with twice as much infantry as his opponents and ten times their cavalry, opened his Sinai offensive on the last day of October 1917, and gained all his immediate objectives.[43] The Ottoman advanced base at Beersheba fell to a surprise attack on the first day. Jaffa was entered a fortnight later, and on 3 December Jerusalem was captured, Allenby's victory ending nearly 700 years of Ottoman rule over the one city in the world sacred to Jews, Christians and Muslims alike. The coming of winter ruled out any further advance, but by the end of the year it seemed, both in Constantinople and in London, as if the Sultan's Arab lands would soon be lost to the Ottomans for all time. Unless, of course, a new wave of Panislamic sentiment could turn the Arab Revolt against its infidel sponsors.

That possibility, discounted by the British, raised Ahmed Cemal's hopes in Damascus. The Bolshevik Revolution of November 1917 was followed by the publication of wartime secret treaties found in the Russian Foreign Ministry archives: the Sultan's subjects thus learned for the first time of the Constantinople Agreement of March 1915, by which the Ottoman capital and the Straits were to be incorporated in the Russian Empire while Britain and France 'achieved their aims in the Near East and elsewhere'; and they were told, too, of the Allied pledge confirming Italy's sovereignty over the Dodecanese and promising the Italians a foothold in Asia Minor by extensive territorial gains in the vilayet of Adana. But the Ottoman authorities made most capital out of the Bolsheviks' publication of the Sykes-Picot agreement, seeing in it a means of winning over the Arabs. The deposed Khedive Abbas II was sent to Damascus, where the Germans set up an 'Arab Bureau' to rival the institution of the same name created by the British in Cairo some twelve months before. When secret overtures to Hussein produced no response, Cemal Pasha delivered a speech at Beirut on 6 December 1917 in which he cited the Bolshevik revelations as proof to all Islam that the Sherif of Mecca was conspiring with the Christian imperialists of the West.[44] One month previously – on 2 November, before the Bolsheviks leaked details of the Sykes-Picot agreement – the famous Balfour Declaration gave notice that the British Government viewed 'with favour the establishment in Palestine of a national home for the Jewish people'. Cemal had already successfully opposed German Foreign Ministry proposals to win Zionist support by a joint German– Ottoman declaration; he maintained that any championship of the Jews would force the Arabs into a closer dependency on the Entente. Now Cemal could cite the Sykes-Picot exchanges and the Balfour Declaration as 'proof' to the Islamic world that Arabs in British pay were handing over their Muslim heritage to the Zionist imperialists.[45]

During that last winter of war Cemal was the only member of the basically secularist Talaat government to affect what might today be described as a 'born-again' Muslim enthusiasm. But other colleagues were willing to accept extensive devolution so long as some form of Ottoman authority was preserved in the Arab lands: thus the Foreign Minister, a kinsman of Enver, let the Americans know in February 1918 that the Porte did not reject the Twelfth of President Wilson's Fourteen Points, which recommended autonomous development for the Ottoman non-Turkish nationalities; and the influential publicist Ziya Gökalp argued in favour of a federalized empire which would link virtually independent Turkish and Arab states.[46] Inevitably the Hashemites were tempted by this apparent change of mood on the Golden Horn, and there were further (almost-) secret exchanges between Emir Feisal and Cemal, and indeed even more confidential contacts between Feisal and Mustafa Kemal, when in the summer the latter returned to the Palestine Front.[47] Lawrence may have encouraged Feisal, in the double hope of spreading dissension among the Young Turk factions and of finding out more about Ottoman intentions. But, if so, it was a risky game to play. In June 1918 the British Foreign Office discovered that Feisal had gone so far as to set down on paper the basic concessions to be met by the Porte before Arab and Turkish armies might again fight 'side by side'. As Lawrence discreetly writes in *Seven Pillars of Wisdom*, 'Events in the end made abortive these complicated negotiations.'[48]

Enver was no longer greatly interested in the fate of the Arab lands within the Empire. Turkestan beckoned him eastwards. The collapse of Russia enabled the Ottoman armies to reoccupy Erzerum, eastern Anatolia and the historic 'Armenian' vilayets lost in three years of war. Provided Enver was allowed a free hand to concentrate Turkish troops in Transcaucasia and thereby secure Central Asia, he was prepared to leave Europe and Asia Minor to the German mission which he had for so long encouraged. Within a few months such mistrust had developed between Enver and the German units around the Black Sea that his staff produced maps marking German outposts in the Caucasus as 'held by the enemy'.[49] But in January 1918 he was by no means displeased that the German ascendancy on the Straits was as strong as ever: Admiral Souchon still commanded the fleet; the Chief of the Ottoman General

Staff was a gifted Prussian strategist, General Hans von Seeckt; and German officers were in command of the Ottoman Fifth Army (Liman von Sanders) and, in the Levant, of the Eighth Army (Kress von Kressenstein) and 'Army Group F' (Falkenhayn). No Ottoman commander could work amicably with Falkenhayn, and there was widespread satisfaction when Seeckt persuaded Berlin to recall him and replace him in Damascus with Liman. Enver regarded these German specialists as shock-absorbers who would contain the expected Allied onslaught in Palestine while he gave his attention to the Caucasus. Thanks to Enver's initiative, the crescent flag flew that autumn over lands which no Sultan had possessed for more than three centuries. Yet while Enver was employing good Turkish regiments to indulge his Caucasian fantasies, his colleagues in government were wondering how long they could count on the crescent flag continuing to fly over Stamboul itself.

By now the British had perfected their strategic plans for a three-pronged blow which would knock the Ottomans out of the war before the coming of winter.[50] The principal offensive would begin in Palestine, with Allenby following the traditional route of Bonaparte and Ibrahim Pasha into Syria and, if necessary, across Cilicia and Anatolia, too. Once at Aleppo Allenby's army would be joined by cavalry advancing up the Euphrates from Ramadi. Feisal's Arabs would give support east of the Jordan valley, with Damascus as their main objective. Meanwhile, on the Salonika Front in the Balkans, the British divisions serving in General Franchet d'Esperey's multinational army would help defeat Germany's ally, Bulgaria, and turn eastwards to follow another familiar route to Constantinople, through the mountains of Thrace. In this Balkan sector the Ottomans had their weakest troops; even in the spring of 1917, at the height of the campaign, no more than eighteen Ottoman battalions fought alongside the Germans, Austrians, Hungarians and Bulgars against the Entente allies in Macedonia; and when the Bulgars concluded their separate armistice with the Allies on 30 September 1918 it was unlikely that this skeleton contingent in Europe would offer serious resistance.

It seemed indeed by the late summer of 1918 as though Young Turk rule were crumbling. There had been a relaxation of political censorship in the press in June, and although Talaat remained Grand Vizier he appointed a liberal Minister of the Interior in July. A few weeks later political exiles were encouraged back to the capital, where new political parties and societies began to spring up.[51] Among them, significantly, was a 'Turkish Wilsonian League' of liberal intellectuals. As the USA was never at war with the Sultan, this could not be regarded as in any sense a treasonable society. Parlour politicians in Constantinople hoped that, by resuscitating Ottoman parliamentarianism, they might gain a sympathetic hearing from the great prophet of democracy in Washington.

Only in Palestine – and at distant Medina – did the Ottoman commanders still show any real determination to withstand the Allied onslaught. Mustafa Kemal had returned to Palestine in the second week of August to command the Seventh Army, one of the three corps in Liman von Sanders's Army Group. He did not think the war could continue much longer, but he wished to save the genuinely Turkish heartland from invasion, enemy occupation or partition. It was therefore primarily as Turkish nationalists, rather than as good Ottomans, that the Seventh Army resisted Allenby's onslaught when, on 18 September, the Allied advance began along the coast north of Jaffa. Constant use of aircraft and imaginative deployment of cavalry enabled the British to defeat the two Ottoman armies west of Jordan within three days, while Feisal's Arabs cut the railway links north of Deraa.

Damascus fell on 1 October.[52] The historic city was officially liberated by the Arabs, who were anxious to gain support for their claims to administer the Syrian capital; but in reality the first troops to reach the centre of Damascus – at six in the morning – were Australians of the 3rd Light Horse Brigade. The French, eager to secure control of the Syrian ports, reached Beirut next day, although here the 'first in' were units of the 7th Indian Division. The loss of Damascus and Beirut had dramatic consequences in Constantinople; the bad news finally toppled the government. Talaat resigned on 8 October, but there was such confusion in the capital that it took the Sultan six days to find a successor whom he could trust. At last, on 14 October, General Ahmed Izzet was able to form a 'Peace Ministry'. By then, in Thrace, the vanguard of General Milne's British Salonika Army was approaching Dedeagatch, while in Mesopotamia British and Indian troops were fighting their way resolutely up the Tigris, heading for the Mosul oil wells (which were not finally secured until 3 November).[53]

Peace talks began on 26 October aboard the flagship of the Mediterranean fleet, HMS *Agamemnon*, moored off Mudros. They lasted for five days; there was confusion over the delineation of provincial boundaries; and Admiral Calthorpe, the chief Allied representative, had the difficult task of reconciling his own practical needs with the demands of an Anglo-Indian pressure group in London and with hardliners in Paris and Rome, too.[54] The Ottoman delegation missed the hidden menace of clauses giving the Allies a right to occupy strategic points 'in case of disorder'. When, on 30 October, an armistice was signed, it was not as harsh as the Turks had feared; there was to be no mandatory occupation of Constantinople. Ottoman garrisons in Palestine, Syria, Mesopotamia and Arabia were to surrender to the Allies, who would establish military administrations pending the conclusion of a peace treaty; Armenian internees would be released; Allied troops would occupy the forts of the Dardanelles and Bosphorus; the Straits would be cleared of mines, enabling warships to enter the Black Sea; Allied commissioners would control the railways; the army would demobilize, except for units needed to safeguard internal order.

The Mudros Armistice was a businesslike document imposing no formal restraints on the Sultan's sovereignty, yet Mehmed VI was soon to see for himself the reality of defeat. By 13 November a line of Allied warships stretched for sixteen miles from the Golden Horn westwards into the Sea of Marmara. 'I can't look out of the window. I hate to see them,' the Sultan is reported to have told a deputation of Turkish parliamentarians who visited him in the Dolmabahche.[55] He was painfully aware that he possessed only a shadow authority. That, however, was more than Kaiser William, Emperor-King Charles, or King Ferdinand of Bulgaria now enjoyed. Of the four defeated rulers, by mid-November only the Sultan retained his throne.

CHAPTER 16

Sovereignty and Sultanate

Constantinople in the winter of 1918–19 was a wretchedly demoralized city. It was overcrowded with refugees, many weakened by typhus and other diseases. Everywhere food was short, and coal for heating almost unobtainable. No trams were running, and few ferries crossed between Europe and Asia. The Ottomans had lost nine wars in the past century and a half, but never before had the people of the capital felt so bitterly the impact of defeat. Allied 'protection' was hardly distinguishable from enemy occupation. In practice little could be done without the permission of the senior Allied High Commissioner, Admiral Calthorpe, who was assisted by French and Italian colleagues. Although the Commissioners personally worked well together, the divergent policies of their respective governments prevented close collaboration or forward planning for the Empire as a whole. In the more distant provinces of northeastern Turkey, the mountainous terrain often left the 'strategic points' occupied by the Allies in remote and ineffectual isolation. Uncertainty over the future of Russia intensified the virtual anarchy in these vilayets.[1]

On the Golden Horn there was at least the semblance of orderly administration. General Sir Henry Maitland Wilson established his headquarters in Pera, while British, French and Italian detachments guarded strategic positions. Yet Turkish units still bore arms. When the victorious French general, Franchet d'Esperey, arrived in the snow-choked city from Salonika in February, Ottoman officers as well as Greeks and Italians joined him in inspecting the British guard of honour; and when a panic report swept Stamboul asserting that Greeks were about to restore Christian symbols in the mosque of Ayasofya, it was Ottoman guards who kept in check an ugly crowd of Muslim demonstrators. Such rumours were common that winter: the Allies were said to be allowing Greeks and Armenians to massacre Muslims and destroy their homes in the disputed vilayets; Christian priests were alleged to be taking over Muslim schools and orphanages, even in the capital; and non-Turks were reputedly receiving preferential treatment by the Allied military administration in every region. There were enough instances of discrimination to give credence to these tales, exaggerated though the reports were in many cases. When forced to choose between the subject-peoples of the Ottoman Empire, Admiral Calthorpe over-simplified: as far as he was concerned, Turks were 'baddies'. 'It has been our consistent policy to show no kind of favour whatsoever to any Turk,' he assured the Foreign Secretary seven months after taking up his duties.[2]

This suspicion and mistrust hampered the growth of the fledgling Ottoman democracy. During November and early December 1918 it looked as if the parliamentary regime, introduced ten years before, would survive the eclipse of the Young Turks. With the CUP triumvirate in exile, there was an immediate revival of the Ottoman Liberal Union, headed by the Sultan's brother-in-law and close friend, Damat Ferid Pasha. But in the absence of strong political leadership more policy decisions depended upon the Sultan's personal inclinations than had seemed likely so long as the war continued. Mehmed VI Vahideddin – as the Sultan was officially styled – was not a natural autocrat. He possessed to the full all the awkward obstinacy of a weak ruler, short of temper and narrow in outlook. A trivial incident soon after his accession was a pointer to his character. Sultans traditionally had beards, any clean-shaven prince hurriedly seeing that his chin became hirsute within weeks of his accession. Not, however, Mehmed VI; at fifty-seven he saw no reason to conform. Despite remonstrances from the *ulema*, he was prepared to strike one defiant note of modernity; he would reign as 'the beardless Sultan'. It was widely felt that, in some strange way, the innovation lessened the sovereign's stature.[3]

For Mehmed Vahideddin this was unfortunate, since he was determined to rule as well as to reign. The Sultan had no liking for parliamentary institutions and did not bother to conceal his prejudices, trying to play the political game in the style his elder half-brother had perfected after the humiliation of San Stefano. Mehmed lacked Abdulhamid's guile and had fewer cards to put on the table; but successive High Commissioners acknowledged his usefulness, however trimmed-down his autocracy had become. Outwardly Sultan and High Commissioners seemed to share common objectives; the latter, too, preferred to govern through decrees rather than respect the wishes of a political forum, especially one in which they thought they detected a nascent socialism.

There were no protests from the High Commissioners when, on 21 December, Mehmed VI dissolved parliament, following this political coup with a return to more traditional ways of government.[4] The authority of the *şeyhülislâm* was re-established, over both education and the interpretation of family law. When, in the first week of March 1919, Mehmed VI appointed Damat Ferid as Grand Vizier, some of the Sultan's most loyal supporters expressed doubts over his brother-in-law's probity and good faith. But Mehmed insisted on upholding the Sultan's prerogatives. He could, he reminded his critics, appoint anyone he wished – 'even the Greek or Armenian Patriarchs or the Chief Rabbi,' he insisted.[5] Soon it became clear that Damat Ferid's 'liberalism' was lightly held. He would comply with most Allied demands, while emphasizing to the High Commissioners the value of the *ulema* as guarantors of good order and discipline. British officials with experience of India were inclined to agree with Damat: better a mullah than a red revolutionary, they believed.

None of the Ottoman ministries in the winter of 1918–19 was harshly repressive. Censorship was selective. 'Societies for the Defence of the Rights of Turks' were tolerated by the Sultan's ministers, despite protests from the High Commissioners. It is probable that Sultan Mehmed knew of the secret 'Outpost Society', a group of officials who smuggled arms along the Black Sea coast to eastern Anatolia or through the Dardanelles to Smyrna. Almost certainly he was aware that his most respected general-in-mufti, Mustafa Kemal, was encouraging the spread of a specifically Turkish nationalism. But he said nothing. He had a curious habit of occasionally shutting his eyes in the presence of ministers and officers to whom he had granted an audience, as Kemal himself noticed when the Sultan engaged him in conversation after a *selamlik*.[6] Was Vahideddin's gesture subconsciously symbolic? At all events, and with or without the Sultan's connivance, an embryonic resistance movement linked the main Turkish towns even before mid-January in 1919, when the Peace Conference opened in Paris. And Kemal was one of three generals on the retired list who knew how extensive were the volunteer militia groups, as they awaited a signal to protect their homes from foreign rule.

The pace of events was determined by what was – or was not – happening in Paris. The statesmen, diplomats and co-opted experts gave priority to the making of peace with Germany and then concentrated on settling the fate of Austria and Hungary before they considered the needs of the Ottoman peoples in any detail. Not until 17 June 1919 was an Ottoman delegation received by the Council of Ten, effectively the Conference's chief executive body; another eleven months passed before the final peace terms reached the Sublime Porte. Long before then a combination of pride, resentment and disillusionment had fostered among the Turks a new sense of national identity.

When the Armistice of Mudros was signed, genuine liberals in Constantinople confidently expected the peace-makers to redraw the map of Europe and Asia to accommodate the principles of the American President, Woodrow Wilson, with their emphasis on self-determination as a cure for the international *malaise*. It was assumed that Wilson's crusading idealism would somehow expunge the secret wartime treaties for the partition of Turkey, the baits tempting Italy into the war, the bargains struck by Sir Mark Sykes and Georges-Picot, and all the other devices of a discredited diplomacy made public by the Bolsheviks. These hopes were, for the most part, dashed. Wilson's self-determination favoured the Armenians, partly because wealthy emigrants could mount a well-organized campaign on both sides of the Atlantic, but also because US missionaries had long been active in the predominantly Armenian vilayets. The Peace Conference recommended the temporary cession of disputed Ottoman lands to the victorious Great Powers as League of Nations 'mandates'. When the League began to function Iraq, Palestine and (later) Transjordan became British mandates while, after fierce wrangling between Paris and London, France gained the mandate for Syria and the Lebanon. In May 1919, in a complete break with the basic tradition of US diplomacy, President Wilson agreed to seek Congressional approval for American mandates over Armenia, and even over Constantinople itself.[7]

Towards one government's ambitions Woodrow Wilson remained as hostile as the Ottoman liberals had hoped. He strongly opposed Italian attempts to secure a foothold in Asia Minor, largely because there were no Italian communities already established there. Yet here, too, Wilson's principles proved disastrous for the Turks; the arguments with which he reproached the 'colonialists' in Rome were twisted by Venizelos, the chief Greek delegate, to further his own ambitions. In Smyrna, the finest Ottoman port on the Aegean, there remained a large Greek community; and it was not difficult for Venizelos to convince Wilson of the need for Greek troops to occupy the port and its hinterland, both to protect their compatriots from the Turks and to forestall an Italian leap from the Dodecanese to the mainland of Asia. Venizelos had long enjoyed the warm backing of the British Prime

Minister, Lloyd George. Within two months of the opening of the Paris Peace Conference, he could count on support from both the British and the American delegations. Reports of violent attacks by Turkish militia upon Greek communities in western Anatolia gave Venizelos his opportunity. A full division of the Greek army was transported to Smyrna on 15 May 1919, their landing protected by British, French and American warships lying out to sea.[8]

This decisive move followed three weeks in which it had seemed likely the Allies would soon occupy every harbour and sizeable town remaining within the Ottoman Empire. Disorder was spreading rapidly through the outlying provinces. A stern warning was delivered to the Sultan by the High Commissioner, who laid particular emphasis on the anarchy prevailing along the Black Sea coast, where the Ottoman Ninth Army seemed incapable of policing a turbulent region.[9] Mehmed VI Vahideddin was most conciliatory: a high-powered military mission, led by a vigorous Inspector-General, should at once be sent to impose discipline on the Ninth Army; and, the British authorities were assured in the last days of April, he had every confidence in the skill of General Mustafa Kemal Pasha to undertake just such a mission. With some hesitancy, the British took the Sultan at his word: a visa was duly stamped authorizing Kemal, as Inspector-General of the Ninth Army, to sail from Constantinople for the small port of Samsun. Accordingly, on the day after the Greeks landed in Smyrna, Kemal boarded a British-built coaster, the *Bandirma*, and set off through the Bosphorus, pledged to restore order along the Black Sea coast. 'Pasha, you can save the country,' the Sultan told him in a farewell audience, with that cryptic obscurity which he found more congenial than clear directives. A few hours later a British officer spotted Kemal's name on a list of dangerous troublemakers. At once the British military attaché set out for the Porte, with orders to see the Grand Vizier and make certain the Inspector-General remained in the capital. 'Too late, Excellency,' Damit blandly told him. 'The bird has flown.'[10]

In the modern Turkish Republic Kemal's arrival at Samsun, on 19 May, is still commemorated each year with a national holiday, as if it were the start of the revolution which was to sweep away Sultan and sultanate. Yet the landing at Samsun was not in itself a remarkable event. For more than a week Kemal behaved cautiously. Only when he set out for the Anatolian plateau, officially to impose order in towns where there had been clashes between the Turks and national minorities, did he begin to show independence. The first genuinely revolutionary act was taken at Amasya, the old Hittite fortress overhanging

Yeşilırmak

the gorge of the river ~~Yesirlimak~~. There, on 21 June, Kemal issued a Declaration of Independence, calling on the Turkish people to send delegates to a national congress, which would be held at Sivas in Anatolia because the Sultan, his capital city and his administration were all under foreign duress. Peremptorily the Inspector-General was summoned back to Constantinople, but he refused to go. On 8 July he resigned his commission.

There followed eight months of political confusion. Kemal was not the first of the military commanders to urge resistance in what was already being called a 'War of Independence', but he was certainly the ablest of the generals to take to the mountains; and his ascendancy was recognized by a congress at Erzerum as well as the Sivas meeting. In some respects the Sivas Congress was a disappointment; only thirty-nine men were able to make the journey there. But at both meetings the delegates endorsed a manifesto whose principles were later clarified and embodied in what became known as the 'National Pact'.[11] The manifesto insisted that ethnic Turks had a right to self-determination, that Anatolia and all European Turkey constituted an indivisible entity in which there could be no Armenian or Greek state, and that the Allies should abandon their plans for partitioning the empire and regulating the government in Constantinople. From Sivas came, too, a call for a new, elected parliament, to meet in a city where deputies would not be intimidated by an Allied military or naval presence.

In this programme there was little to which the Sultan or his Grand Vizier could object. Although the Sultan confirmed orders for Kemal's arrest, contact was maintained between Constantinople and the Nationalists. Eleven days after the Sivas Congress finished, a US fact-finding team, commissioned by the President to discover whether an American mandate was a feasible proposition, visited Sivas and discussed the problems of self-determination with Mustafa Kemal. Four weeks later the rebellious general received the Ottoman Minister of Marine at Amasya, and sent him back to the capital with a version of the National Pact. As chairman of the Nationalist Representative Committee, Kemal asked for elections to be held for a parliament which would meet in a town free from foreign domination, and he also requested that the NRC should have the opportunity of vetoing the appointment of Ottoman delegates to the Peace Conference. These terms were rejected by Ali Riza Pasha, who had succeeded Damat Ferid as Grand Vizier on 2 October.[12] For parliament to meet in any town where its work could not be scrutinized by the Sultan seemed unthinkable to Mehmed VI. He had no wish to exchange the comfortable security of his Bosphorus palaces for some remote, impromptu capital in Anatolia. Elections were duly held; Kemal's Nationalists won more seats in the lower House than any other party; but when parliament met, in the second week of January 1920, the deputies still gathered in Stamboul.

Surviving letters show that the British authorities could not make up their minds over Kemal.[13] To some he was a bandit, to others a brigand; it was a fine distinction. None looked upon him as a responsible spokesman for the Turkish people. He had been elected to represent Erzerum, but he stayed away from a city where he would almost certainly have been arrested or killed. As an absentee deputy, he may even have made a greater impact on the parliament than had he spoken in the chamber. Immediately after the Sultan's formal opening speech, a message of welcome telegraphed by Kemal from Ankara (then Angora) was read to the deputies; and throughout the nine weeks of the parliamentary session, the Nationalists determined the day-to-day work of the chamber. A group of deputies secretly sought to have him elected as President (Speaker) of the Chamber, hoping that official status would give him immunity from arrest. The proposal was dropped for fear it might prompt the Sultan to dissolve the assembly. By keeping parliament in session, the deputies were able to endorse Kemal's National Pact in the second week of February, thus giving constitutional recognition to the Sivas manifesto.

The defiant mood of the Ottoman Parliament alarmed the British High Commissioner, Admiral Sir John de Robeck, who had succeeded Admiral Calthorpe a few months earlier. He was already concerned by reports that substantial stocks of arms were reaching Kemal, some from French and Italian sources. Against whom would they be employed? In London, detailed discussion of the treaty terms to be offered the Sultan continued throughout the weeks that the Ottoman Parliament was in session. If these demands ran counter to the National Pact, Sir John de Robeck anticipated prolonged resistance from the Turks. He sought permission for the High Commissioners to take preventive action strengthening Allied control over the Sultan and the administration in Constantinople.[14]

This request posed awkward problems at the highest level. The United States was fast withdrawing into isolation: Wilson's grave illness and the hostility of many Democrats and all Republicans to the League of Nations ensured that the proposed American mandates were already being written off as historical aberrations, though it was not until June that Congress formally declined to accept them. The three Allied Powers had difficulty in agreeing on policy or objectives. Friction between Britain and France over the Levant antedated the World War: 'So far as Syria is concerned it is France and not Turkey that is the enemy,' T. E. Lawrence had written in February 1915 (though in a private letter home, rather than an official report).[15] The French, for their part, deeply resented the speed with which the British had seized Mosul in the last days of the war, for Sykes and Picot had considered that rich oil-producing district to fall within the French sphere of influence. Nor were Anglo-Italian relations any easier. For four years Italy had opposed British support for Venizelist Greece, whether in Macedonia, Albania or the Aegean; and the government in Rome resented Lloyd George's patronage of the Greek adventure in Anatolia. The actions of both their Allies continued to puzzle the British. François Georges-Picot had travelled to Anatolia and met Kemal personally towards the end of 1919 and, although Kemalist troops subsequently fired on French forces occupying the predominantly Armenian districts around Marash, by the following spring it was clear that the French were preparing to pull back from their advanced line in Cilicia, to make sure of their hold on Syria. The Italians, too, appeared to seek an understanding with Kemal, provided always that they could retain the Dodecanese. Yet, despite such disunity and mistrust among the Allies, the Supreme Council responded favourably to Robeck's request: the High Commissioners might complete the occupation of the Ottoman capital, arrest dangerous dissidents, and send them to Malta for internment.[16]

The military occupation of Constantinople was not a joint Allied operation: neither the French nor the Italians made any move on the first day. Early in the morning of 16 March 1920 British soldiers, marines and seamen took over the principal buildings of Stamboul and Pera, while their armoured cars patrolled the streets. The Turkish War Office was occupied and searched by British officers, thereafter remaining jointly under the control of the three Allies. Eighty-five parliamentary deputies and some sixty army officers or senior bureaucrats were arrested. The Ottoman Parliament was formally dissolved on 18 March, never to meet again. Martial law prevailed throughout the Sultan's capital. The odium for interfering so drastically in Turkey's internal affairs was directed at the British.

A few weeks earlier Lord Curzon, the British Foreign Secretary, had urged his cabinet colleagues to seek the end of Ottoman rule in Constantinople and thereby 'settle once and for all a question which more than any single cause has corrupted the public life of Europe for nearly 500 years'.[17] His memorandum, which runs to more than eight pages of close print in the published British documents, was prompted by two developments: a visit to Downing Street by the French Prime Minister, Clemenceau, who favoured the retention of Ottoman rule in the city; and claims by the Indian Secretary, Edwin Montagu, that the expulsion of the Sultan-Caliph from his palaces in Europe would provoke grave unrest among the Muslims of the sub-continent. 'There never has been till in the last two or three years any pronounced feeling among Indian Moslems in favour of Constantinople as the seat of the Khalifate or the capital of Islam,' Curzon declared, with all the authority of a distinguished ex-Viceroy. 'Personally I think that if we rob the Turks of Smyrna we shall do more to fan the flame of racial religious animosity in Turkey in Asia than by any steps we might take with regard to Constantinople.'[18] He therefore recommended some form of international status for the city and the Straits. But Curzon failed to carry the cabinet with him: Montagu's fears of what might happen in Muslim India if the Caliph were to be unceremoniously booted across the Bosphorus prevailed. Far better, it was felt, to have a temporary occupation of the city, followed by the appointment of a career diplomat as High Commissioner, someone who would convince the Sultan of his need for 'the friendship of England': Admiral de Robeck was succeeded by Sir Horace Rumbold in November.

The burdens assumed by these British High Commissioners were considerable. They became responsible for policing and administering a city which faced bankruptcy and was troubled by the constant arrival of refugees fleeing from Bolshevik vengeance across the Black Sea; sixty ships, with 12,000 Russian refugees aboard, were moored in the crowded waters of the Sea of Marmara in the week Rumbold reached Constantinople. For almost three years a British colonel, Colin Ballard, commanded the Inter-Allied Police Commission in the Sultan's capital, and when the Ottoman authorities could not find the money to pay their gendarmerie it was the High Commissioner who had to safeguard their monthly salaries. Presiding ineffectually over what remained of his empire was Sultan Mehmed VI, who had reappointed Damat Ferid Pasha as Grand Vizier early in April 1920. A strong Sultan would have slipped away from the capital and put himself at the head of the Turkish Nationalists in Anatolia; a wily Sultan might have pursued a policy of passive non-compliance; but Mehmed and Damat were so weak in character that they collaborated as closely as possible with the High Commissioners. Even the pusillanimous *şeyhülislâm* proclaimed Kemal and his Representative Committee to be faithless betrayers of the *şeriat* who might be shot dead on sight.[19]

Such fulminations did not unduly disturb Kemal. In Ankara he established a Grand National Assembly to continue the work of the Ottoman Parliament. On 23 April the Assembly confirmed Kemal's status as executive president of a Council of State, although no formal constitutional act was presented to the Grand National Assembly for another nine months. 'The Sultan-Caliph', Kemal ambiguously proposed, 'shall take his place within the constitutional system in a manner to be determined by the Assembly as soon as he is free from the coercion to which he submits.'[20] No member of the Assembly dissented.

While the Grand National Assembly was in session, the Allies met in conference at San Remo to decide on the final terms of the peace treaty. It had been drafted by British, French and Italian experts, some of whom knew the Middle East well. Bargains were struck, notably concessions by Britain to France over the Mosul oilfields, an agreement giving the French favourable treatment and the right to draw on the yield of the oilfields to service their development of Syria. Repeatedly Lloyd George's cabinet colleagues and expert advisers tried to dissuade the Prime Minister from backing the demands of Venizelos for a permanent Greek zone around Smyrna. It 'would be a canker for years to come, the constant irritant that will perpetuate bloodshed in Asia Minor probably for generations,' Admiral de Robeck wrote to Curzon in the second week of March.[21] The Foreign Secretary agreed with him, even though he was basically sympathetic to the Greek cause; he would have liked to see the Greeks holding the Gallipoli peninsula, thus making the Dardanelles a frontier as well as a channel between Europe and Asia. No arguments could persuade Lloyd George to change his policy; he remained a staunch champion of Venizelos.

The peace terms were presented to the Sultan's delegates in the second week of June 1920.[22] Soon afterwards they became public knowledge, through leaked information in Athens. The treaty was harsher than the Turks had anticipated. They were resigned to the loss of the Sultan's Arab lands, but were shocked by the proposed border in Europe; by advancing the Greek frontier eastwards to include Edirne and the whole of Thrace up to the Lines of Chatalja, the new map would leave Constantinople with only twenty-five miles of hinterland in Europe. At the same time, Greece was to gain eight islands in the Aegean, while Smyrna would be placed under Greek control but nominal Ottoman sovereignty for five years, after which there would be a plebiscite to decide whether the region should remain Greek or Turkish. Rhodes and the Dodecanese were ceded to Italy. An independent Armenian state, with access to the Black Sea, was to include most of the six disputed vilayets, together with Russia's Armenian provinces; Woodrow Wilson – or those Americans acting in the stricken President's name – accepted an offer to determine the state's boundaries after arbitration, and astonished even the turcophobe Lloyd George by assigning the fortress of Erzerum and the port of Trebizond to the Armenians. The treaty also proposed an autonomous Kurdistan east of the Euphrates, with the Kurds having the right after twelve months to choose independence. The Straits were to be demilitarized, and controlled by an international commission; the Ottoman Army would be limited to 50,000 men and the navy restricted to coastal defence vessels; the Capitulations were restored, to benefit foreign traders; Britain, France and Italy would jointly control the Ottoman state budget and public loans.

Marshal Foch thought the proposed treaty a threat to peace. To enforce such terms on a reluctant Turkey the Allies would need an army of 27 divisions (about 325,000 men), he warned in April.[23] No war-weary government would contemplate such a commitment. When, a few months later, Sir Charles ('Tim') Harington was given the high-sounding post of 'General Officer Commanding the Allied Forces in Turkey', he found he could call on no more than 8,000 British soldiers to hold Constantinople and the Straits. Only Venizelos was prepared to authorize a campaign in Anatolia to try to crush the Nationalists. For the moment the Allies held him back, awaiting the reaction of the Turks – which, when it came, was bad. The proposed frontiers aroused such resentment among Turkish soldiers hitherto loyal to the Sultan that they deserted to Kemal, whose troops advanced to the Sea of Marmara. There they were halted by shellfire from Allied warships and fell back into the hinterland, beyond the range of naval guns.

At this point the Allies lifted their veto on a Greek campaign. Venizelos proposed that the Greek army should advance into Thrace and stamp out any Kemalist guerrilla forces operating in Europe, while the main Greek expeditionary force based upon Smyrna should be used to clear Kemal's Nationalists from western Anatolia. On 22 June the Greek regiments went forward and met only sporadic resistance. Within two and a half weeks they had forced the Kemalists back into the mountains and cleared the whole of south-western Anatolia. A month later the Sultan's plenipotentiaries, having failed to achieve any revision of the settlement, signed the peace treaty in the Parisian suburb of Sèvres. But, even as they signed, they protested strongly at the harsh terms laid down by the Allies. It would be several months before the Porte could ratify the treaty, thereby making it effective. Before then, the Sultan's ministers had every hope of securing the annulment of the treaty's more vindictive terms.

Long negotiations, constant bargaining, elaborate exchanges between viziers and ambassadors, the playing off of one Great Power against another – all these ploys were familiar features of Ottoman diplomacy. And the published documents confirm that Ahmed Tevfik, the last Grand Vizier, and his ministers were skilled players of this traditional game.[24] But the decisive contest took place not on the Straits, but in Anatolia; and it followed other rules. Kemal, did not, for example, simply protest at the proposed establishment of an Armenian state. Seven weeks after the Treaty of Sèvres was signed, Nationalist forces advanced through the Armenian vilayets and captured Kars while, soon afterwards, the Soviet Red Army established a puppet Armenian republic at Erivan. By the first week of December the Ankara Government and the Soviet authorities had signed the Treaty of Gümrü, thereby establishing, across a divided Armenia, a Russo-Turkish frontier which was to survive longer than the Soviet Union itself. Not only did Kemal safeguard his eastern flank, he was able to count on Russian arms and equipment in his fight against 'western imperialism'. By January 1921 he was better placed to withstand a Greek offensive than in the previous summer. That month four Greek infantry divisions advanced from Bursa along the main Anatolian railway, through difficult mountain terrain towards the important junction at Eskişehir. They were checked near the small town of Inönü, on the last ridge before road and railway descend to the Eskişehir plain. Two months later a second battle was fought at Inönü, to coincide with a Greek thrust inland from Smyrna. Once more the Kemalists held their ground, and the Greeks failed to make progress.[25]

The French and Italians never felt so strongly committed to the Sèvres settlement and the maintenance of the Sultan's government as did the British; and in March both France and Italy concluded agreements of their own with Kemal's representatives. Ironically, these understandings were reached in London, where Curzon had invited representatives of both the Sultan's government and the Nationalists in Ankara to meet the three Allied Powers and discuss possible modifications of the Treaty. By now the British were wavering in their support of the Greeks, for Venizelos was no longer in office and the sudden death of the young King Alexander of the Hellenes had brought back to the throne his father, King Constantine I, whom the British and French had forced into exile in 1917 as an alleged 'pro-German'. Yet, though Lloyd George mistrusted Constantine, he was too heavily committed to the Anatolian venture to follow the example of the French and Italians.[26]

More and more the Sultan was being forced to appear to be a British puppet, a state of servility the Foreign Office had never wanted; better far that he should be seen to reign as an enlightened autocrat. Soon after his arrival in Constantinople, Sir Horace Rumbold set out on the traditional task of strengthening the Ottoman government through the Sultanate; this, as Rumbold telegraphed to Curzon, involved the use of 'the Sultan as corner-stone. . . . giving him definite and whole-hearted assistance with a view to reconstruction of administration on sound financial basis'.[27] But Mehmed VI Vahideddin was too brittle for such a task. Rumbold's first audience with the Sultan left the High Commissioner puzzled and disappointed. 'He remained absolutely silent for a considerable time, his mouth twitching nervously,' reported Rumbold to King George V a week later.[28]

There were moments when Mehmed impressed foreign officers in his capital by a sudden assertion of the Islamic sovereignty he had inherited: towards the end of his life General Tim Harington recalled how, on the holiest night of Ramadan, the *Leilat al-Kadir*, the Sultan arrived at the Ayasofya mosque resplendent on a white horse, while ten thousand worshippers bent in prayer beneath the vast dome of the old basilica.[29] But these occasions were rare. For much of September 1921, a critical period in the war between Kemal's Nationalists and the Greeks, no minister or foreign diplomat could transact business with the Sultan. On the first of the month, so Mehmed's friend Šerif Ali Hayder recalls, 'he had taken a new wife, who so demanded his attention that he refused to see any visitors'. Mehmed was sixty; his 'new wife', Nevzad, was nineteen.[30]

Not surprisingly, Rumbold's dispatches to London paid increasingly detailed attention to the qualities of the Nationalist leaders, even if he could not travel to Ankara to meet them. Both the High Commissioner and the military commander were impressed by reports of the resilient spirit of the Turks in Anatolia. Harington irritated Lloyd George by reiterating his conviction that, though the Greek army was impressive during an offensive, there would be little resistance if Kemal once successfully broke the Greek lines. As early as the first week in April 1921 Harington was assessing the prospects of holding the approaches to Üsküdar and the Sea of Marmara, should the Kemalists pursue the Greeks back down the railway route from Eskişehir to Haydarpaša.[31]

Four months later a twenty-two-day battle was fought along the river Sakarya, barely fifty miles from Ankara. Rumbold hoped the

Greeks and Kemalists would exhaust each other, allowing the British and the Sultan to come forward as mediators. The Greeks were indeed exhausted, but not the Turks, who knew the terrain and the climate. Over the following winter Kemal was able to draw on new resources and create a formidable army out of the desperate defenders who had triumphed along the Sakarya. On 26 August 1922 Kemal launched, in person, a surprise offensive against Greek positions in the mountains, 200 miles inland from Smyrna. General Harington's warnings to London were justified. Within a fortnight Kemal had gained an outright victory. By 13 September a wall of fire two miles long was consuming the Greek and Armenian quarters of Smyrna. Nearly a quarter of a million Christians and Jews sought refuge aboard the foreign warships which lay off the burning city.[32]

The magnitude of Kemal's victory left the fate of the Ottomans in his hands. His immediate objectives were clear: the replacement of the Treaty of Sèvres by a new settlement which would restore to the Turkish people the cities they knew as İstanbul and Edirne. His troops pressed forward towards the Dardanelles, entering a neutral zone established by the Treaty of Sèvres, some fifty miles in depth and based upon Çanakkale, 'Chanak' as it was generally called during these critical weeks. The flags of the three Allies – Great Britain, France and Italy – flew over the quay at Chanak, but in reality only a token British force was deployed around the town. A single infantry battalion, a squadron of Hussars, and an artillery battery protected Britain's foothold in Asia Minor, the twelve-mile deep 'Zone of the Straits', although this meagre garrison was supported by three battleships in the Narrows of the Dardanelles. Within ten days of the great fire of Smyrna, British and Turkish troops were ominously facing each other, entrenched behind barbed wire close to the excavations of ancient Troy. Throughout the third and fourth weeks of September 1922 there were alarmist headlines in the British press. War between Great Britain and Kemalist Turkey seemed imminent.[33]

It was avoided by the common sense and moderation of General Tim Harington and Sir Horace Rumbold. Harington declined to present an ultimatum from Lloyd George's cabinet to the Nationalists, as he thought it would 'put a match' to the crisis; and Rumbold induced Turkish delegates to come to Mudanya and discuss there the future of the Straits and eastern Thrace, and the need for the Kemalists to respect the Neutral Zone. After ten days of talks at Mudanya a formal convention was signed on 11 October, providing for the withdrawal of Kemal's troops from the Neutral Zone and leaving the Allies in occupation of Constantinople, Chanak and the Gallipoli peninsula, pending the negotiation of a new peace treaty to replace Sèvres. At first it was thought the negotiations would be held in Venice, but Italy was convulsed by the political crisis which, at the end of October, brought Mussolini to power and inaugurated the 'Fascist Era'. It was agreed instead that the peace conference would meet at Lausanne.[34]

During the talks at Mudanya, there was still technically an imperial sovereign of the Ottoman Empire. But by now the Sultan's dominions had contracted to what Mehmed VI Vahideddin could see about him as he strolled around his Yildiz parkland. Mustafa Kemal, ever a realist, regarded the Sultanate as an anachronistic institution, to be swept away with the autumn leaves. But, though no member of the Nationalist inner circle wished to keep Vahideddin on the throne, there were several who still respected the traditions of Sultanate and Caliphate. They feared that any drastic constitutional change favouring the growth of republicanism would alienate the Faithful; nowhere in the world was there, in 1922, an Islamic republic. For the moment, Kemal was prepared not to force the issue. He appointed his close friend Colonel Refet Pasha as Military Governor of eastern Thrace, with his headquarters in Stamboul. On 19 October Refet crossed the Sea of Marmara from Mudanya in the steamer *Gulnihal* and landed at the quay of Eminonü, beside the Galata Bridge. Festooned arches covered the narrower streets of Stamboul, flags flew from the minarets, banners proclaimed the glory of the Turkish people, reborn by the victories of Ghazi Mustafa Kemal's army. Everywhere the triumph of the Turkish Revolution was celebrated for the next three days.[35]

Everywhere, that is, except at Yildiz. Refet made it clear that he did not acknowledge the Sultan's government, although he had respect for the 'high office of the Caliphate'. When he was received in audience by Mehmed VI he urged him to abdicate. The Sultan, as ever, played for time. His fate was settled by the insistence of the Allies on observing diplomatic protocol; they invited to the Lausanne Conference a delegation from the Grand National Assembly in Ankara, and a delegation from the Sublime Porte. This misguided courtesy so angered the deputies at Ankara that Kemal drafted a motion calling on the Assembly to abolish the Sultanate. An Ottoman prince would hold office as Caliph; the secularist Kemal did not wish to offend the 'Holy Men' who supported him. But henceforth temporal power would be vested in the sovereignty of the Turkish people.[36]

The Grand National Assembly was not a supine institution. When the motion was debated on 1 November, many members were uneasy.

The breach with the past was too drastic. It was Kemal himself who made the decisive speech:

> Gentlemen, sovereignty and Sultanate are not given to anyone by anyone because scholarship proves that they should be, or through discussion or debate. Sovereignty and Sultanate are taken by strength, by power, and by force. It was by force that the sons of Osman seized the sovereignty and Sultanate of the Turkish nation; they have maintained this usurpation for six centuries. Now the Turkish nation has rebelled, has put a stop to these usurpers, and has effectively taken sovereignty and Sultanate into its own hands. This is an accomplished fact. The question under discussion is not whether or not we should leave Sultanate and sovereignty to the nation. That is already an accomplished fact – the question is merely how to give expression to it.[37]

Five years later Kemal recalled how 'finally the chairman put the motion to the vote and announced that it had been unanimously accepted. Only one opposing voice was heard saying "I am against it" . . . In this way, gentlemen, the final obsequies of the decline and fall of the Ottoman Sultanate were completed.'

On 4 November Tevfik surrendered to the Sultan-Caliph the seals of office of the last Government of the Ottoman Empire; and on the following Friday Mehmed VI heard the muezzin call for prayers for him as Caliph, no longer as sovereign too. The experience unnerved him; he had no wish to be in Constantinople for another Friday *selamlik*. With most of his personal suite deserting him, he turned for help to General Harington: 'Considering my life in danger in Constantinople, I take refuge with the British Government and request my transfer as soon as possible from Constantinople to another place,' he wrote in a note to the General dated 16 November 1922 and signed, significantly, 'Mehmed Vahideddin, Caliph of the Mussulmans'.[38] Once approval had been telegraphed from London, Harington's staff perfected elaborate plans for whisking the last of the Sultans secretly away from Yildiz on the following Friday morning, long before the *selamlik*.

It was never likely that Mehmed VI would be able to make a dignified departure, worthy of the heir to six centuries of sovereignty. No one, however, could have predicted that his exit would be quite so Chaplinesque.[39] The plans were, in themselves, perfect. On Thursday evening Mehmed told his staff he would sleep at the Meraşim Kiosk in the Yildiz complex, which was close to a gate adjoining barracks where Harington had quartered the Grenadier Guards. The weather was wet and blustery: on the Friday morning, had they been awake, the spies employed by Refet Pasha to keep watch on the deposed ruler might have thought it curious that a detachment of Grenadiers should have been drilling in the pouring rain, more than an hour before dawn. They might also have found it odd that two ambulances should be waiting on the edge of the parade ground. A party of eleven men emerged through the gate into the Yildiz unobserved; but a Turkish naval officer under Refet's orders recognized the sexagenarian who was helped into the first of the ambulances, which drove away as soon as the umbrella of its distinguished passenger could be extricated from the door in which it was wedged. Most of the party, and some heavy trunks, went aboard the second ambulance, which left ten minutes later.

The Turkish naval officer hurriedly threw on some clothes and, still wearing carpet slippers, began running through the rainswept streets towards the Galata Bridge and Refet's headquarters in Stamboul. He does not seem to have observed the small group waiting on the naval quay near the Dolmabahche, prominent among whom were General Harington and the British chargé d'affaires, Nevile Henderson (who was to be ambassador in Berlin when the Second World War broke out). The second ambulance arrived safely: but, to the dignitaries' consternation, the first ambulance, with the fallen Sultan aboard, had gone missing. When it eventually appeared, to the relief of Harington and Henderson, the driver explained that a tyre had punctured, and he had been forced to change a wheel in a dark side-street in pouring rain. A naval launch carried the Sultan and his suite with greater dignity out to HMS *Malaya*, lying with steam up off the Golden Horn. As the launch drew near to the battleship, Mehmed Vahededdin had one final request for General Harington: would he please take care of the five wives left behind at Yildiz, and send them on? By nine o'clock in the morning, while Refet was trying to reassure his distraught agent in the rain-soaked carpet slippers, *Malaya* was steaming out into the Sea of Marmara. Would His Imperial Majesty be content to sail to Malta, Henderson had asked? No objection was raised. When at noon the muezzin called the faithful to the *selamlik* prayers, the battleship was ploughing through heavy seas towards the Dardanelles. Once more 'the bird had flown'. For this migrant, there would be no return.

EPILOGUE:

Ottomans Moribund

Imperial Ottoman sovereignty was dead: the vestigial authority of the dynasty was not. It lingered for fifteen months in a changing world, delaying the emergence of the Turkish Republic, as Kemal sought to find a compromise which would have retained a made-to-measure Ottoman caliphate as a symbol of cohesion and spiritual unity in the strictly secularized state which he was creating. This proved to be an impossible objective, at variance with the whole character of Islam.

As soon as news of Mehmed VI's flight was confirmed in Ankara, the Minister of Religious Affairs issued a *fetva* of deposition: Mehmed was accused of abandoning the Caliphate in collusion with Turkey's enemies on the eve of the opening of the Lausanne conference summoned to revise the peace settlement.[1] Next day the Grand National Assembly elected Abdulaziz's eldest surviving son, Abdulmecid II, to succeed his cousin as Caliph. The new leader of the Faithful was an amiable aesthete in his mid-fifties. Twenty-two years before, he had achieved a unique distinction for an Ottoman prince when one of his paintings was exhibited at the Paris Salon. Politics held no interest for him. He had rejected approaches from Talaat in the summer of 1918 and from Mustafa Kemal two years later. When, on 24 November, he was invested as Caliph, there was no *kiliç kuşanmaci* out at Eyüp, with all the pomp of sword-girding. George Young, the only British observer of the investiture in the Topkapi Sarayi, thought the ceremony a travesty: 'a delegation of Angora deputies notifying an elderly dilettante that he has been elected by a majority vote like any Labour leader,' Young wrote. As for the new Caliph himself, Abdulmecid seemed 'a portly person in a fez, frock-coat and green ribbon'. Refet Pasha, Kemal's representative at the investiture, watched Abdulmecid like 'a sparrow-hawk,' Young thought: 'The Caliph has been denied his Sword of

Othman, but he has been given his Sword of Damocles', he commented.[2] Perhaps so; but Abdulmecid seemed content with Refet's role. Despite the traditional Muslim taboo on the artistic representation of living things, he even painted Refet's portrait.

The investiture emphasized the anachronistic character of Turkey's international status during the Lausanne negotiations. Islamic states were basically theocratic: their sovereigns received temporal power from God, reigning thereafter as His trustee on earth; a republic, on the other hand, was a secular institution created by the godless Infidel and as yet unknown in the Islamic world. If the Ottoman Sultanate had ceased to exist, Muslim purists might argue that the head of state was the Caliph, a prince ordained to defend the faith in a community where the business of government was left in other hands; and when the new Caliph adopted an Imperial style of life, signing himself 'Abdulmecid bin Abdullah Han' as if to emphasize his Ottoman heredity, the *ulema* gave their spiritual leader full support, even beyond some of the frontiers of the new Turkey. Traditionally the name of the ruler was invoked each Friday in the allocution at the midday prayers: from the end of November 1922 that religious courtesy was accorded to Caliph Abdulmecid II, not only in Turkish mosques, but in Baghdad and throughout all the former Ottoman vilayets of Iraq. The Caliphate was a supra-national institution; and the more conservative deputies in the Grand National Assembly argued that its retention gave the new Turkey world status as a leader of Islam. To abolish it would, they declared, 'be an action totally incompatible with reason, loyalty and national feeling'.[3]

Mustafa Kemal had every intention of cultivating nationalist sentiment, but he wished it to be patriotically Turkish in character, rather than Islamic. Under his instructions Ismet Pasha – the later President, Ismet Inönü – sought to convince the British, French and Italian delegates at the Lausanne Conference that the Ankara Government favoured the creation of a homogeneous Turkish national state, which would be both free from outside interference and disinclined to embark on foreign adventures of its own. Those National Assembly deputies who championed the Caliphate therefore threatened to make Ismet's task more difficult; and it is hardly surprising that the Turkish delegation to the Conference was determined to concentrate on purely secular issues. So, too, by now, were the old wartime Allies. British backing for an Arab caliphate effectively went down with Kitchener, in the wreck of HMS *Hampshire*, for more knowledgeable specialists in Arab affairs convinced Whitehall that a caliph could never be simply a spiritual leader, like a post-1870 pope (as Kitchener seems to have believed); no imperial Power asserting sovereignty over the Indian subcontinent could welcome the association of Muslim peoples under a single caliph, in whatever country he resided. Throughout the seven months of negotiations at Lausanne, both Ankara and London preferred to ignore the existence of the Caliphate.

Ismet's efforts were, in the end, astonishingly successful.[4] The principal task of the conference was to replace the Treaty of Sèvres by a negotiated settlement which would both recognize the transition from Ottoman rule to national sovereignty in the Middle East, and safeguard the new Turkey's foothold in Europe. The Treaty of Lausanne – signed on 24 July 1923 – accepted the division of Thrace, with the river Maritsa forming a frontier between Greece and Turkey, but with Edirne confirmed as a Turkish city. Greece's tragic misadventure in Asia Minor was at an end: the Turks retained Smyrna and its hinterland in full sovereignty, as well as the islands of Tenedos and Imbros and the shores of the Dardanelles and the Bosphorus, although there were to be demilitarized zones on the Straits as well as along the Thracian frontier. No Arab lands were claimed by the Turkish delegates, but an attempt was made to recover some of the predominantly Kurdish districts around Mosul, and it was not until 1926 that the League of Nations finally decided Mosul should remain in British-mandated Iraq, with Turkey promised ten per cent of the revenue from the British-owned oilfields of the region. The greatest problems at Lausanne were caused by the attempts of the British and French, and to a lesser extent the Italians, to reimpose Capitulations and other forms of financial control and economic supervision. So deep was the conflict over this question that the conference broke down in the first week of February 1923 and did not reconvene until the last week in April. Ultimately Ismet's wishes prevailed. The Capitulations were discarded for all time and, apart from a temporary limitation on Turkish tariff rates, the Ankara Government was left free to prepare its own economic plans. Unlike Germany, Austria, Hungary or Bulgaria, Kemal's Turkey was not required to pay reparations to the victorious Allies.

Some questions went unresolved at Lausanne. Talks over the future fate of the Turkish and Greek minorities antedated the first sessions of the Conference, but it was not until after the Lausanne Treaty was ratified that bilateral agreements between Ankara and Athens provided for an exchange of populations. More than a million Greeks left Asia Minor; some 350,000 Turks emigrated from Macedonia to seek a new life in Anatolia. Both these uprooted communities suffered great hardship from the drawing of the new frontier lines.

So, too, in a different way, did two other nationalities, ancient enemies of one another. The claims of the Armenians and the Kurds were virtually ignored at the Conference. Nothing more was heard of an independent Armenia, nor of an autonomous Kurdistan.[5] Proposals were put forward for the creation of an Armenian 'National Home', but the Turks refused to consider the matter and it was not pressed by the French or the British. The Armenians therefore remained a divided people, some in the Soviet Union, many settling in Syria and Lebanon, others keeping their heads down in the city which was now known as İstanbul. The Kurds, on the other hand, technically became a 'non-people' in Kemal's national state, where they were identified quite simply as 'mountain Turks'. A Kurdish rebellion two years after the signing of the treaty was brutally suppressed. There were further risings in 1929 and 1930, while in 1987 the guerrilla campaign initiated by the PKK (Kurdish Workers' Party) in south-eastern Turkey led to the imposition of martial law in eight of modern Turkey's seventy-one provinces; and the terrible cycle of terrorism and repression has continued into the last decade of the century. Like the Armenians, the Kurds were a people split asunder by the frontiers of the post-Ottoman map of the Middle East; and their sufferings were intensified by a thirty-year struggle in Iraq (where in 1961 the Kurdish minority formed a fifth of the population).

In three respects the Lausanne terms disappointed the Grand National Assembly in Ankara. There was some resentment at the creation of an International Straits Commission, based at İstanbul and committed to upholding freedom of navigation along the great waterway linking the Black Sea and the Mediterranean. Other deputies regretted the failure to secure Mosul, and criticized the inclusion in French-mandated Syria of the district of Hatay, with the port of İskenderun and the historic city of Antioch (Antakya). But in an assembly of two hundred and fifty delegates, only fourteen voted against ratification of the Lausanne Treaty.[6]

Ismet's success at Lausanne enabled Kemal to seal his revolution. Within ten weeks of the signing of the treaty, the Allied occupation of the Ottoman capital came to an end, General Tim Harington leaving a city in which he had enjoyed astonishing popularity. On 2 October 1923 a battalion of the Coldstream Guards paraded in the square outside the Caliph's residence, the Dolmabahche Palace, before boarding the troop-ship *Arabic*, at anchor in the Bosphorus.[7] Turkish troops marched back into İstanbul four days later. Their reception was, however, not as warm as the Nationalists had anticipated, possibly because Kemal never hid his mistrust of the Sultans' capital, with its notorious record of political intrigue and corruption. Less than a fortnight later, the imperial city was deposed. On 13 October the Grand National Assembly adopted a constitutional amendment, proposed four days earlier by Ismet Pasha, declaring that 'Ankara is the seat of government of the Turkish State'. Finally, on the evening of 29 October the Assembly resolved that 'the form of government of the Turkish State is a Republic'. Within a quarter of an hour the Assembly elected Mustafa Kemal as Turkey's first President, thereby confirming the national leadership he had exercised for the past four years.[8]

Abdulmecid II may, perhaps, have envisaged a dual system, with İstanbul providing a home for the Caliphate while all the business of politics took place in central Anatolia. If so, he was swiftly disillusioned. The Republic was only eleven weeks old when a stern Presidential rebuke warned him not to follow 'the path of his ancestors the Sultans'; as Kemal explained, 'We cannot sacrifice the Republic of Turkey for the sake of courtesy or sophistry. The Caliph must be content to know who he is and what his office is.'[9] But what exactly was this office? That problem perplexed two prominent Muslims on the Indian subcontinent, Ameer Ali and the Aga Khan, who wrote to Ismet, now Turkey's Prime Minister, recommending that the Republic should bestow a special international status on the Caliphate since it 'commanded the confidence and esteem of the Muslim peoples'. The letter, leaked to the press ahead of its arrival at Ankara, was exploited by the President. The Assembly was told that, so long as the Caliphate was retained in İstanbul, it would provide outsiders with an opportunity to interfere in Turkey's internal affairs. Conversely, abolition of the Caliphate would 'enrich the Islamic religion', enabling the Republic to purge the *ulema*. Dutifully the National Assembly voted for the final breach with the Ottoman past: on 3 March 1924 the Caliphate was abolished, Abdulmecid II formally deposed, and all members of the former ruling dynasty expelled from the Turkish Republic.[10]

Abdulmecid was hustled out of the Dolmabahche next morning before the newspapers announcing his deposition could go on sale in the streets. A car sped him to Chatalja, well outside the sprawling city. There he waited throughout that Tuesday, while other members of the family were brought to the small town. In the evening the most famous of Balkan locomotives stopped briefly at Chatalja; and it was aboard the Orient Express that the Ottomans were carried, bag and baggage, into Europe.[11]

No leading Ottoman politician served the new Republic. Nor, indeed, did any ministers who had held office under the Young Turk regime. Most were already dead. Enver, clinging still to his ideal of an independent Turkestan in Central Asia, was killed in 1922 during an obscure cavalry skirmish with the Red Army; and by then Cemal, Said Halim and Talaat had all been assassinated in exile by Armenian extremists, seeking to avenge the sufferings of their compatriots. Two prominent Young Turks of the pre-war period, Mehmed Cavit and Dr Nazim, chose to remain in the Republic and in 1926 were, on the flimsiest evidence, found guilty of alleged conspiracy to kill President Kemal; they were publicly hanged in the centre of Ankara. More than a dozen lesser luminaries of the old CUP sat as deputies in the Grand National Assembly. Apart from Ismet himself, they gained no particular distinction in the chamber.[12]

Yet the Ottoman dynasty left a greater legacy in the Middle East than either the Turkish Republic or its other successor states cared to acknowledge.[13] *Tanzimat* restructuring had made possible the emergence of a well-educated bureaucracy, trained as civil servants at the *Mülkiye*, and a highly professional officer corps, graduates of the war college, the *Harbiye*. The remarkable programme of modernization achieved in Kemal's Turkey would have been impossible without the skills of administrative officials from the *Mülkiye*; and it might well be argued that the final vindication of *Harbiye* teaching came as late as November 1950, when the Turkish brigade serving in Korea met the first onslaught of the Chinese Red Army with disciplined good order. Ottoman-trained personnel administered Syria, Lebanon, Transjordan and to a lesser extent Iraq between the two world wars, often in conflict with the mandatory powers, France and Britain; and the Ottoman military tradition remained strong among the armies of all the Middle Eastern states, even in the Free Officers' Committee which became the powerhouse of Egypt's national revolution. The *Mecelle*, the code of law drawn up in the early 1870s to help modernize the empire, provided a framework for the Turkish republic too, although the civil code promulgated in 1926 also borrowed extensively from Swiss practice. Outside republican Turkey, the *Mecelle* remained a model for all communities seeking to reconcile Islamic traditions with Western legal concepts. In many parts of the old Ottoman Empire, local government was little changed until mid-century. Nor, indeed, was the influence of the absentee landowning political élite, who simply transferred their service from the Ottomans to the successor governments. These 'notables' were thus able to bring a surprising stability into what appeared on the map to be a fragmented region; they maintained a delicate balance of power until a new generation succeeded them during the very years when the old European governments ceased to dominate the region. A shadow Ottoman paternalism long outlived the empire of the Sultans.

Why, then, did the Ottoman Empire, which had survived so many challenges to its existence, finally fall in the aftermath of the First World War? The Kemalists were prepared to advance a determinist theory of history which was almost as mechanical as the workings of Marxist dialectic. They gloried in the Asiatic origins of the Turkish people and argued that, once the Sultans had crossed into Europe and accepted the role of legatees for the Byzantine Emperors, they became ensnared by their new acquisitions; the inheritance fatally weakened what was essentially a warrior empire, and the House of Osman was therefore doomed from the moment it settled on the shores of the Bosphorus. There is some truth behind this much simplified thesis. For as long as the Empire was expanding, Constantinople served as the natural base for the penetration of the Balkan peninsula and the Danube Basin; but as the Ottoman lands receded the city became a dangerously exposed foothold on an alien continent. Some later Sultans, notably Abdulhamid II, accepted that the Empire still had a mission to fulfil in Asia and, less certainly, in North Africa; but they could not shake off the bonds of Rumelia. Had these later Sultans not been encumbered by their European inheritance, they could have developed the resources of Anatolia, Mesopotamia and the Levant for the profit of their empire. An enlightened Sultan could thus have brought stable government and effective administration to those regions of the Middle East where, even without the benefit of such improbably wise rule, Ottoman habits and traditions survived for almost half a century after the fall of the dynasty.

Theorizing of this nature is, of course, idle speculation. More relevant to the question is the relationship between the Sultanate and Islam; the essentially religious basis of the Ottoman State gave the empire both its strength and its weakness. That 'firm grasp on the strong cord of the law of Muhammad', of which Mustafa Koçi wrote in the early seventeenth century,[14] enabled the sultans to draw on the religious loyalty of their peoples in a succession of foreign wars against infidel Christians; and, so long as government could be seen to rest upon the *şeriat*, the *ulema* formed staunch pillars of the state. But the Western European revolutionary years at the end of the eighteenth century allowed new concepts of centralized government to filter into the Ottoman Empire. Thereafter the politics of the laity increasingly encroached on prerogatives tenaciously held by the religious hierarchy, raising doubts over the viability in an Ottoman state of such westernized institutions as a conscript army or a parliament. Yet, just as the sultans looked to preserve both their European and their Asian lands, so too they sought the best of both worlds, secular and spiritual. The claims of the Ottoman Caliphate were never so strongly asserted as in the late nineteenth and early twentieth centuries, even though these were the decades in which a sceptical intellectualism and a popular Turkish nationalism made the greatest inroads on traditional ways of thought and behaviour. The incomplete Young Turk revolution destroyed the Sultan's autocracy and championed the concept of religious disestablishment without finding adequate alternatives, political or spiritual, before plunging the empire into a disastrous war from which wiser councillors might have stood aside, as did Ismet Inönü's government a quarter of a century later. Fear of Mustafa Kemal's veiled laicism led in April 1920 to the proscription of the National movement by the Sultan-Caliph and the *şeyhülislâm*, thus emphasizing how remote were the sovereign and the spiritual leader from their peoples. When, four months later, Mehmed authorized the signing of the Sèvres Treaty, he distanced himself still further from his subjects.

'May God preserve us from such a weak-kneed Sultan,' Ali Hayder, an Arabian prince loyal to the dynasty, wrote in his journal when he heard of Mehmed VI's flight. 'The Turkish Imperial Family are largely to blame' for the 'disintegration' of the Muslim world, Ali added in a later diary entry.[15] Although it remains unfashionable to stress the influence of individual rulers on great events, there is no doubt that the Ottomans were ill-served by Abdulhamid's successors. Significantly, once he had sailed off to Malta, the last Sultan was content to drop out of the pages of history. He settled in San Remo, on the Italian Riviera, making no attempt to establish a court-in-exile. Only once did his movements arouse even passing interest and that was when, soon after his deposition, he decided to go on pilgrimage to Mecca. Thus, so he believed, he would fulfil an obligation binding on every good Muslim and shamefully neglected by all thirty-five of his predecessors on the throne.

Yet, even though he no longer ruled as Sultan or Caliph, those knees remained pathetically weak. Mehmed VI duly sailed through the Suez Canal and disembarked at Jeddah. He made the fifty-four-mile journey from the coast into the barren valleys of the limestone hills, and saw for himself the Great Mosque around the sacred Kaaba. But he did not wait to perform the full pilgrimage at the Sacred House, with its sevenfold

OTTOMAN SULTANS

```
 1 Osman  I     c.1280-1326
 2 Orhan         1326-1359
 3 Murat  I      1359-1389
 4 Bayezit I     1389-1402
        Interregnum
 5 Mehmet I      1413-1421
 6 Murat  II     1421-1451
 7 Mehmet II(1444)1451-1481
 8 Bayezit II*   1481-1512
 9 Selim  I      1512-1520
10 Süleyman I    1520-1566
11 Selim  II     1566-1574
12 Murat  III    1574-1595
13 Mehmet III    1595-1603
```

Direct succession father to son

Ahmet I 1603-17   15 Mustafa I 1617-18 & 1622-23*

16 Osman II*!   17 Murat IV   18 İbrahim*!
  1618-22   1623-40   1640-48   48 ?

19 Mehmet IV*   20 Süleyman II   21 Ahmet II
  1648-87   1687-91   1691-95

22 Mustafa II 1695-1703*   23 Ahmet III 1703-30*

24 Mahmut I 1730-54   25 Osman III 1754-57

26 Mustafa III 1757-74   27 Abdulhamit I 1774-89   88 ?

28 Selim III 1789-1807*!

29 Mustafa IV 1807-08*!   30 Mahmut II 1808-39

31 Abdulmecit I 1839-61   32 Abdulaziz 1861-76*

urat V* 34 Abdulhamit II* 35 Mehmet V 36 Mehmet VI*
876   1876-1909   1909-18   1918-22

        Abdulmecit II (Caliph only) 1922-24*

* Deposed   ! Murdered
```
```

circumambulation of the Kaaba and the contrite kissing of the black stone. While Mehmed was in Mecca, he heard that his one-time rebellious vassal, King Hussein of the Hejaz, was again seeking to secure for himself the title of Caliph. Rather than risk being caught up in the intrigues of Arabian politics, the ex-Sultan hurried back to his sanctuary in Mussolini's Italy. There he died on 15 May 1926, three months after his sixty-fifth birthday. He was the first Sultan since the fall of Constantinople who could not be buried in the city which his namesake had conquered; but French mandatory officialdom relented, allowing his body to be brought to territory over which he was briefly the ruler. His tomb lies in Damascus.[16]

A stranger fate was reserved for the last Ottoman Caliph. While Mehmed VI survived his deposition for only forty-two months, Abdulmecid II had more than twenty years of exile ahead of him when he stepped down from the Orient Express; as a man of exquisite culture, he chose to spend his last days in Paris, the city where his artistry had once been exhibited. He lived quietly, virtually forgotten in the inter-war world of strutting dictators, and he lived longer than any previous head of the Ottoman dynasty. When death came to him in his seventy-seventh year, his passing went unnoticed in the wider world, not even a brief obituary being slipped into *The Times* of London.[17] But this is hardly surprising: Abdulmecid died on 23 August 1944 – an abnormal day in the history of Paris, with the Grand Palais in flames as Free French tanks and American infantry hurried to liberate his chosen city of exile from Nazi occupation. As if to atone for upstaging Abdulmecid's final exit, the Allied authorities gave permission for his body to be conveyed to the second Holy City of Islam. Alone among Ottoman rulers, the last Caliph was interred at Medina.

Sultans Since the Ottoman Capture of Constantinople

Mehmed II	reigned 1444–1481
Bayazed II	1481–1512
Selim I	1512–1520
Suleiman I, the Magnificent	1520–1566
Selim II, the Sot	1566–1574
Murad III	1574–1595
Mehmed III	1595–1603
Ahmed I	1603–1617
Mustafa I	1617–1618 & 1622–1623
Osman II	1618–1622
Murad IV	1623–1640
Ibrahim	1640–1649
Mehmed IV	1649–1687
Suleiman II	1687–1691
Ahmed II	1691–1695
Mustafa II	1695–1703
Ahmed III	1703–1730
Mahmud I	1730–1754
Osman III	1754–1757
Mustafa III	1757–1774
Abdulhamid I	1774–1788
Selim III	1788–1807
Mustafa IV	1807–1808
Mahmud II	1808–1839
Abdulmecid I	1839–1861
Abdulaziz	1861–1876
Murad V	1876
Abdulhamid II	1876–1909
Mehmed V	1909–1918
Mehmed VI Vahideddin	1918–1922
Caliph Abdulmecid (II)	1922–1924

Alternative Place Names

Versions printed first are those generally used in the book.

Aleppo	Halab
Ankara	Angora
Brusa	Bursa
Chanak	Çanakkale
Constantinople	İstanbul
Dedeagatch	Alexandroúpolis
Edirne	Adrianople
Gallipoli	Gelibolu
Ioánnina	Janinà
İskenderun	Alexandretta
Jassy	Iaşi
Karlowitz	Sremski Karlovici
Kuchuk Kainardji	Kainardzhi
Lepanto	Návpaktos
Monastir	Bitola
Mudanya	Mudaniya (Mundanya)
Peloponnese	(The) Morea
Pera/Galata	Beyoğlu
Plovdiv	Philippopolis
Prinkipo	Büyükada
Ruschuk	Ruşe
Salonika	Thessaloniki
San Stefano	Yesilköy
Scutari (Albania)	Shkodra
Smyrna	İzmir
Tenedos	Bozcaada
Trebizond	Trabzon
Üsküb	Skopje
Üsküdar	Scutari (Turkey)

Glossary

*:'ş' is sometimes transliterated 'sh'

aga: chief palace official; commander

akinji: irregular horsemen in early Ottoman armies

Bab-i Âli: 'the high gate', 'Sublime Porte'; administrative office of the Grand Vizier

bailo: ambassador of the Venetian republic

başi bozuka: 'bashibazooks'; irregular military volunteers employed in Balkans in late XIXth century

bayrakdar: standard bearer

bey: a vassal ruler in early Ottoman empire; later, the governor of a *sanjak*

beylerbey: provincial governor (of a *beylerbik*)

caliph: (Arabic, *khalifa*), 'Succesor to the Prophet'

Capitulations: system of extraterritorial jurisdiction and favoured trade tariffs established by bilateral treaties

ceşme: fountain

devşirme : tribute of Christian boys for conversion to Islam and service to the Sultan, raised from conquered Balkan lands mid-XVIIth century

Divan: Sultan's imperial council and court of law

dragoman: interpreter to a foreign envoy

Effendi: Turkish title of respect

Ethnike Hetairia: Greek nationalist society in late XIXth century

evkaf (sing. *vakif*): Muslim religious charitable endowments

firman: imperial edict (later replaced by *irade*)

fetva: legal opinion given by a mufti skilled in Muslim Holy Law

Galatasaray: Imperial *lycée*; school opened in 1869; also known as *Mekteb-i Sultani*

Ghazi: honorific title denoting a warrior hero of Islam

Grand Vizier: Sultan's chief minister

haiduk (hajduk): Balkan bandit, generally a Bulgar or Serb

hamidiye: auxiliary gendarmerie, mainly of Kurds, raised by Abdulhamid II

hafiye: secret police

hamam: bath

Harbiye: Military Academy in Pera

Glossary

harem: women in the Sultan's household; their part of a house
hatt-i hümayun: imperial rescript (decree)
hospodar: governor of Wallachia–Moldavia
Hümbaraciyan: bombardier corps
ilmiye: religious cultural institution, constituting the Muslim 'Establishment'
iltizam: tax farm
imam: prayer leader in mosque
irade: imperial order (successor of firman)
Janissaries: *Yeni Çeri*; Sultan's standing army, an élite corps until 1826
jihad: A Holy War against the Infidel
jurnalcis: police informers
kafe: 'cage'; guarded palace apartments where Ottoman princes lived as virtual
　　prisoners
kaimakan: deputy Grand Vizier
kaime: paper money
kapetanate: powerful Muslim ruling military caste in Bosnia
Kapudan Pasha: Grand Admiral
Khedive: Ottoman vassal ruler in Egypt, 1867–1914
kiliç kuşanmaci: sword-girding ceremony, equivalent to a sultan's coronation
klephts: Greek bandits
Lale Devri: 'Tulip Era' (1718–30)
madresse: Muslim college of higher education
Mamelukes: Originally slaves, became ruling caste in Egypt
Mecelle: Ottoman code of civil law, issued 1869–78
Meclis-i Ayan: Chamber of Notables; Senate (upper house of Ottoman
　　parliament)
Meclis-i Mebusan: Chamber of Deputies (lower house of Ottoman
　　parliament)
'*Mehmedchik*': nickname given to Ottoman private soldiery (cf. 'Tommy
　　Atkins', 'poilu' etc.)
millet: legal status given to a recognized religious sect (Orthodox Christians;
　　Jews, etc.); later signifies a nation
mufti: an expounder of Muslim Holy Law
Mulkiye: Ottoman civil service school (*Mekteb-i Mulkiye*)
mullah: high ranking Muslim judge and member of the *ulema*
namaz: The offering of prayers
Nizam-i Cedid: 'New Order' of Sultan Selim III, especially his reformed army
orta: battalion of Janissaries
Pasha: courtesy title for a senior official
Philike Hetairia: Society of Friends, a Greek nationalist movement
Porte: short for 'Sublime Porte; see *Bab-i Âli*
redif: military reservists
rusdiye: secondary schools
sancaci şerif: Holy banner of Islam
sanjak: Local administrative unit, a county
sarayi (sarai): palace
segban-i cedit: military bodyguard; 'keepers of the hounds'
selamlik: The gathering of men at the ceremony of midday Friday prayers

serdengeçi: crack Janissary infantry assault force

şeriat: Islamic Holy Law, regulating the Muslim code of behaviour

şeyhülislâm: Grand Mufti; head of Muslim hierarchy in Ottoman Empire

Shi'ites: fundamentalist Islamic believers; practitioners of Shi'a

silahtar: Imperial bodyguard of Janissary dragoons

sipahi: cavalryman, originally the holder of a *timar* or a horseman in the Sultan's lifeguards

Sublime Porte: see *Bab-i Âli*

Sunni (Sunnites): orthodox Muslim worshippers

tanzimat: re-structuring of government: XIXth century reform era

timar: grant of revenue received from a particular area of land (but not the freehold of the land)

turbe: mausoleum

ulema: Muslim hierarchy

Valide Sultana: reigning Sultan's mother

vladika: Montenegrin Prince-Bishop

vilayet: province

yamak: Young Janissary mercenaries

Notes

ABREVIATIONS USED IN THE NOTES

Add. MSS: Additional Manuscripts in the British Library.

Ahmad: Feroz Ahmad, *The Young Turks*

Alderson: A. D. Alderson, *The Structure of the Ottoman Dynasty*

Anderson: M. S. Anderson, *The Eastern Question*

Barker: T. M. Barker, *Double Eagle and Crescent*

BDD: G. P. Gooch and H. Temperley, *British Documents on the Origins of the War, 1898–1914*

Cemal: Djemal Pasha, *Memoirs of a Turkish Statesman*

Corr. Nap.: *Correspondance de Napoléon I*

Davison, *Essays*: R. Davison, *Essays in Ottoman and Turkish History*.

Davison, *Reform*: R. Davison, *Reform in the Ottoman Empire, 1856–1876*

DBF: *Documents of British Foreign Policy, Series I*

DDF: *Documents Diplomatiques Françaises*, série 2 or 3

DDI: *I Documenti Diplomatici italiani*

EI i: *The Encyclopaedia of Islam*, first ed., 1913–1938

EI ii: *The Encyclopedia of Islam*, second ed., 1954–

FO: Foreign Office Papers in the Public Record Office.

Gibb and Bowen: Sir Hamilton Gibb and H. Bowen, *Islamic Society and the West*

GP: J. Lepsius, A. Mendelssohn Bartholdy, F. Thimme, *Die Grosse Politik der europäischen Kabinette*

HJ: *Historical Journal* (Cambridge)

Hinsley: F. H. Hinsley (ed.), *British Foreign Policy under Sir Edward Grey*

Hurewitz: J. C. Hurewitz, *Diplomacy in the Near and Middle East, A Documentary Record*

IJMES: *International Journal of Middle East Studies*

JMH: *Journal of Modern History*

Kedourie: E. Kedourie, *England and the Middle East*

Kemal *Sp.*: M. K. Atatürk, *Speech delivered by Ghazi Mustapha Kemal, October 1927*

Kent: Marian Kent (ed.), *The Great Powers and the End of the Ottoman Empire*

Langer: W. L. Langer, *The Diplomacy of Imperialism* (rev. single volume edition)

Lewis: Bernard Lewis, *The Emergence of Modern Turkey*

L-P: Stanley Lane-Poole, *Life . . . of Viscount Stratford de Redcliffe*

PRO: Public Record Office, Kew.

SEER: *Slavic and East European Review*

Shaw *Between*: S.J. Shaw, *Between Old and New: The Ottoman Empire under Sultan Selim III*

Shaw, *Gazis*: S.J. Shaw, *History of the Ottoman Empire and Modern Turkey*, vol. 1, *Empire of the Gazis*

Shaws: S.J. Shaw and E.K. Shaw, *History of the Ottoman Empire and Modern Turkey*, vol. 2, *The Rise of Modern Turkey*.

Sumner: B.H. Sumner, *Russia and the Balkans*

Temp.: H.W.V. Temperley, *Britain and the Near East; The Crimea*

Trump.: Ulrich Trumpener, *Germany and the Ottoman Empire, 1914–1918*

Prologue: Ottomans Triumphant

1. 'Dreadful happening', cited from Agarathos monastery codex by Steven Runciman in *The Fall of Constantinople 1453*, p. 160. Runciman's account remains the finest study of the event and makes an interesting contrast to chapter 68 of Gibbon's *Decline and Fall of the Roman Empire*. See also Halil Inalcik, 'The Policy of Mehmed II towards the Greek Population of Istanbul and the Byzantine Buildings of the City', *Dumbarton Oaks Papers*, no. 23, pp. 213–49; and, in general, his *The Ottoman Empire, 1300–1600*.
2. Lewis, pp. 317–18; Shaw, *Gazis*, p. 78.
3. N. Machiavelli, *The Prince*, fourth paragraph of Chapter IV.
4. Lewis, pp. 89–92; Shaw, *Gazis*, pp. 159–63; see also the entries in EI i on *timar* and *wakf* (Arabic spelling of *vakif*).
5. Shaw, *Gazis*, pp. 132–49.
6. Alderson, pp. 74–6.
7. Davison, *Essays*, pp. 16–17. Halil Inalcik, 'The Heyday and Decline of the Ottoman Empire' in *Cambridge History of Islam*, I, pp. 324–53. M.A. Cooke (ed.), *A History of the Ottoman Empire to 1730* is a useful selection of relevant chapters from the Cambridge histories. Andrina Stiles, *The Ottoman Empire 1450–1700*, is an excellent and stimulating introduction, a model of compression.

Chapter 1: Floodtide of Islam

1. Barker, pp. 244–5. Thomas M. Barker's book is less well-known than John Stoye's dramatic narrative *The Siege of Vienna*, but with great clarity he puts the whole campaign and its aftermath in a general historical perspective.
2. Ibid., pp. 68–71. The eminent German scholar Franz Babinger contributed a detailed biographical entry on Kara Mustafa to EI i.
3. Count Frosaco's letters, originally printed in *Revue de Hongrie*, III, are cited by Barker, with this extract on p. 257.
4. Stoye, op. cit., and cf. E. Crankshaw, *Maria Theresa*, pp. 121–3.
5. The finest modern account of the battle of the Kahlenberg is in Barker, pp. 321–34.
6. For the diplomat (Benetti) and his report, see N. Barber, *Lords of the Golden Horn*, p. 105.
7. Richard Kreutel, *Kara Mustafa vor Wien*, pp. 121–4 and 184, an annotated translation of a diary kept by an anonymous Ottoman official. Kreutel's work is critically examined by Barker, p. 403 (and cf. p. 364).

Chapter 2: Challenge from the West

1. Barker, pp. 369–70; Lord Kinross, *The Ottoman Centuries*, p. 349.
2. M. A. Cooke (ed.), *Ottoman Empire to 1730*, p. 190; N. Cheetham, *Mediaeval Greece*, pp. 300–1.
3. Shaw, *Gazis*, p. 219; Alderson, pp. 65–6.
4. Ibid., pp. 32–6.
5. Selim II biography in *EI* i; Barber, p. 108.
6. Gibb and Bowen I, pp. 314–28; Nahsom Weissmann, *Les Janissaries*, pp. 30–48.
7. Gibb and Bowen II, pp. 191–2.
8. Shaw, *Gazis*, p. 223; Kinross, op. cit., p. 353; Cooke, op. cit., p. 193.
9. Lord Acton, *Lectures on Modern History*, p. 259.
10. Rifat Abou El-Haj, 'Ottoman Diplomacy at Karlowitz', *Journal of American Oriental Society*, vol. 87 (1967), pp. 498–512; Barker, pp. 373–4; Davison, *Essays*, p. 20; Shaw, *Gazis*, pp. 223–5; Kinross, op. cit., pp. 356–7, 373–6.
11. Alderson, p. 66; Shaw, *Gazis*, p. 228. See also the biographical entry by Bowen on Ahmed III in *EI* ii.
12. Gibb and Bowen II, p. 216 and pp. 233–4; C. A. Frazee, *Christians and Sultans*, pp. 6–7; G. G. Arnakis, 'The Greek church of Constantinople and the Ottoman Empire', *JMH*, vol. 24, September 1952, especially pp. 242–50.
13. A. de la Moutraye, *Travels*, vol. 1, p. 333.
14. Davison, *Essays*, p. 20; Kinross, op. cit., pp. 376 and 383. The saying about the turban seems to have originated with the Byzantine historian Michael Ducas.

Chapter 3: Tulip Time and After

1. Lewis, p. 437; for Koçi Bey, see C. H. Imber's entry on him in *EI* ii, vol. 5.
2. M. L. Shay, *Ottoman Empire from 1720 to 1734*, pp. 17–27; Kinross, *Ottoman Centuries*, p. 378, pp. 380–2.
3. Lewis, pp. 45–6; Shaw, *Gazis*, p. 235.
4. Shay, op. cit., p. 19.
5. Letter to Lady Bristol, 10 April 1718, E. Halsband, *Complete Letters of Lady Mary Wortley Montagu*, vol. 1, p. 397.
6. L. Cassels, *The Struggle for the Ottoman Empire*, p. 52; L. A. Vandal, *Une ambassade française en Orient sous Louis XV*, p. 88.
7. Ibid., p. 85.
8. Shay, op. cit., p. 22.
9. Kinross, *Ottoman Centuries*, p. 380; Shaw, *Gazis*, pp. 234, 293–4.
10. Ibid., pp. 236–7; N. Berkes, *The Development of Secularization in Turkey*, pp. 42–5; M. Daley, *The Turkish Legacy*, pp. 17–24; Lewis, pp. 50–1.
11. Jean-Claude Flachat, *Observations sur le Commerce et sur les arts . . . même des Indes Orientales*, p. 111.
12. Shay, op. cit. (14 January 1724), p. 22.
13. Ibid., p. 23.
14. Ibid., pp. 27–8; Vandal, op. cit., pp. 27–8.
15. Lewis, p. 47.
16. Vandal, op. cit., pp. 116–46. The following paragraphs are based on H. Benedikt, *Der Pascha-Graf Alexander von Bonneval*, especially pp. 82–160.
17. Shaws, *Gazis*, pp. 246–7.
18. Anderson, p. xv; P. M. Holt, *Egypt and the Fertile Crescent*, p. 111; A. Hourani, 'The

Changing Face of the Fertile Crescent in the Eighteenth Century', *Studia Islamica*, 8 (1953), pp. 89–122.

19. For the fullest modern account of the Treaty of Kuchuk Kainardji, see Davison, *Essays*, pp. 29–44. English text, Hurewitz, I, pp. 54–61. For Franz Thugut's report to Vienna of 17 August 1774 see Davison, *Essays*, p. 32, with comments on pp. 43–4.
20. The various forms of the treaty are further discussed by Professor Davison in his paper on 'The Dosografa church in the Treaty of Kuchuk Kainardji', (*Essays*, pp. 51–9), from which I have drawn for the final paragraphs of this chapter. See also his article, 'The Treaty of Kuchuk Kainardji, A Note on the Italian text', *International History Review*, vol. 10, no. 4 (1988), pp. 611–21.

Chapter 4: Western Approaches

1. L. Cassels, *Struggle for the Ottoman Empire*, p. 110; Vandal, *Une ambassade française*, pp. 197 and 291; Kinross, *Ottoman Centuries*, p. 396.
2. W. R. Polk, *The Opening of South Lebanon*, pp. 10–18; P. Holt, *Egypt and the Fertile Crescent*, pp. 120–3.
3. On Ali Pasha in general see: D. N. Skiotis's article, 'From Bandit to Pasha' in *IJMES*, vol. 2 (1971), pp. 219–44; William Plomer's biography, *Ali the Lion*; and G. Remerland's more scholarly study, *Ali de Tekelen, Pasha de Janina*, largely based on French diplomatic archives; Shaw, pp. 253–4.
4. Kinross, op. cit., pp. 410–13; G. S. Thomson, *Catherine the Great and the Expansion of Russia*, pp. 170–93.
5. Anderson, p. 20; Shaw, *Between*, pp. 64–8.
6. Ibid., pp. 14–17, with Louis XVI's letter in full (pp. 16–17).
7. B. Lewis 'The Impact of the French Revolution on Turkey', *Journal of World History*, vol. 1 (1953), pp. 105–25, summarized Lewis, p. 63.
8. Lewis, p. 65.
9. Lewis, p. 59.
10. Alderson, p. 87 and his genealogical table XLIV; see also the article by Deny in *EI* i under 'Valide Sultanlar'. For the more romantic assumptions, See N. Barber, *Lords of the Golden Horn*, pp. 118–19 and, at greater length, B. A. Morton, *The Veiled Empress*, and Lesley Blanch, *The Wilder Shores of Love*.
11. *Corr. Nap.* vol. 1, nos. 61 and 65.
12. Miot, *Mémoires I*, p. 235; J. F. Bernard, *Talleyrand*, pp. 201–4; C. Herold, *Bonaparte in Egypt*, pp. 127–9; D. Chandler, *The Campaigns of Napoleon*, pp. 211–12.
13. *Corr. Nap.* vol. 4, pp. 191–2; Ottoman reactions: Shaw, *Between*, pp. 258–71.
14. Herold, op. cit., pp. 286–99.
15. Shaw, *Between*, pp. 278–81; Anderson, p. 33.

Chapter 5: The Strange Fate of Sultan Selim

1. P. Holt, *Egypt and the Fertile Crescent*, pp. 176–92; Shaw, *Between*, pp. 286–91.
2. Ibid., pp. 317–27. On the Serb revolt and its background, M. Boro Petrovich, *History of Modern Serbia*, vol. 1, pp. 23–81; Temperley, *History of Serbia*, chapter 10.
3. V. Puryear, *Napoleon and the Dardanelles*, pp. 2–39.
4. This may have been a higher figure than usual; cf. C. Issawi, *Economic History of Turkey*, pp. 80 and 83–4 and Anderson, p. 60.

5. Napoleon to Selim III, 30 January 1805, *Corr. Nap.* vol. 10 no. 8298.
6. Napoleon to Talleyrand, 9 June 1806, *Corr. Nap.* vol. 12 no. 10339.
7. Napoleon to Caulaincourt, 31 May 1808, L. Lecaistre, *Lettres inédites de Napoleon I*, vol. 1, p. 198; and see A. Palmer, *Alexander I*, pp. 143 and 155.
8. M. P. Coquelle, 'Sébastiani, ambassadeur à Constantinople', *Revue Historique Diplomatique*, vol. 18 (1904), pp. 574–611.
9. P. Mackesy, *The War in the Mediterranean, 1803–10*, p. 161.
10. Ibid., pp. 166–7.
11. Ibid., pp. 170–4, supplemented by Arbuthnot's reports in FO 78/55.
12. Mackesy, pp. 176–7; C. Frazee, *Orthodox Church and Independent Greece*, p. 8.
13. Mackesy, op. cit., pp. 186–94.
14. Shaw, *Between*, pp. 373–5.
15. Ibid., pp. 378–95.
16. Puryear, op. cit., pp. 207–27; Mackesy, op. cit., pp. 206–11.
17. Shaw, *Between*, pp. 403–4.
18. Temp., p. 6 and p. 401.
19. A. Juchéreau de St Denys, *Les Révolutions de Constantinople en 1807–08*, vol. 2, pp. 217–392; Shaws, pp. 2 and 3; Lewis, pp. 74–5.
20. Juchereau, op. cit., vol. 2, pp. 199–208.

Chapter 6: Mahmud II, the Enigma

1. C. Macfarlane, *Constantinople in 1828*, p. 111; L. A. Marchand, (ed.) Byron *Letters*, vol. 1, pp. 241–56; J. C. Hobhouse, *Journey through Albania . . . to Constantinople*, vol. 1, p. 365.
2. Temperley, *Hist. of Serbia*, p. 190: the book was published in 1917, with this section probably written during the Balkan Wars; Shaws, p. 6; Davison, *Essays*, p. 23.
3. L-P, vol. 1, pp. 49–53 and p. 513; Slade, *Travels in Turkey, etc.*, chapters 8 and 9.
4. L-P, vol. 1, p. 49.
5. S. Canning to R. Wellesley, 9 November 1809, L-P, vol. 1, p. 71.
6. Ibid., p. 63; C. W. Crawley, *The Question of Greek Independence*, pp. 55–6.
7. Kinross, *Ottoman Centuries*, pp. 443–4 and works cited for chapter 4, note 3, above.
8. H. Holland, *Travels in Ionian Islands, Albania, etc.*, vol. 1, p. 204.
9. For following paragraphs: D. Dakin, *Unification of Greece*, pp. 39–43; C. W. Crawley, op. cit., pp. 18–20; R. Clogg (ed.), *The Movement for Greek Independence*, pp. 175–200.
10. Exhortation of 1798 translated, ibid., pp. 56–64.
11. Palmer, *Alexander I*, pp. 377–80; C. M. Woodhouse, *Capodistria*, pp. 267–70.
12. Chabert to Strangford, 31 March 1821, Add. MSS 36299, no. 59.
13. Chabert to Strangford, 16 April 1821, Add MSS 36299, no. 88; Pisani Memorandum of same date, Add. MSS. 36301, no. 4.
14. Anathema of March 1821, Clogg, op. cit., pp. 203–6; cf. C. A. Frazee, *Orthodox Church and Independent Greece*, pp. 28–9.
15. Patriarch's death: eyewitness account, R. Walsh, *A Residence at Constantinople*, pp. 314–17; Memorandum by Pisani, 25 April 1821, Add MSS 36301, no. 5; formal dispatch, Strangford to Castlereagh (?25) April 1821, FO 78/98/27; later account, Strangford to Castlereagh, 12 June 1821, FO 78/99/47; Frazee, op. cit., pp. 32–3; Crawley, op. cit., pp. 17–18.
16. Strangford to Castlereagh, 23 July 1821, FO 78/99/71.
17. Frazee, op. cit., pp. 36–9.
18. Walsh, op. cit. I, pp. 316–17; Pisani Memorandum, 1 June 1821, Add. MSS 36301, no. 54.

19. Temperley, *Foreign Policy of Canning*, pp. 336–8; Ibrahim in Greece, Crawley, op. cit., pp. 38–59.
20. G. Canning to S. Canning, 9 January 1826, L–P, vol. 1, p. 396; A. Palmer, *The Chancelleries of Europe*, p. 46.
21. Hobhouse, op. cit. I, p. 213.
22. For the Turkish Court Chronicler see Temp., p. 16, p. 402.
23. S. Canning to G. Canning, 19 April 1826, L–P, vol. 1, p. 401.
24. L–P, vol. 1, p. 417; Stratford's account was written some 40 years later.
25. Ibid., pp. 418–20; Walsh, op. cit. vol. 2, pp. 264–6 and his Appendix VII, pp. 502–25; see also Temp., pp. 18–22 and the French account translated in Laurence Kelly's *Istanbul*, pp. 266–71.
26. S. Canning to G. Canning, 12 August 1821, L–P, vol. 1, p. 424.

Chapter 7: Egyptian Style

1. Mahmud's reforms: Lewis, pp. 75–103; Shaws, pp. 21–9, 35–40, 46–8.
2. Lewis, pp. 89–92.
3. C. Issawi, *Economic History of Turkey*, p. 161.
4. Anderson, pp. 67–74; Crawley, *Question of Greek Independence*, pp. 86–112; Palmer, *Chancelleries of Europe*, pp. 48–9.
5. For the diplomatic background as well as the naval events see C. M. Woodhouse's *The Battle of Navarino*.
6. Crawley, op. cit., pp. 164–75; Shaws, pp. 31–2; Hurst, *Key Treaties*, vol. 1, pp. 188–203.
7. N. Shilder, *Imperator Nikolaus I*, vol. 2, pp. 250–1.
8. Palmerston to Granville, 6 November 1832, C. Webster, *Foreign Policy of Palmerston*, vol. 1, p. 282. Webster's chapter 4 is a valuable source for Great Power policies in this crisis; P. Holt, *Egypt and the Fertile Crescent*, pp. 232–5; P. Vatikiotis, *History of Modern Egypt*, p. 65; Temp., pp. 89–136.
9. Anderson, pp. 81–6; P. E. Moseley, *Russian Diplomacy and the Opening of the Eastern Question*, p. 21.
10. Palmer, *Chancelleries*, pp. 64–5; J. Norris, *The First Afghan War*, pp. 214–6.
11. Moltke's letter of 12 July 1839, H. von Moltke, *Briefe aus dem Turkei*, pp. 377–400 (for the battle and its preliminaries).

Chapter 8: Sick Man?

1. Temp., p. 242.
2. Shaws, pp. 58–9; Temp. pp. 98–9, 157, 163, 243–7; L–P, vol. 2, pp. 101–14.
3. Temp., pp. 158–61. The official French language text of the Gülhane Decree is in Young, *Coup de droit Ottoman*, vol. 1, pp. 257–61. Extensive quotations, Shaws, pp. 58–9.
4. Diplomats' comments, Temp., p. 162. See also Temperley's article, 'British Policy towards Parliamentary Reform and Constitutionalism in Turkey', *Cambridge Historical Journal*, 1933, especially pp. 150–60.
5. See discussion in Palmer, *Chancelleries of Europe*, pp. 65–7.
6. Hurst, *Key Treaties*, vol. 1, pp. 252–8; C. Webster, *Foreign Policy of Palmerston*, vol. 2, p. 644–737; Anderson, pp. 100–4.
7. Hurst, *Key Treaties*, vol. 1, pp. 259–60.

8. For an account of Nicholas's visit to London, based on the Aberdeen Papers and Russian sources, see A. Palmer, *The Banner of Battle*, pp. 1–7.

9. For the *Tanzimat* reforms in general: Lewis, pp. 75–125; Shaws, pp. 61–118; Davison, *Essays*, pp. 114–28.

10. Temp., pp. 242–3. This opinion, probably written in 1934, occurs in a strange paragraph comparing the methods used by Stratford de Redcliffe and T. E. Lawrence in 'reforming Orientals'.

11. See the article 'The First Ottoman Experiment with Paper Money' in Davison, *Essays*, pp. 60–72.

12. Detailed figures cited by Shaws, p. 107, from sources in İstanbul.

13. Stratford de Redcliffe to Palmerston, 5 April 1851, Temp., p. 242.

14. Temp., pp. 188–97 and p. 446, may be supplemented by Colonel Rose's journal in the Strathnairn Papers, Add. MSS 42834.

15. On Maronites in the Lebanon see Yapp, *Making of the Modern Near East*, p. 136; P. M. Holt, *Egypt and the Fertile Crescent 1576–1922*, pp. 236–41.

16. The chief biographical source for Omer is a memoir by his physician, published in Sarajevo when Bosnia was under Austro-Hungarian administration: J. Koetscheck, *Aus dem Leben Serdar Ekrem Omer pasha*.

17. Lord Cowley (in Vienna) to Palmerston, 3 January 1849, FO 30/122/10 mentions two occasions, basing his report on talks with Archduke John. The other occasion is cited below (note 18).

18. Vienna visit of December 1845: T. Schiemann, *Geschichte Russlands unter Kaiser Nikolaus I*, vol. 4, p. 377; A. Palmer, *Metternich*, pp. 290–1.

19. Temp., pp. 259–65. A British government bluebook, 'Correspondence respecting Refugees within the Turkish dominions', was published in 1851 (no. 1324, in volume 50 of Accounts and Papers).

20. Temp., pp. 265–66, 502–6.

21. Temp., pp. 292–5.

22. H. Rose to Clarendon, 28 December 1852, FO 78/894/170.

23. A. A. Zaionchkovskii, *Vostochnaia voina v sviazi s sovremennoi i politeschkoi obstanovki*, vol. 1, pp. 356–7.

24. The fullest treatment of these talks is in G. H. Bolsover, 'Nicholas I and the Partition of Turkey', *SEER*, vol. 27 (1948–9) pp. 139–43. But this article must be supplemented by Seymour's Journal, Add. MSS 60306. For this reference see the Journal for 9 January 1853.

25. Palmer, *Banner of Battle*, pp. 14–15.

26. Russell to Seymour, 9 February 1853, FO 65/649/38; Temp., pp. 274–5.

27. Ibid., Palmer, op. cit., p. 16.

28. H. Rose to Admiral Dundas, 5 March 1853, Add. MSS 42801; Rose to Clarendon, 6 March, FO 78/930/73.

29. Stratford to Clarendon, 11 April 1853, FO 78/931/12. See also the valuable article by J. L. Herkless, 'Stratford, the Cabinet and the Outbreak of the Crimean War', *HJ*, vol. 18 iii (1975), pp. 497–523.

30. Blakely's report, 23 April 1853, Stratford de Redcliffe Papers, FO 352/36; Slade's report, 21 May, is enclosed in Stratford to Clarendon, 28 May, FO 78/932/70.

31. Herkless, loc. cit., pp. 498, 501, 522.

32. Palmer, *Banner of Battle*, p. 20.

33. Stratford to Clarendon, 14 August 1853, FO 78/939/220.

34. Palmer, op. cit., p. 23.

35. Vatikiotis, *History of Modern Egypt*, p. 72; Temp., p. 346.

36. Temp., p. 475; Herkless, loc. cit., p. 517.

37. Temp., p. 363.

Chapter 9: Dolmabahche

1. J. Curtiss, *Russia's Crimean War*, pp. 186-8.
2. Palmer, *Banner of Battle*, pp. 30-2.
3. Rose's Journal, 25 October 1854, Add. MSS 42837.
4. On Kars: A.J. Barker, *The Vainglorious War*, pp. 274-9.
5. Shaws, p. 140; Lewis, p. 115; see also the biographical entries in *EI* i and *EI* ii.
6. Text of treaties, Hurst, *Key Treaties*, vol. 1, pp. 317-37. For Palmerston's comments, see his letter to Clarendon, 26 September 1855, Add. MSS 48579. On the receipt, see also Shaws, pp. 87, 124-5, 140; Lewis, pp. 113-15 and 131; Davison, *Reform*, pp. 52-80.
7. Anderson, pp. 156-7.
8. Lewis, p. 339; Shaws, pp. 116 and 141.
9. R.G. Richardson, *Nurse Sarah Anne*, p. 80; Cook; *Florence Nightingale*, p. 85.
10. Charles Gordon to Lord Aberdeen, 10 May 1854, Add. MSS 43225.
11. Celik Gulbersoy's *Dolmabahche* is a beautifully illustrated book which, though written in Turkish, gives non-Turkish readers a clear impression of the palace's magnificence.
12. Shaws, pp. 63, 82-3.
13. For a detailed study of the effect of the electric telegraph in the Ottoman Empire, see Davison, *Essays*, pp. 133-65.
14. Vatikiotis, *History of Modern Egypt*, pp. 71-4, 84.
15. See Sumner, p. 140.
16. Lebanon settlement: Holt, *Egypt and Fertile Crescent*, p. 241; text of Lebanon statute of 1861, Hurewitz, I, pp. 165-68; Hurst, *Key Treaties*, vol. 1, pp. 408-10.
17. Queen Victoria to Crown Princess of Prussia, 13 July 1867, R. Fulford (ed.), *Your Dear Letter*, p. 143.
18. Shaws, pp. 83-91, 106-11, 119.
19. Lewis, pp. 145-51; Shaws, pp. 130-3.
20. Edward Hornby, *Autobiography* p. 74, cited by Davison, *Essays*, p. 111.
21. Sumner, p. 101; H. Feis, *Europe, The World's Banker*, pp. 312-4; C. Issawi, *Economic History of Turkey*, pp. 321-4.
22. Queen Victoria to Crown Princess of Prussia, 20 July 1867, Fulford, op. cit., p. 145; *The Times*, 19 July 1867.
23. Sumner, p. 103.
24. C. Issawi, *Economic History of the Middle East*, pp. 90-1.
25. Shaws, p. 153.
26. Sumner, p. 101; Shaws, pp. 154-6.
27. R.W. Seton-Watson, *Disraeli, Gladstone and the Eastern Question*, pp. 32 and 37; A.P. Vacalopoulos, *History of Thessaloniki*, pp. 116-20.
28. Sir Henry Elliot, *Some Revolutions and Other Diplomatic Experiences*, p. 231; Lewis, pp. 156-8; Shaws, p. 163.
29. Davison, *Reform*, pp. 330-9; Alderson, p. 69; J. Haslip, *The Sultan*, pp. 70-2.
30. Davison, *Reform*, pp. 317-49, while his Appendix D (p. 418) discusses the fate of Abdulaziz. For Çerkes Hasan affair see also: Shaws, p. 164; Lewis, p. 159; Alderson, p. 70.
31. H. Elliot to Lord Derby, 17 August 1876, FO 78/2462/867; Seton-Watson, op. cit., p. 36.
32. *The Times*, 3 August 1876, printing a report from Therapia dated 26 July.
33. Elliot to Derby, 25 September 1876, FO 78/2464/1079.

Chapter 10: Yildiz

1. J. Haslip, *The Sultan*, p. 84; cf. the extract from Pierre Loti's *Aziyade* in L. Kelly (ed.), *Istanbul*, pp. 208–10. See also R. Devereux, *The First Ottoman Constitutional Period*, pp. 41–6.
2. H. Elliot to Derby, 15 September 1876, FO 78/2463/1016.
3. Haslip, op. cit., pp. 76–8; Shaws, p. 172; for Sir Henry Elliot and 'the Englishman' see his dispatch to Lord Derby, 27 August 1876, FO 78/2462/915.
4. Constitution of 1876: R. Devereux, op. cit., p. 80; Davison, *Reform*, pp. 358–408; and the article 'Dustur' by Bernard Lewis in *EI* ii. See also Shaws, pp. 174–8.
5. Sumner, pp. 198–234; Seton-Watson, *Disraeli, Gladstone, etc.*, pp. 51–105.
6. Kenneth Rose, *The Later Cecils*, p. 62, citing from the Hatfield archives (C51/1–2) a private letter from Salisbury to Lord Robert Cecil, 25 December 1876.
7. Kennedy, *Salisbury*, p. 100; Seton-Watson, op. cit., pp. 133–7; Sumner, pp. 235–51. See also the diary kept during the ambassadors' conference by the German diplomat C. A. Busch and edited by one of his colleagues, Leopold Raschdau, for publication in *Deutsche Rundschau*, vol. 141 (Berlin, 1909), especially pp. 22–7.
8. Ali Haydar Midhat, *Midhat Pasha*, p. 145; Devereux, op. cit., p. 110; Davison, *Reforms*, pp. 400–2.
9. For the elections and composition of parliament see Devereux, op. cit., pp. 123–45; opening ceremony, ibid., p. 108–13.
10. Sumner, p. 271; Anderson, p. 193.
11. Sumner, pp. 319–33 and 339.
12. Devereux, op. cit., pp. 186–7.
13. Layard to Derby, 30 April and 18 May 1877, cited from Add. MSS by Seton-Watson, op. cit., p. 207.
14. Layard to Beaconsfield, 5 February 1878, ibid., p. 354.
15. Devereux, op. cit., pp. 236–48.
16. Sumner, p. 373; Seton-Watson, op. cit., p. 311.
17. Layard to Derby, 15 February 1878, copy in Add. MSS 39131; cf. Seton-Watson, op. cit., p. 317.
18. Derby to Layard, 14 February 1878, Add. MSS 39137; cf. Seton-Watson, op. cit., pp. 331–2.
19. E. Corti, *The Downfall of Three Dynasties*, p. 241.
20. Joan Haslip, *The Sultan*, p. 131.
21. Text of San Stefano Treaty: Sumner, pp. 627–37; Hurst, *Key Treaties*, vol. 2, pp. 528–46.
22. Anderson, pp. 210–16; Sumner, pp. 434–8.
23. Layard to Derby, 13 March 1878, FO 195/1176/343. For 'place of arms' proposals, Seton-Watson, op. cit., pp. 324–5.
24. Sumner, pp. 475–95 and 637–51.
25. Seton-Watson, op. cit., p. 325 and p. 423.
26. Sumner, p. 510, citing Colonel Dmitri Anuchin's diary, from *Russkaya Starina*, vol. 150.
27. Lewis, p. 172; Shaws, p. 189.
28. Seton-Watson, op. cit., pp. 427–9.
29. Shaws, pp. 213–25, using Yildiz Palace archives; Haslip, op. cit., p. 184; Kinross, *Ottoman Centuries*, pp. 533–5.
30. Haslip, op. cit., pp. 152–3. Sir Edwin Pears's *Life of Abd ul-Hamid* was written by a diplomat with considerable personal knowledge of Yildiz and supplements his *Forty Years at Constantinople*. G. Dorys, *Abdul Hamid Intime*, and Paul Regla, *Les Secrets*

de Yildiz, are good quarries for fiction; they were written during Abdulhamid's later years.

31. Layard to Sir Henry Elliot, 5 July 1878, Add. MSS 39138. See also Sumner, p. 506 and Seton-Watson, op. cit., pp. 419–20 and 509–12.
32. Berlin Treaty text: Sumner, pp. 658–69; Hurst, *Key Treaties*, vol. 2, pp. 551–77.
33. Stratford de Redcliffe, *The Eastern Question*, p. 49.
34. Lewis, p. 447; C. Issawi, *Economic History of Turkey*, pp. 361–5; D. C. Blaisdell, *European Financial Control in the Ottoman Empire*, pp. 88–93; Shaws, p. 223 and p. 225.

Chapter 11: The Hamidian Empire

1. Sumner, pp. 563–8; Anderson, pp. 227–31; C. Jelavich, *Tsarist Russia and Balkan Nationalism*, pp. 215–43; R. Crampton, *A History of Bulgaria 1878–1918*, pp. 85–114.
2. P. J. Vatikiotis, *History of Modern Egypt*, p. 73.
3. For Ismail: P. Holt, *Egypt and the Fertile Crescent*, pp. 195–210. See also Anderson, pp. 242–3, and M. E. Yapp, *Making of the Modern Near East*, pp. 213–32.
4. Anderson, pp. 244–51; Lewis, p. 402; Yapp, op. cit., p. 181.
5. Foreign Office to Treasury, 7 November 1898, FO 78/4967, cited by G. Papadopoulos, *England and the Near East*, p. 27.
6. Layard to Beaconsfield, 1 August 1877, copy Add. MSS 39137.
7. E. M. Earle, *Turkey, the Great Powers and the Baghdad Railway*, pp. 107–10.
8. Ulrich Trumpener in Kent, pp. 115–16; Goltz, *Denkwürdigkeiten*, pp. 120–6.
9. Intelligence report of 22 May 1890, enclosure in FO 195/2053.
10. Shaws, p. 246; Langer, p. 160.
11. Full account is in Sir Charles Eliot ('Odysseus'), *Turkey in Europe*, pp. 115–17; a long extract is in Laurence Kelly, *Istanbul*, pp. 272–3.
12. White to Salisbury, 17 August 1888, FO 78/4102/320, cited in C. L. Smith, *The Embassy of Sir William White*, p. 116. For comments on the railway terminus see Frances Elliot's account of arriving by train, printed in Kelly, op. cit., pp. 259–60.
13. H. Nicolson, *Lord Carnock*, pp. 88–9.

Chapter 12: Armenia, Crete and the Thirty-Day War

1. A. O. Sarkissian, *History of the Armenian Question*, chapters 1–2.
2. S. H. Longrigg, *Oil in the Middle East*, p. 13. See also on Armenians: Langer, chapter 5; Sumner, pp. 16–17, 513, 547, 572; and L. Arpee, *The Armenian Awakening, History of the Armenian Church 1820-60*.
3. Sarkis Atamian, *The Armenian Community*, pp. 51–130; growth of Armenian revolutionary movement, Louise Nalbandian, *The Armenian Revolutionary Movement*, pp. 80–98, 104–18, 151–63.
4. Langer, p. 162.
5. Hatzfeldt to Holstein, 30 July 1895, *GP* vol. 10, no. 2371.
6. Staal to Lobanov, 13 August 1895, Meyendorff (ed.), *Correspondence de M. de Staal*, p. 256; Salisbury's telegram to Currie, 9 October 1895, FO 195/1862/177.
7. Shaws, p. 204; Langer, p. 161.

8. A. Marder, *British Naval Policy*, p. 245; Papadopoulos, *England and the Near East*, p. 55.

9. Chermside's report enclosed in Currie to Salisbury, 29 January 1896, FO 78/4884/78, reaching London on 10 February. For its assessment in London, Marder, op. cit., pp. 249–50.

10. Goschen's speech, 11 February 1896, Hansard, *Parliamentary Debates*, 4th Series, vol. XXVII, p. 162.

11. Consul-General Blunt to Salisbury, 20 January 1896, FO 78/4734/1. D. Dakin, *The Unification of Greece, 1770–1923*, covers both the Cretan problem (pp. 149–51) and the Macedonian imbroglio (pp. 159–79).

12. Herbert to Salisbury, 4 July 1896, FO 78/4724/263.

13. Salisbury to Sanderson, 25 July 1896, FO 7/1240; for reply to Vienna, see *Queen Victoria's Letters*, ser. 3, vol. 3, p. 58.

14. Papadopoulos, op. cit., pp. 77–9.

15. Details of these events were telegraphed by Herbert to Salisbury, 30 and 31 August, 1896, FO 78/4724/365 and 374. Eyewitness account in an anonymous article, 'The Constantinople Massacres', in *Contemporary Review* for October 1896, pp. 457–65.

16. Papadopoulos, op. cit., pp. 82–3.

17. William II's comment appears as a footnote to *GP* vol. 12, no. 2901; see also Haslip, *The Sultan*, pp. 225–6.

18. Herbert to Salisbury, 31 August 1896, FO 78/4724/tel. 374. Other questions: telegrams 368 (30 August) and 386 (5 September); and Herbert's dispatch of 2 September, FO 78/4714/695.

19. Details of the Nelidov Plan were revealed in V. Khvostov's article for *Krasnyi Arkhiv*, vol. 47 (1931), with English summary in Boutelle and Thayer's *Digest of the Krasnyi Arkhiv*, p. 384; see also Langer, pp. 337–40. Full reports on movements of the Black Sea Fleet were sent to London from the consul-general in Odessa: see FO 65/1540; the earliest (no. 10) is dated 5 February 1897. For the ambassadorial conference, see Currie's telegrams to Salisbury in FO 78/4724 and 4797; also see Papadopoulos, op. cit., pp. 112–20.

20. For declaration of war, ibid., pp. 140–2; and Papadopoulos also prints as his Appendix 3 a military assessment of the war made in Pera by Captain H. A. Lawrence (originally in FO 78/4993). Langer, chapter 11, has a good survey of the war, with maps. For optimism in Athens, see G. W. E. Russell, *Malcolm MacColl*, pp. 195–7. See also Dakin, op. cit., pp. 152–4.

21. Prince Nicholas of Greece, *My Fifty Years*, p. 157.

22. Salisbury to O'Conor, 15 May 1897, FO 65/1535/tel. 244; answered, O'Conor to Salisbury, 17 May, FO 65/1536/tel. 59 and FO 65/1532/ dispatch 112.

23. Papadopoulos, op. cit., p. 222.

24. Shaws, pp. 207–11; Crampton, op. cit., pp. 229–40; D. Dakin, *Unification of Greece*, pp. 159–79, succinctly covers material more exhaustively assessed in his *The Greek Struggle in Macedonia, 1897–1913*; Stoyan Pribicevich, *Macedonia, Its People and History*, pp. 119–36, takes a (moderate) Yugoslav approach to what is still a highly-charged topic.

25. Currie to Salisbury, 2 June 1897, FO 78/4802/372; printed in full as Appendix 2 in Papadopoulos, pp. 245–7.

26. *Punch*, 18 January 1896; included in a special supplement, 'The Unspeakable Turk', which reprinted 24 anti-Ottoman cartoons published between September 1876 and November 1914, and was distributed with the issue of *Punch* on 16 December 1914.

Chapter 13: Ancient Peoples and Young Turks

1. *GP*, vol. 12, chapter 83 contains relevant German diplomatic documents. Contemporary reports in G. Gaulis, *La Ruine d'une Empire*, pp. 156–242. See A. Palmer, *The Kaiser*, pp. 91–2. Very strangely, the detailed and scholarly first volume of Lamar Cecil's biography (*Wilhelm II, Prince and Emperor 1859–1900*) ignores the Kaiser's visits to Constantinople, Palestine and Syria entirely.
2. F. Fischer, *Germany's Aims in the First World War*, pp. 20–2 and 39–40; C. Issawi, *Economic History of Modern Turkey*, pp. 188–91.
3. Haslip, *The Sultan*, p. 236.
4. Longrigg, *Oil in the Middle East*, p. 27.
5. These comments – some 400 words – were made by William II in 1931 on p. 120 of a copy of *Die Verschworung der Diplomaten*, the German edition of Nicolson's *Lord Carnock*, which is in my possession. The page annotated corresponds to p. 89 of the English edition.
6. Prince von Bülow, *Memoirs, 1897–1903*, p. 249.
7. William II to Nicholas II, 9 November 1898, N. Grant, *The Kaiser's Letters to the Tsar*, pp. 65–70.
8. Bülow, op. cit., p. 254.
9. Trumpener, in Kent, pp. 117–20. On the Hejaz Railway, see Kinross, *Ottoman Centuries*, p. 567, and the specialist study, W. Ochsenwald, *The Hijaz Railroad*.
10. M. Lowenthal (ed.), *Diaries of Theodor Herzl*, pp. 266–7 and 282. For Herzl's meetings with the Kaiser see I. Friedman, *Germany, Turkey and Zionism*, pp. 75–81, with a detailed study of earlier contacts between Herzl and the German imperial circle (pp. 56–62 and 65–74). For Herzl's meetings with the Sultan, ibid., pp. 97–8.
11. Ibid., pp. 154–70.
12. Derek Wilson, *Rothschild*, pp. 289–98.
13. See Currie's dispatch noted above, chapter 12, note 25, which may be supplemented by an interesting report on military dissidents by Colonel Chermside, 30 March 1896, FO 78/4705. See also O'Conor to Salisbury, 21 December 1898, FO 78/4920/659.
14. Lewis, pp. 208–10; Kinross, *Ottoman Centuries*, pp. 504–7.
15. Ahmad, pp. 166–81; E. F. Ramsaur, *The Young Turks*, pp. 55–7; and for Sabaheddin, ibid., pp. 65–7 and 124–9.
16. J. Swire, *Balkan Conspiracy*, pp. 84 and 94–7.
17. A. P. Vacalopoulos, *History of Thesssaloniki*, p. 127.
18. David Porter, *Mother Teresa, The Early Years*; S. Skendi, *The Albanian National Awakening*, pp. 380–404.
19. B. Jelavich, *History of the Balkans, vol. 2, XXth Century*, pp. 89–90; Albertini, *Origins of the War of 1914*, vol. 1, pp. 132–8.
20. Haslip, *The Sultan*, p. 234; Kent, pp. 122–3.
21. Ramsaur, op. cit., pp. 94–5; Kinross, *Atatürk*, pp. 24, 25, 28.
22. Incident at Drama; Ahmad, op. cit., p. 12, citing FO 371/544/423. The works of Ramsaur and Ahmad complement Lewis, pp. 206–9.
23. Shaws, p. 267.

Chapter 14: Seeking Union and Progress

1. Shaws, p. 273; Haslip, *The Sultan*, pp. 263–4.
2. Ahmad, pp. 20–1, 172, 175.

Notes

3. Lowther to Grey, 4 August 1908, *BDD*, vol. 5, no. 205; see also Lowther's private letter of 25 August, no. 209.
4. Shaws, p. 276; Lewis, p. 226.
5. Kent, pp. 37–9; Palmer, *Chancelleries*, pp. 214–15; Albertini, *Origins of the War of 1914*, vol. 1, pp. 206–10.
6. Grey to Lowther, 13 November 1908, cited from the Grey Papers in PRO by Feroz Ahmad, 'Great Britain's Relations with the Young Turks', *Middle East Studies*, vol. 2, no. 4 (1966), p. 306 and p. 309.
7. Grey to Lowther, 11 August 1908, *BDD*, vol. 5, no. 207.
8. B. C. Busch, *Britain and the Persian Gulf 1894–1914*, pp. 187–234 and 304–47; Longrigg, *Oil in the Middle East*, pp. 18–19.
9. M. K. Chapman, *Great Britain and the Baghdad Railway 1888–1914*, chapter 4. The Anglo-Russian exchanges may be traced in *BDD*, vol. 5, nos 535–41.
10. Ahmad, pp. 39–42; Shaws, pp. 279–81; Lewis, pp. 211–12; Francis McCullagh, 'The Constantinople Mutiny of April 13th', *Fortnightly Review*, vol. 86 pp. 58–69, and his book *The Fall of Abdul Hamid*; Sir Andrew Ryan, *The Last of the Dragomans*, pp. 54–6.
11. Ahmad, pp. 43–8.
12. Shaws, p. 282; Anderton, p. 71. For *fetva* of deposition: Abbot, *Turkey in Transition*, p. 258.
13. Kinross, *Ottoman Centuries*, p. 578; Haslip, *Sultan* pp. 285–7.
14. M. Gilbert, *Winston S. Churchill*, vol. 3, p. 189, and Companion to vol. 3, pt. 1, p. 39. See also Ahmad, pp. 49–51.
15. Ahmad, pp. 58–61.
16. Shaws, pp. 284–6.
17. Ahmad, pp. 45–8, 106–7, 179. Feroz Ahmad has also contributed a valuable article on Shevket to *EI* ii.
18. S. Skendi, *The Albanian National Awakening, 1878–1912*, pp. 398–404; Shaws, p. 288.
19. Timothy W. Childs, *Italo-Turkish Diplomacy and the War over Libya, 1911–1912*, p. 25. For events in the Yemen, P. Mansfield, *The Ottoman Empire and its Successors*, p. 30; Yapp, *Making of Modern Near East*, pp. 174–5.
20. This theme is developed in Childs, op. cit; chapters 2 and 3. See also Albertini, op. cit., vol. 1, chapter 6.
21. Childs, op. cit., pp. 70–91; G. F. Abbot, *The Holy War in Tripoli*, is a contemporary English account, sympathetic to the Ottomans. See also E. N. Bennett, *With the Turks in Tripoli*.
22. Ahmad, pp. 94 and 107.
23. Childs, op. cit., p. 24: Mallet to Grey, 5 December 1913, *BDD*, X (i) no. 403 is informative on British naval mission.
24. B. Jelavich, *History of the Balkans, Vol. 2, XXth Century*, pp. 95–100; Dakin, *Unification of Greece*, pp. 195–200; R. Crampton, *History of Bulgaria*, pp. 401–28; W. Miller, *The Ottoman Empire and its Successors*, pp. 498–522.
25. Ahmad, pp. 113–16, 172–3.
26. The diplomat was Gerald Fitzmaurice, whose report on the affair is in FO 195/2451/340, dated 5 February 1913; cf. Ryan, op. cit., p. 80. For the Sublime Porte Raid see: Ahmad, pp. 116–21; Shaws, pp. 295 and 299; Djemal, *Memoirs of a Turkish Statesman*, pp. 1–3; Sir E. Pears, *Forty Years in Constantinople*, p. 331–2.
27. Ahmad, p. 128.
28. E. C. Helmreich, *The Diplomacy of the Balkan Wars*, pp. 324–32 may be supplemented by Crampton's account; see also Albertini, op. cit., vol. 1, pp. 450–53.
29. See, in general, Ahmad, chapter 7.

30. Wangenheim to Foreign Ministry, 17 May 1913, *GP* vol. 38, no. 15303.
31. F. Fischer, *War of Illusions*, pp. 333–4.

Chapter 15: Germany's Ally

1. Longrigg, *Oil in the Middle East*, p. 30: Gilbert, *Winston S. Churchill*, vol. 3, pp. 188–90.
2. Fischer, *War of Illusions*, pp. 334–5.
3. Wangenheim to German Foreign Ministry, 18 July 1914, cited by H. S. W. Corrigan in his article, 'German-Turkish Relations and the Outbreak of War in 1914', *Past and Present*, no. 36, p. 151. See also Howard, *Partition of Turkey*, pp. 96–102 and Trumpener, pp. 15–20. For Baghdad Railway: Chapman's final chapter and Hurst, *Key Treaties*, vol. 2, pp. 867–73.
4. Fischer, op. cit., p. 336.
5. Corrigan, loc. cit., p. 168; Bompard to Doumergue, 27 May 1914, *DDF*, sér. 3, vol. 10 no. 291.
6. Note de Departement, 13 July 1914, *DDF*, sér. 3, vol. 10, no. 504. Djemal, *Memoirs*, p. 106 and p. 113, is less reliable.
7. Shaws, p. 311. For Turkish reactions to the coming of the war: H. Morgenthau, *Secrets of the Bosphorus*; Lewis Einstein, *Inside Constantinople* (a journal for 1915 and 1916); and for the impact of these events on a child, Irfan Orga's fascinating *Portrait of a Turkish Family*.
8. Gilbert, op. cit., vol. 3, pp. 191–3 and Companion vol. 3 pp. 9, 10, 19; Fromkin, *Peace to End All Peace*, pp. 54–61.
9. A. J. P. Taylor, *Struggle for Mastery in Europe*, p. 533. For the alliance, see also Howard, op. cit., pp. 83–91.
10. Gilbert, op. cit., vol. 3, p. 196.
11. Churchill to Limpus, 9 September 1914, Gilbert, Companion vol. 3, pt. 1, p. 105.
12. Limpus to Churchill, 26 August 1914, ibid., pp. 56–60; Souchon description is by Lewis Einstein, op. cit., p. 43.
13. Shaws, p. 312; Ahmad, p. 157.
14. Gilbert, op. cit., vol. 3, pp. 212–13 clarifies this matter.
15. Trumpener, pp. 23–57; Howard, op. cit., pp. 106–15; Yapp, *Making of Modern Near East*, p. 272.
16. Holt, *Egypt and Fertile Crescent*, p. 263.
17. Russian ambassador to Russian Foreign Minister, 13 November 1914, cited by Taylor (op. cit., p. 541) from Russian diplomatic documents. See also Michael Ekstein on 'Russia, Constantinople, and the Straits 1914–15' in Hinsley, pp. 423–35.
18. Fromkin, op. cit., pp. 126–37; Gilbert, op. cit., vol. 3, pp. 202–3; 217–19; 229–35.
19. Ibid., p. 222, quoting Churchill's testimony to the Dardanelles Commissioners in September 1916.
20. The grand strategy behind the Gallipoli campaign may be traced in vol. 3 of Martin Gilbert's *Churchill*. Robert Rhodes James's *Gallipoli* is fine narrative, and analysis, of the tragedy.
21. Aspinall-Oglander, *Military Operations; Gallipoli*, pp. 485–6.
22. William II marginal note of 30 July 1914, cited from German diplomatic documents by Fischer, *Germany's Aims . . .*, p. 121.
23. Ibid., p. 127; Fromkin, op. cit., p. 209.
24. Holt, op. cit., pp. 273, 276, 290.

25. Fischer, op. cit., pp. 127–8. For problems behind the lines in the southern provinces, see Emin, *Turkey in the World War*, p. 88.
26. Gilbert, op. cit., vol. 3, pp. 279, 281, 291; Vatikiotis, *History of Modern Egypt*, pp. 253–4; Shaws, p. 320; Trumpener, pp. 111–12.
27. Holt, op. cit., pp. 260–1; Fromkin, op. cit., pp. 176–8.
28. Ibid., p. 106–10; Kedourie, *Anglo-Arab Labyrinth*, pp. 47–52.
29. Expedition to Fao had been planned as early as 1912, see Busch, *Britain and Persian Gulf*, p. 329. See A. T. Wilson, *Mesopotamia; Loyalties 1914–17*; the account of the campaign in A. J. Barker's *The Neglected War*; M. Fitzherbert, *The Man Who Was Greenmantle*, pp. 169–81; J. Wilson, *Lawrence of Arabia*, pp. 253–78 (with Kitchener's bribery offer discussed on p. 270); and Russell Braddon's moving narrative of Kut, *The Siege*.
30. Trumpener, *passim*; and see also Emin, op. cit., and Morgenthau's *Secrets*.
31. Yapp, op. cit., pp. 267–72; A. Hayder, *A Prince of Arabia*, pp. 106–9; Reinhold Lorenz, *Kaiser Karl*, pp. 461–5.
32. Richard Hovannissian, *Armenia on the Road to Independence*, pp. 45–56; Shaws, pp. 315–16.
33. T. E. Lawrence, *The Seven Pillars of Wisdom*, p. 48; Jeremy Wilson, op. cit., p. 201.
34. Foreign Office telegram (containing Kitchener's message) to M. Cheetham (Cairo), 31 October 1914, FO 371/2139/303. See Fromkin, op. cit., pp. 96–100; and the contrasting arguments of Kedourie, *In the Anglo-Arab Labyrinth*, pp. 17–20, and of J. Wilson, op. cit., p. 165 and p. 1003.
35. Ibid., pp. 214–6 and 1014–16. There is a judicious assessment of this much-disputed question by Professor Marian Kent in Hinsley, pp. 444–7. The correspondence was published as a British Government bluebook (Cmd. 5957) in 1939. See also L. Friedman, 'The Hussein–McMahon Correspondence and the Question of Palestine', *Journal of Contemporary History*, vol. 5, no. 2 (1970), and the subsequent exchanges between A. J. Toynbee and Friedman in issue no. 4 of the same year.
36. Hinsley, p. 446.
37. *DBF* Series 1, vol. 4, pp. 241–51; Kedourie, pp. 4–5, 65–6, 107–13; Bruce Felton's contribution to Kent, pp. 163–4; Marian Kent's contribution to Hinsley, pp. 447–51; Yapp, op. cit., pp. 277–8.
38. J. Wilson, op. cit., p. 288; Fromkin, op. cit., p. 207 and pp. 218–28.
39. J. Wilson, op. cit., p. 300.
40. Ibid., pp. 412–13 and 1069–70.
41. Kinross, *Atatürk*, pp. 104, 108, 112; Trumpener, pp. 311–33.
42. Papen, *Memoirs*, p. 72. Interest in Papen's later career has inclined historians to ignore his shrewd judgements on the Asia Corps commanders and their relations with the Turks, pp. 69–82.
43. Fromkin, op. cit., pp. 311–13 is the most recent account.
44. Kedourie, p. 107.
45. On the Balfour Declaration, see the specialist study by L. J. Stein, and Fromkin, op. cit., pp. 274–300. For the German Jews, Germany and the Declaration see Friedman, *Germany, Turkey and Zionism*, pp. 339–41.
46. Anderson, p. 348.
47. J. Wilson, op. cit., pp. 469–70, 558, 1087.
48. Lawrence, *Seven Pillars*, p. 556.
49. Trumpener, pp. 167–90.
50. The clearest account is in C. Falls, *Armageddon*; see also Fromkin, op. cit., pp. 332–42. For the Balkan Front: Palmer, *The Gardeners of Salonika*, pp. 229–31.
51. Kinross, *Atatürk*, p. 126; Shaws, pp. 332–3; Anderson, pp. 348–9.
52. There has been a long-running historical dispute over the capture of Damascus.

Notes

Effectively the argument began forty years ago with Elie Kedourie's research, challenging the accepted view of the role of Feisal's Arab army (cf. Kedourie, pp. 2 and 119–21). Many of Kedourie's contentions were refuted by Jeremy Wilson in his definitive biography of Lawrence, pp. 559–62, and the accompanying notes, pp. 1103–8. See also later contributions to the debate in Fromkin's narrative, op. cit., pp. 334–47.

53. Longrigg, op. cit., p. 44; Barker, op. cit., p. 222.
54. See the two-part article by Gwynne Dyer, 'The Turkish Armistice of 1918' in *Middle East Studies*, vol. 8, for May and October 1972. English text of armistice, E. G. Mears, *Modern Turkey*, pp. 624–6. See also Kinross, *Atatürk*, pp. 127–34.
55. Ibid., p. 136.

Chapter 16: Sovereignty and Sultanate

1. Ryan, *Last of the Dragomans*, pp. 122–6; Lewis, pp. 234–5; Davison, *Essays*, p. 208; Edib, *Turkish Ordeal*, pp. 7–20.
2. Calthorpe to Curzon, 6 June 1919, FO 406/41/58; Shaws, p. 329.
3. See the biographical entry on Mehmed VI in *EI* ii.
4. Shaws, p. 333.
5. Quoted in *EI* ii entry cited above.
6. Kinross, *Atatürk*, p. 137.
7. Fromkin, *Peace to End All Peace*, provides the most recent and detailed commentary on these events, which may also be followed in *DBF*, series 1, vol. 4. For the American side, H. N. Howard, *Turkey, the Straits and U.S. Policy*, pp. 51–109.
8. M. Llewellyn-Smith, *Ionian Vision*, gives the best modern account of Greek activities, with Toynbee's *Western Question in Greece and Turkey* providing a contemporary attempt to place these events in a historical setting.
9. Ryan, op. cit., pp. 129–31.
10. Kinross, op. cit., p. 158. Kemal described his activities in considerable detail in his thirty-six-hour *Speech* to the Grand National Assembly of October 1927. The 724-page English-language version covers these events on pp. 24–57.
11. National Pact: Mears, *Modern Turkey*, pp. 629–31; summarized by Kinross, pp. 531–2; Davison, *Essays*, pp. 211–12.
12. Chapter 23 of Kinross, op. cit.; Ryan, op. cit., p. 141.
13. Ibid., pp. 142–7; Gilbert, *Churchill*, vol. 4, chapter 27, notably pp. 476 and 487.
14. See the letters from Robeck to Curzon in *DBF*, vol. 13, especially nos 17 and 32.
15. Lawrence's letter of February 1915 is cited by Kedourie, p. 98.
16. See the record of Allied conferences in *DBF*, vol. 7, nos 36–8, no. 50 and no. 55.
17. Memorandum by Earl Curzon on the future of Constantinople, *DBF*, vol. 4, no. 646; Nicolson, *Curzon*, pp. 212–15.
18. Curzon Memorandum (as above).
19. Martin Gilbert, *Sir Horace Rumbold*, pp. 219–24; Shaws, p. 349; Lewis, p. 246.
20. Kinross, op. cit., p. 222.
21. Robeck to Curzon, 9 March 1920, *DBF*, vol. 13, no. 17, p. 18.
22. Davison, *Essays*, p. 215; Anderson, pp. 367–8; Gilbert, *Churchill*, vol. 4, pp. 485–8.
23. Anderson, p. 368; Kinross, op. cit., p. 233.
24. Nicolson, *Curzon*, pp. 160–74 may be supplemented by relevant documents in *DBF*, vol. 12.
25. Kinross, op. cit., chapter 32.
26. Gilbert, *Churchill*, vol. 4., pp. 600–01.

290

27. Rumbold to Curzon, 20 January 1921; Gilbert, *Rumbold*, pp. 228–30.
28. Rumbold to King George V, 13 December 1930, ibid., p. 224.
29. C. Harington, *Tim Harington Looks Back*, p. 90.
30. A. Hayder, *A Prince of Arabia*, p. 242.
31. Gilbert, *Rumbold*, p. 238.
32. Ward Price, *Extra Special Correspondent*, p. 129 and Kinross, op. cit., chapter 40.
33. D. Walder, *The Chanak Affair*, pp. 303–18; Gilbert, *Churchill*, vol. 4, chapter 45; Harington, op. cit., pp. 100–28.
34. On Mudanya: Harington, pp. 117–28; Davison, *Essays*, p. 224.
35. Kinross, op. cit., p. 344.
36. Ibid., p. 348; Shaws, p. 365.
37. Kemal, *Speech*, pp. 377–9.
38. A photograph of the document is among the illustrations in Harington's book.
39. Much of Harington's vivid account (pp. 129–31) is reproduced in Kinross, op. cit., pp. 349–51. Turkish newspaper reminiscences were used by Alderson, p. 72. See also Hayder, op. cit., pp. 249–50 and Walder, op. cit., pp. 333–5.

Epilogue: Ottomans Moribund

1. Alderson, p. 73.
2. G. Young, *Constantinople*, pp. 111–12; reprinted in L. Kelly's *Istanbul*, pp. 253–4.
3. Lewis, pp. 256–8; Kemal, *Speech*, p. 668–9.
4. Davison, *Essays*, pp. 225–31; and compare the classic account of the Conference in Nicolson, *Curzon*, chapters 10 and 11. See also Gilbert, *Rumbold*, pp. 280–9, and Ryan, *Last of the Dragomans*, pp. 174–98.
5. Lewis, p. 350; Yapp, *Near East since the First World War*, pp. 78–9, 147, 156–7.
6. Kinross, *Atatürk*, p. 357.
7. C. Harington, *Tim Harington Looks Back*, p. 134; Walder, *Chanak*, pp. 349–52.
8. Kemal, *Speech*, pp. 657–9; Lewis, pp. 254–6; Shaws, p. 368.
9. Kemal, *Speech*, p. 683.
10. Lewis, p. 258; A. Hayder, *A Prince of Arabia*, pp. 268–70.
11. Ryan, op. cit., p. 213.
12. Enver's fate, Fromkin, *Peace to End All Peace*, pp. 485–90; Cavit and Nazim's fate, Kinross, *Atatürk*, pp. 428–33. For later careers of CUP members, Ahmad, pp. 166–81.
13. Yapp, op. cit., pp. 3–4, 37–8, 227–9.
14. Lewis, p. 437; and see above, chapter 3, p. 32.
15. A. Hayder, op. cit., p 250 ('weak-kneed'), p. 266 ('disintegration').
16. Pilgrimage, Alderson p. 126; death and burial; ibid., pp. 109 and 111.
17. Alderson, p. 109 and p. 111.

Select Bibliography

All books were published in London unless otherwise stated.

MANUSCRIPT SOURCES

Selected files from:
Aberdeen Papers, British Library
Ardagh Papers, Public Record Office
Foreign Office Papers (including Stratford Canning Papers), Public Record Office
Layard Papers, British Library.
Palmerston Letterbooks, British Library
Seymour Papers (Sir Hamilton Seymour), British Library
Smythe Papers (Lord Strangford; Francois Chabert; Bartolomeo Pisani), British Library
Strathnairn Papers (Sir Hugh Rose), British Library

PUBLISHED COLLECTIONS OF OFFICIAL DOCUMENTS

Documents Diplomatiques Françaises 1871–1914 (Paris, 1929–55)
Gooch, G. P. and Temperley, H. W. V. (eds), *British Documents on the Origins of the War, 1898–1914* (1926–38)
Hurewitz, J. C., *Diplomacy in the Near and Middle East*, 2 vols (Princeton, 1956)
Hurst M. (ed.), *Key Treaties for the Great Powers 1814–1914*, 2 vols (Newton Abbot, 1972)
Lepsius, J., Mendelsohn Bartholdy A., Thimme F. (eds), *Die Grosse Politik der europäischen Kabinette* (Berlin, 1922–7)
Woodward, E. L., Butler, Rohan and others (eds), *Documents on British Foreign Policy 1919–1939* Series 1 (1947–72)
Young, George (ed.), *Corps de droit civil Ottoman* (Oxford, 1907–8)

GENERAL BOOKS

Abbot, G. F., *Turkey in Transition* (1909)
—— *The Holy War in Tripoli* (1912)
Acton, Lord, *Lectures on Modern History* (1906)
Ahmad, F., *The Young Turks* (Oxford, 1957)
Albertini, L., *The Origins of the War of 1914*, vol. 1 (Oxford, 1951)
Alderson, A. D., *The Structure of the Ottoman Dynasty* (Oxford, 1956)
Anderson, M. S., *The Eastern Question* (1966)
Andrew, Prince, of Greece, *Towards Disaster* (1930)
Antonius, G., *The Arab Awakening* (Beirut, n.d.)
Arpee, L., *The Armenian Awakening, History of the Armenian Church 1820–60* (Chicago, 1909)
Aspinall-Oglander, C. F., *Military Operations, Gallipoli*, 2 vols (1929–32)
Atamian, S., *The Armenian Community* (New York, 1955)
Atatürk, M. K., *A Speech Delivered by Ghazi Mustapha Kemal, President of the Turkish Republic, October 1927* (Leipzig, 1929)
Barber, N., *The Lords of the Golden Horn* (1973)
Barker A. J., *The Neglected War; Mesopotamia 1914–1918* (1967)
—— *The Vainglorious War, 1854–56* (1970)
Barker, Thomas N., *Double Eagle and Crescent* (New York, 1957)
Benedikt, N., *Der Pascha-Graf Alexander von Bonneval* (Cologne and Graz, 1959)
Bennett, E. N., *With the Turks in Tripoli* (1912)
Berkes, N., *The Development of Secularization in Turkey* (Montreal, 1964)
Bernard, J. F., *Talleyrand* (1973)
Blaisdell, D. C., *European Financial Control in the Ottoman Empire* (New York, 1929)
Boutelle, L. M. and Thayer, G. W., *A Digest of the Krasnyi Arkhiv volumes 1–40* (Cleveland, 1947)
Bülow, Prince B. von, *Memoirs, 1897–1903* (1932)
Busch, B. C., *Britain and the Persian Gulf 1894–1914* (1976)
Cassels, L., *The Struggle for the Ottoman Empire 1717–1740* (1966)
Chandler, David, *The Campaigns of Napoleon* (1966)
Chapman, M. K., *Great Britain and the Baghdad Railway 1888–1914* (Northampton, Mass., 1948)
Cheetham, Sir Nicholas, *Mediaeval Greece* (New Haven, Conn., 1981)
Childs, Timothy W., *Italo-Turkish Diplomacy and the War over Libya, 1911–1912* (Leiden, 1990)
Clogg R. (ed.), *The Struggle for Greek Independence* (Manchester 1973)
—— *The Movement for Greek Independence* (1976)
Cook E., *Short Life of Florence Nightingale* (1925)
Cooke, M. A. (ed.), *A History of the Ottoman Empire to 1730* (Cambridge, 1976)
Corti, E., *The Downfall of Three Dynasties* (1934)
Crampton, R. J., *A History of Bulgaria, 1878–1918* (New York, 1983)
Crawley, C. W., *The Question of Greek Independence* (Cambridge, 1930)
Curtiss, J. S., *Russia's Crimean War* (Durham, NC, 1979)
Dakin, D., *The Greek Struggle in Macedonia* (Salonika, 1966)
—— *The Unification of Greece* (1972)

Davison, Roderic H., *Reform in the Ottoman Empire, 1856–1876* (Princeton, 1963)
—— *Essays in Ottoman and Turkish History* (Austin, Texas, 1990)
Devereux, R., *The First Ottoman Constitutional Period* (Baltimore, 1963)
Djemal Pasha, *Memoirs of a Turkish Statesman, 1913–19* (1922)
Djevad Bey, A., *État militaire ottoman* (Constantinople, 1882)
Earle, E. M., *Turkey, the Great Powers and the Baghdad Railway* (New York, 1923)
Einstein, Lewis, *Inside Constantinople* (1917)
Eliot, Sir Charles ('Odysseus'), *Turkey in Europe* (1900)
Feis, Herbert, *Europe, the World's Banker* (New Haven, Conn., 1930)
Edib, Halide, *The Turkish Ordeal* (1928)
Elliot, Sir Henry, *Some Revolutions and Other Diplomatic Experiences* (1922)
Emin (Yalman), Ahmed, *Turkey in the World War* (Newhaven, Conn., 1930)
Encyclopaedia of Islam, first edition (Leiden, 1913–38)
Encyclopaedia of Islam, second edition (Leiden, 1954 continuing)
Falls, Cyril, *Armageddon* (1964)
Fischer, F., *Germany's Aims in the First World War* (1967)
—— *War of Illusions, German Policies 1911 to 1914* (1975)
Fitzherbert M., *The Man Who Was Greenmantle* (1983)
Flachat, Jean-Claude: *Observations sur le Commerce et sur les art . . . même des Indes Orientales* (Lyons, 1766)
Frazee, C. A., *Orthodox Church and Independent Greece* (1969)
—— *Christians and Sultans* (1980)
Friedman, Isaiah, *Germany, Turkey and Zionism* (Oxford, 1977)
Fromkin, David, *A Peace to End All Peace* (1989)
Fulford, Roger (ed.), *Your Dear Letter* (1971)
Gaulis, G., *La Ruine d'une Empire* (Paris, 1921)
Gibb, Sir Hamilton and Bowen, H., *Islamic Society and the West*, two parts (1950, 1957)
Gilbert, Martin, *Winston S. Churchill*, vol. 3 (1982), Companion to vol. 3 (1972), and vol. 4 (1985)
—— *Sir Horace Rumbold, Portrait of a Diplomat, 1869–1941* (1973)
Gillard, D., *The Struggle for Asia* (1977)
Göltz, W. L. C. von der, *Die Thessalische Krieg und die türkische Armee* (Berlin, 1898)
—— *The Turkish Army, characteristics and capabilities* (1898)
—— *Denkwürdigkeiten* (ed. F. von der Göltz and W. Foerster, Berlin, 1929)
Grant, N., *The Kaiser's Letters to the Tsar* (1920)
Gulbersoy, Celik, *Dolmabahche* (Istanbul, 1984) (in Turkish)
Halsband, R., *The Complete Letters of Lady Mary Wortley Montagu*, vol. 1 (Oxford, 1965)
Harington, Sir Charles, *Tim Harington Looks Back* (1940)
Haslip, Joan, *The Sultan* (1958)
Hayder, Ali, *A Prince of Arabia* (ed. G. Stitt) (1948)
Helmreich, E. C., *Diplomacy of the Balkan Wars* (Cambridge, Mass., 1938)
Herold, C., *Bonaparte in Egypt* (1963)
Hinsley, F. H. (ed.), *British Foreign Policy under Sir Edward Grey* (Cambridge, 1977)

Hobhouse, J. C., *A Journey through Albania . . . to Constantinople during the Years 1809 and 1810* (1913)

Holland, Sir Henry, *Travels in Ionian Islands, Albania . . .*, vol. 1 (1819)

Holt, P. M., *Egypt and the Fertile Crescent, 1576–1922* (1965)

Holt, P. M., Lambton, A. K. S. and Lewis, B. (eds), *Cambridge History of Islam* (1970)

Hovannissian, Richard, *Armenia on the Road to Independence* (Berkeley, 1967)

Howard, H. N., *The Partition of Turkey 1913–1923* (Norman, Oklahoma, 1931)

—— *An American Enquiry in the Middle East: the King–Crane Commission* (Beirut, 1963)

—— *Turkey, the Straits and U.S. Policy* (Baltimore, 1974)

Inalcik, Halil, *The Ottoman Empire, 1300–1600* (1973)

Issawi, C., *The Economic History of the Middle East* (Chicago, 1966)

—— *The Economic History of Turkey 1800–1914* (Chicago, 1980)

James, Robert Rhodes, *Gallipoli* (1965)

Jelavich, Barbara, *History of the Balkans, Vol. 2, XXth Century* (Cambridge, 1983)

Jelavich, C., *Tsarist Russia and Balkan Nationalism* (Westport, Connecticut, 1978)

Juchereau de St Denys, A., *Les Revolutions de Constantinople en 1807–08* (Paris, 1819)

Kedourie, Elie, *England and the Middle East, The Destruction of the Ottoman Empire 1914–21* (1956: rev. ed. 1987)

—— *The Chatham House Version* (1970)

—— *In the Anglo-Arab Labyrinth* (Cambridge, 1976)

Kelly, Laurence, *Istanbul, A Traveller's Companion* (1987)

Kannengeisser, Hans, *The Campaign in Gallipoli* (1927)

Kennedy, A. L., *Salisbury, 1830–1903* (1953)

Kent, Marian (ed.), *The Great Powers and the End of the Ottoman Empire* (1984)

Kinross, Lord, *Atatürk, The Rebirth of a Nation* (1964)

—— *The Ottoman Centuries; The Rise and Fall of the Turkish Empire* (1987)

Koetschek, J., *Aus dem Leben Serdar Ekrem Omer pasha* (Sarajevo,? 1890)

—— *Aus Bosniens letzer Turkenzeit* (Vienna, 1905)

Kreutel, Richard, *Kara Mustafa vor Wien* (Graz, 1955)

Lane-Poole, S., *Life of Stratford Canning, Viscount Stratford de Redcliffe*, 2 vols (1888)

Langer, W. L., *The Diplomacy of Imperialism* (New York, rev. ed. 1951)

Lawrence, T. E., *The Seven Pillars of Wisdom* (1935)

Lecestre, L., *Lettres inédites de Napoléon I*, vol. 1 (Paris, 1897)

Lewis, Bernard, *The Emergence of Modern Turkey* (Oxford 1968)

Llewellyn-Smith, Michael, *Ionian Vision: Greece in Asia Minor, 1919–22* (1973)

Longrigg, S., *Oil in the Middle East* (3rd ed., Oxford, 1968)

Lorenz, Reinhold, *Kaiser Karl und der Untergang der Donaumonarchie* (Graz, 1959)

Lowenthal, M. (ed.), *Diaries of Theodor Herzl* (1958)

McCullagh, F., *The Fall of Abd-el-Hamid* (1910)

Macfarlane, C., *Constantinople in 1828* (1829)

Mackesy, Piers, *The War in the Mediterranean, 1803–10* (1957)

MacMunn, Sir George and Falls, Cyril, *Military Operations in Egypt and Palestine*, 2 vols (1930–39)

Mansfield, P., *The Ottoman Empire and its Successors* (1973)
—— *The Arabs* (2nd ed. 1985)
Marchand, L. A. (ed.), *Byron Letters*, vol. 1 (1973)
Marder, A. J., *British Naval Policy 1890–1905* (1941)
Mears E. G., and others, *Modern Turkey* (New York, 1924)
Meyendorff, A. (ed.), *Correspondence Diplomatique de M. de Staal*, vol. 2 (Paris, 1929)
Midhat, Ali Haydar, *The Life of Midhat Pasha* (1903)
Miot de Melito, A. F., *Mémoires I* (Paris, 1858)
Miller, W., *The Ottoman Empire and its Successors* (4th ed. Cambridge, 1936)
Moltke, H. von, *Briefe aus dem Turkei* (Berlin, 1873)
Morgenthau, Henry, *Secrets of the Bosphorus* (1918)
Moseley, P. E., *Russian Diplomacy and the Opening of the Eastern Question in 1838 and 1839* (Cambridge, Mass., 1934)
Moutraye, Aubrey de la, *Travels*, vol. 1 (1723)
Nalbandian, L., *The Armenian Revolutionary Movement* (Berkeley, 1963)
Napoleon I., *Corréspondence de Napoléon I* (Paris, 1854–69)
Nicholas, Prince, of Greece, *My Fifty Years* (1926)
Nicolson, Harold, *Lord Carnock* (1930)
—— *Peacemaking 1919* (1933)
—— *Curzon, The Last Phase* (1934)
Norris, J., *The First Afghan War* (Cambridge, 1967)
Ochsenwald, W., *The Hijaz Railroad* (Charlottesville, 1980)
Orga, Irfan, *Portrait of a Turkish Family* (1988)
Palmer, Alan, *The Gardeners of Salonika* (1965)
—— *Metternich* (1972)
—— *Alexander I, Tsar of War and Peace* (1974)
—— *The Kaiser* (1976)
—— *The Chancelleries of Europe* (1983)
—— *The Banner of Battle* (1987)
Papadopoulos, George S., *England and the Near East, 1896–1898* (Salonika, 1969)
Papen, Franz von, *Memoirs* (1952)
Pears E., *Forty Years at Constantinople* (1916)
—— *Life of Abd ul-Hamid* (1917)
Petrovich, M. Boro, *History of Modern Serbia*, vol. 1 (New York, 1976)
Plomer, William, *Ali the Lion* (1936)
Polk, W. R., *The Opening of South Lebanon* (Cambridge, Mass., 1963)
Porter, D., *Mother Teresa, The Early Years* (1986)
Pribicevich, Stoyan, *Macedonia, Its People and History* (Pittsburgh, Penn., 1982)
Puryear, V., *Napoleon and the Dardanelles* (Berkeley, 1951)
Ramsaur, E. F., *The Young Turks* (Princeton, 1957)
Remerland, G., *Ali de Tekelen, Pasha de Janina* (Paris, 1928)
Rose, Kenneth, *The Later Cecils* (1975)
Runciman, Sir Stephen, *The Fall of Constantinople 1453* (1969)
Russell, Braddon, *The Siege* (1969)
Russell, G. W. E., *Malcolm MacColl* (1914)
Ryan, Sir Andrew, *The Last of the Dragomans* (1951)

Sanders, Liman von, *Five Years in Turkey* (Annapolis, 1927): original German version, *Funf Jahre Turkei* (Berlin, 1920), is preferable

Sarkissian, A.O., *History of the Armenian Question to 1885* (Urbana, 1938)

Schiemann, T., *Geschichte Russlands unter Kaiser Nikolaus I*, 4 vols (Berlin, 1904–19)

Seton-Watson, R.W., *Disraeli, Gladstone and the Eastern Question* (1933)

—— *History of the Rumanians* (Cambridge, 1934)

Shaw, S.J., *Between Old and New: The Ottoman Empire under Sultan Selim III* (Cambridge, Mass., 1971)

—— *History of the Ottoman Empire and Modern Turkey: Empire of the Gazis* (Cambridge, 1977)

Shaw, S.J. and E.K., *History of the Ottoman Empire and Modern Turkey: Reform, Revolution and Republic* (Cambridge, 1977)

Shay, M.L., *Ottoman Empire from 1720 to 1734 as revealed in despatches of the Venetian bailo* (Urbana, 1944)

Shilder, N., *Imperator Nikolaus I* (St Petersburg, 1903)

Skendi, S., *The Albanian National Awakening, 1878–1912* (Princeton, 1967)

Slade, Adolphus, *Record of Travels in Turkey, Greece, etc.* (1854)

Smith, C.L., *The Embassy of Sir William White at Constantinople 1886–1891* (Oxford, 1957)

Stein, L.J., *The Balfour Declaration* (1961)

Stiles, Andrina, *The Ottoman Empire 1450–1700* (1989)

Stoye, John, *The Siege of Vienna* (1967)

Stratford de Redcliffe, Lord, *The Eastern Question* (1881)

Sumner, B.H., *Russia and the Balkans, 1870–1880* (Oxford, 1937)

Swire, J., *Balkan Conspiracy* (1939)

Taylor, A.J.P., *The Struggle for Mastery in Europe* (Oxford, 1954)

Temperley, H.W.V., *History of Serbia* (1917)

—— *The Foreign Policy of Canning, 1822–27* (1925)

—— *England and the Near East, The Crimea* (1936)

Thomson, Gladys Scott, *Catherine the Great and the Expansion of Russia* (1950)

Toynbee, A.J., *The Western Question in Greece and Turkey* (1922)

Trumpener, U., *Germany and the Ottoman Empire 1914–1918* (Princeton, 1968)

Vacalopoulos, Apostolos P., *A History of Thessaloniki* (Salonika, 1963)

Vandal, L.J.A., *Une Ambassade Française en Orient sous Louis XV* (Paris, 1887)

Vatikiotis, P.J., *The History of Modern Egypt* (1991)

Victoria, Queen, *Letters*, 3rd Series, vol. 3 (1930)

Volkan, V.D. and Itzkowitz, N., *The Immortal Atatürk* (Chicago and London, 1984)

Walder, David, *The Chanak Affair* (1969)

Walsh, R., *A Residence at Constantinople* (1836)

Ward Price, G., *Extra-Special Correspondent* (1957)

Webster, Sir Charles, *The Foreign Policy of Palmerston*, vol. 1 (1951)

Weissmann, Nahoum, *Les Janissaries* (Paris, 1964)

Wilson, A.T., *Mesopotamia: Loyalties 1914–17* (1930)

Wilson, Derek, *Rothschild* (1988)

Wilson, Jeremy, *Lawrence of Arabia* (1989)

Wolf, J.B., *The Diplomatic History of the Baghdad Railroad* (Missouri, 1936)

Woodhouse, Hon. C.M., *The Greek War of Independence* (1952)
—— *The Battle of Navarino* (1965)
—— *Capodistria* (Oxford, 1973)
Yapp, M.E., *The Making of the Modern Near East* (1987)
—— *The Near East since the First World War* (1991)
Young, George, *Constantinople* (1926)
Zaionchkovskii, A.A., *Vostochnaia voina v sviazi s sovremennoi i politeschloi obstanovki* (St Petersburg, 1908–13)

ARTICLES IN PERIODICALS

Ahmad, Feroz, 'Great Britain's Relations with the Young Turks', *Middle East Studies*, vol. 2, no. 4 (1966)
Arnakis, G.G., 'The Greek church of Constantinople and the Ottoman Empire', *JMH*, vol. 24, Sept. 1952
Bolsover, G.H., 'Nicholas I and the Partition of Turkey', *SEER*, vol. 27 (1948–9)
Coquelle, M.P., 'Sébastiani, ambassadeur à Constantinople', *Revue Historique Diplomatique*, vol. 18 (1904)
Corrigan, H.S.R., 'German-Turkish Relations and the Outbreak of War in 1914, A Re-Assessment', *Past and Present*, 36 (1967)
Davison, R., 'The Treaty of Kuchuk Kainardji, A Note on the Italian text', *International History Review*, vol. 10 no. 4 (1988)
Dyer, Gwynne, 'The Turkish Armistice of 1918' in *Middle East Studies*, vol. 8, for May and Oct. 1972
Friedman, I., 'The Hussein–McMahon Correspondence and the Question of Palestine', *Journal of Contemporary History*, vol. 5, no. 2 (1970); and correspondence in no. 4 of 1970
Herkless, J.L., 'Stratford, the Cabinet and the Crimean War', *HJ*, vol. 18, no. 3 (1975)
Hourani, A., 'The Changing Face of the Fertile Crescent in the Eighteenth Century', *Studia Islamica*, 8 (1953)
Kedourie, E., 'The Surrender of Medina, January 1919', *Middle East Studies*, vol. 13, no. 1 (1977)
Lewis, B., 'The Impact of the French Revolution on Turkey', *Journal of World History*, vol. 1 (1953)
McCullagh, Francis, 'The Constantinople Mutiny of April 13th', *Fortnightly Review*, vol. 86 (1908)
Rifat Abou El-Haj, 'Ottoman Diplomacy at Karlowitz', *Journal of American Oriental Society*, vol. 87 (1967)
Skiotis, D.N., 'From Bandit to Pasha' in *International Journal of Middle Eastern Studies*, vol. 2 (1971)
Swanson, V.R., 'The Military Rising in Istanbul, 1909', *Journal of Contemporary History*, 5 (1970)
Temperley, H.W.V., 'British Policy towards Parliamentary Rule and Constitutionalism in Turkey', *Cambridge HJ*, vol. 4, no. 2 (Oct. 1933)
Trumpener, U., 'Turkey's Entry into World War I', *JMH*, vol. 39 (1962)

Index

299

Index

Index

Index

Index

305